TEXTUAL SIGNPOSTS IN THE ARGUMENT OF ROMANS

EARLY CHRISTIANITY AND ITS LITERATURE

Shelly Matthews, General Editor

Editorial Board:
Jennifer A. Glancy
Joseph A. Marchal
Anders Runesson
Janet Spittler
Matthew Thiessen

Number 25

TEXTUAL SIGNPOSTS IN THE ARGUMENT OF ROMANS

A Relevance-Theory Approach

Sarah H. Casson

SBL PRESS

Atlanta

Copyright © 2019 by Sarah H. Casson

All rights reserved. No part of this work may be reproduced or transmitted in any form or by any means, electronic or mechanical, including photocopying and recording, or by means of any information storage or retrieval system, except as may be expressly permitted by the 1976 Copyright Act or in writing from the publisher. Requests for permission should be addressed in writing to the Rights and Permissions Office, SBL Press, 825 Houston Mill Road, Atlanta, GA 30329 USA.

Library of Congress Cataloging-in-Publication Data

Names: Casson, Sarah H., author.
Title: Textual signposts in the argument of Romans : a relevance-theory approach / by Sarah H. Casson.
Description: Atlanta : SBL Press, 2019. | Series: Early Christianity and its literature ; Number 25 | Includes bibliographical references and index.
Identifiers: LCCN 2019000485 (print) | LCCN 2019011400 (ebook) | ISBN 9780884143598 (ebk.) | ISBN 9781628372397 (pbk. : alk. paper) | ISBN 9780884143581 (hbk. : alk. paper)
Subjects: LCSH: Bible. Romans—Criticism, interpretation, etc.
Classification: LCC BS2665.52 (ebook) | LCC BS2665.52 .C37 2019 (print) | DDC 227/.1066—dc23
LC record available at https://lccn.loc.gov/2019000485

Printed on acid-free paper.

In memory of Trevor Patterson, 1960–2017

evangelist, pastor, and friend

Romans 5:5

Contents

Foreword by Edward Adams..ix
Acknowledgments...xiii
Abbreviations..xv

1. Why Study γάρ in Romans? 1
   1.1. Traditional Accounts of γάρ   4
   1.2. Linguistic Accounts of γάρ   15
   1.3. New Light on γάρ, New Light on Romans: Contours,
        Contributions, and Claims of the Study   21

2. Relevance Theory and Perspectives on Romans 27
   2.1. Introducing Relevance Theory   27
   2.2. Pointing to Inferences: Procedural Meaning   35
   2.3. Relevance Theory and Biblical Interpretation   40
   2.4. Background Issues   45

3. Consistent Yet Context-Sensitive: The Guidance γάρ Gives.......61
   3.1. Methodological Matters   62
   3.2. Straightforward but Backward: Instructions for
        Strengthening   70
   3.3. Strengthening Guidance in More Complex Cases:
        Romans 7:7–20   84
   3.4. Flagging Up Reinforcements: Romans 14:1–12   106

4. What Kind of Strengthening? Problematic Examples..................123
   4.1. Romans 2:25: Questions of Coherence   125
   4.2. Romans 5:6–7: Parenthesis or Adjustment?   131
   4.3. Romans 9:11–12: Complex Syntax   143
   4.4. Romans 7:1: An Aside   148
   4.5. Romans 6:19–20: A Supporting Exhortation?   153

4.6. Romans 15:24: A Delicate Request	161
4.7. The Procedural Guidance γάρ Gives: A Summary	167

5. γάρ as Exegetical Signpost: Pointing a Path through the Undergrowth 173
    5.1. Romans 4:1–2: Testing Interpretations   174
    5.2. Romans 10:4–5: Respecting Coherence   187

6. γάρ as Communicative Signpost: Guidance in Tracing Paul's Argument...203
    6.1. Direction and Center of the Argument of Romans   204
    6.2. Romans 1:15–18: Which Way Lies Relevance?   207
    6.3. Romans 15:7–13: Bringing It All Together   245
    6.4. Tracing the Path of Argument in Romans 1–4   263
    6.5. A Roman-Focused Reading   267

7. Relevance for Romans and Beyond 269
    7.1. A Crucial Communicative Clue   269
    7.2. Interpretative Implications and Interdisciplinary Fruit   273

Appendix A: Glossary..283
Appendix B: Occurrences of γάρ in Romans...289
Bibliography...293
Ancient Sources Index...309
Modern Authors Index..317

Foreword

I have long been convinced that linguistics has a great deal to offer New Testament scholarship. The field of Bible translation has been particularly receptive to new developments in linguistics, rather more so than has been New Testament studies. A recent development within linguistics and pragmatics that has had quite an influence in Bible translation circles but is less known to New Testament scholars is relevance theory—a broad framework for explaining how human communication works and why it is (usually) successful. The theory posits that communication is based on a shared understanding between a communicator and her addressees that the message being communicated will be relevant to the latter. Addressees will process the message, within a particular context, in order to arrive at the most relevant, which is to say the most readily accessible, interpretation of it. That interpretation will often enough coincide with the interpretation intended by the communicator. Languages tend to be equipped with expressions that a speaker may employ to direct her hearers toward inferences to be drawn in interpretation (in English, expressions such as "you see," "indeed"). These words do not convey conceptual meaning; rather they serve as "procedural markers," giving guidance to hearers as to how to construe a given utterance. Sarah Casson, the author of this volume, is experienced in the field of Bible translation in minority languages, and has found relevance theory helpful for her translation work. In this book, she applies the theoretical framework, and in particular the notion of procedural meaning, to the Greek word γάρ in Paul's Letter to the Romans.

The lexeme γάρ is one of the most frequently occurring words in the New Testament. It occurs in every book of the New Testament, in some books more than others (just once each in 2 John and Jude). Romans has the highest concentration of instances (144). The word is found in verses widely regarded as theologically significant or pivotal in Paul's argument (Rom 1:16, 17, 18, etc.). Traditionally, γάρ is regarded as a causal or explanatory particle, and thus rendered "for" in English, but in many cases, in both Romans and more widely, the causal and explanatory senses do not seem to fit. In an effort to accommodate the diversity of actual usage, lexical entries on γάρ are often complex, adding a host of subdefinitions to the primary causal and explanatory meanings. Commentators on the Greek text of Romans exhibit one of two tendencies as they deal with γάρ: either they treat it as a particle with a fixed causal or explanatory meaning; or, swayed by lists of subclassifications in standard lexicons, they view it as a malleable word whose meaning varies from cotext to cotext. Both tendencies are problematic: the former struggles to account for seemingly irregular uses; the latter misses the potential importance of γάρ as a consistent discourse signal. Taking up and extending a hypothesis first mooted by the linguist and Bible translation scholar Regina Blass, and working through a range of examples in Romans, Sarah makes a compelling case that γάρ is best understood as a procedural cue, guiding towards particular inferences to be drawn, thus reducing ambiguity. In giving a procedural account of γάρ in Romans, she is able to attribute to the word a single and stable communicative function, while satisfactorily explaining all the variations in usage.

This is a significant achievement on its own, but Sarah goes further. She shows that a procedural view of γάρ is a valuable aid to the interpretation of Romans, whether at the close-up level of the exegesis of individual verses or the wider horizon of the letter's larger argument. On an exegetical level, it helps to constrain interpretation, permitting some readings of a verse while excluding others. On a wider plane, it helps interpreters to track the flow and coherence of Paul's argument and discern his main points and concerns. Sarah thus intervenes in scholarly disputes about the interpretation of particular verses, such as 1:18, 4:2 and 10:4, showing how some influential readings are rendered unlikely by a procedural view of γάρ. She also offers fresh insight into the much-debated structure of Rom 1–4 and makes a distinctive contribution to the Romans Debate, the discussion about Paul's purpose in writing the letter.

So, then, this volume is not just about a tiny Greek connecting word; it is about how to read Romans, Paul's most influential letter, indeed the most influential letter ever written. I am confident that Sarah's book will become a standard reference point for exegetes of Romans. The book is an example of the merits of interdisciplinary research for New Testament studies, showing how developments in related fields can shed fresh light on the interpretation of the biblical text. It is to be hoped that the book will help to foster greater dialogue between the often-separate worlds of Bible translation studies and New Testament studies, based on a mutual recognition of the value of linguistics for illuminating the biblical text.

Edward Adams

Acknowledgments

The seeds of this project were sown while grappling with γάρ as I worked with Congolese translators of the Bible into minority languages in the Democratic Republic of Congo. Searching for the best way to render γάρ in fresh languages threw up fundamental questions about its communicative role.

I owe a particular debt of gratitude to Eddie Adams, without whose encouragement I would never have embarked on this research, nor stayed the course. I am tremendously grateful for his incisive criticism, thorough reading of my copious drafts, and openness to debating all kinds of perspectives. I am also thankful to John Barclay and Sarah Whittle for their rigorous criticism, and their encouragement to publish my work, and for John Barclay's gracious and meticulous correction of errors in my manuscript. Many thanks also go to David Horrell for reading the manuscript and accepting it for publication in the Early Christianity and Its Literature series of SBL Press. I have greatly appreciated his painstaking engagement with my manuscript, his detailed suggestions for improvements, and his encouragement. All remaining errors are my own responsibility. I am also grateful to Nicole Tilford of SBL Press for her patient and invaluable guidance in the editing process.

I would like to thank various colleagues and friends for their moral support, and their willingness to act as sounding boards during this research, in particular, Margaret Sim, Ronnie Sim, Steve Nicolle, Stephen Lim, Philip Richardson, John Casson, Johnny Patterson, Rieko Ishibuchi, Elizabeth and Eddie Thomas, and Nick Cocking. I am particularly grateful to my colleagues at Shalom University, Bunia, Democratic Republic of Congo, for their enthusiasm for my research, for their inspiring example of resilience and perseverance against all the odds, and for being willing to release me for a time to complete this project. Finally, my thanks go to many generous friends and financial partners who have supported me over many years of work in Bible translation in Africa. I am particularly grateful to Holy Trinity Church, Richmond, and to our former vicar, Trevor Patterson, so greatly missed. His last words to me were an enthusiastic exhortation to publish this research as a book.

Abbreviations

AB   Anchor Bible Commentary
ASCP   Amsterdam Studies in Classical Philology
BDAG   Danker, Fredrick W., Walter Bauer, William F. Arndt, and F. Wilbur Gingrich. *A Greek-English Lexicon of the New Testament and Other Early Christian Literature*. 3rd ed. Chicago: University of Chicago Press, 2000.
BDF   Blass, Friedrich, Albert Debrunner, and Robert W. Funk. *A Greek Grammar of the New Testament and Other Early Christian Literature*. Chicago: University of Chicago Press, 1961.
BHL   Blackwell Handbooks in Linguistics
B.J.   Josephus, *Bellum judaicum*
BLG   Biblical Languages: Greek
BNTC   Black's New Testament Commentaries
BSac   *Biblia Sacra*
BZNW   Beiheft zur Zeitschrift für die neutestamentliche Wissenschaft und die Kunde der älteren Kirche
C. Ap.   Josephus, *Contra Apionem*
CBET   Contributions to Biblical Exegesis and Theology
CBQ   *Catholic Biblical Quarterly*
ConBNT   Coniectanea Biblica New Testament
CSCO   Corpus scriptorum Christianorum orientalium
CSEL   Corpus scriptorum ecclesiasticorum latinorum
CSL   Cambridge Studies in Linguistics
CurBR   *Currents in Biblical Research*
Disc.   Epictetus, *Discourses*
EBib   Etudes bibliques
EKKNT   Evangelisch-katholischer Kommentar zum Neuen Testament
Ep.   Seneca, *Epistulae morales*

ESV	English Standard Version
FC	*La Bible Ancien et Nouveau Testament en français courant*. Pierrefitte: Société biblique française, 1982.
GBS	Guides to Biblical Scholarship
GN	*Die Bibel in heutigem Deutsch: Die Gute Nachricht des Alten und Neuen Testaments*. Stuttgart: Deutsche Bibelgesellschaft, 1984.
HDC	High Definition Commentary
HNT	Handbuch zum Neuen Testament
HThKNT	Herders theologischer Kommentar zum Neuen Testament
IBC	Interpretation: A Bible Commentary for Teaching and Preaching
ICC	International Critical Commentary
JBL	*Journal of Biblical Literature*
JSNT	*Journal for the Study of the New Testament*
JSNTSup	Journal for the Study of the New Testament Supplement Series
KEK	Kritisch-exegetischer Kommentar über das Neue Testament
KJV	King James Version
KNT	Kommentar zum Neuen Testament
LCC	Library of Christian Classics
LCL	Loeb Classical Library
LNTS	Library of New Testament Studies
LSJ	Liddell, Henry G., Robert Scott, and Henry S. Jones. *A Greek-English Lexicon*. 9th ed. with revised supplement. Oxford: Clarendon, 1996.
LXX	Rahlfs, Alfred. *Septuaginta: Id est Vetus Testamentum Graece iuxta LXX interpres*. Stuttgart: Deutsche Bibelgesellschaft, 1935.
Metam.	Ovid, *Metamorphoses*
MNTC	Moffatt New Testament Commentary
MS	Mnemosyne Supplementum
NA[28]	Aland, Barbara, Kurt Aland, Johannes Karavidopoulos, Carlo M. Martini, and Bruce M. Metzger, eds. *Novum Testamentum Graece*. 28th ed. Stuttgart: Deutsche Bibelgesellschaft, 2012.
NBS	*La nouvelle Bible Segond*. Société biblique française, 2002.

NET	New English Translation
NICNT	New International Commentary on the New Testament
NIV	New International Version, 1984.
NLT	New Living Translation
Notes	*Notes on Translation*
NovT	*Novum Testamentum*
NRSV	New Revised Standard Version
NTL	New Testament Library
NTS	*New Testament Studies*
NTTS	New Testament Tools and Studies
PdV	*Bible Parole de Vie*. Société biblique française, 2000.
PTSDSSP	Princeton Theological Seminary Dead Sea Scrolls Project
RBS	Resources for Biblical Study
REB	Revised English Bible
Rhet.	Aristotle, *Rhetoric*
RSV	Revised Standard Version
SBLDS	Society of Biblical Literature Dissertation Series
SBLMS	Society of Biblical Literature Monograph Series
SBT	Studies in Biblical Theology
ScEs	*Science et Esprit*
SD	Studies and Documents
Semeur	*La Bible Version du Semeur*. Société biblique internationale, 2000.
SIGC	Studien zur interkulturellen Geschichte des Christentums
SNTSMS	Society for New Testament Studies Monograph Series
SubBi	Subsidia Biblica
SymS	Symposium Series
TB	Theologische Bücherei
UBS[5]	Aland, Barbara, Kurt Aland, Johannes Karavidopoulos, Carlo M. Martini, and Bruce M. Metzger, eds. *The Greek New Testament*. 5th ed. Stuttgart: Deutsche Bibelgesellschaft; United Bible Societies, 2014.
WMANT	Wissenschaftliche Monographien zum Alten und Neuen Testament
WUNT	Wissenschaftliche Untersuchungen zum Neuen Testament

1

Why Study γάρ in Romans?

Why should we be concerned at all with the small connective γάρ in the Letter to the Romans?[1] It has long been glossed *for* in English; is there anything of fresh relevance to say about it as we interpret the epistle? First, γάρ occurs 144 times in the epistle, its highest concentration in any New Testament text. Second, it is by no means as unambiguous as the gloss *for* might suggest. In Romans, in New Testament Greek more generally, and, indeed, in Classical Greek, many instances of the connective defy easy definition, and the English translation *for* is inadequate, obscuring the clue that γάρ gives to the direction of the communicator's thought.[2] Agreement continues to elude grammarians and exegetes as to its grammatical status and semantic or conceptual content.[3] The initial impetus for this research

---

1. Traditionally scholars have referred to γάρ as a particle (e.g., John D. Denniston, *The Greek Particles* [Oxford: Clarendon, 1934]) or as a conjunction (e.g., LSJ, s.v. "γάρ"; Raphael Kuehner and Bernhard Gerth, *Ausführliche Grammatik der griechischen Sprache*, 3rd ed., vol. 2 [Hannover: Hahn, 1966]). I will use the general term *connective*, in keeping with more recent terminology employed in relevance theory and in biblical studies, e.g., Deirdre Wilson, "The Conceptual-Procedural Distinction: Past, Present and Future," in *Procedural Meaning: Problems and Perspectives*, ed. Victoria Escandell-Vidal, Manuel Leonetti, and Aoife Ahern (Bingley: Emerald, 2011), 3–31; and N. T. Wright, *Paul and the Faithfulness of God: Parts III and IV*, Christian Origins and the Question of God 4 (London: SPCK, 2013), 764.

2. As Wright points out, *for* is somewhat archaic in contemporary English. This adds an additional layer to the confusion regarding its interpretation (Wright, *Paul and the Faithfulness of God*, 765).

3. It is variously described as a causal particle (e.g., Georg B. Winer, *A Treatise on the Grammar of New Testament Greek: Regarded as the Basis of New Testament Exegesis* [Edinburgh: T&T Clark, 1870], 558), a common particle (A. T. Robertson, *A Short Grammar of the Greek New Testament: For Students Familiar with the Elements of Greek*, 4th ed. [New York: Hodder & Stoughton, 1908], 159), a coordinating conjunction (e.g., BDF, s.v. "γάρ"), a subordinating conjunction (e.g., Neil Elliott, *The*

came from Bible translation work in minority languages. Finding appropriate terms in fresh host languages to render the apparent range of uses of γάρ presents a considerable challenge. This is compounded by the lack of clarity and consensus regarding the role of γάρ.

The variety of classifications among scholars of New Testament Greek is evidence of this uncertainty in relation to γάρ, both in clauses and in the wider discourse. A glance at the standard New Testament Greek lexicon BDAG reveals a confusing categorization of different examples. It lists three main definitions, the first of which alone has six subcategories.[4] There is considerable overlap between categories and an extensive listing of diverse New Testament examples, but there is no explanation as to why particular uses are found in different contexts. As a result of such a plethora of subdefinitions, there is an implicit assumption among many New Testament exegetes that γάρ cannot be relied upon as a consistent communicative signal. When confronted with a seemingly problematic occurrence, each scholar tends to interpret it in accordance with her prior reading of the cotext.[5] Instances that are perceived as problematic because they do not sit easily with a preferred interpretation are not infrequently overlooked.

This brings us to a third reason for reexamining γάρ in Romans. It is found in some of the most exegetically contested passages of the letter, and in some that have been made to bear considerable doctrinal weight. Moreover, it occurs at various pivotal points that have a bearing on wider

---

Arrogance of Nations: Reading Romans in the Shadow of Empire [Minneapolis: Fortress, 2008], 74), a conjunction having either a logical or adverbial function (Daniel B. Wallace, *Greek Grammar Beyond the Basics: An Exegetical Syntax of the New Testament* [Grand Rapids: Zondervan, 1996], 673–74), etc.

4. BDAG, s.v. "γάρ," "1. marker of cause or reason: *for* ... 2. marker of clarification: *for, you see* ... 3. marker of inference: *certainly, by all means, so, then*." Subcategories include: "1b. used with other particles and conjunctions"; "1c. γάρ is sometimes repeated"; "1d. the general is confirmed by the specific ... the specific by the general"; and "1e. oft. the thought to be supported is not expressed, but needs to be supplied fr. the context."

5. I will use feminine pronouns when referring in the singular to an addressee, reader, or interpreter of a text, and masculine pronouns when referring to the author/communicator. This convention is motivated not only by considerations of inclusivity but also by ease of reference, given that the author of Romans is male. By *cotext*, I mean the surrounding communicated text, both preceding and following, i.e., the literary context, whether sentence, paragraph, section, or entire piece of communication.

unresolved questions such as the letter's purpose and the center of its argument. The most notorious and thoroughly discussed example is found in 1:18, but there are other seemingly ambiguous occurrences that are potentially of considerable exegetical importance (e.g., 3:9; 4:2; 5:6–7; 10:4–5; 11:25). The tendency among interpreters to overlook the potentially significant exegetical guidance given by γάρ means that an important clue to communicator intentions is neglected at points where it could provide valuable assistance in making crucial exegetical choices and in deciding on the direction of the argument.

A final reason for this study is a gap in scholarship in relation to the role of γάρ in New Testament nonnarrative material, and, in particular, in argumentation.[6] My research has not uncovered any systematic study of γάρ in the Letter to the Romans in its entirety, nor indeed in any single Pauline epistle, nor other piece of New Testament argumentation considered as a communicative whole. Studies have instead focused largely on γάρ in narrative texts and on isolated problematic occurrences.[7] This is despite the fact that the large majority of New Testament occurrences are found in nonnarrative material, and, in particular, in argumentation. According to Steven Runge's statistical analysis, of the 1,041 occurrences of γάρ in the New Testament, only 10 percent are to be found in narrative proper.[8] Stephanie Black's investigation of γάρ in Matthew's Gospel shows a similar pattern: out of 124 occurrences, only 10 are found in the narrative framework (6 percent of all occurrences), even though the narrative sections account for 31 percent of all material in Matthew.[9] The handful of studies that have investigated γάρ in New Testament argumentation have concentrated on examples in selected passages in Romans and other epistles or have considered γάρ together with other connectives in the Pas-

---

6. For my definition of argumentation, see §3.1.1, below.

7. E.g., Stephanie Black, *Sentence Conjunctions in the Gospel of Matthew: καί, δέ, γάρ, οὖν and Asyndeton in Narrative Discourse*, JSNTSup 216 (Sheffield: Sheffield Academic, 2002); Richard A. Edwards, "Narrative Implications of Gar in Matthew," *CBQ* 52 (1990): 636–55; Margaret E. Thrall, *Greek Particles in the New Testament: Linguistic and Exegetical Studies*, NTTS 3 (Leiden: Brill, 1962); Samuel Zakowski, "She Was Twelve Years Old: On Γάρ and Mark 5:42," *Glotta* 92 (2016): 305–17; Stanley K. Stowers, "*Peri Men Gar* and the Integrity of 2 Cor. 8 and 9," *NovT* 32 (1990): 340–48; C. H. Bird, "Some Γάρ Clauses in St. Mark's Gospel," *JTS* 4 (1953): 171–87.

8. Steven Runge, *A Discourse Grammar of New Testament Greek* (Peabody, MA: Hendrickson, 2010), 52.

9. Black, *Sentence Conjunctions*, 254.

toral Epistles.[10] A systematic study of all occurrences of γάρ in Romans is needed in order to ascertain its role in a piece of argumentation considered as a communicative whole. Romans is the obvious choice for such a study, not only because of its preponderance of occurrences, but also because it is the prime example of sustained argumentation within the New Testament. Such a study will enable us to explore the possibility of a more satisfactory account of the role of connective as a consistent communicative signal.

1.1. Traditional Accounts of γάρ

In considering previous scholarship, three distinct areas are pertinent: first, traditional grammatical and lexicographical accounts of γάρ in New Testament Greek in general (which often build upon accounts of the connective in Classical Greek); second, more recent linguistic accounts; and third, the treatment of γάρ in recent Romans scholarship. Since the latter relies in large part on traditional accounts, I will begin with these and then move on to consider how Romans scholarship makes use of them. After that I will consider some more recent linguistically motivated analyses of γάρ.

1.1.1. Grammatical and Lexicographical Accounts

The focus of this book is the role of γάρ in the Koine Greek of Paul's Letter to the Romans. It is generally agreed, however, that the use of γάρ in New Testament Greek has not changed significantly from Classical Greek.[11] Standard New Testament lexicons and grammars thus tend to reflect

---

10. See Regina Blass, "Constraints on Relevance in Koine Greek in the Pauline Letters" (paper presented at a SIL International seminar, Nairobi, Kenya, May 1993); Iver Larsen, "Notes on the Function of γάρ, οὖν, μέν, δέ, καί, and τέ in the Greek New Testament," *Notes* 5 (1991): 35–47; Jakob A. Heckert, *Discourse Function of Conjoiners in the Pastoral Epistles* (Dallas: SIL International, 1996). Rudolph's doctoral thesis promises much, but, as far as Romans is concerned, focuses almost exclusively on a handful of occurrences in Rom 8. Michael A. Rudolph, "Reclaiming ΓAP: The Semantic Constraints and Structural Significance of ΓAP as an Intersentential Conjunction in Romans through Hebrews" (PhD diss., Southeastern Baptist Theological Seminary, 2014).

11. E.g., Black, *Sentence Conjunctions*, 257; Nigel Turner, *Syntax*, vol. 3 of *A Grammar of New Testament Greek* (Edinburgh: T&T Clark, 1963), 331; BDF.

the categories of their Classical Greek counterparts.[12] Up to the present, the vast majority of New Testament and Classical Greek lexicons alike adopt a traditional account of the connective that is based on a "semantic apparatus" essentially unchanged since classical times.[13] They show little awareness of the principles and methods of modern linguistics but are instead based largely on an outmoded comparative and diachronic philological analysis of language.[14]

The ambiguity surrounding the role of γάρ is related in part to the fact that the connective is grammatically and syntactically optional in any sentence. Any attempt at a sentence level explanation of its function will thus founder.[15] On a traditional account, γάρ is regarded as a causal or explanatory particle, expressing a semantic relationship of cause, reason, or grounds, usually between two adjacent sentences, though the precise reach or scope of γάρ is little discussed.[16] A variation on this traditional causal view is Raphael Kuehner and Bernhard Gerth's identification (in Classical Greek) of an adverbial, confirmatory use alongside a causal/grounds-giving use.[17] In addition, other traditional analyses suggest that in certain instances, such as exclamations and questions, γάρ has an "inferential force."[18] As Stanley Porter points out, a failing of the traditional approach is the erroneous assumption that the way a particle such

---

12. E.g., BDAG, s.v. "γάρ," reflects various definitions and subdefinitions of LSJ, s.v. "γάρ."

13. Standard examples of this traditional approach are LSJ, s.v. "γάρ," and Kuehner and Gerth, *Grammatik*, vol. 2, for Classical Greek; and for New Testament Greek, BDF, s.v. "γάρ," and BDAG, s.v. "γάρ."

14. Stanley E. Porter, "An Introduction to Other Topics in Biblical Greek Language and Linguistics," in *Biblical Greek Language and Linguistics: Open Questions in Current Research*, ed. Stanley E. Porter and D. A. Carson, JSNTSup 80 (Sheffield: JSOT Press, 1993), 85. See also Black, *Sentence Conjunctions*, 28.

15. See Black, *Sentence Conjunctions*, 37.

16. For γάρ as causal particle, see Winer, *Treatise on the Grammar of New Testament Greek*, 558; A. T. Robertson, *A Grammar of the Greek New Testament in the Light of Historical Research*, 3rd ed. (London: Hodder & Stoughton, 1919), 1190. For its use in relation to adjacent sentences, see BDF §235; Kuehner and Gerth, *Grammatik*, 2:335.

17. For the affirmative use, similar to the use of the German particle *ja*, see Kuehner and Gerth, *Grammatik*, 2:330. For the causal use, see Kuehner and Gerth, *Grammatik*, 2:335. Wallace broadly follows this division of the uses of γάρ into "logical" and "adverbial" (Wallace, *Greek Grammar*, 673–74).

18. See Winer, *Treatise on the Grammar of New Testament Greek*, 559.

as γάρ may be translated in English throws light on its function in Greek.[19] Accordingly, γάρ is usually glossed as "for," masking the fact that in various instances "for" may not adequately render its function.

Particularly influential within this traditional approach has been John D. Denniston's comprehensive discussion of particles in Classical Greek. The work broke new ground in providing a detailed examination of a wealth of data and in paying attention to cotext. Denniston identifies the primary use of γάρ as "confirmatory and causal, giving the ground for belief or the motive for action."[20] His study nevertheless displays and reinforces many of the limitations of the traditional approach.[21] His impressive treatment of a range of diverse examples results in a proliferation of subcategories.[22] His work is strong on descriptive detail but says little about the communicative role of γάρ and provides no satisfying, unified account of its function. In general, the traditional approach does not adequately account for examples that involve implicit information or information communicated further back in the cotext than immediately adjacent material. Moreover, it shows little awareness of the interplay between the connective and the semantic content of the particular cotexts in which it occurs.[23] Instead, there is an attempt to read conceptual content from the cotext into the meaning of the connective itself, multiplying the apparent functions of γάρ.

Most recent New Testament lexicons and grammars continue to tread the traditional path reinforced by Denniston, attempting to identify one or two basic definitions or uses for the connective, while listing an array of subdefinitions and categories.[24] These are of limited usefulness in the eluci-

---

19. Porter, "Introduction," 84–85. This implies a naïve view of cross-linguistic equivalence, a notion that is a fiction.

20. Denniston, *Greek Particles*, 58.

21. Denniston's approach has been challenged in recent years by Dutch scholars working on Classical Greek particles; see, e.g., Albert Rijksbaron, ed., *New Approaches to Greek Particles*, ASCP 7 (Amsterdam: Gieben, 1997); C. M. J. Sicking and J. M. van Ophuijsen, *Two Studies in Attic Particle Usage*, MS 129 (Leiden: Brill, 1993).

22. Black, *Sentence Conjunctions*, 19.

23. See Black, *Sentence Conjunctions*, 19.

24. E.g., Wallace, *Greek Grammar*; BDAG, s.v. "γάρ." Porter, while acknowledging the importance of a discourse-analytic approach, does not allow this to shape significantly his analysis of New Testament particles. Stanley E. Porter, *Idioms of the Greek New Testament*, BLG 2 (Sheffield: Sheffield Academic, 1992), 298–307; for his discussion of particles, see 204–17.

dation of apparently problematic instances of γάρ and in the understanding of the connective's communicative role or of the interplay between γάρ and information communicated in the surrounding cotext.

1.1.2. Treatment of γάρ in Romans: Commentaries

The majority of commentaries of Romans, including the most recent, essentially adopt this traditional view of γάρ, following standard New Testament grammars and lexicons, albeit in different ways.[25] The following choices of interpretations for discussion from the vast sea of Romans scholarship are based upon four criteria: (1) the relative prominence given to the discussion of γάρ; (2) the recognition, in theory, at least, of the need to account for γάρ as part of the task of exegesis; (3) the influential and sometimes controversial character of those interpretations chosen; and (4) the representation of a range of diverging perspectives on Romans. The majority of works discussed here are commentaries that deal systematically with the exegesis of the entire epistle. These are particularly appropriate as conversation partners since they engage with the majority of cases of γάρ in the letter, rather than selected occurrences only. After discussing various relatively recent commentaries, we will move on to consider two monographs in which the specific approach taken to γάρ influences the distinctive interpretation of the entire epistle.

Approaches to γάρ in commentaries on Romans, while broadly traditional, can be split into two streams. First, there are those that attempt to pay consistent attention to the connective's causal or explanatory role, in keeping with the basic uses of γάρ identified by traditional grammarians. Second, there are those that, in view of the wide range of subcategories traditionally proposed, begin from the assumption that γάρ expresses diverse "connections of thought," some of which are "light" or "bland." For this latter stream, γάρ is not a consistent exegetical signal and need not be given consideration in all contexts. This perspective on γάρ has been characterized by one of its critics as the "loose" approach.[26]

---

25. E.g., Stanley E. Porter, *The Letter to the Romans: A Linguistic and Literary Commentary*, New Testament Monographs 37 (Sheffield: Sheffield Phoenix, 2015); Michael Wolter, *Röm 1–8*, vol. 1 of *Der Brief an die Römer*, EKKNT 6.1 (Neukirchen-Vluyn: Neukirchener Verlag, 2014); Robert Jewett, *Romans: A Commentary*, Hermeneia (Minneapolis: Fortress, 2007).

26. Wright, *Paul and the Faithfulness of God*, 764.

Representative of the first stream is C. E. B. Cranfield's commentary, which, although published in the 1970s, stands out among commentaries in its careful and consistent treatment of γάρ.[27] Cranfield represents a traditional Reformed reading of Romans. He regards γάρ as an important piece of linguistic evidence contributing not only to the meaning of the clause in which it occurs, but also signaling relationships between larger chunks of thought. As he puts it, "Where there is continuous argument, [connectives] are a most important clue to the author's meaning, of which full use should be made. In the exegesis of Romans one is well advised to watch the connectives with utmost attentiveness."[28]

Cranfield glosses γάρ as "for" but consistently discusses it in terms of its function, explaining its role in almost all contexts as explaining, confirming, or supporting assertions in the previous cotext. He has a flexible view of its scope, maintaining that in some contexts γάρ indicates a relationship between several clauses, or even an entire section, and what precedes it.[29] Cranfield's characterization of γάρ as a "clue to the author's meaning" implies a communicative role. Insights from a linguistic and cognitive-pragmatic understanding of connectives can help to put his reading on a firmer theoretical, linguistic, and cognitive foundation. At the same time, the light shone by these insights may expose the cognitive implausibility of some of Cranfield's claims regarding the scope of γάρ over entire sections.

Ulrich Wilckens's commentary, published shortly after Cranfield's, though less systematic and thorough in its attention to γάρ, nevertheless also attempts to interpret the connective consistently.[30] Wilckens, while coming from a Lutheran perspective, emphasizes the continuity between God's covenant with Israel and salvation through faith in Christ. He essentially reads γάρ as introducing grounds ("begründend"), or a rationale, for preceding material, which in certain contexts he describes as an explanation.[31] This does not prevent him from at times viewing material introduced by γάρ as the beginning of a fresh line of thought or a new

---

27. C. E. B. Cranfield, *The Epistle to the Romans*, 2 vols., ICC (Edinburgh: T&T Clark, 1975).

28. Cranfield, *Epistle to the Romans*, 1:27.

29. In 1:18, Cranfield asserts that γάρ introduces the whole of the section 1:18–3:20, which supports the statement in 1:17 (Cranfield, *Epistle to the Romans*, 1:108).

30. Ulrich Wilckens, *Der Brief an die Römer*, 3 vols., EKKNT 6 (Neukirchen-Vluyn: Neukirchener Verlag, 1978–1982).

31. E.g., on 7:22 (Wilckens, *Der Brief an die Römer*, 2:89).

section (see, e.g., 1:18; 2:12; 8:18; 11:25), which in some cases he analyzes as a "thesis" (1:18; 8:18). In such cases Wilckens acknowledges the tension between the signal given by γάρ and the imposition of the traditional divisions on the text but stops short of challenging these. Instead, while maintaining them, he attempts to emphasize the close connection between the beginning of the supposed new line of thought introduced by γάρ and what precedes.[32]

A third advocate of the consistent causal approach is N. T. Wright, who pays systematic attention to γάρ in his various treatments of Romans.[33] Wright's reading of Romans has been characterized as part of the so-called New Perspective on Paul.[34] The distinctive characteristics of his interpretation are an emphasis on the renewal and fulfilment, in Christ, of God's covenant with Israel, so as to include gentiles together with Jews as members of God's multiethnic family through faith in Jesus, Israel's messiah.[35] Wright argues forcefully against any reading of γάρ that implies that Paul uses his connectives in what he terms a "loose" way. He maintains that γάρ should be read as indicating a causal connection, though with the caveat "until it is definitely proved otherwise," leaving the door open for alternative analyses.[36] Wright understands causal connection in

---

32. E.g., the discussion of 1:18 (Wilckens, *Der Brief an die Römer*, 1:101) and 8:18 (2:147).

33. N. T. Wright, *The Climax of the Covenant: Christ and Law in Pauline Theology* (Edinburgh: T&T Clark, 1991); Wright, "Romans," in *Acts; Introduction to Epistolary Literature; Romans; 1 Corinthians*, NIB 10 (Nashville: Abingdon, 2002), 393–770; Wright, *Paul and the Faithfulness of God*. Of these, only the New Interpreter's Bible is a commentary.

34. By the *New Perspective* is meant a family of related readings of Paul, developed in the wake of E. P. Sanders's paradigm-shifting analysis of Second Temple Judaism found in *Paul and Palestinian Judaism: A Comparison of Patterns of Religion* (London: SCM, 1977). See N. T. Wright, "Romans 9–11 and the 'New Perspective,'" in *Between Gospel and Election: Explorations in the Interpretation of Romans 9–11*, ed. Florian Wilk and J. Ross Wagner, WUNT 257 (Tübingen: Mohr Siebeck, 2010), 37, though Wright elsewhere finds the label unhelpful (Wright, *Paul and the Faithfulness of God*, 925 n. 426). These share the view that Paul's teaching about justification by faith was occasioned by a specific historical situation in the early church and thus has a social and ethnic dimension. See James D. G. Dunn, *The New Perspective on Paul: Collected Essays*, WUNT 185 (Tübingen: Mohr Siebeck, 2005), 26. Justification by faith is essentially about the inclusion of the gentiles into God's people.

35. The kernel of Wright's reading is set out in *Climax of the Covenant*.

36. Wright, *Paul and the Faithfulness of God*, 764–65.

its broadest sense of a relationship of reason, rationale, or explanation. He consistently analyzes γάρ as introducing further explanation of preceding material. This works well in many cases but is not able to account for all peculiarities of the use of γάρ in Romans. In a minority of cases, such as 2:25 and 9:17, where an explanatory reading of γάρ does not obviously fit, Wright passes over the connective in silence. Like Cranfield, he views its scope flexibly but does not provide an explanation of how addressees are to identify the scope in different cotexts.[37]

In his 2002 discussion, Wright draws attention to the series of "successive explanations" in 1:16–17, each introduced by γάρ, which he sees as characteristic of a particular style of argumentation found often in Romans. He maintains that in such a series, the final explanatory clause (v. 17) expresses "the deepest thing Paul wishes to say ... the foundation of the whole sequence," but he passes over the fact that the chain of successive explanations introduced by γάρ in fact continues into 1:18.[38] In other passages too, Wright asserts that explanatory theological material introduced by γάρ represents the main thrust of the argument, carrying Paul's emphasis.[39] This is in tension, however, with the causal understanding of γάρ he espouses, which regards γάρ as introducing a rationale that is essentially in a supporting relation with something that has previously been asserted.[40] We will explore how far a linguistic and cognitive-pragmatic account of the connective is compatible with Wright's view that certain explanatory theological statements introduced by γάρ represent the heart of the argument and how far it challenges this particular tracking of Paul's argumentative thrust.

The second stream of traditional approaches to γάρ is influenced by the multiplication of subcategories found in standard New Testament lexicons such as BDAG. James D. G. Dunn's influential 1988 commentary is representative of this stream. This classic example of a New Perspective

---

37. See, e.g., Wright's 2002 discussion of 1:18 and 10:5–9 (Wright, "Romans," 428–29, 652).

38. Wright, "Romans," 423–24. In Wright's 2013 work, however, he draws attention to the sequence of γάρ clauses in 1:16–18, but nevertheless views 1:18 as the beginning of a major new section in Paul's argument (Wright, *Paul and the Faithfulness of God*, 764).

39. See Wright's 2002 discussion of 8:3–4; 9:11b; 15:8–9 (Wright, "Romans," 574, 637, 747).

40. See, e.g., BDAG, s.v. "γάρ," 1e; Denniston, *Greek Particles*, 62; Cranfield, *Epistle to the Romans*, 1:240.

reading of Romans finds the "integrating motif for the whole letter" in the tension between "Jew first but also Greek."[41] Dunn maintains that the significance of γάρ should not be "overloaded," since it can indicate "lighter connections of thought."[42] In 1:18, for instance, Dunn suggests that γάρ may be read as introducing the first stage of the larger argument and that the connection indicated may be "as much as contrast as of cause."[43] In other contexts, γάρ is interpreted variously as indicating an explanation, elaboration, or development of thought. In 10:4–5, meanwhile, Dunn insists that the "full force" of γάρ must be appreciated. The inconsistency of Dunn's approach is striking when one compares his light reading of the connective in 1:18 with the weightier reading he chooses in 10:4–5. The importance of the close link between 10:4–5 and the immediately preceding argument is crucial to Dunn's reading of the Jewish law as the symbol and instrument of Jewish privilege.[44] His variable approach to γάρ appears to be determined by his prior interpretation of particular passages. The communicative account of γάρ proposed in this study will not only expose the inconsistency of his treatment of γάρ, but also throw into question certain of his prior assumptions about the thrust of Paul's argument.

This second stream of approaches to γάρ is represented in German scholarship by Ernst Käsemann's 1973 commentary, and, most recently, by Michael Wolter's commentary on Rom 1–8.[45] Both come to Romans from a Lutheran perspective, emphasizing the universal theological significance of the doctrine of justification by faith and its central role in the epistle's argument. Käsemann's treatment of γάρ is multifarious. He asserts a range of different uses but at no point discusses his general view of the connective's role. His readings range from "begründend," to "explaining the consequence" of a previous statement (2:12), introducing a result of the previous paragraph (7:14), introducing a theme (8:18), summarizing (8:22), communicating the sense *indeed* ("in der Tat," 15:27), and an argumentative use that starts a new train of thought (2:25, etc.).[46] In many instances, Käsemann simply asserts the connective's function in the brief-

---

41. James D. G. Dunn, *Romans 1–8*, WBC 38A (Waco, TX: Word, 1988), lxii.
42. Dunn, *Romans 1–8*, 38.
43. Dunn, *Romans 1–8*, 70, 54.
44. James D. G. Dunn, *Romans 9–16*, WBC 38B (Waco, TX: Word, 1988b), 589–96.
45. Ernst Käsemann, *An die Römer*, HNT 8a (Tübingen: Mohr, 1973); Wolter, *Röm 1–8*.
46. Käsemann, *An die Römer*, 31, 57, 189, 220, 226, 381, 367.

est of terms, without explaining the rationale for his reading. In contrast to Wilckens, he seems untroubled by occurrences of the connective at the beginning of supposed new subsections or fresh lines of thought. Like Dunn, his readings of γάρ appear to be predetermined by his interpretation of the cotext. As we shall see, the unified and communicative account of γάρ presented in this book will throw into question aspects of Käsemann's reading of the contours of the argument of Romans and expose his apparent lack of concern with the clear connection it indicates with the preceding cotext at certain points (see, e.g., 2:25; 4:13; 8:18).

Wolter, on the other hand, explicitly acknowledges his dependence on Walter Bauer's analysis of γάρ.[47] The latter asserts not only a grounds-giving ("begründend") use, but also a connective-continuative use ("anknüpfend/fortführend"), and even an adversative use in certain contexts.[48] In 1:18, Wolter argues that γάρ can be read anaphorically ("begründend") or kataphorically ("anknüpfend/fortführend/adversativ"). In order to decide between these, he jumps forward in the text to 3:21–22, ascertaining the relationship indicated by γάρ in 1:18 by analogy with the one indicated by γάρ in 3:22b. In both cases, γάρ introduces grounds for the claim that salvation is for all, without exception, through faith alone.[49] Wolter's strategy is thus to begin with the wider argument and to use it to clarify seemingly ambiguous occurrences of γάρ. In other words, the connective is in no sense a basic piece of exegetical evidence that helps to inform and direct an understanding of the argument. Wolter's treatment of γάρ is curiously patchy: while commenting on some seemingly problematic instances, there are others that are passed over in silence.[50] The fresh communicative account of γάρ put forward in this book will challenge Wolter's reliance on older lexicographical analyses such as Bauer's. More significantly, it will revolutionize the connective's contribution to exegesis, transforming it into a signpost guiding toward communicator intentions, instead of a whiteboard onto which interpreters impose their prior perspective.

---

47. Walter Bauer, *Griechisch-deutsches Wörterbuch zu den Schriften des Neuen Testaments und der übrigen urchristlichen Literatur*, ed. Kurt Aland, 6th ed. (Berlin: de Gruyter, 1988). Bauer's German work forms the basis of BDAG.

48. Wolter, *Röm 1–8*, 130, 330, citing Bauer, *Griechisch-deutsches Wörterbuch*, s.v. "γάρ."

49. Wolter, *Röm 1–8*, 130–31.

50. E.g., the occurrences in 2:25; 4:13; 5:6–7; 7:22 are not discussed.

1.1.3. Treatment of γάρ in Romans: Monographs

One might not ordinarily look to monographs on Romans for the detailed discussion of γάρ that one would expect in a commentary. Neil Elliott's and Douglas Campbell's recent monographs, however, both pay attention to the connective at certain key points in the letter's argument.[51] Both are explicit in articulating their approach to the connective, but their approaches stand in stark contrast to each other.

Campbell's work is an "apocalyptic rereading of justification in Paul" that focuses in particular on a rereading of Rom 1–4. Campbell's aim is to challenge the distorting interpretative grid of a justification theory that, in his view, has been imposed upon Romans by generations of interpreters. Campbell advocates a loose approach to γάρ, much like Dunn's and Wolter's. While recognizing that γάρ often carries causal force, it is, in his view, best viewed as a "bland signifier" in various contexts.[52] It is not clear, however, what criteria Campbell uses to distinguish between instances of causal force and blander uses. He insists that for ambiguous occurrences, the cotext and wider argument are determinative for ascertaining the particular use of γάρ. Campbell is explicit about wishing to avoid placing too much interpretative weight on the connective. For him, "γάρ is not an unambiguous signal concerning Paul's argumentative strategy; rather, the strategy that we conclude is operative ... will signal how we are to interpret γάρ."[53]

The attention Campbell gives to the connective is concentrated primarily in his discussion of 1:18, on which his reading of Rom 1–4 hinges. By dismissing γάρ as a communicative clue, he is able to argue that 1:18 represents the beginning of the presentation of an opposing gospel to Paul's, spoken in the voice of Paul's opponent, which is in fundamental discontinuity with what precedes it in 1:16–17.[54] In other passages that are also discussed in considerable detail, however, he is silent regarding γάρ, despite the fact that the signal it gives could potentially support his

---

51. Neil Elliott, *The Rhetoric of Romans: Argumentative Constraint and Strategy and Paul's Dialogue with Judaism*, JSNTSup 45 (Sheffield: Sheffield Academic, 1990); Elliott, *Arrogance of Nations*; and Douglas A. Campbell, *The Deliverance of God: An Apocalyptic Rereading of Justification in Paul* (Grand Rapids: Eerdmans, 2009).

52. Campbell, *Deliverance of God*, 340. See also 1021 n. 6, for a range of senses of γάρ, inspired by BDAG, s.v. "γάρ."

53. Campbell, *Deliverance of God*, 340.

54. Campbell, *Deliverance of God*, 542–43.

interpretation.⁵⁵ Ultimately, Campbell's disregard for γάρ as a consistent communicative signpost deprives him of an important clue to communicator intentions and the direction of the argument. His strategy of disambiguating γάρ from his construal of the wider argument threatens to undermine his own valid concern to reject the imposition of prior interpretative grids. As we shall see, the communicative account of γάρ offered by the present study poses a serious challenge to Campbell's reading of γάρ at the pivotal point of 1:18. As such, it threatens to undermine his entire rereading of the argument of Romans.

In contrast, Elliott emphasizes the importance of taking into account the clear indications given by γάρ as to the argumentative flow of the epistle. In his 1990 work, he takes a rhetorical-critical approach, while in his 2008 monograph he reads Romans from an ideological-critical, anti-imperial perspective.⁵⁶ For Elliott, γάρ is a subordinating conjunction, a "grammatical marker" that indicates a close connection with what precedes.⁵⁷ Elliott is scathing of interpretations that disregard the clear indication given by chains of γάρ clauses (see 1:15–18 and 2:1–16) as to the direction of Paul's argument. In his view, these interpretations tear statements such as those in 1:16–17 from their context and isolate them as self-contained units. This encourages a distorted theological reading of the letter that privileges the doctrine of justification by faith.⁵⁸ It is notable that here Campbell and Elliott's wider concerns coincide, and yet Campbell employs precisely the treatment of γάρ that Elliott criticizes as an "interpretive misstep" leading to particular theological readings of the letter.⁵⁹

Elliott's audience-orientated approach, which views the epistle as a piece of persuasion, encourages an essentially communicative view of γάρ, in which the connective helps guide addressees towards the thrust of the argument.⁶⁰ In both works, Elliott argues for a reading of Romans that takes account of the fact that the argumentative flow of these passages is from supporting axioms introduced by γάρ backward toward

---

55. See Campbell's discussion of 1:16b (Campbell, *Deliverance of God*, 702–3).
56. Elliott, *Arrogance of Nations*, 11.
57. Elliott, *Rhetoric of Romans*, 80; Elliott, *Arrogance of Nations*, 74 n. 80.
58. Elliott, *Arrogance of Nations*, 74–75; Elliott, *Rhetoric of Romans*, 122.
59. Elliott, *Arrogance of Nations*, 75.
60. Elliott, *Arrogance of Nations*, 19.

a main argumentative point.⁶¹ That is, information introduced by γάρ, however theologically weighty, represents premises that support other more argumentatively salient information. Elliott's view suggests that γάρ allows us to trace the direction of the argument and distinguish between salient argumentative points, on the one hand, and weighty supporting theological statements, on the other. But he applies this insight only selectively in his 2008 reading. He does not consider other examples of chains of γάρ clauses, or indeed pivotal single occurrences, that could have implications for identifying the center of the argument, possibly challenging aspects of his anti-imperial interpretation (e.g., 8:17–30; 10:1–13; 15:7–13). A fresh, cognitively grounded analysis of γάρ could enhance Elliott's important insights regarding the direction of argumentation by placing them within a theoretical and communicative framework, ensuring that they are applied more generally to the whole argument of the epistle.

1.2. Linguistic Accounts of γάρ

While contemporary scholars of Romans have continued in large part to rely upon traditional analyses of γάρ, in the past half century attempts have been made, particularly by some working in the domain of Bible translation, to apply modern linguistic principles to the study of γάρ in New Testament Greek. These studies are distinguished by a particular awareness of the biblical text as a piece of communication with an audience and by the assumption that Biblical Greek is a human language like any other. This perspective enables an investigation of the language from outside the straitjacket of traditional grammatical categories, using the methodology of descriptive linguistics. Such studies are, however, limited in their scope: most focus on isolated and problematic occurrences of γάρ, particularly within New Testament narrative.⁶²

---

61. Elliott, *Rhetoric of Romans*, 122.
62. E.g., J. A. Harbeck, "Mark's Use of 'Gar' in Narration," *Notes* 38 (1970): 10–15; Stephen H. Levinsohn, *Textual Connections in Acts*, SBLMS 31 (Atlanta: Scholars Press, 1987); Larsen, "Notes on the Function"; Larsen, "The Use of 'γάρ' and the Meaning of Fire in Mark 9:49," *Notes* 8 (1994): 33–39; S. Swartz, "Hiding the Light: Another Look at Luke 8:16–18," *Notes* 8 (1994): 53–59.

1.2.1. Discourse-Analytic Approaches

Stephen Levinsohn, also working within the field of Bible translation, harnesses a discourse-analytic approach in order to explain features of New Testament Greek, including connectives.[63] He characterizes his approach as eclectic and functional.[64] His work focuses mainly on New Testament narrative material, particularly Acts, and is distinctive in its identification of a single function for γάρ: "to introduce background material that strengthens some aspect of what has just been presented."[65] This material does not advance the main line of the narrative or argument but instead provides an explanation or exposition of the previous assertion. This explanation is a clear departure from the traditional listing of various uses of γάρ in different contexts. The notion of strengthening previous information does, however, pick up on a strand in traditional accounts that recognizes a confirmatory role for γάρ.[66] Levinsohn's analysis accords with the views of Dutch scholars applying a pragmatically orientated discourse-analytic approach to Classical Greek, who view γάρ as a particle that "pushes [or subordinates] the utterance [that it introduces] to a lower level than the preceding discourse."[67]

Levinsohn's analysis represents a step forward in its attempt to provide a unified account of the function of γάρ in New Testament texts and its recognition of the connective as essentially a structural signal that indicates background information. But his account has limitations.[68] It suggests a

---

63. See the discussion of discourse analysis in §2.2.2 n. 42, below.

64. Stephen H. Levinsohn, *Discourse Features of New Testament Greek: A Coursebook on the Information Structure of New Testament Greek*, 2nd ed. (Dallas: SIL International, 2000), vii.

65. Levinsohn, *Discourse Features*, 90.

66. E.g., LSJ, s.v. "γάρ," 3b, "to confirm or strengthen something said"; Winer, who states that γάρ can express "generally an affirmation or assent (γε) which stands in relation to what precedes (ἀρά)" (Winer, *Treatise on the Grammar of New Testament Greek*, 558), and Denniston's identification of a "confirmatory use" (Denniston, *Greek Particles*, 58).

67. Simon R. Slings, "Adversative Relators Between PUSH and POP," in Rijksbaron, *New Approaches to Greek Particles*, cited by Stéphanie J. Bakker, "On the Curious Combination of the Particles Γάρ and Οὖν," in *Discourse Cohesion in Ancient Greek*, ed. Stéphanie J. Bakker and Gerry C. Wakker, ASCP 16 (Leiden: Brill, 2009), 41.

68. See Porter's critique in which he criticizes Levinsohn for failing to consider discourse features in a range of New Testament text types and authors: Stanley E.

close strengthening relationship between information introduced by γάρ and the immediately preceding assertion but does not address the issue of γάρ clauses that seem to relate to preceding material not immediately adjacent, nor of the strengthening of implicitly communicated information. Despite using the terminology of strengthening, Levinsohn stops short of a cognitive, inferential account of γάρ that would explain in what sense strengthening occurs and what this means in terms of communicative and persuasive effects for addressees.

Other scholars have built on Levinsohn's discourse-analytic approach, applying it to a wider range of material. Jakob A. Heckert uses it to investigate the use of γάρ in the Pastoral Epistles. He argues that γάρ has one "semantic function" but "one or two pragmatic uses," concluding that its basic function is "to introduce propositions which confirm and strengthen a preceding conjunct, usually one that immediately precedes."[69] His study is not a systematic exploration of all occurrences in the Pastoral Epistles, however, and contains little illustration or explanation of how γάρ does in fact introduce strengthening material. Runge, meanwhile, in his innovative discourse-analytic grammar of New Testament Greek, adopts Levinsohn's basic view of γάρ. He describes its function thus: "the information introduced [by γάρ] does not advance the discourse but adds background information that strengthens or supports what precedes."[70] Runge applies this analysis consistently in his 2014 reading of Romans.[71] Like Levinsohn, however, his work does not consider the possible cognitive and inferential aspects of the role of γάρ and is ultimately focused on the text itself and its structure, rather than on the text as a communicative stimulus for an audience.

1.2.2. A Cognitive-Pragmatic Approach: Procedural Meaning

The discourse-analytic approach represented by Levinsohn and Runge makes some progress, then, in identifying a core function for γάρ but

---

Porter, "How Can Biblical Discourse Be Analyzed? A Response to Several Attempts," in *Discourse Analysis and Other Topics in Biblical Greek*, ed. Stanley E. Porter and D. A. Carson, JSNTSup 113 (Sheffield: JSOT Press, 1995), 107–10.

69. Heckert, *Discourse Function of Conjoiners*, 9.
70. Runge, *Discourse Grammar*, 52.
71. Steven Runge, *Romans: A Visual and Textual Guide*, HDC (Bellingham, WA: Lexham, 2014).

still leaves aspects of its use unexplained, in Romans and elsewhere. The approach needs to be supplemented by more pragmatic and context-sensitive models, which emphasize that a focus on the text or linguistic form itself, without due attention to its cognitive implications, is not enough to discover its meanings.[72] In recent years, the increasing interest among linguists in the phenomenon of connectives in many languages has generated a wealth of research from a variety of theoretical perspectives.[73] In particular, developments in cognitive pragmatics have opened up possibilities for a new understanding of the role of connectives in terms of giving guidance toward inferences that are drawn by addressees as part of the comprehension process. The groundbreaking notion of procedural meaning, first proposed by Diane Blakemore within the framework of relevance theory, has served as a basis for unified accounts of a whole host of connectives in diverse languages.[74] Relevance theory is a theory of communication that seeks to explain how the interpretation of linguistic communication works. One of its fundamental insights

---

72. By *pragmatic* I mean dealing with language in use, not to be confused with philosophical pragmatism; see Stephen Pattemore, *The People of God in the Apocalypse: Discourse, Structure, and Exegesis*, SNTSMS 128 (Cambridge: Cambridge University Press, 2004), 13 n. 2; Stephen C. Levinson, *Pragmatics*, CSL (Cambridge: Cambridge University Press, 1983), 1. See §2.1, below, for a discussion of pragmatics as a subbranch of linguistics. See Teun A. van Dijk's critique of systemic-functional approaches to context. Teun A. van Dijk, *Discourse and Context: A Sociocognitive Approach* (Cambridge: Cambridge University Press, 2008), 28–55.

73. E.g., Levinson, *Pragmatics*; Deborah Schiffrin, *Discourse Markers* (Cambridge: Cambridge University Press, 1987); Diane Blakemore, *Semantic Constraints on Relevance* (Oxford: Blackwell, 1987); Black, *Sentence Conjunctions*. Depending on the approach adopted, connectives are also referred to by some as "discourse markers" or "connectors."

74. See Blakemore, *Semantic Constraints*, though she does not use the term *procedural* in her early work. Wilson, "Conceptual-Procedural Distinction" gives an overview of the development of the notion of procedural meaning. E.g., Corinne Iten, *Linguistic Meaning, Truth Conditions and Relevance: The Case of Concessives* (New York: Palgrave MacMillan, 2005); Tomoko Matsui, "Semantics and Pragmatics of a Japanese Discourse Marker *Dakara* (so/in Other Words): A Unitary Account," *Journal of Pragmatics* 24 (2002): 867–91; Jacques Moeschler, "Connecteurs pragmatiques, inférences directionnelles et représentations mentales," *Cahiers Chronos* 12 (2005): 35–50; Ryoko Sasamoto, "Japanese Discourse Connectives *Dakara* and *Sorede*: A Reassessment of Procedural Meaning," *Journal of Pragmatics* (2008): 127–54; Sandrine Zufferey, *Lexical Pragmatics and Theory of Mind* (Amsterdam: Benjamins, 2010).

is that the comprehension of all language involves not only decoding but also inferences. Procedural meaning, meanwhile, is to be distinguished from conceptual meaning. It involves the linguistic representation not of concepts, but of instructions that guide addressees toward the derivation of inferences. Blakemore argues that connectives are used by communicators as procedural markers that constrain addressees' inferential processes, reducing ambiguity. A more detailed account of both relevance theory and the notion of procedural meaning will be given in chapter 2.

The notion of procedural meaning has the potential to provide a unifying explanation for the variety of uses of γάρ in Romans and beyond within an overarching, cognitively grounded theoretical framework that recognizes the fundamental role of communicator, context, and addressees in the interpretative process. Indeed, its potential in relation to New Testament Greek was recognized in the 1990s by Regina Blass, a linguist and pragmatician with a background in Bible translation. In a brief but insightful unpublished sketch, Blass sought to apply Blakemore's procedural account to various Greek connectives in Pauline epistles, in an attempt to find a more coherent explanation of these for the purposes of translation into fresh languages. Blass attempted to explain their particular roles in terms of "constraining relevance," that is, in guiding in a particular direction the inferences drawn by addressees.[75] She posited a backward strengthening or confirming function for γάρ that is able to accommodate a variety of uses in different contexts (see further under §2.2, below). Blass's account makes intuitive sense and has the advantage of explaining the functions of various Greek connectives as part of a single cognitive account, allowing for comparison and enhanced understanding of their contrasting yet related roles. Her study limits itself to a handful of relatively straightforward examples of γάρ from Romans, however. A systematic examination of all occurrences in Romans is needed to discover how far such a procedural hypothesis is able to provide a consistent and unifying account of a diversity of examples and how it may need to be refined or extended.

Blass thus briefly considers procedural meaning in relation to New Testament Greek connectives but comes at the subject from the perspective of pragmatics rather than biblical studies. Indeed, although the

---

75. Blass, "Constraints on Relevance."

notion of procedural meaning has proved influential in pragmatics, it has hitherto had relatively little impact on biblical studies. In general, while older structuralist and functionalist linguistic approaches have gained traction to some extent, innovative insights from pragmatics have yet to make a significant impact on the understanding of New Testament Greek.[76] Two forward-looking exceptions, however, are Stephanie Black's examination of sentence conjunctions in Matthew's Gospel and Margaret Sim's monograph examining ἵνα and ὅτι in Koine Greek.[77] Both bridge the gap between biblical studies and linguistics/pragmatics by applying the notion of procedural meaning to New Testament connectives, offering innovative, unifying accounts of their communicative function across a range of uses. Black starts from a systemic-functional perspective but is eclectic in her approach, drawing from other streams in her application of new linguistic tools to the study of New Testament Greek. Her analysis of γάρ is limited in its scope: her chapter on γάρ deals with the ten occurrences found in narrative material in Matthew. Nevertheless, her work is a model of how one may integrate the concept of procedural meaning with aspects of other cognitive approaches and produce a pragmatic account of connectives that is accessible to biblical scholars.[78] For Black, in narrative material γάρ has a single pragmatic function of directing addressees to "strengthen a preceding proposition, confirming it as part of the mental representation they construct of the discourse." Her analysis emphasizes the interplay between the connective and the semantics of the linguistic cotext, but stops short of discussing the inferential processes that may be involved in comprehending this. Like Levinsohn and Runge, Black

---

76. See Margaret Sim, *Marking Thought and Talk in New Testament Greek: New Light from Linguistics on the Particles ἵνα and ὅτι* (Eugene, OR: Pickwick, 2010), 21. For an overview of studies applying structuralist and functionalist linguistic approaches to aspects of New Testament Greek, see Stanley E. Porter and Andrew W. Pitts, "Greek Language and Linguistics in Recent Research," *CurBR* 6 (2008): 214–55; and Joseph D. Fantin, *The Lord of the Entire World: Lord Jesus, a Challenge to Lord Caesar?* New Testament Monographs 31 (Sheffield: Sheffield Phoenix, 2011), 23–24.

77. Black, *Sentence Conjunctions*; Sim, *Marking Thought*. See also Zakowski ("She Was Twelve Years Old"), who uses the notion of procedural meaning to explain γάρ in Mark 5:42.

78. E.g., Philip N. Johnson-Laird's theory of mental models. Johnson-Laird, *Mental Models: Towards a Cognitive Science of Language, Inference, and Consciousness* (Cambridge: Cambridge University Press, 1983).

emphasizes that γάρ introduces material that is "off-line with respect to the sequence of narrative events."[79]

Sim, meanwhile, taking a relevance-theoretic approach, argues that ἵνα does not carry a fixed lexical meaning but instead gives procedural instructions to addressees to process information that follows as representing a potential rather than an actual state of affairs. Such an account is superior to a traditional explanation because it enables an understanding of ἵνα in terms of the author's communicative intention, and the inferences it encourages addressees to draw.[80] Sim's study serves as an illuminating example of how a relevant-theoretic framework can be employed to throw fresh light on features of New Testament Greek that continue to resist satisfactory analysis using traditional categories.

In brief, insights from the evolving domain of pragmatics not only have the potential to unlock more satisfying and theoretically grounded explanations of connectives in New Testament Greek, but also, more generally, encourage the recovery of a communicative view of the biblical text, in which communicator, context, and addressees all play a fundamental role. Unlike biblical studies, modern linguistics and pragmatics are relatively recent fields of study, unencumbered by the weight of tradition. They enable the application of fresh cross-linguistic discoveries about the functioning and use of human language to the elucidation of both ancient and modern languages. As cousin disciplines closely related to some of the concerns of biblical studies, they have much to offer their older relative. Their innovative insights need to be seized and applied within biblical studies in order to find new ways forward for intransigent exegetical problems. With these new linguistic tools at our disposal, the time is ripe for a systematic exploration of γάρ in Romans.

1.3. New Light on γάρ, New Light on Romans: Contours, Contributions, and Claims of the Study

Given this research context, the present work takes a fresh look at γάρ in Romans, using an original interdisciplinary method that harnesses the cognitive approach of relevance theory. The theoretical framework of relevance theory is concisely presented in chapter 2, showing its usefulness

---

79. Black, *Sentence Conjunctions*, 280, 51–52, 261.
80. Sim, *Marking Thought*, 59, 197.

as a tool for the interpretation of biblical texts. In chapters 3 and 4, taking into account all the examples of γάρ in Romans, the book proposes a fresh understanding of the connective as a crucial communicative signal with a consistent role as a procedural indicator in the epistle's discourse. Put another way, γάρ does not carry conceptual meaning but instead guides addressees in drawing inferences that result in the strengthening of points already made in the argument. This fresh, cognitively based account does far more than simply provide a unified yet contextually sensitive account of γάρ. It enables us to find a way forward out of the confusion of traditional explanations to a more exegetically useful understanding of the connective's communicative role. The procedural explanation of γάρ has real significance for the exegesis of Romans and the interpretation of its argument, as chapters 5 and 6 of the book demonstrate, assisting us in adjudicating between major interpretations of disputed verses and sections. As a procedural indicator, γάρ is an indispensable clue to the coherence and direction of Paul's argument.

The Letter to the Romans continues to generate vigorous scholarly debate like no other epistle. Paul's reasons for writing, the center and coherence of his argument, his likely intended audience, and the importance or otherwise of the Roman situation to which he wrote, all remain lively subjects of discussion and lead to a bewildering variety of alternative construals of the epistle. As already noted, a number of the most notoriously contested sections of Romans, which give rise to divergent interpretations, are peppered with examples of γάρ, and some contain high profile instances at key points in the argument. Consider, for example, the four occurrences in 1:16–18. These verses are read in various ways, for example, as a thematic statement (vv. 16–17) followed by a heading (v. 18) that begins Paul's main argument and the indictment that forms its first section.[81] They have also been read as a programmatic statement of Paul's gospel followed by the presentation of an opposing gospel.[82] Others still have interpreted them as a statement of Paul's gospel about God's justice as a challenge to imperial pretension, followed by an explanation of God's wrath against imperial injustice.[83]

---

81. E.g., Dunn, *Romans 1–8*, 36–51; Wilckens, *Der Brief an die Römer*, 1:77, 93–95; Peter Stuhlmacher, *Paul's Letter to the Romans: A Commentary* (Louisville: Westminster John Knox, 1994), 33–34.

82. See Campbell, *Deliverance of God*, 542–43.

83. Elliott, *Arrogance of Nations*, 51, 74–83.

Other examples abound of γάρ occurring at points where the exegetical stakes are high. Take, for example, the instance in 4:2, which occurs at the beginning of a section regarded as a key text both for a traditional Lutheran reading and for a new perspective construal of the epistle, or the four instances in 10:1–5, which are similarly central to the debate between these two perspectives (see chapter 4, below). We could also cite the ten instances found in the famously disputed 7:7–25 or those occurring in the interpretative minefield of 11:11–32, particularly the example found in 11:25. Similarly, we find an occurrence of γάρ in 15:8, a verse containing serious exegetical difficulties in the closing section of the letter body, regarded by some as the culmination of Paul's entire argument.[84]

In all these instances and others still, a reading of γάρ as a consistent exegetical signal that can be relied upon serves as an important tool for deciding between certain interpretations. It can save much exegetical effort by enabling interpreters to swiftly rule out readings that plainly contradict the clear guidance that γάρ gives to the coherence of the argument. Equally, it provides support for other readings that take account of the connective's indications of supporting and background information as distinct from the salient main points of the argument. The procedural explanation of γάρ thus provides a way forward out of various exegetical thickets in Romans.

Chapter 5 of the book demonstrates how a procedural understanding of γάρ sheds light on long-disputed exegetical difficulties in individual verses. It rules out Richard Hays's influential New Perspective reading of 4:1, since this does not respect the indication given by γάρ in 4:2 of coherence with the preceding context in 3:27–31.[85] Similarly, we shall see how the indication given by γάρ in 10:4 undermines the Lutheran reading of τέλος ... νόμου as the termination of the law but confirms the increasingly accepted goal or fulfilment interpretation. In 10:5, too, the guidance given by γάρ rules out the interpretation advocated by Käsemann, Francis Watson, and others that regards 10:5 and 10:6 as being in sharp contrast to one another.[86] In contrast, it provides support for the view put forward by

---

84. Wright, *Paul and the Faithfulness of God*, 819, 1494–95.

85. Richard Hays, "Have We Found Abraham to Be Our Forefather according to the Flesh? A Reconsideration of Rom. 4:1," *NovT* 27 (1985): 76–98.

86. Käsemann, *An die Römer*, 273; Francis B. Watson, *Paul and the Hermeneutics of Faith* (London: T&T Clark, 2004), 331–40.

Robert Badenas and others that the voice of righteousness by faith in 10:6 reinterprets the citation in 10:5.[87]

Meanwhile, chapter 6 of the book demonstrates how, at the macrolevel of whole sections of the letter's argument, a procedural understanding of γάρ enables us to trace more clearly the direction and point of Paul's argument at pivotal points where its coherence is contested. The chapter focuses on the discussion of two hinge texts already mentioned, 1:15–18 and 15:7–13. It shows how a procedural reading of γάρ seriously undermines Campbell's controversial construal of 1:18–32 as the voice of Paul's opponent, a reading that ignores the clear signals given by γάρ as to the close strengthening connection between 1:18 and the thought of 1:15–17.[88] At the other end of the letter's argument, Wright's contention that 15:8–12 communicates an implicit challenge to Roman imperial power is also thrown into question by the guidance γάρ gives in 15:8 as to the main thrust of the argument in this section.[89]

The illumination thrown by γάρ on the coherence and argumentative thrust of these sections also has a bearing on major discussions regarding the purpose and the likely intended audience of the epistle. We will discover that the procedural guidance γάρ gives in these passages leads to a Rome-specific reading of the letter's purposes and a construal of Paul's probable addressees as a mixture of Jews and gentiles. In this way the fresh account of γάρ offered constitutes a new method for determining whom Paul was writing to and why.

More generally, it is the book's claim that a procedural understanding of γάρ allows us to distinguish the argumentative wood from the trees, facilitating a focus on the main line of the argument. It throws into question interpretations that are distracted from the main thrust of what Paul has to say by weighty but supporting theological explanations or proofs, which serve as ballast for the argument's most salient points. It likewise casts doubt on readings of Romans that are determined by a prior interpretative grid and ride roughshod over the explicit textual clues as to the letter's coherence. Instead, it fosters a respect for the coherence of the epistle as a communicative whole. In sum, this communicative account of γάρ

---

87. Robert Badenas, *Christ the End of the Law: Romans 10.4 in Pauline Perspective*, JSNTSup 10 (Sheffield: JSOT Press, 1985), 124, 129.

88. Campbell, *Deliverance of God*, 542–43.

89. Wright, "Romans," 746, 748; Wright, *Paul and the Faithfulness of God*, 1300, 1308, etc.

encourages interpreters to remove their theological spectacles and take a fresh look at the argumentative thrust of Romans, reexamining their presuppositions regarding its direction and likely intended relevance.

2
Relevance Theory and Perspectives on Romans

This chapter will first present the theoretical framework and methodology of the study, setting out some basic aspects of relevance theory that are pertinent to the investigation of γάρ in Romans. Second, it will show how relevance theory is a new tool that is particularly well adapted to a reexamination of the old problem of the role of γάρ and will justify its application to the interpretation of an ancient text. Third, taking relevance theory's notion of cognitive environments as a starting point, it will discuss briefly some background issues related to Romans, touching on questions of the possible shared context of author and addressees and giving a concise overview of some major perspectives on the epistle and its likely purpose.

2.1. Introducing Relevance Theory

Relevance theory belongs within a cognitive-pragmatic approach to communication and the interpretation of language.[1] Within the discipline of linguistics, the branch of pragmatics deals with language in use, that is, in relation to users and interpreters, and with the contribution of context to meaning.[2] This emphasis on communicators, addressees, and context is highly pertinent to biblical studies. Pragmatic approaches inspired by

---

1. Cognitive pragmatics has been described as "the interdisciplinary study of language use and verbal communication within the methodological and theoretical framework of the cognitive sciences." See Marina Sbisà, Jan-Ola Östman, and Jef Verschueren, eds., *Philosophical Perspectives for Pragmatics* (Amsterdam: Benjamins, 2011), 241.

2. Laurence R. Horn and Gregory E. Ward, eds., *Handbook of Pragmatics*, BHL (Oxford: Blackwell, 2004), xi. For a discussion of different definitions of pragmatics based on diverse linguistic perspectives, see Pattemore, *People of God*, 13 n. 2.

the philosopher of language, H. P. Grice, define pragmatics in terms of a semantics/pragmatics distinction, in which semantics is concerned with "what the words say" and pragmatics with "what the speaker means."[3] On this view, linguistic semantics is understood as the linguistic encoding of meaning, while linguistic pragmatics deals with meaning that must be inferred from contextual information. Grice assumed that pragmatic interpretation is based on human rationality and accorded a central role to speaker intention in determining meaning.[4]

Cognitive pragmatics affirms these Gricean assumptions. It differs from Grice, however, in its use of the methods of cognitive science and its concern with empirical cognitive processes. It assumes that the inferring of a communicator's intention from the communication context involves a specific kind of information processing.[5] Relevance theory, first proposed by Dan Sperber and Deirdre Wilson in the 1980s, represents one specific approach within cognitive pragmatics. It aims to explain how the human cognitive system does the interpretative work needed to understand utterances in communication.[6] It holds that the interpretation of language involves subpersonal cognitive processes that are automatically geared toward the maximization of relevance and guided by the search for it.[7]

Relevance theory aims to provide a general, unifying explanation of human communication applicable cross-linguistically. In the years since its initial appearance, relevance theory has stimulated vigorous debate and a wide range of research into linguistic and pragmatic phenomena in many languages. It continues to evolve in the light of this.[8] It has likewise been applied within various related disciplines: philosophy and psychol-

---

3. Robyn Carston, *Thoughts and Utterances: The Pragmatics of Explicit Communication* (Oxford: Blackwell, 2002), 3.

4. Billy Clark, *Relevance Theory*, CSL (Cambridge: Cambridge University Press, 2013), 18, 21, 357.

5. Sbisà, Östman, and Verschueren, *Philosophical Perspectives*, 241.

6. Diane Blakemore, *Relevance and Linguistic Meaning: The Semantics and Pragmatics of Discourse Markers*, CSL 99 (Cambridge: Cambridge University Press, 2002), 154-55.

7. I.e., automatic computations that are not under conscious control. See Clark, *Relevance Theory*, 34, and Carston, *Thoughts and Utterances*, 7.

8. See, e.g., the "Open Peer Commentary" in Dan Sperber and Deirdre Wilson, "Précis of Relevance: Communication and Cognition," *Behavioral and Brain Sciences* 10 (1987): 697-754, and the modifications in Sperber and Wilson, *Relevance: Communication and Cognition*, 2nd ed. (Oxford: Blackwell, 1995), 255-60, 295-98.

ogy, literary, media, and translation studies, experimental pragmatics, and cognitive science.[9]

2.1.1. Cognition, Relevance, and Ostensive-Inferential Communication

Relevance theory is concerned with what it terms ostensive-inferential communication. This involves an overt intention to communicate on the part of the communicator and inferencing on the part of the addressee.[10] Relevance theory asserts that "intentional communication gives rise to expectations which help us to decide what the communicator intends to convey" and that language functions as a clue to those intentions.[11] It works from the presupposition that human minds automatically pay attention to whatever in their environment brings them most cognitive benefits or effects. Relevance theory defines cognitive effects as "worthwhile differences to the individual's representation of the world."[12] The aim of ostensive communication is to bring about changes and expansion to the addressee's cognitive environment (see §2.1.3, below), that is, to the set of assumptions that are manifest to her.[13] Within relevance theory, *assumption* is a technical term referring to a thought or idea that is held as true by, or accessible to, an individual (see glossary for a more complete definition).

Cognitive processes demand processing effort, however. Relevance theory conceives of relevance in terms of a trade-off between worthwhile cognitive effects and the processing effort involved in acquiring them. Something is optimally relevant to an individual if cognitive effects gained outweigh processing effort. Relevance theory claims that "to communicate is to claim someone's attention."[14] By the act of communicating verbally (i.e., ostensively), we automatically claim that the information communicated is relevant enough to our addressees to be worth the effort needed to process it. The mutual recognition by communicator and

---

9. See Pattemore for a short overview (*People of God*, 21) and the relevance theory Online Bibliographic Service, available at https://tinyurl.com/SBL4528b.
10. See Clark, *Relevance Theory*, 113, and the glossary in appendix A, below.
11. Clark, *Relevance Theory*, 4.
12. Deirdre Wilson and Dan Sperber, "Relevance Theory," in *The Handbook of Pragmatics*, ed. Laurence R. Horn and Gregory E. Ward (Oxford: Blackwell, 2004), 608.
13. Assumptions are manifest to an individual if they are perceptible or inferable to her (Sperber and Wilson, "Précis of Relevance," 699).
14. Sperber and Wilson, "Précis of Relevance," 697.

addressee of the communicator's intentions acts as a guarantee that what is said will give rise to an interpretation that will be optimally relevant.[15] Relevance theory claims that this presumption or principle of relevance automatically guides inferential comprehension processes.[16] It enables the addressee's comprehension processes to select a relevant set of contextual assumptions (i.e., a context) in order to draw inferences and arrive at a relevant interpretation.[17]

2.1.2. Decoding, Inference, and Underdeterminacy

In contrast to older code models of communication, relevance theory claims that interpretation of linguistic communication involves two distinct mechanisms: decoding and inference.[18] On this view, decoding involves subpersonal computations that translate the linguistic forms used by the communicator into mental representations. These are then combined with, and adjusted in relation to, contextual information by means of inferential processes in the search for an optimally relevant interpretation.

Relevance theory claims that the linguistic code of all utterances is, for reasons of efficiency, underdetermined in terms of meaning. To make every detail of a communicator's intention explicit would involve unnecessary effort for both communicator and addressee. Instead, the linguistic code is merely a stimulus supplying necessary clues from which the addressee infers the communicator's likely intention. Interpretation involves drawing inferences to disambiguate and enrich the underdetermined linguistic stimulus using contextual information to arrive at a semantically complete propositional form.[19] In many cases it also involves drawing inferences from implicit information in order to arrive at the intended relevant interpretation. A communicator tailors the linguistic stimulus in order to provide an optimal amount of explicit information: neither too little, which would lead to extra inferential work, nor too much, which would result in

---

15. Sperber and Wilson, *Relevance*, 267.
16. Sperber and Wilson, *Relevance*, 267–70.
17. I.e., background assumptions used in the interpretation of an utterance. See glossary and further discussion under §2.1.3, below.
18. For a critique of older code models of interpretation, see Pattemore, *People of God*, 13.
19. Sperber and Wilson, *Relevance*, 72–73.

distracting overload. If a communicator misjudges what is required, an addressee may fail to arrive at a relevant interpretation.

2.1.3. Context and Contextual Assumptions

In relevance theory terms, the context of an utterance or piece of communication is the set of premises used in comprehension, chosen in the interpretative process: "a context is a psychological construct, a subset of the hearer's assumptions about the world."[20] Communicators and addressees have a unique body of knowledge accessible to them that relevance theory refers to as encyclopedic knowledge.[21] The context of an utterance may include information from the physical environment and immediately preceding utterances, but also from encyclopedic knowledge. An addressee may draw on all kinds of manifest contextual information to combine with the information communicated by the linguistic code in order to comprehend the communicator's intention. It is the principle of relevance that ensures that addressees select the appropriate contextual assumptions from all manifest information. In the comprehension of a written text, the immediately preceding cotext represents the most highly accessible contextual information.

Furthermore, relevance theory talks in terms of the cognitive environment of individuals. At any given time, individuals have a set of facts or assumptions that are manifest to them, determined by physical environment, cognitive abilities, encyclopedic knowledge, and more.[22] This set of assumptions makes up their unique cognitive environment. The cognitive environments of individuals can overlap to a greater or lesser extent.[23] In order for communication to succeed, communicator and addressees must share an overlapping cognitive environment.

---

20. Sperber and Wilson, *Relevance*, 15–16. Relevance theory uses the term *premise* in a technical sense to refer to an assumption that is used in a process of inferences that leads to a conclusion (see glossary). This does not imply, however, as in strict logic, that the truth of a premise guarantees the truth of the conclusion.

21. Encyclopedic knowledge comes from the experiences of an individual and consists of contextual assumptions in the form of beliefs, memories, cultural information, and values, etc.; see glossary.

22. Sperber and Wilson, *Relevance*, 39.

23. This stops short of the problematic notion of mutual knowledge. See Sperber and Wilson, *Relevance*, 15–21.

2.1.4. A Relevance-Guided Comprehension Heuristic

How does the principle of relevance ensure that an addressee selects the intended contextual assumptions as premises in the inferential interpretation process? Because of the presumption of relevance, an addressee's subpersonal interpretative processes follow what relevance theory terms a relevance-guided comprehension heuristic. That is, the addressee's inferential comprehension processes automatically follow "a path of least effort" as they compute cognitive effects.[24] In constructing hypotheses about the intended meaning of a linguistic stimulus, the most accessible (the most obvious) interpretation is considered first, and the process of testing interpretative hypotheses stops as soon as the addressee's expectations of relevance are satisfied. The next most accessible interpretation will only be considered if adequate cognitive effects are not gained from the first.

2.1.5. Types of Cognitive Effect

Relevance theory identifies different kinds of cognitive effect, that is, ways in which the cognitive environment of addressees can be modified. These result from different kinds of inferential procedures undertaken. The most notable effect is a contextual implication. This is a new conclusion, derivable from a combination of the input provided by the linguistic stimulus plus contextual assumptions.[25] A second cognitive effect is particularly pertinent to our study of γάρ: the strengthening of existing assumptions already held by an addressee, so that she adheres to them more strongly. Blass states that, "the strength of an existing assumption may ... be modified by the acquisition of new information ... [and] new information may achieve relevance by strengthening an existing assumption."[26] Other

---

24. Wilson and Sperber, "Relevance Theory," 613.
25. Wilson and Sperber, "Relevance Theory," 608.
26. Regina Blass, *Relevance Relations in Discourse: A Study with Special Reference to Sissala*, CSL 55 (Cambridge: Cambridge University Press, 1990), 45. The relevance theory notion of strengthening has much in common with Chaïm Perelman and Lucie Olbrecht-Tyteca's view that beliefs, once established, can be intensified by argumentation that reinforces them by means of new reasons supporting them. Chaïm Perelman and Lucie Olbrecht-Tyteca, *The New Rhetoric: A Treatise on Argumentation* (Notre Dame: University of Notre Dame Press, 1969), 44.

types of cognitive effect include the revision or the abandonment of available assumptions.[27]

2.1.6. Explaining the Strengthening Effect

According to Blakemore, in the inferential procedure of strengthening, an addressee draws certain inferences about the relationship between a newly presented statement and a previously communicated assumption (claim). The new statement is processed as a premise or evidence that provides support for the previous claim, so that it is held more strongly as valid by the addressee. Relevance theory uses *premise* to refer to an assumption in a process of inference that functions as support for a conclusion (for a more complete definition, see glossary). Strengthening involves combining the new premise with highly accessible contextual assumptions in an inferential series. This leads to a conclusion that is a reiteration, and confirmation, of the previously communicated claim, based on independent evidence.[28] By independent evidence is meant information already known and accepted by the addressee, which she is able to access independently of the communicator. As a result of the fact that this independent evidence substantiates the communicator's previous claim, its validity is confirmed, and it is adhered to more strongly by the addressee.

To illustrate the difference between the procedure of strengthening and the procedure of drawing a contextual implication, Blakemore uses the following example:

(1) Tom can open Ben's safe. (2) He knows the combination.[29]

Depending on the context, statement (2) can be processed either as a strengthening premise for (1) or as a new conclusion inferred from (1). An addressee must use contextual information in order to infer the rela-

---

27. Wilson and Sperber, "Relevance Theory," 608.
28. See Blakemore, *Semantic Constraints*, 84–85, 88–90. Relevance theory proposes a model of nondemonstrable inferences in which the truth of a premise does not guarantee the truth of the conclusion. The process of nondemonstrable inferences is "less a logical process than a form of suitably constrained guesswork" involving hypothesis formation. It uses "deductive rules, but is not totally governed by them" (Sperber and Wilson, *Relevance*, 69).
29. Blakemore, *Relevance and Linguistic Meaning*, 78.

tionship and thus the relevance of (2). In a context where (1) has been interpreted as a new claim, when an addressee hears (2), her subpersonal comprehension processes infer that this is intended as confirming evidence. These processes then search for the most easily accessible contextual assumption(s) to use as premises to be combined with (2) in an inferential series leading to the independent deduction of (1) as a conclusion. In this case, the most highly accessible assumption activated by (2) from the addressee's encyclopedic knowledge will be something like (3): "If someone knows the combination of a safe, that person is able to open the safe."

We can represent the assumptions involved in this procedure as a logical argument something like the following:

Series A: strengthening
Explicitly communicated premise (1): Tom can open Ben's safe.
Explicitly communicated premise (2): Tom knows the combination to Ben's safe.
Background premise (3): If someone knows the combination of a safe, that person is able to open the safe.
Conclusion (independently confirming, and reiterating, [1]): Tom can open Ben's safe.

Since (1) is independently deduced by the addressee as a conclusion on the basis of (2) plus background assumptions already available and accepted as valid, the result is an increase in the strength with which claim (1) is held as valid. Statement (2) is thus relevant in relation to (1), contributing to an increase in its relevance.

On the other hand, in a different context, where (1) has been understood as a premise, (2) will be interpreted as a new conclusion. We can imagine the following scenario: Ben is unconscious, and his friends urgently need to know the combination to his safe. They suddenly remember that another friend, Tom, has opened the safe in the past. This leads them to infer, and to state explicitly, (2), that he knows the combination. In terms of cognitive effects, this represents a contextual implication that is relevant in its own right, bringing fresh changes in thought, rather than strengthening existing assumptions. In this case, addressees' comprehension processes will draw a different set of inferences to establish the relevant relation between (1) and (2), along the following lines:

Series B: new conclusion/implication
> **Explicitly communicated premise** (1): Tom can open Ben's safe.
> **Conclusion** (explicitly communicated in utterance [2]): Tom knows the combination to Ben's safe.
> **Background premise**: If a person can open a safe, that person knows the combination to the safe.

It is possible for an addressee to infer these differing cognitive effects in different contexts from statements (1) and (2) without additional procedural guidance from the communicator. But Blakemore argues that the insertion of a connective at the beginning of (2) (either "you see/after all" indicating strengthening) or "therefore/so" (indicating a new implication) will facilitate comprehension, constraining interpretation and reducing processing effort.[30] Such connectives encode instructions for inferential procedures to be followed.

2.2. Pointing to Inferences: Procedural Meaning

Blakemore's notion of procedural meaning is based on a distinction between conceptual information, which, when decoded, becomes input for the construction of mental representations and procedural information, which encodes instructions guiding towards inferential procedures. This distinction corresponds to the two distinct modes of ostensive-inferential communication: decoding and inference. The conceptual/procedural distinction has proved influential both within and outside the framework of relevance theory and has been applied not only to connectives, but also to the analysis of a whole range of linguistic phenomena.[31] The notion of procedural meaning continues to evolve as it is applied to fresh areas such as the study of mental states and epistemic vigilance.

Indeed, as already noted, Blakemore's notion of procedural meaning has been applied to aspects of New Testament Greek by scholars working in the domain of Bible translation. In her unpublished but influential article, Blass, a linguist and Bible translator working within relevance theory, suggests that Blakemore's procedural account may be applied to the New Testament Greek connectives οὖν, γάρ, καί, δέ, and ἀλλά in the Pauline

---

30. Blakemore, *Relevance and Linguistic Meaning*, 78.
31. See Wilson, "Conceptual-Procedural Distinction."

epistles. She proposes that γάρ is a procedural marker that indicates that the assumptions that it introduces should be interpreted as "premises, backwards confirming and strengthening other propositions." Blass argues that it is the principle of relevance that determines the exact scope of the material introduced by γάρ and which elements of the previous communication it strengthens. She recognizes the particular difficulties faced by secondary interpreters of the biblical text, given the fact that the original communication context is no longer available.[32] She argues that procedural markers such as γάρ provide valuable constraints on interpretation for contemporary interpreters, guiding toward certain inferences and thus assisting with the selection of contextual assumptions.[33]

Based on Blakemore's proposed model, Blass lays out the strengthening procedure triggered by γάρ in Rom 3:22–23 as a logical argument, as below. It is important to note that this is a hypothetical analysis of how the interpretation process *may* go, rather than a representation of what was *actually thought*.[34] This is the case for the construction of hypothetical inferential series throughout this study.

> Romans 3:22–23: The righteousness of God through faith in Jesus Christ (is) for all who believe, γάρ there is no distinction, γάρ all have sinned and fall short of the glory of God.
>
> **Premise 1**: If there is no distinction, then the righteousness of God through faith in Jesus Christ (is) for all who believe. (Inference drawn from background assumptions.)
> **Premise 2 introduced by** γάρ: There is no distinction. (v. 22b)
> **Conclusion**: The righteousness of God through faith in Jesus Christ (is) for all who believe. (Backward strengthening v. 22a)

Similarly, she lays out the strengthening series triggered by γάρ in 3:23 as follows:

---

32. I use Ernst-August Gutt's terminology of "secondary communication situation" to refer to any interpretation undertaken in a situation where the cognitive environment of the first addressees is no longer accessible. Ernst-August Gutt, *Translation and Relevance: Cognition and Context* (Manchester: St. Jerome, 2000), 76.
33. Blass, "Constraints on Relevance," 6–9.
34. See Blass, *Relevance Relations*, 13.

Premise 1: If all have sinned and fall short of the glory of God, then there is no distinction (between Jews and gentiles).[35] (Inference drawn from background assumptions.)
Premise 2 introduced by γάρ: All have sinned and fall short of the glory of God.
Conclusion: There is no distinction (between Jews and gentiles). (Backward strengthening v. 22b)[36]

In each case, Blass identifies a single background assumption that is involved in the inferential procedure. Her account provides a theoretically coherent, cognitively grounded account of the handful of isolated occurrences of γάρ she discusses from Romans, all of which are unambiguous instances introducing substantiation or confirming evidence for a previous claim. It does not, however, deal with more problematic occurrences, nor does it consider a range of diverse biblical data from a piece of communication in its entirety.

Blass's study represents an insightful hypothesis for a fresh analysis of γάρ. It makes intuitive sense and opens up new possibilities for a more cognitively coherent and useful explanation. Her proposal requires a systematic investigation of all the data in Romans, however, in order to test its capacity to provide a unified yet flexible explanation for the apparent range of uses of γάρ, in contrast to the confusion of multiple functions that results from traditional approaches. Her proposal needs exploration and development in order to account for apparently problematic occurrences. It thus serves as a springboard for the thorough reexamination of all occurrences of γάρ in Romans undertaken in the present study. Our goal is twofold: first to demonstrate how in every case γάρ functions as a consistent exegetical signal guiding addressees toward inferences that strengthen previous claims, and second to explore how this fresh account of γάρ sheds significant light on major exegetical debates and discussions regarding the coherence of the epistle's argument.

2.2.1. Benefits of a Procedural Approach

A relevance-theoretic, procedural approach to connectives has a number of strengths that make it a well-adapted tool as we seek a more satisfactory

---

35. Blass translates as "gentiles" rather than "Greeks."
36. Taken from Blass, "Constraints on Relevance," 8.

explanation of γάρ in Romans. First, it provides a cognitively grounded explanation for the phenomenon of connectives within a wider explanatory theory affirming the importance of communicative intention, context, and interpretative choices in interpretation. Cross-linguistic evidence from a wide range of languages suggests that procedural meaning may be a universal linguistic phenomenon, just as inferences are a fundamental part of all human communication.[37]

Second, the notion of procedural meaning opens up new possibilities for a unified account of diverse occurrences of γάρ. The range of partially overlapping meanings or functions traditionally identified can potentially be accounted for by a single set of instructions. This is flexible enough to account for different outworkings in diverse contexts, as we shall see. Thus a procedural account has the potential to explain various problematic instances where a causal or supporting relationship with immediately preceding material is not obvious.

Third, the proposal that connectives encode processing instructions, not concepts, liberates us from the difficulties encountered when we attempt to find a conceptual definition or an explanation of its nongrammatical status and optional use. The notion of procedural instructions makes sense of the fact that γάρ is used at the communicator's discretion, depending on his assessment of how much guidance a particular audience needs toward a relevant interpretation. In short, a procedural account potentially untangles various knots in the task of defining and explaining γάρ.

2.2.2. Guidance toward Different Contributions to Relevance

According to relevance theory, over the course of a piece of communication, an addressee's cognitive environment is adjusted and expanded as a result of different cognitive effects. A cognitive environment is not a fixed construct but is "progressively created as the text is processed."[38] The interpretation of one utterance contributes to the contextual assumptions available for establishing the relevance of the next.[39] Consequently, the preceding cotext of any utterance plays a vital role in its interpretation, particularly immediately preceding utterances. Information commu-

---

37. See Blass, *Relevance Relations*, 14.
38. Pattemore, *People of God*, 49.
39. Blass, *Relevance Relations*, 78.

nicated further back in the cotext may also be made freshly salient by repetition or by the activation of associated assumptions at a particular point, contributing to the cognitive effects derived.[40]

Within an extended piece of communication such as a literary text, various parts make different contributions to its overall relevance. Some represent highly salient pieces of information from which many contextual implications are drawn; for example, the climax of a story, or the beginning or conclusion of a section of argumentation. Others represent premises that prepare for subsequent conclusions, while still others represent information that strengthens previous assumptions.[41] Procedural markers or indicators such as γάρ help to flag up the salience or relative relevance of different pieces of information in relation to the wider argument. We can define salience in terms of relatively high numbers of cognitive effects derived from particular communicated assumptions. Less salient parts of a text (background or supporting information) make a contribution to overall relevance by activating assumptions that prepare for and support the most salient points. In the case of strengthening, a statement contributes to relevance in relation to previously communicated information, increasing the strength with which it is held as valid and thereby increasing its salience. Without the contributions to relevance made by less salient information, there would be fewer cognitive effects gained at key salient points. Punch lines would have only weak punch, since contextual assumptions necessary for maximal cognitive effects would not be easily accessible.

A relevance-theoretic approach thus requires that interpreters pay careful attention to the whole previous cotext as potentially relevant contextual information. For this reason, I have chosen to use the entire Letter to the Romans as a corpus for the study of γάρ. I will examine occurrences of γάρ in Romans within their wider cotext to explore how γάρ may guide the interpreter at each point in the argument and thus contribute to the argument as a whole. In every case, I will consider previously communicated assumptions that are highly accessible and likely to be involved in the inferential processes of interpretation.

---

40. See Pattemore, *People of God*, 53–54: "a subsequent passage may provide the missing component of the cognitive environment of an earlier passage … allowing [this] to achieve optimal relevance *as the reading proceeds*" (emphasis original).

41. Christophe Unger, "On the Cognitive Role of Genre: A Relevance-Theoretic Perspective" (PhD diss., University of London, 2002), 134–38.

Whereas various discourse-analytic approaches focus on the structure of a text, and on coherence between units of text or discourse that may be indicated by linguistic signals such as discourse markers (connectives), relevance theory focuses on the relationship between the linguistic code of the text and its context and how this relationship may achieve effects in addressees' minds.[42] Thus the contours and structure of a piece of communication are ultimately psychological rather than textual, arising from cognitive processes and effects. This is not to say that the linguistic structure of a text, nor its study, is unimportant, but rather that it serves as a series of clues to cognitive realities beyond it.[43] Discourse analysis allows us to analyze more effectively these clues, and the ways they are organized. Insights from discourse analysis will be harnessed in this study to throw light on matters of text type (see §3.1, below).

2.3. Relevance Theory and Biblical Interpretation

While relevance theory is a well-adapted tool for the reexamination of a connective such as γάρ, is it more generally suited to the investigation of an ancient literary text? Although the theory has been applied in diverse ways by a handful of biblical scholars, concerns have been raised about the appropriateness of applying a modern cognitive approach to the study of the biblical text.[44] Relevance theory claims that the interpretation of literary

---

42. Discourse analysis encompasses a diversity of approaches, definitions, and methodology. See Deborah Schiffrin, *Approaches to Discourse* (Oxford: Blackwell, 1994), for a detailed comparison of differing theoretical perspectives within discourse analysis; and Blass, *Relevance Relations*, 7–40. For an overview of a variety of discourse-analytic approaches applied to biblical studies, see Porter and Pitts, "Greek Language," 235–41. See also Runge, *Discourse Grammar*, and Levinsohn, *Discourse Features*. Porter and Runge take two distinct discourse-analytic approaches to Romans (Porter, *Letter to the Romans*, and Runge, *Romans*).

43. Blass, *Relevance Relations*, 14, 24. Relevance theory understands the contours of an extended piece of communication in terms of continuity created by sets of closely associated assumptions versus discontinuity caused by switches in psychological context. See Blakemore, *Relevance and Linguistic Meaning*, 156–57.

44. Among those applying relevance theory, see, e.g., Fantin, *Lord of the Entire World*; Margaret Sim, *A Relevant Way to Read: A New Approach to Exegesis and Communication* (Cambridge: Clarke, 2016); and Sim, *Marking Thought*; Pattemore, *People of God*; Black, *Sentence Conjunctions*. See Pattemore, *People of God*, 22–32 for a response to concerns about applying relevance theory to biblical texts.

works involves the same cognitive and communicative abilities as spoken communication and that the same theoretical notions and principles apply.[45] Since linguistic interpretation takes place in the mind of the addressee and affects thought, any account of interpretation, whether of spoken or written language, must be psychologically plausible. Relevance theory allows us to bring recent insights about the way the mind interprets linguistic communication to bear on our interpretation of the biblical text. Moreover, it holds together two fundamentally important concerns for biblical interpretation: a focus on the linguistic code of the text, on the one hand, and on its communicative purpose, on the other. Relevance theory leads us to take the linguistic form of the text seriously as a starting point, but also to recognize it as an incomplete stimulus for first audience and secondary interpreters alike, beyond which addressees need to go by means of inferences.

In the light of the problematization of the notion of authorial intention, some have criticized relevance theory for the role that it accords to communicator intentions.[46] The role of authorial intention is, however, currently being explored in fresh ways by some literary theorists.[47] Indeed, literary critic Stanley Fish, a well-known advocate of reader-response theory, recently affirmed the importance of communicator intention: "Words always mean what their speakers intend, and they fail or multiply in their meaning if no intention is attached to them."[48] Moreover, relevance theory's recognition of communicator intentions fits well with the attention paid by historical-critical biblical exegesis to possible authorial intention.

---

45. Sperber and Wilson, *Relevance*, 32; Deirdre Wilson, "Relevance and the Interpretation of Literary Works," *UCL Working Papers in Linguistics* 23 (2011): 70. For a defense of relevance theory as an effective tool in literary interpretation, see Ian MacKenzie, *Paradigms of Reading: Relevance Theory and Deconstruction* (New York: Palgrave Macmillan, 2002).

46. See Wilson's and Pattemore's discussions (Wilson, "Literary Works," 70; Pattemore, *People of God*, 23).

47. E.g., Seán Burke, *The Death and Return of the Author: Criticism and Subjectivity in Barthes, Foucault and Derrida*, 3rd ed. (Edinburgh: Edinburgh University Press, 2010). Raymond W. Gibbs suggests that "people immediately, and unconsciously, seek out authorial intentions when they read." Raymond W. Gibbs, *Intentions in the Experience of Meaning* (Cambridge: Cambridge University Press, 1999), 28, cited by Pattemore, *People of God*, 28.

48. Stanley Fish, "On King v. Burwell: What Is a Natural Reading?," *Huffington Post*, 29 June 2015, https://tinyurl.com/SBL4528a.

Relevance theory's affirmation of the role of communicator intentions in shaping a piece of communication is, however, only part of the story. The theory affirms equally the role of addressees' interpretative processes in fulfilling those informative intentions by inferring a relevant interpretation.[49] This brings us to another potential criticism of the application of relevance theory to the study of the biblical text. While the theory may leave room for a reader-response approach to interpretation, is it able to assist us with a more historical-critical concern with the recovery of the possible perspectives of the first audience?[50] Relevance theory insists upon an overlapping cognitive environment between communicator and addressees within which a relevant interpretation can be inferred. Biblical interpreters are, however, secondary interpreters, listening in on a communication between biblical authors and the first addressees, whose cognitive environment and contextual assumptions cannot be recovered with any certainty.[51] How is relevance theory able to help secondary interpreters recover the most important probable inferences derived by the first addressees?

First, relevance theory raises our awareness of the text as "a record of a genuine communication event."[52] It compels interpreters to ask questions about the text's first addressees, the important contextual assumptions probably available to them, and the inferences they might plausibly have drawn in interpretation. It draws attention to the fact that we as secondary interpreters are also limited by our cognitive environments. We likewise constantly make use of contextual assumptions and inferences in order to fill in the gaps left by the textual clues, inferences that may be different from those of the first audience.[53] In short, relevance theory draws attention to the otherness of the text's first addressees, to our own limited

---

49. Pattemore, *People of God*, 29.

50. By *first audience* I mean the Roman audiences that first heard the letter, in distinction from subsequent secondary audiences. This raises the question of *implied audience* versus actual or empirical audience, a distinction that is not as clear as Stanley K. Stowers suggests. Stanley K. Stowers, *A Rereading of Romans: Justice, Jews and Gentiles* (New Haven: Yale University Press, 1994), 21–22. See Philip Esler's critique in *Conflict and Identity in Romans: The Social Setting of Paul's Letter* (Minneapolis: Fortress, 2003), 110, and §2.4.1, below.

51. For a discussion of the importance and difficulty of reconstructing such perspectives, see John M. G. Barclay, "Mirror-Reading a Polemical Letter: Galatians as a Test Case," *JSNT* 10 (1987): 73–93.

52. Pattemore, *People of God*, 28.

53. Fantin, *Lord of the Entire World*, 4.

interpretative perspective, and to the inevitability of drawing inferences as part of the interpretative process.[54] It encourages interpreters to be aware of two sets of interpretative inferences: those probably drawn by the first audience and those we draw ourselves in interpretation.[55]

Furthermore, relevance theory suggests a way forward for secondary interpreters confronted with the problem of the inaccessibility of contextual information available to the first addressees. It encourages the positing of a basic shared cognitive environment for communicator and first audience, within which hypotheses can be made about probable inferences that might plausibly have been drawn.[56] It affirms the contribution of historical-critical research in the reconstruction of a plausible shared cognitive environment that makes most relevant sense of the textual data.[57]

Most importantly, relevance theory stipulates a principle by which potential contextual information can be judged and selected as input into the interpretation process. As Stephen Pattemore points out, according to relevance theory, it is not the context of communication but the assumption of relevance that is a constant. Addressees assume that the communication is relevant and search for the appropriate context in order to infer optimal cognitive effects.[58] Following the principle of relevance, secondary interpreters, too, begin with the textual linguistic clues and are constrained to consider only the most highly accessible contextual information as plausible input into the reconstruction of inferential processes.[59] This will be background information that is easily suggested by the textual clues (i.e., does not involve undue processing effort to

---

54. See William S. Campbell, "The Addressees of Paul's Letter to the Romans: Assemblies of God in House Churches and Synagogues?," in Wilk and Wagner, *Between Gospel and Election*, 176.

55. See Pattemore's discussion, which talks in terms of "synchronic"/"diachronic" communication situations, rather than primary/secondary (Pattemore, *People of God*, 29).

56. Pattemore suggests that this will consist of shared assumptions derived from membership of a particular community. In the case of a community of faith, as with the audience of Romans, shared assumptions may concern texts, beliefs, and traditions (Pattemore, *People of God*, 30).

57. See Wilson, "Literary Works," 72.

58. Pattemore, *People of God*, 17.

59. This will be not only assumptions communicated by the cotext but plausible historical information that the text makes highly accessible.

access) and that produces a coherent construal of as much of the textual data as possible. Such a construal will represent the most relevant interpretation of the text. On the other hand, background historical information that is more tangential and speculative, and less obviously suggested by the textual stimulus, can be left out of consideration, since it requires more processing effort.[60] Finally, as well as providing a principle for the identification of likely contextual assumptions, relevance theory also provides models of inferential series, suggesting how interpretative hypotheses may be constructed using contextual information. This study will make much use of relevance theory's proposed model for the incorporation of probable contextual assumptions in the inferential procedure of strengthening (as demonstrated by Blakemore and Blass).

Of course, there is no guarantee of the validity of the proposed reconstructions of cognitive environments, contextual assumptions, and inferences drawn by the first addressees. We can aim for probability and plausibility in such reconstructive work, but not certainty. In response to this, some within biblical studies embrace the epistemological perspective of critical realism.[61] This acknowledges that biblical exegesis is a particularly complex and uncertain task, that interpretative objectivity is unattainable, and that there can be no guarantee of recovery of the communicator's intention or first interpreters' context. Nevertheless, it assumes that the biblical text was shaped by the communicative intention of its authors and that, on the basis of the textual and historical data available to us, it is worth attempting to trace probable communicator intentions and to suggest interpretations that might plausibly have been reached by the first addressees. The subjectivity of our perspective calls for a basic attitude of humility in the interpretative task, however, holding on to our conclusions lightly. I will adopt a critical-realist perspective in this study, onto which relevance theory maps well. Relevance theory, too, argues that there is no guarantee that an addressee will arrive at the interpretation intended by the communicator, since "intentions cannot be decoded but only nondemonstratively inferred," so communication and interpretation

---

60. See Pattemore, *People of God*, 50–51. Cf. Barclay's discussion of categories of plausibility for possible background information (Barclay, "Mirror-Reading a Polemical Letter," 84–86).

61. This method is set out by N. T. Wright in relation to the study of the New Testament. N. T. Wright, *The New Testament and the People of God*, Christian Origins and the Question of God 1 (London: SPCK, 1992).

always take place at a risk.⁶² Nevertheless, just as we all engage in the risky business of communication because of its potential benefits, so also this interpretative risk is worth taking because of the potential gains.

2.4. Background Issues

2.4.1. Author, Audience, and Their Cognitive Environment

Relevance theory encourages us, then, to posit basic common sense elements of a likely mutual cognitive environment for Paul and his likely Roman addressees, within which relevant contextual assumptions would have been selected during the inferential interpretation process.⁶³ As stated above, this cognitive environment will be posited primarily on the basis of textual clues, but also using plausible and generally accepted historical information made highly accessible by the text. The identity of the author and recipients, as well as the specification of a probable date and location for the letter, all fit within the establishment of this cognitive environment. We will make use of some widely accepted general assumptions about Paul, and some consensus views regarding his likely Roman audience, in order to posit foundational aspects of their probable cognitive environments.

The apostle Paul is the undisputed author of Romans. Three broad areas of generally accepted basic assumptions regarding the apostle allow us to identify some basic building blocks of his cognitive environment. The first area includes Paul's Jewish ethnicity, his training as a Pharisee, and his knowledge of the Jewish scriptures.⁶⁴ The second is his Hellenistic first-century diaspora Jewish background, though precisely what this

---

62. Wilson, "Literary Works," 72. See also Pattemore, *People of God*, 28.
63. Pattemore, *People of God*, 51–60; Fantin, *Lord of the Entire World*, 18.
64. On the first point, see Rom 11:1; Gal 1:13–14; Phil 3:5; 2 Cor 11:22; Martin Hengel, "Der vorchristliche Paulus," in *Paulus und das antike Judentum*, ed. Martin Hengel and Ulrich Heckel, WUNT 58 (Tübingen: Mohr Siebeck, 1991), 177–291; Sanders, *Paul and Palestinian Judaism*. On the second, see Phil 3:5; Paul McKechnie, "Paul among the Jews," in *All Things to All Cultures: Paul Among Jews, Greeks and Romans*, ed. Mark Harding and Alanna Nobbs (Grand Rapid: Eerdmans, 2013), 107–11; Hengel, "Der vorchristliche Paulus," 225–32. On the third, see Stanley E. Porter and Christopher D. Stanley, eds., *As It Is Written: Studying Paul's Use of Scripture*, SymS 50 (Atlanta: Society of Biblical Literature, 2008); Watson, *Paul and the Hermeneutics of Faith*.

background entails is a complex question with various uncertain elements occasioning debate.⁶⁵ Although Paul was born in the Cilician city of Tarsus, how long he lived there and how far he was educated in Hellenistic culture is a moot point (aee Acts 21:39; 22:3; 9:11).⁶⁶ Though some have argued that Paul was thoroughly Greek in his thought and writing and versed in Greek rhetoric, the evidence from his letters suggests not more than a general familiarity with Hellenistic philosophy, rhetoric, and literature.⁶⁷ His Greek does not show evidence of formal Hellenistic education. As Barclay points out, it is good but not polished, and despite making use of the popular style of the diatribe in Romans, Paul does not display the techniques of a trained orator.⁶⁸ The third broad set of widely accepted assumptions relates to Paul's faith in Christ and his calling as an apostle of Christ to gentile believers (see Gal 1:15–16; 2:7–8). These led him to adapt his understanding of his ancestral faith and its law and traditions, though how radically and in what ways is a subject of ongoing debate. This adaptation of his ancestral faith in the light of his faith in Christ resulted in tensions and conflict with some of his fellow Jews.⁶⁹

The identification of a probable date for the epistle provides a broad historical constraint for outlining elements of a shared cognitive environment for Paul and his likely Roman addressees. There is general consensus that the letter was written between 54 CE and 59 CE, in the early years of the emperor Nero's reign, probably in Corinth.⁷⁰

When we come to the probable recipients of the epistle, the positing of basic elements of their likely cognitive environment becomes more problematic. While the epistle's authorship is undisputed, the question of the

---

65. For a recent discussion, see Chris Forbes, "Paul among the Greeks," in Harding and Nobbs, *All Things to All Cultures*, 124–42. See also John M. G. Barclay, *Jews in the Mediterranean Diaspora: From Alexander to Trajan (323 BCE–117 CE)* (Edinburgh: T&T Clark, 1996); Hengel, "Der vorchristliche Paulus."

66. Hengel, "Der vorchristliche Paulus," 186. The question of Paul's Roman citizenship is likewise contested. Consequently we cannot assume that background knowledge relating to this status would have formed part of his cognitive environment. For a discussion of this question, see Hengel, "Der vorchristliche Paulus," 193–208.

67. Hengel, "Der vorchristliche Paulus," 183–86.

68. John M. G. Barclay, *Jews in the Mediterranean Diaspora*, 383.

69. Barclay, *Jews in the Mediterranean Diaspora*, 384.

70. There is some scholarly disagreement over the more precise dating of the letter within this period. See Wolter, *Röm 1–8*, 29–30. For a detailed justification of Corinth as the location of writing, see Wolter, *Röm 1–8*, 28–29.

identity of its addressees is highly contested. Nevertheless, we can make use of some broad consensus views to guide us in identifying some basic assumptions that would probably have formed part of the Roman addressees' general cognitive environment. These will be enough to allow us to construct plausible inferential series that the Roman addressees might well have inferred in interpreting the epistle.

The issue of the identity of the recipients of the letter has often been framed in terms of their ethnic-religious background, which has produced a multiplicity of varying explanations.[71] Descriptions of Paul's Roman audience range from exclusively gentile, through various construals of a mixed gentile-Jewish audience, to Ferdinand C. Baur's proposal that Paul addresses exclusively Jewish Christians.[72] A current consensus

---

71. Richard N. Longenecker suggests, however, following Raymond Brown, that it is the theological outlook of the Roman addressees, not their ethnic identity, that is of most relevance. See Richard N. Longenecker, *Introducing Romans: Critical Issues in Paul's Most Famous Letter* [Grand Rapids: Eerdmans, 2011], 134). Moreover, the terms *Jew* and *gentile* have been criticized in recent scholarship as anachronistic. See Elliott, *Arrogance of Nations*, 16, 46. Nevertheless I follow scholarly convention in using these terms to refer to those of Jewish and those of non-Jewish ethnicity/descent.

72. Ferdinand C. Baur, *The Apostle of Jesus Christ, His Life and Work, His Epistles and His Doctrine*, 2nd ed. (London: Williams & Norgate, 1876), 331. Runar M. Thorsteinsson, Matthew Thiessen, and Rafael Rodríguez argue that Paul addresses torah-observant gentiles ("Paul's Interlocutor in Romans: The Problem of Identification," in *The So-Called Jew in Paul's Letter to the Romans*, ed. Rafael Rodríguez and Matthew Thiessen [Minneapolis: Fortress, 2016], 15). Magnus Zetterholm asserts that the crucial issue in Romans is the status of non-Jews ("The Non-Jewish Interlocutor in Romans 2:17 and the Salvation of the Nations: Contextualizing Romans 1:18–32," in Rodríguez and Thiessen, *So-Called Jew in Paul's Letter to the Romans*, 40). Andrew A. Das proposes exclusively gentile addressees, familiar with Judaism, but worshiping separately ("The Gentile-Encoded Audience of Romans: The Church Outside the Synagogue," in *Reading Paul's Letter to the Romans.*, ed. Jerry L. Sumney, RBS 73 [Atlanta: Society of Biblical Literature, 2012], 29–46). See also Wolter, *Röm 1–8*, 44; Stowers, *Rereading of Romans*. John M. G. Barclay argues that Paul writes to his addressees as *gentiles* (the "implied audience") but nevertheless knows that the actual audience will include Jews (*Paul and the Gift* [Grand Rapids: Eerdmans, 2015], 458). For construals of a mixed gentile-Jewish audience, see, e.g., Longenecker, *Introducing Romans*, 83; Esler, *Conflict and Identity in Romans*, 119. Alexander J. M. Wedderburn views the audience as composed of "Gentiles with a leaning towards Judaism and Gentiles believing in a law-free gospel (as well as probably some Jews of both persuasions)." ("The Purpose and Occasion of Romans Again," in *The Romans Debate*, ed. Karl P. Donfried, rev. and exp. ed. [Edinburgh: T&T Clark, 1991], 201). For Francis Watson,

has emerged, however, in as far as most now view Paul's Roman audience as predominantly gentile (11:13, 15:16) but suggest varying orientations towards Judaism and torah among them: some are Jewish-orientated and torah-observant, while others may have no association with the Jewish faith or negative attitudes toward it.[73] Another area of debate is the question of whether Paul writes to one or more groups of believers in Rome and what the relationship may have been between them. Here, too, something of a consensus has been reached, in that most scholars now problematize the notion of a single Roman church.[74]

Before outlining a tentative construal of Paul's addressees for the purposes of this study, we need to consider the question of the implied or encoded audience.[75] This notion, drawn from literary criticism, is an interpretative construct referring to "the audience as visualized and entextualized" by the author, which the latter seeks to persuade by means of the communication.[76] It is distinct from the actual audience, with which

---

the audience consists of Jewish as well as gentile believers (*Paul, Judaism and the Gentiles: Beyond the New Perspective*, 2nd ed. [Grand Rapids: Eerdmans, 2007], 188–89). Wolfgang Wiefel and Dunn speak of a gentile majority among Roman believers (Wolfgang Wiefel, "The Jewish Community in Ancient Rome and the Origins of Roman Christianity," in Donfried, *Romans Debate* [2nd ed.], 100; Dunn, *Romans 1–8*, liii). William L. Lane posits a "primarily Gentile constituency" but also a "Jewish presence" among Paul's addressees, claiming that Romans is "incomprehensible" without the assumption of the latter in the Roman church ("Social Perspectives on Roman Christianity during the Formative Years from Nero to Nerva: Romans, Hebrews, 1 Clement," in *Judaism and Christianity in First-Century Rome*, ed. Karl P. Donfried and Peter Richardson [Grand Rapids: Eerdmans, 1998], 206–7). Wright argues the letter is written to a "largely Gentile church" but deals with "deep-rooted issues of the interrelationship between Jews and Gentiles within God's purposes" (Wright, *Paul and the Faithfulness of God*, 1:206; Wright, "Romans," 406–7). William S. Campbell asserts that Romans is addressed "almost exclusively" to gentiles, who are, however, "in the context and presence of Jews" (Christ-followers or not) "listening in on the conversation" ("Addressees of Paul's Letter to the Romans," 193–95).

73. E.g., Campbell, "Addressees of Paul's Letter to the Romans," 187.

74. See Edward Adams, *The Earliest Christian Meeting Places: Almost Exclusively Houses?*, LNTS 450 (London: T&T Clark, 2013), 31–33; Jewett, *Romans*, 62; Paul Minear, *The Obedience of Faith: The Purposes of Paul in the Epistle to the Romans*, SBT 2.19 (London: SCM, 1971), 7–8; Peter Lampe, *From Paul to Valentinus: Christians at Rome in the First Two Centuries*, trans. Michael Steinhauser (Minneapolis: Fortress, 2003), 359; Esler, *Conflict and Identity in Romans*, 358.

75. Stowers, *Rereading of Romans*, 21–22.

76. Johannes N. Vorster, "Strategies of Persuasion in Romans 1:16–17," in *Rheto-*

it may correspond partially.[77] This raises the question of how the implied audience is "entextualized" and how a secondary reader detects this construct. In his application of the concept, Stanley Stowers makes a distinction between the "encoded explicit" and "encoded implicit" audience. The former is manifest in explicit references and direct addresses, including the use of the second person. The implicit audience, on the other hand, is inferred from the content of the letter and from the use of sources and literary devices within it. This is a construct built from the "assumptions, knowledge, frames of reference and horizon of expectations" that the communicator assumes the audience to have.[78]

Stowers acknowledges that the boundary between encoded explicit and implicit audience is blurred. From a relevance-theoretic perspective, this makes good sense. As we have seen, relevance theory recognizes that even textually encoded information represents only a clue to a relevant interpretation. In all cases, addressees and interpreters must and do draw inferences from this code in order to achieve cognitive effects, with diverse addressees sometimes drawing different inferences, depending on the context selected.[79] For example, the second-person plural, while encoded in the text, is always an underdetermined clue, and inferences must be drawn to ascertain its referent in any particular context.

It is therefore not as simple as some imply to identify the limits of encoded textual information relating to the envisaged audience or to restrict ourselves to this in our construal of Paul's addressees.[80] Interpreters begin with textual clues as basic evidence regarding Paul's audience, but these limited explicit clues ("you in Rome" [1:6], "you gentiles"

---

ric and the New Testament: Essays from the 1992 Heidelberg Conference, ed. Stanley E. Porter and Thomas H. Olbricht, JSNTSup 90 (Sheffield: JSOT Press, 1993), 152; Mark D. Nanos, "To the Churches Within the Synagogues of Rome," in Sumney, *Reading Paul's Letter to the Romans*, 22.

77. Stowers, *Rereading of Romans*, 21–22.
78. Stowers, *Rereading of Romans*, 21.
79. Thus the statement in 7:1 that Paul's audience "knows the law" gives rise to diverse inferences concerning the Jewish or non-Jewish identity of Paul's addressees, depending on contextual assumptions accessed.
80. *Pace* Barclay, *Paul and the Gift*, 456, 458; Nanos, "To the Churches," 22; Das, "Gentile-Encoded Audience," 29. Stowers's assertion that "I can know with certainty that the audience in the text is gentiles at Rome who know something about Jewish scripture and Jesus Christ" is simplistic and misleading (Stowers, *Rereading of Romans*, 22).

[11:13], and "those who know the law" [7:1]) must be disambiguated and enriched. Moreover, the letter also communicates a wealth of assumptions more indirectly by means of its argument. These also serve as stimuli for inferences regarding the audience's background knowledge, frames of reference, and more. In our construal of the implied audience we need to consider all these and infer a plausible reconstruction that makes the most coherent sense of all the data, explicitly and implicitly communicated.[81] While there is no guarantee that the textual data and the most plausible inferences drawn from them reflect the actual first audience, I will work from the presupposition that there is considerable overlap between implied and actual audiences and that the textual clues enable us to draw some common sense conclusions regarding Paul's probable first audience. These are enough to help us identify the basic elements of a broad cognitive environment that the Roman addressees plausibly shared with Paul. They lead to a common-sense construal of some general characteristics of Paul's addressees, which is sufficient to guide our interpretation in certain key directions, allowing us to attribute to them access to certain probable contextual assumptions.[82]

With these considerations in mind, I propose the following tentative general profile of Paul's envisaged audience, inferred from a mixture of textual clues and basic historical information. The addressees live in the multicultural setting of imperial Rome (1:7, 15).[83] They are a diverse group of predominantly non-Jewish Christ-believers (11:13), but with a minority of Jewish believers, or at least, torah-observant believers, among them.[84] Certain textual clues seem to suggest that Paul assumes that Jewish believers will be part of his audience, in particular, the references to Paul's συγγενεῖς in chapter 16 and the repeated use of Jewish scripture and references to Jewish faith and tradition.[85] In view of the latter, it also seems

---

81. See Alexander J. M. Wedderburn's discussion of the inevitable "reading between the lines" involved in any interpretation of Paul's letters in *The Reasons for Romans* (Edinburgh: T&T Clark, 1988), 63–64. This includes drawing inferences from plausible historical data, where these help to make coherent sense of textual clues. See Campbell, "Addressees of Paul's Letter to the Romans," 175.

82. See Pattemore's model (Pattemore, *People of God*, 51).

83. Esler, *Conflict and Identity in Romans*, 84–85; James C. Walters, *Ethnic Issues in Paul's Letter to the Romans: Changing Self-Definition in Earliest Roman Christianity* (Valley Forge, PA: Trinity Press International, 1993), 7–18.

84. See Esler, *Conflict and Identity in Romans*, 119.

85. On the reference to συγγενεῖς, see Campbell, "Addressees of Paul's Letter to

reasonable to assume that the majority of Paul's addressees, whether Jewish or gentile, are familiar with Jewish scriptures, teaching, and customs. For his gentile addressees, such familiarity would presumably be the result of considerable contact with Jews and Jewish synagogues.[86]

Paul's addressees do not seem to represent one cohesive community.[87] This is inferred partly from chapter 16, where Paul greets at least five different groups of believers and does not use the term ἐκκλησία to refer to the Christ-believers in Rome as a whole.[88] There is some evidence in chapters 14 and 15 that the envisaged addressees may be going through a period of transition or tension.[89] Some are stronger and some weaker in their faith (14:1–15:13) and they are dealing with issues of mutual acceptance and with arrogant judgmental attitudes toward others who do not share their lifestyle or convictions.[90] We can infer that the addressees may be dealing with uncertainty concerning their relationship to the Jewish law (e.g., Rom 3; 6–8; 9:30–10:13; 13).[91] There is also some evidence that they are a vulner-

---

the Romans," 181; Barclay, *Paul and the Gift*, 458 n. 20; Watson, *Paul, Judaism and the Gentiles*, 182–88. Following Harry Y. Gamble Jr.'s text-critical study, most recent scholars regard ch. 16 as an integral part of the letter. See Harry Y. Gamble Jr., *The Textual History of the Letter to the Romans: A Study in Textual and Literary Criticism*, SD42 (Grand Rapids: Eerdmans, 1977); Adams, *Earliest Christian Meeting Places*, 31. On the references to Jewish faith and tradition, see Antoinette C. Wire, "'Since God Is One': Rhetoric as Theology and History in Paul's Romans," in *The New Literary Criticism and the New Testament*, ed. Elizabeth S. Malbon and Edgar V. McKnight, JSNTSup 109 (Sheffield: JSOT Press, 1994), 217. For a different explanation of these elements as addressed to an exclusively gentile audience, see, e.g., Das, "Gentile-Encoded Audience."

86. See Lampe, *Paul to Valentinus*, 70. Lampe argues that Paul's gentile addressees may have been in large part former σεβόμενοι, worshiping on synagogue fringes before believing in Christ. See also Thomas H. Tobin, *Paul's Rhetoric in Its Contexts: The Argument of Romans* (Peabody, MA: Hendrickson, 2004), 41.

87. See above, n. 74.

88. See Esler, *Conflict and Identity in Romans*, 121; Adams, *Earliest Christian Meeting Places*, 31. Minear also takes the discussion of disputes between the weak and the strong in chs.14–15 as evidence that Paul is addressing several disparate groups (Minear, *Obedience of Faith*, 7–8).

89. See, e.g., Tobin, *Paul's Rhetoric in Its Contexts*, 41; Wire, "Rhetoric as Theology," 218.

90. See, e.g., Esler, *Conflict and Identity in Romans*, 353–56; Jewett, *Romans*, 59, 72; Walters, *Ethnic Issues in Paul's Letter to the Romans*, 90–91.

91. Lampe asserts that "questions about Jewish Torah observance are central to the conflict" alluded to in chs. 14–15 (Lampe, *Paul to Valentinus*, 73). See also Tobin, *Paul's Rhetoric in Its Contexts*, 41.

able minority within the wider Roman culture, experiencing discrimination (see, e.g., 12:14–21).[92] It is probable that Paul's addressees are somewhat diverse in their socioeconomic status but most are of low social standing.[93] Many may come from slave backgrounds or are freed slaves, though not all.[94] Some, however, may be people of considerable material means (such as the mother of Rufus: 16:13), able to support others with their resources.[95]

The question of the probable educational and literacy level of Paul's addressees is pertinent, given the kinds of inferential series I will suggest that Paul's addressees may have drawn in interpretation (while bearing in mind that the posited inferential series take place at a subpersonal rather than conscious level). The text only gives us the most general clues: the envisaged addressees know the Jewish law (7:1), and they are familiar with and able to interpret not only Jewish midrash (see, e.g., Rom 4), but also the rhetorical techniques of diatribe (see, e.g., Rom 2).[96] Research into literacy and orality in first-century Rome suggests that we can assume that only a minority of Paul's addressees might have been highly literate, especially if the majority were of lower economic status.[97] Familiarity with

---

92. See Edward Adams, *Constructing the World: A Study in Paul's Cosmological Language* (Edinburgh: T&T Clark, 2000), 210–16; Mark Reasoner, *The Strong and the Weak: Romans 14.1–15.13 in Context*, SNTSMS 103 (Cambridge: Cambridge University Press, 1999), 161.

93. See Jewett, *Romans*, 955–72; Lampe, *Paul to Valentinus*, 170–95.

94. See Lampe's analysis of the names in ch.16, many of which he identifies as of slave origin (Lampe, *Paul to Valentinus*, 170–95).

95. Jewett, *Romans*, 969.

96. By *midrash*, I mean Jewish exegetical exposition of the Hebrew scriptures, following Jacob Neusner, who cites examples from the Hebrew Bible (e.g., Ps 106:32–33), the Dead Sea Scrolls (e.g., a midrash from the Damascus Rule focusing on Num 21:18), and Matthew's Gospel (1:18–23; 2:1–6; 2:16–18; 3:1–3). See Jacob Neusner, *What Is Midrash?*, GBS (Philadelphia: Fortress, 1987), 9–10, 19, 35. By *diatribe*, I mean, following Stanley K. Stowers, a dialogical discourse involving questions and answers, used for rhetorical effect (*The Diatribe and Paul's Letter to the Romans*, SBLDS 57 [Chico, CA: Scholars Press, 1980]). Diatribe is intended to lead addressees to change their point of view, sometimes by means of an apostrophe to an imaginary interlocutor with whom they identify in some way. Stowers cites as examples the *Discourses* of Epictetus (e.g., 1.12.9, 1.29.3, 2.12) and certain of the *Orationes* of Dio Chrysostom (e.g., 74.28).

97. Carolyn Osiek, "The Oral World of Early Christianity in Rome: The Case of Hermas," in Donfried and Richardson, *Judaism and Christianity in First Century Rome*, 156–58. See, however, Larry W. Hurtado's challenge to the oversimplification of

Jewish midrashic and Greco-Roman diatribal techniques need not imply a high level of literacy, however, since oratory and the practice of oral/aural interpretation were pervasive in ancient Greco-Roman society.[98] Moreover, a low level of literacy on the part of an audience does not imply a low level of understanding or an inability to follow relatively sophisticated logical arguments. Indeed, the predominance of oral forms of communication would have meant that addressees would have had a greater capacity to process and commit to memory information communicated orally.[99] I suggest that Paul's audience would have been able to retain relatively large chunks of the argument in their short-term memory as they listened to the letter being read. They would thus have been able to make associations between assumptions communicated at different stages and draw fresh implications from previously made points. In addition, we can envisage that the letter may have been read out a number of times to its Roman recipients so that they could discuss and meditate on its contents.[100] This would have given them the opportunity to grasp the fundamentals of Paul's argument at whatever level was relevant to them.

Related to this is the question of how Paul's letter might have been read to its first addressees. The recent growth in performance criticism has led to the suggestion that it would have been dramatically performed multiple times to various groups of believers by the letter carrier, using a "plethora of nonverbal signals."[101] It seems more probable, however, that the letter would not have been acted so much as simply read aloud as a written text to groups of gathered believers.[102] If so, it may have been read

---

the claim that only a small minority of "the Roman-era populace" were literate ("Oral Fixation and New Testament Studies? 'Orality', 'Performance' and Reading Texts in Early Christianity," *NTS* 60 [2014]: 330–31).

98. See Hurtado, "Oral Fixation," 323; Paul J. Achtemeier, "*Omne Verbum Sonat*: The New Testament and the Oral Environment of Late Western Antiquity," *JBL* 109 (1990): 20.

99. Personal observation of contemporary cultures with a high degree of orality (predominantly oral cultures in Burkina Faso, Uganda, and the Democratic Republic of Congo) suggests a much greater capacity for retention and memorization of information communicated orally than in highly literate cultures.

100. See Pattemore, *People of God*, 54.

101. Campbell, *Deliverance of God*, 530–32.

102. Hurtado cites Luke 4:16–21; 2 Cor 10:9–10; 1 Thess 5:27; Col 4:16 as evidence of texts being read out in synagogal or early church contexts (Hurtado, "Oral Fixation," 336–39).

out by a different reader to diverse groups on different occasions, and it is not necessary to speculate regarding a single, rehearsed performer.

To conclude, our brief discussion of author and addressees allows us to identify some core elements of their cognitive environments, which they in all probability shared. These include their faith in Christ and knowledge of basic elements of Christian teaching, their experience of daily life in the multicultural environment of the Roman Empire, living under Roman authority as a minority within the wider Greco-Roman culture, their knowledge of Jewish scripture, teaching, and traditions, and some familiarity with pervasive aspects of Greco-Roman culture such as oratory and popular diatribal techniques. These elements provide the outline of a broad, common-sense construal of a plausible mutual cognitive environment for author and addressees. Within the context of this construal, we can posit inferential series involving highly accessible contextual assumptions, series that might plausibly have been drawn by the letter's Roman addressees as they interpreted the letter.

2.4.2. Purpose of Romans

Closely related to the question of the audience of Romans is the highly contested issue of the epistle's purpose. From a methodological point of view, however, these two questions need to be distinguished. The common sense historical assumptions, supplemented by explicit textual clues, which were discussed in §2.4.1 in relation to the likely audience, represent basic building blocks in our construal of a probable shared cognitive environment. This serves as a plausible background against which to interpret the argument of the letter (a construal which may, however, be adjusted in this process of interpretation). The matter of the letter's purpose, on the other hand, is a question that can only be addressed and resolved by interpreting the letter's argument. Thus, the identity and characteristics of the likely audience represent background information against which the question of the purpose of the letter, that is, its argumentative thrust or relevance, can be understood. The issue of the reasons for Romans is, in fact, one of the major interpretative questions that, I suggest, can be illuminated by a consistent procedural analysis of γάρ, as discussed in chapter 6 of this book. Since some of the questions relating to purpose intersect with issues discussed under §2.4.1, however, and are relevant to an introduction to the letter, I will present an overview of the debate here.

The issue of the letter's purpose remains resistant to consensus.[103] Romans displays various characteristics which complicate the question. First, there is an apparent tension between content and encoded audience (though as we have noted, any explicit textual encoding itself represents only a fragmentary clue that will need to be filled out by inferencing). The letter is explicitly addressed to gentile Christ-believers in Rome, but much of its argument focuses on issues relating to ethnic Israel and the Mosaic law, and it is steeped in references to Jewish scripture and tradition.[104] Moreover, in contrast to Paul's other epistles, there is an absence of detailed references to concrete phenomena in the Christ-believing communities in Rome, and no specific evidence of Paul's personal knowledge of them.[105] Instead, we find sustained theological argument and some possible allusions to objections to Paul's gospel and to possible opponents of Paul, both Judaizing and antinomian (e.g., 3:8; 6:1, 15; 7:7, 13; 9:1–2; 16:17–20).

This blend of apparently contradictory characteristics leads to ongoing scholarly disagreement and to a plethora of explanations regarding the occasion and purpose of the epistle, which can nevertheless be grouped into major perspectives. Before Baur's paradigm-shifting scholarship, Romans was viewed (following Melanchthon and the Reformers) essentially as a normative theological treatise which presented a summary of Paul's gospel, the argument of which could be interpreted without paying detailed attention to the historical situation in which it arose.[106] Baur's groundbreaking insight was to claim, in contrast, that the argument could not be properly understood without a consideration of the historical circumstances of author and addressees.[107] Post-Baur, the debate has often

---

103. Barclay, *Paul and the Gift*, 455.

104. Werner G. Kümmel famously referred to this apparent mismatch as the "double character" of the letter (Werner G. Kümmel, *Introduction to the New Testament*, trans. H. C. Kee, rev. ed. [Nashville: Abingdon, 1975], 30). On this question, see, most recently, Wolter, *Röm 1–8*, 44.

105. Other than the greetings in ch. 16, which do not provide conclusive proof of personal knowledge. See Watson, *Paul, Judaism and the Gentiles*, 182–83; Thorsteinsson, Thiessen, and Rodríguez, "Paul's Interlocutor in Romans," 12.

106. See Campbell's discussion of Melanchthon's *Loci Communes Theologici* and his commentary on Romans, in which he treats the epistle essentially as a *christianae religionis compendium* (Campbell, *Deliverance of God*, 258–60). For the neglect of the background, see Watson, *Paul, Judaism and the Gentiles*, 166.

107. Baur, *Apostle of Jesus Christ*, 310–13.

been framed in terms of two main contrasting positions: the view that the epistle's purpose is to be located within "Paul's own ministry and consciousness," versus the view that its purpose is motivated by the social situation of Paul's Roman addressees.[108] Wolter criticizes this polarization of the debate, insisting that all theological discussions arise from a specific historical and cultural context.[109] Along similar lines, Watson points out that in all Paul's letters he writes not only for the sake of his addressees, but also for his own; at one level the two concerns cannot be separated.[110] The two supposedly opposing alternatives are thus inextricably linked and are best thought of as different emphases rather than polarized positions.

These different emphases continue to manifest themselves in recent scholarship. Some interpreters read Romans as essentially a theological presentation of Paul's gospel, finding the specific historical occasion for the epistle primarily in the concerns of Paul's apostolate and ministry plans.[111] This is not, however, to deny the importance of the fact that the epistle is written to Rome; rather it is to emphasize that it is not primarily directed to *problems* in the Roman congregations.[112] Others advocate a Rome-focused reading, arguing that it is the specifics of the historical situ-

---

108. Longenecker, *Introducing Romans*, 111. Donfried provides a compilation of views representing these two positions (Donfried, *Romans Debate* [2nd ed.]).

109. Wolter, *Röm 1–8*, 55.

110. Watson, *Paul, Judaism and the Gentiles*, 165, referencing Jacob Jervell, "The Letter to Jerusalem," in *The Romans Debate*, ed. Karl P. Donfried (Minneapolis: Augsburg, 1977), 62.

111. E.g., Barclay argues that Paul's purpose is to present himself to the Roman believers as "apostle to the gentiles" and thus *their* apostle, before visiting them and enlisting their support for his mission to Spain (Barclay, *Paul and the Gift*, 456–57). Michael Wolter proposes that the letter not only serves to introduce Paul to the Romans before he visits them and solicits support, but also as a kind of self-evaluation of his theological path thus far (*Paulus: Ein Grundriss seiner Theologie* [Neukirchen-Vluyn: Neukirchener Verlag, 2011], 424–25). Jervell argues that in the epistle Paul rehearses his arguments for his visit to Jerusalem ("The Letter to Jerusalem," in Donfried, *Romans Debate* [2nd ed.], 53–64). See also, e.g., Dunn, *Romans 1–8*, lx; Nils A. Dahl, "The Missionary Theology in the Epistle to the Romans," in *Studies in Paul: Theology for the Early Christian Mission*, trans. Paul Donahue (Minneapolis: Augsburg, 1977), 78; Ulrich Wilckens, "Über Abfassungszweck und Aufbau des Römerbriefes," in *Rechtfertigung als Freiheit: Paulusstudien* (Neukirchen-Vluyn: Neukirchener Verlag, 1974), 139.

112. Barclay, *Paul and the Gift*, 459 n. 23.

ation of the Roman believers that are the key to understanding the letter's purpose and thus its argument.[113]

Many scholars, though by no means all, accept the broad outline of Wolfgang Wiefel's influential hypothesis regarding the historical circumstances of Paul's addressees in Rome.[114] Wiefel's reconstruction is based on Suetonius's account of the expulsion of Jews from Rome under Claudius.[115] John Barclay notes that the basic elements of this hypothesis now form a consensus reading. He himself critiques this as a "tissue of speculation" but nevertheless offers a helpful summary of it:[116]

> The Christian movement in Rome began in the Jewish synagogues, and ... caused controversy there during the 40s, climaxing in the expulsion of Jewish-Christians ... in 49 CE on the order of Claudius. During their absence, the Christian movement in Rome became largely separate from the synagogues and developed mostly Gentile-Christian leadership, so that, when the Jewish-Christians returned (on Claudius's death, 54 CE), there arose internal tension within the Christian communities.[117]

---

113. Elliott and Wright find in Romans a challenge to imperial pretension (Elliott, *Arrogance of Nations*, 6; Wright, "Romans," 404). For Watson, Paul writes "to encourage Jewish and Gentile Christians in Rome ... to set aside their differences and to worship together" (Watson, *Paul, Judaism and the Gentiles*, 186). For Campbell, Paul's purpose is to counter the opposing gospel of Judaizing countermissionaries (Campbell, *Deliverance of God*, 495–511). For Thorsteinsson, Paul aims to persuade his gentile addressees that "the proper path for them is not to try to become Ἰουδαῖοι" (Thorsteinsson, Thiessen, and Rodríguez, "Paul's Interlocutor in Romans," 31).

114. Wiefel, "Jewish Community." Among those who show scepticism regarding Wiefel's hypothesis are Wolter, *Röm 1–8*, 41; John M. G. Barclay, "Is It Good News That God Is Impartial? A Response to Robert Jewett, *Romans: A Commentary*," *JSNT* 31 (2008): 89–111; Barclay, *Paul and the Gift*, 456; Campbell, *Deliverance of God*, 494, 1068 n. 61.

115. See Watson's detailed discussion of the various sources that refer to restrictions of Jewish freedoms under Claudius (Watson, *Paul, Judaism and the Gentiles*, 167–74).

116. Barclay, "Is It Good News?," 93.

117. Barclay, "Is It Good News?," 91. Wiefel's specific hypothesis further proposes that there was widespread anti-Jewish sentiment in Rome when the Jewish exiles returned (Wiefel, "Jewish Community," 100). Consequently, Paul writes to counter anti-Jewish prejudice and to ensure that belief in Christ does not become an anti-Jewish movement (Elliott, *Rhetoric of Romans*, 51).

Various scholars use elements of Wiefel's reconstruction as support for the identification in chapters 14–15 of "the weak" as Jewish believers and "the strong" as gentile.[118] More recent scholarship has nuanced this, recognizing that some of the "weak" may be torah-observant gentiles and some of the strong, non-torah-observant Jews, like Paul himself (see §3.4.1, below).[119] On the basis of this identification of weak and strong, some argue specifically that Paul's primary purpose in writing is to address the tensions between Jewish Christ-believers and gentile Christ-believers (or between torah-observant and non-torah-observant believers) evidenced in these chapters.[120]

Finally, various scholars propose a mix of multiple reasons why Paul wrote the letter.[121] Such construals demonstrate an awareness, perhaps, of the limitations of polarized positions (as highlighted by Wolter and Watson). Thus Alexander Wedderburn sums up the reasons for Romans as

> a cluster of different interlocking factors: the presence of both Judaizing and Law-free Christians in the church there, the present situation of the church in Rome and the present situation of Paul, the visit to Jerusalem now being undertaken and the prospect of a future visit to Rome. All played their part in provoking Paul to write to the Roman Christians as he did.[122]

In sum, the reasons that provoked Paul to write the letter, and his purpose in doing so, remain a source of ongoing disagreement in Romans research. We will leave these questions open for now, while noting that a proce-

---

118. E.g., Dunn, *Romans 1–8*, lvii; Wedderburn, *Reasons for Romans*, 58; Elliott, *Rhetoric of Romans*, 51–57.

119. See Barclay, *Paul and the Gift*, 511; Campbell, "Addressees of Paul's Letter to the Romans," 187.

120. E.g., Esler, *Conflict and Identity in Romans*; Walters, *Ethnic Issues in Paul's Letter to the Romans*; Watson, *Paul, Judaism and the Gentiles*, 175–82; Walter B. Russell, "An Alternative Suggestion for the Purpose of Romans," *BSac* 45 (1988): 174–84. For a critique of this position, see Campbell, *Deliverance of God*, 487–93. See also Robert Karris, "Romans 14:1–15:13 and the Occasion of Romans," in Donfried, *Romans Debate* (2nd ed.), 65–84.

121. E.g., Michael F. Bird, "The Letter to the Romans," in Harding and Nobbs, *All Things to All Cultures*, 190–92; Longenecker, *Introducing Romans*, 158–59; Cranfield, *Epistle to the Romans*; John A. Ziesler, *Paul's Letter to the Romans* (London: SCM, 1989), 16; Wedderburn, *Reasons for Romans*.

122. Wedderburn, *Reasons for Romans*, 142.

dural reading of γάρ could potentially illuminate this important debate. The issue will be pursued further in chapter 6, where we will see how a relevance-theoretic, procedural account of γάρ lends support to a Roman-focused reading of the letter's purpose.

To conclude this chapter: we have seen that relevance theory's approach overlaps with key preoccupations in biblical studies, affirming the shaping role of communicator, the varying perspectives of diverse addressees, and the crucial role of context in interpretation. Its recognition both of the importance of the linguistic code of the text, and of its communicative purpose, coincides with the concerns of biblical interpretation. Its insistence on the linguistic form as starting point, and on the need to go beyond this by means of inferences in order to derive communicative effects, is invaluable for biblical scholars. The principle of relevance, the notion of mutual cognitive environments, and the construction of plausible inferential series suggest a method for identifying probable contextual information available to the first audience.

Using widely recognized basic assumptions about author and addressees, drawn from textual clues and generally accepted, plausible historical information, we have been able to outline a common sense, shared cognitive environment for Paul and his Roman addressees. This broad outline will serve as a context within which hypotheses can be made about likely inferences that might plausibly have been drawn by the letter's addressees on the basis of the linguistic clues of the text. The reconstruction of likely inferences from within a posited cognitive environment is undertaken in full recognition of the inherent subjectivity and uncertainty of the task and the possible charge of circularity. Nevertheless, we can be satisfied that the attempt is plausible and worthwhile, given the constraints imposed on the process by the use of only generally accepted historical information and of contextual information immediately suggested by textual clues. In addition, this task is valuable in that it raises our awareness of our own subconscious inferences involved in our interpretation of the text and of the fact that inferencing using contextual information is an unavoidable part of the interpretation process.

More specifically, the notion of procedural meaning is an innovative tool that is well suited to the reexamination of the role of γάρ, as Blass has suggested. It offers exciting possibilities for a way forward in relation to the intransigent and oft-overlooked problem of the connective's role in Romans. Relevance theory has the potential to provide a cognitively grounded, consistent, and communicative account of the function of γάρ.

This account has the potential to transform the contribution γάρ makes to the exegesis of Romans, revealing its role as a signpost to the coherence and thrust of the argument and illuminating some major unresolved interpretative questions. It is to the demonstration of this account that we now turn.

3
Consistent Yet Context-Sensitive: The Guidance γάρ Gives

In this chapter I will begin to demonstrate how a relevance-theoretic, procedural account of γάρ provides a unified and consistent explanation of diverse occurrences of the connective in Romans, showing that all occurrences can be accounted for in terms of core procedural instructions toward backward strengthening. I will use insights from discourse analysis to categorize different types of argumentation in the epistle, expository and hortatory, and follow a rough categorization of occurrences of γάρ into three types, straightforward, somewhat complex, and problematic, to facilitate analysis.

There are, in total, 144 instances of γάρ in Romans.[1] The greatest concentration is found in chapters 7 (thirteen in twenty-five verses), 14 (twelve in twenty-three verses), 10 (ten in twenty-one verses), 11 (ten in twenty-four verses), and 8 (sixteen in thirty-nine verses). Clusters occur in particular subsections of the argument, where several consecutive clauses are introduced by γάρ in a series; for example, 1:16–18; 7:14–22; 8:2–7; 10:10–13; 13:1b–7; and 14:3–11. The majority of these clusters follows the presentation of a key claim or point in the argument and often involves a tightly argued logical sequence.[2] Other chapters, by contrast, have a relatively sparse sprinkling of occurrences: chapter 12 has only four in twenty-one verses, while the final greetings of chapter 16 contain just three examples in twenty-seven verses.

---

1. Including the variants followed in the UBS[5] and NA[28] Greek texts.
2. The relationship between 1:16–17 and both what follows and what precedes it is notoriously disputed. See §6.2.2, below.

3.1. Methodological Matters

We start with the investigation of five isolated, straightforward instances of γάρ that occur in diverse contexts, in order to demonstrate various ways in which the connective's core strengthening function works itself out. For some of these cases, the demonstration of a strengthening series might at first glance seem too obvious to merit discussion. The purpose of the chapter, however, is to establish the validity and common-sense nature of a procedural explanation first from these uncontroversial examples before testing it out in relation to more ambiguous and complex examples. We then move on to somewhat more complex instances, demonstrating how the procedural strengthening hypothesis can be adapted and expanded to explain these. For this second category, we will consider several instances in two stretches of text, 7:7–20 and 14:1–12, in order to take better account of information in the preceding cotext as we trace the inferences γάρ potentially triggers. The chapter will finish by considering briefly some of the implications of this procedural account of γάρ for tracing the contours of the argument in the two passages investigated in preparation for the later discussion in chapter 6, below. Once the validity of the procedural account has been clearly demonstrated in this chapter from unproblematic cases, followed by somewhat complex examples, we will be ready in chapter 4 to apply it to apparently problematic and atypical examples of γάρ.

3.1.1. Romans as Argumentation

The Letter to the Romans is a piece of argumentation contained within an epistolary frame. The frame is generally identified as 1:1–15 and 15:14–16:27.[3] In argumentation, a communicator's overt aim is to persuade addressees of the validity or truth of certain claims. As Chaïm Perelman and Lucie Olbrechts-Tyteca argue in continuity with ancient theories of rhetoric such as Aristotle's, "argumentation is a function of the audience being addressed" and aims to "induce or increase the mind's adherence ... to the theses presented for its assent." It is future-oriented since it "sets out to bring about some action or to prepare for it" by influencing the minds of addressees.[4] This may be achieved by means of various

---

3. The precise extent of the letter's epistolary opening is debated. See §6.2.1, below.
4. Perelman and Olbrechts-Tyteca, *New Rhetoric*, 3, 30, 47.

persuasive strategies: rational argument involving evidence and premises and leading to logical conclusions, the marshalling of authoritative and accepted material in order to gain addressees' trust, and the deployment of rhetorical forms that create an impressive persuasive display.[5] In argumentation, the communicator aims to gain the audience's trust in relation to his own trustworthiness as a source and in relation to the rationality and coherence of the content of his communication.[6] The procedure of strengthening previously held assumptions, identified by relevance theory as a basic type of cognitive effect (see §§2.1.5 and 2.1.6, above), represents a core aspect of this influencing of the minds of addressees, increasing their adherence to the claims presented for their assent.

The Letter to the Romans contains various types of argumentation, including tight logical argument, Jewish midrashic exposition, passages in a diatribal style employing devices such as rhetorical questions and repetition, and exhortations backed up by authoritative justifications and proofs.[7] With the exception of parts of chapters 6 and 8, chapters 1–11 consist broadly of the presentation of claims and substantiation, with the aim of persuading addressees to accept the validity of these claims. Chapters 12:1–15:13, on the other hand, consist of exhortations and supporting rationale, the aim of which is to motivate addressees to certain kinds of behavior and action.[8] It is not the focus of this book to discuss different

---

5. For gaining trust, see Steve Moyise, "Quotations," in Porter and Stanley, *As It Is Written*, 17–18. For the deployment of rhetorical forms, see D. Hellholm, "Enthymemic Argumentation in Paul: The Case of Romans 6," in *Paul in His Hellenistic Context*, ed. Troels Engberg-Pedersen (Edinburgh: T&T Clark, 1994), 119–20 n. 7. Hellholm identifies two main types of argumentation: "texts with predominantly logical-theoretical argumentation with the aim of convincing.... And texts with predominantly practical pragmatic argumentation with the aim of persuading the interlocutors emotionally."

6. See Dan Sperber et al., "Epistemic Vigilance," *Mind & Language* 25 (2010): 369, 274. Throughout this study I use the masculine pronoun to refer to the communicator and the feminine to the addressee; see ch. 1 n. 5.

7. See ch. 2 n. 96.

8. There is discussion among scholars as to the nature of the paraenesis in chs. 12–15 and how it differs from that in chs. 6 and 8. Some view chs. 12–15 as generalized exhortation. See Günther Bornkamm, "The Letter to the Romans as Paul's Last Will and Testament," in Donfried, *Romans Debate* (2nd ed.), 16–28; Karris, "Romans 14:1–15:13." Many others, however, read chs. 14–15 in particular as addressing real problems in the Roman congregations. See Barclay, *Paul and the Gift*, 511; Barclay, "Do We Undermine the Law? A Study of Romans 14:1–15:6," in *Pauline Churches*

text types within Romans, but we need to be alert to the fact that the guidance γάρ gives works itself out differently in Romans depending on the diverse persuasive strategies employed in different passages.

3.1.2. Longacre's Parameters for Text Types

Defining and identifying text types, or literary genres, is a complex and contested task that is beyond the scope of this study. In their practical handbook dealing with the discourse analysis of texts, Robert Dooley and Stephen Levinsohn argue that text types are culturally specific and maintain that "each text type has a particular social or cultural purpose, around which clusters a characteristic combination of linguistic or textual properties."[9] They note that diverse text types may be embedded in one piece of communication.

Dooley and Levinsohn draw attention to Robert Longacre's proposal of four very broad categories for text types across different cultures. This proposal is useful as a general-purpose tool that recognizes certain basic characteristics of texts, helping us to distinguish between very general types. It is based on two primary parameters, agent orientation and contingent temporal succession:

		agent orientation	
		+	−
contingent temporal succession	+	narrative	procedural
	−	behavioral	expository

---

and Diaspora Jews, WUNT 275 (Tübingen: Mohr Siebeck, 2011), 41; Watson, *Paul, Judaism and the Gentiles*; Wright, "Romans"; Wilckens, *Der Brief an die Römer*, 3:79. See Reasoner, *Strong and the Weak*, 37–41 for a detailed discussion. Adams argues that the exhortations in chs. 12–13 are also context-specific (Adams, *Constructing the World*, 210–16). In contrast, the exhortations in chs. 6 and 8 (in particular 6:11–13, 19; 8:12–13) do not have the same specificity and are not practical, dealing with more fundamental issues of mindset, orientation, and allegiance. See Barclay, *Paul and the Gift*, 506.

9. Robert Dooley and Stephen Levinsohn, *Analyzing Discourse: A Manual of Basic Concepts* (Dallas: SIL International, 2000), 4.

To these primary parameters are added two more, projection and tension. According to this schema, any text can be categorized as minus or plus each of these parameters, with the different combinations of values yielding different text types. Agent orientation relates to whether or not a text deals with events or doings controlled by agents "with at least a partial identity of agent running through the discourse." Contingent temporal succession has to do with whether a text is structured around a temporal sequence in which most events and actions are contingent on previous ones (as is the case with narrative). According to this scheme, behavioral discourse (exhortation, eulogy, political speeches, etc.) is minus contingent temporal succession but plus agent orientation, since it "deals with how people did or should behave" and addressees are potential agents. Expository discourse, on the other hand, is minus both temporal succession and agent orientation. A positive value for projection, meanwhile, indicates "a situation or action which is contemplated, enjoined or anticipated but not realized," while tension relates to "whether a discourse reflects a struggle or polarization of some sort." Thus hortatory material would be plus projection, while a polemical academic article would be judged plus tension.[10]

Longacre's primary parameters, in particular, are of value in tracing very broad text types in Romans. According to his scheme, we can categorize the paraenetic or hortatory material of chapters 12:1–15:13 as behavioral. Chapters 1–11, on the other hand (with the exception of the letter opening and elements of chapter 6), are both minus- contingent-temporal succession and minus-agent orientation and are therefore expository material.[11] Longacre's schema thus allows us to identify two very broad types of material in the argumentation of Romans, which correspond to a generally recognized distinction between two modes. Even so the boundary between these two is sometimes blurred, as, for example, in chapter 6, which is viewed by many scholars as hortatory and dealing with ethics, but also contains stretches of expository, nonagent orientated material.[12] We

---

10. Robert E. Longacre, *The Grammar of Discourse*, 2nd ed. (New York: Plenum, 1996), 9–10.

11. Within this broad characterization of expository text are found diverse types of material, however: Jewish critique of idolatry, Hellenistic vice lists, diatribe, midrashic exegesis, hymnic paeans of praise, etc.

12. It is viewed as hortatory by, e.g., Käsemann, *An die Römer*, 149; Dunn, *Romans 1–8*, 305.

will see that paraenesis in Romans is very often supported by expository material that grounds the exhortations in rational argumentation and a theological framework.

Given these two broad categories of persuasive material in Romans, we will need to demonstrate that a procedural account of γάρ accommodates occurrences found in both types. In my analysis I will thus consider examples, both straightforward and more complex, from both. The connective is fairly evenly distributed between them: certain passages in expository argumentation such as chapters 7 and 8 contain a high concentration, as do certain stretches of hortatory material such as Rom 13:1–7 and Rom 14. On the other hand, certain sections of exposition contain relatively few occurrences (1:24–31 has a single case, and chapter 4 has six instances in twenty-five verses), as do certain sections of exhortation, such as chapter 12.

3.1.3. Categorizing Occurrences of γάρ

My investigation of a procedural strengthening role for occurrences of γάρ in Romans has led me to group examples into three rough categories for the purposes of manageable discussion: straightforward, somewhat complex, and highly problematic (see table of occurrences of γάρ in appendix B). This categorization is impressionistic, formed on the basis of consensus or otherwise among commentators about a particular occurrence, ease with which a strengthening series can be constructed and contextual assumptions identified, and perceived exegetical significance of an occurrence. There is some overlap between the three categories, so that another analyst might evaluate certain examples differently. The categorization does not underpin the validity of a procedural account but serves rather to organize the analysis and to facilitate the choice and ordering of representative examples. Furthermore, it allows us to ascertain at a glance that the largest percentage of occurrences fits intuitively with a procedural explanation of γάρ.

Straightforward examples are those where a simple strengthening inferential series reinforcing immediately preceding material is intuitive, can be immediately established, and involves only one or two contextual assumptions. For these occurrences, most commentators agree on the supporting role of γάρ as indicating grounds/proof, confirmation, or explanation. This category includes examples where γάρ introduces a scriptural citation as authoritative proof for a previous claim.

On my analysis, this category accounts for 49 percent of occurrences.[13] Somewhat complex occurrences are those for which the strengthening relation with preceding material is less easy to reconstruct. The posited inferential series is somewhat more complex, involving several deductive steps and perhaps some contextual assumptions that are less easily accessible. The strengthened claim may not immediately precede the γάρ clause but occur further back in the cotext, or may be implicitly communicated. In some cases, the extent of the material introduced by γάρ may also be a subject of disagreement. Alternatively, in certain cases, a strengthening relation may be relatively easy to trace but not commonly acknowledged by interpreters, because of the exegetical ambiguity of the cotext (e.g., 1:17). According to my analysis, this category accounts for 33 percent of occurrences. Highly problematic occurrences are those for which an obvious logical strengthening series is difficult to construct and may involve the positing of uncertain contextual assumptions. The strengthened claim may not be easily identifiable in the immediately preceding cotext. In addition, these occurrences are exegetically problematic, occurring in contexts where there is considerable ambiguity. Some are found at points where much is at stake exegetically, with differing readings of γάρ leading to divergent interpretations of the epistle's wider argument. In my evaluation, this category represents 18 percent of occurrences.

3.1.4. Presuppositions, Method, and Template for Analysis

The analysis takes as its starting point Blakemore's deductive paradigm for the inferential procedure of strengthening. As explained under §2.1.6, above, this follows a relevance-theoretic template, constructing series of nondemonstrable inferences between a premise and a previously communicated claim, in order to confirm that claim independently by means of access to contextual assumptions already held by the addressee. The analysis assumes a relevance-theoretic view of the interpretation process, involving decoding and disambiguating of the linguistic clues of the text and the drawing of inferences from contextual information in order to arrive at a relevant understanding of the text.

---

13. Bearing in mind the impressionistic categorization of occurrences and the porous nature of the category boundaries.

Following the procedural strengthening hypothesis proposed by Blass (see §2.2, above), I assume that γάρ is a procedural indicator giving processing instructions, in order to specify "the sort of inferential relation which the utterance [it prefixes] enters into with existing contextual assumptions."[14] It indicates that the assumptions it introduces "are meant to function as premises, backwards confirming and strengthening" other assumptions.[15] That is, when an interpreter comes across γάρ, the connective triggers an automatic mental procedure that takes the statement (or complex of assumptions) introduced by γάρ as a premise (which we will refer to as Q) that strengthens a previously communicated assumption or proposition (referred to in this study as P). It then searches for a contextual (implicit) assumption (IA) to combine with Q in an inferential series that yields a conclusion (C) that independently confirms P.[16] This independent confirmation gives rise to the cognitive effect of the strengthening of assumption P so that it is held more strongly as valid in interpreters' minds. The confirmation is independent in the sense that it involves information already known and accepted by addressees and thus serves as corroborating evidence that comes from a source other than the communicator. Although at first glance C might seem to be simply a repetition of P, C in fact represents a strengthened version of P, adhered to more strongly by addressees. That is, addressees are more strongly persuaded of claim P as a result of the inferences triggered by γάρ. This is crucially important, given that we are dealing with argumentation. We will refer to the inferential procedure triggered by γάρ as procedure G.[17]

We have seen in chapter 2 that Blass in her analysis identifies for each example of γάρ a single implicit contextual assumption that is involved in the inferential strengthening procedure triggered. For more complex examples of γάρ, however, additional contextual assumptions will need to be accessed in order to achieve the cognitive effect of strengthening. I will adapt and extend the template suggested by Blass to accommodate such instances. In the case of some problematic occurrences, the analytical work undertaken for this study involved the construction of several

---

14. Carston, *Thoughts and Utterances*, 256.
15. Blass, "Constraints on Relevance," 6.
16. See Christophe Unger, "Epistemic Vigilance and the Function of Procedural Indicators in Communication and Comprehension," in *Relevance Theory: More Than Understanding* (Newcastle upon Tyne: Cambridge Scholars Publishing, 2012), 47.
17. G standing for γάρ.

different strengthening series using different plausible accessible contextual assumptions, in order to ascertain the most plausible and efficient. In the discussion below, for each example I will present only the constructed series judged, as a result of the analysis, to be most relevant (bringing most effects for least effort).

I will reorganize the presentation of the strengthening sequence of premises and conclusion suggested by Blass so that it corresponds more obviously to the order in which assumptions are communicated in the text. Thus for each occurrence discussed, I will present:

P: the propositional form of the information needing strengthening
Q: the propositional form of the premise introduced by γάρ
IA(s): the contextual assumption(s) made accessible in the cotext
C: the conclusion, a reiteration of P, confirmed by backward strengthening, which thus represents a more firmly held version of P.

By *propositional form*, I mean an utterance that has been disambiguated and filled out in key aspects for the purposes of my analysis (e.g., key pronouns are assigned referents, ellipses filled out, imperatives are stated as propositions) so that it represents a state of affairs capable of functioning as input into inferential processes.[18] This means that P and Q in my analysis will sometimes take the form of a disambiguated reformulation or summary of the utterances involved in a particular series.

Following my schema, we can lay out the analysis of 3:22b as follows:

P (v. 22a): The righteousness of God through faith in Jesus Christ (is) for all who believe.
Q introduced by γάρ (v. 22b): There is no distinction.
IA: If there is no distinction, then the righteousness of God through faith in Jesus Christ (is) for all who believe.
C (strengthening v. 22a): The righteousness of God through faith in Jesus Christ (is) for all who believe.

For each occurrence, the analysis begins with the linguistic code of the text as a clue to communicator intentions. It regards the preceding cotext as the most important source of highly accessible contextual assumptions. It

---

18. See the glossary for a complete definition of *propositional form*.

also posits contextual information that, following our basic reconstruction of the shared cognitive environment of author and addressees (see §2.4.1, above), would probably have been highly accessible to the first audience. This involves close exegetical work at pertinent points, and interaction with a variety of commentators, in an attempt to identify the probable highly accessible assumptions at play. The analysis makes hypotheses about strengthening series of inferences that γάρ may plausibly have triggered for Paul's audience. Following a relevance-guided heuristic, it reconstructs a likely inferential series leading to the strengthening of preceding assumptions. In each case, the constructed series represents a hypothetical analysis of how the interpretation process might plausibly have gone, rather than a representation of what was actually thought.[19]

3.2. Straightforward but Backward: Instructions for Strengthening

I will begin by discussing five straightforward occurrences of γάρ, three from expository and two from hortatory material. These isolated examples will be briefly considered in their cotext but have been selected as instances where a strengthening relation is obvious even without a detailed awareness of the literary context. It is beyond the scope of this book to give more than the briefest of summaries of the cotext of the straightforward examples of γάρ discussed, and I will deal with points of exegetical detail only in as far as these have a direct bearing on the analysis of γάρ.

3.2.1. Romans 8:2

Romans 8:1–11 forms part of the second major section of the epistle that many commentators consider coterminous with chapters 5–8.[20] It is preceded in 7:7–25 by the notoriously disputed exploration of the role of the law in the light of the new reality in Christ (see discussion under §3.3.1, below). This is expressed in terms of the intense inner conflict experienced by the *I* who wants to obey God's law, as a result of the two-sidedness of the law and its manipulation by the power of sin, which results in the law's powerlessness to enable human righteousness and to

---

19. See Blass, *Relevance Relations*, 13.
20. For different views of the transitional status of ch. 5, see §4.2.1, below.

bring life.[21] In 8:1–11 there is a dramatic shift in perspective, picking up the themes and confident tone of 5:1–7:6 and developing them from the perspective of the antithesis between life in the flesh and life in the Spirit. Romans 8:1, presented as a conclusion drawn from what precedes, is an emphatic statement of assurance regarding the freedom from condemnation enjoyed by those who are "in Christ Jesus." Jewett characterizes this statement as a "thesis," and Dunn as "the restatement of the major theme of the composition."[22]

8:1: οὐδὲν ἄρα νῦν κατάκριμα τοῖς ἐν Χριστῷ Ἰησοῦ
8:2: ὁ γὰρ νόμος τοῦ πνεύματος τῆς ζωῆς ἐν Χριστῷ Ἰησοῦ ἠλευθέρωσέν σε ἀπὸ τοῦ νόμου τῆς ἁμαρτίας καὶ τοῦ θανάτου[23]

Commentators variously describe the role of γάρ in 8:2 as explanatory, as introducing the beginning of an exposition or grounding for the theme stated in verse 1, as introducing grounds for what precedes in both 8:1 and 7:25a, or as a confirmation of the truth of verse 1.[24] Given the preceding discussion of the law in 7:7–25 and the clear reference to the torah in 8:3, it makes best sense to read both occurrences of νόμος in 8:2 as referring to the Mosaic law.[25] The genitive construction τοῦ πνεύματος τῆς ζωῆς can be understood as "the Spirit that brings life," and the double genitive ὁ ... νόμος τοῦ πνεύματος τῆς ζωῆς in terms of the Spirit acting upon the law, making its fulfillment possible; that is, the law as fulfilled and enabled by the life-bringing Spirit.[26] Conversely, τοῦ νόμου τῆς ἁμαρτίας καὶ τοῦ

---

21. See Dunn, *Romans 1–8*, 398.
22. Jewett, *Romans*, 478; Dunn, *Romans 1–8*, 416.
23. Throughout the study, I work from the UBS⁵ Greek text. English translations are my own unless stated otherwise.
24. Wright, "Romans," 574; Dunn, *Romans 1–8*, 416; Wilckens, *Der Brief an die Römer*, 2:118; Wolter, *Röm 1–8*, 470; Henning Paulsen, *Überlieferung und Auslegung in Römer 8*, WMANT 43 (Neukirchen-Vluyn: Neukirchener Verlag, 1974), 32; Cranfield, *Epistle to the Romans*, 372.
25. Ulrich Wilckens, *Der Brief an die Römer: Studienausgabe* (Ostfeldern: Theologie Patmos Verlag, 2014), 122; Dunn, *Romans 1–8*, 416–17; Wright, "Romans," 576–77. In contrast, Wolter and Käsemann read νόμος in 8:2 metaphorically as "ein den Menschen bestimmendes und ihn festlegendes Prinzip" (Wolter, *Röm 1–8*, 473 and Käsemann, *An die Römer*, 207). See also Cranfield, *Epistle to the Romans*, 374–76.
26. See Wolter, *Röm 1–8*, 123.

θανάτου can be understood in terms of sin acting upon and manipulating the law, which results in condemnation and death (see 7:7–25).[27]

Using the relevance-theoretic template for an inferential strengthening series, we can explain γάρ in 8:2 in terms of procedural strengthening as follows. When addressees hear the statement in verse 1 followed by verse 2, their comprehension processes check for relevance and compute cognitive effects. I propose that procedure G is triggered by γάρ in verse 2, giving instructions to process what follows as backward strengthening a previous claim. That is, expectations of relevance are raised that the material in verse 2 will be relevant as strengthening material in relation to a previously communicated claim. The procedure includes the instruction to search for the most accessible implicit assumptions that, together with the information introduced by γάρ, lead to the confirmation of the first appropriate preceding claim available. The search follows a relevance-guided heuristic that takes the path of least effort and stops at the first relevant interpretation.

Following procedure G, addressees' inferential processes search for the information that is to be processed as input into the strengthening procedure and construct a hypothesis. We can suggest that it is inferred that the entire statement in verse 2 is to be processed as a single complex of assumptions, premise Q (introduced by γάρ), since it consists of a balanced antithetical statement with a single verb. The search for a relevant inferential strengthening relation is immediately satisfied by hypothesizing a relationship between the statement in verse 2 and the immediately preceding claim in verse 1. The subpersonal procedure searches for contextual assumptions made highly accessible by Q. I propose that the following assumption is likely identified, which is highly accessible from assumptions communicated in the previous cotext, in which the concepts of law, sin, condemnation, and death are closely associated: "If a person is set free from the law of sin and death, there is no condemnation for that person."[28] A series is then constructed along the following lines:

Explicit claim P (v. 1): There is now no condemnation for those who are in Christ Jesus.

---

27. See Wilckens, *Der Brief an die Römer*, 122; Dunn, *Romans 1–8*, 419.
28. See, in particular, 5:12, 15–21; 7:7–14, 21–25.

Premise Q introduced by γάρ (v. 2): The law of the Spirit of life in Christ Jesus has set those in Christ Jesus free from the law of sin and death.[29]
Implicit premise IA: If a person is set free from the law of sin and death, there is no condemnation for that person.
Conclusion C deduced from Q and IA (reiterating, independently confirming, and thus strengthening P in v. 1): There is no condemnation for those who are in Christ Jesus.

As a result of the hypothesizing of this inferential series triggered by γάρ, a strengthening relationship is established between verse 2 and verse 1. In this way, claim P in verse 1 is confirmed and strengthened with the help of independent evidence supplied from addressees' own encyclopedic knowledge. That is, the cognitive effect of strengthening has taken place. Addressees now adhere more strongly to claim P and are more strongly persuaded of its validity. This procedural analysis of γάρ corresponds with Cranfield's reading, which views verse 2 as "confirming the truth of verse 1." Equally, the combination of Q and IA leading to C could be understood as an explanation or exposition of P, as other commentators suggest. In this case, the inferential procedure increases the comprehensibility of the latter by connecting it with existing assumptions addressees hold about the world. This is also a case of the cognitive effect of strengthening: P becomes more plausible and is thus held more strongly as valid.

Within a relevance-theoretic framework, then, the strengthening procedure may be relevant to different addressees and interpreters in different ways, depending on what leads to the most cognitive effects for them in the context. If P raises questions of plausibility because an addressee is not yet fully convinced of its validity, then her comprehension processes will search for a series that is relevant as confirmation. If, on the other hand, assumption P raises implicit questions of comprehensibility for certain addressees, then they will process γάρ followed by Q by searching for an inferential strengthening series that is relevant as an explanation. Either way, a relevance-theoretic framework allows us to account for the connective as a procedural indicator that guides toward the inferential procedure of strengthening, constraining interpretation and thereby reducing pro-

---

29. In the cotext, the referent of σέ is most naturally identified as an addressee who is one of "those in Christ Jesus." Even if we were to follow the textual variant μέ, this would still be the case (see Wolter, *Röm 1–8*, 469 n. 2, for a discussion of the variants).

cessing costs. The connective raises expectations that the information that follows will be relevant in relation to a previously communicated assumption or claim. The information introduced by γάρ in verse 2 increases the cognitive effects derived from verse 1 and thus augments its argumentative salience and its persuasiveness.

3.2.2. Romans 10:10

This example occurs in the middle of the sustained argumentation of chapters 9–11, the epistle's third major section, that deals with the question of the continuing role of ethnic Israel in God's purposes, in the light of God's righteousness as revealed in the gospel of Christ. Many scholars regard 10:1–13 as explaining and developing the thought of 9:30–33.[30] Romans 10:5–13 are viewed by some as a typical Jewish exposition of scriptural passages that develops and supports Paul's claim in 10:4: τέλος ... νόμου Χριστὸς εἰς δικαιοσύνην παντὶ τῷ πιστεύοντι.[31] The exegesis in verse 8d of the citation from Deut 30:14, introduced by τοῦτ' ἔστιν, is further developed by the assertion in verse 9. The occurrence of γάρ in verse 10 is the first in a series of five that form a tight chain of strengthening statements running from verse 10 to verse 13.

10:9a: ὅτι ἐὰν ὁμολογήσῃς ἐν τῷ στόματί σου κύριον Ἰησοῦν
10:9b: καὶ πιστεύσῃς ἐν τῇ καρδίᾳ σου ὅτι ὁ θεὸς αὐτὸν ἤγειρεν ἐκ νεκρῶν, σωθήσῃ·
10:10: καρδίᾳ γὰρ πιστεύεται εἰς δικαιοσύνην, στόματι δὲ ὁμολογεῖται εἰς σωτηρίαν.

The occurrence of γάρ in 10:10 is uncontroversial. Commentators generally regard it as introducing an explanation that clarifies and supports the

---

30. E.g., Paul W. Meyer, "Romans 10:4 and the 'End' of the Law," in *The Word in This World: Essays in New Testament Exegesis and Theology*, ed. John T. Carroll (Louisville: Westminster John Knox, 2004), 81; Dunn, *Romans 9–16*, 579; Badenas, *Christ the End of the Law*, 108; Cranfield, *Epistle to the Romans*, 2:504–5; Käsemann, *An die Römer*, 264. See Florian Wilk, "Rahmen Und Aufbau von Römer 9–11," in Wilk and Wagner, *Between Gospel and Election*, 23–31, 53, for contrasting analyses.

31. Dunn, *Romans 9–16*, 603; Jewett, *Romans*, 624. See the fuller discussion of 10:4 under §5.2, below.

statement of 10:9.³² There is not room at this juncture to discuss πιστεύω nor δικαιοσύνη.³³ Pending further discussion, I will translate πιστεύω "have faith" and follow Maximilian Zerwick's translation of εἰς δικαιοσύνην, "leading to righteousness."³⁴ Using the relevance-theoretic template, I propose the following procedural account of γάρ in 10:10. The connective triggers procedure G. The statement following γάρ in verse 10 is identified as premise Q and, following a relevance-guided heuristic, comprehension processes automatically search for preceding information in relation to which this premise is relevant as strengthening material. The preceding statement in verse 9 is identified as the most likely candidate. This identification is facilitated by the repetition in verse 10 of the vocabulary from verse 9, "believe with heart," "confess with lips." Addressees' comprehension processes then search for contextual assumptions made highly accessible by verse 10 and verse 9. We can posit that the following inferential series may likely be involved:

P (v. 9): If a person confesses with her mouth that Jesus is Lord and has faith in her heart that God raised him from the dead, she will be saved.
Q introduced by γάρ (v. 10): It is with the heart that a person has faith, leading to righteousness, and it is with the mouth that a person confesses, leading to salvation.
IA: If it is with the heart that a person has faith, leading to righteousness, and with the mouth that a person confesses, leading to salvation, then if a person confesses with her mouth that Jesus is Lord and has faith in her heart that God raised him from the dead, that person will be saved. (Inferable from common sense, plus from encyclopedic knowledge of the concept of salvation/being saved and its association with the concepts of faith and righteousness, highly accessible from the wider preceding cotext, e.g., 3:22–26.)
C (strengthening P): If a person confesses with her mouth that Jesus is Lord and has faith in her heart that God has raised him from the dead, she will be saved.

---

32. E.g., Cranfield, *Epistle to the Romans*, 530; Jewett, *Romans*, 630. Dunn regards 10:5–10 as "the scriptural underpinning of 9:30–10:4" (Dunn, *Romans 9–16*, 616, 599).
33. See the discussion of πιστεύω and δικαιοσύνη under §6.2.3 nn. 48 and 52, below.
34. See Jewett, *Romans*, 621, 630; Maximilian Zerwick, *A Grammatical Analysis of the Greek New Testament*, trans. Mary Grosvenor, 4th ed., SubBi 39 (Rome: Pontifical Biblical Institute, 1993), 482.

As a result of the deductive procedure, the statement in verse 9 is adhered to more strongly by addressees, that is, it results in the cognitive effect of strengthening. The statement is confirmed independently, by inference, with the help of evidence supplied from addressees' own background knowledge of the world. In this cotext, which consists of intricate exposition rather than strong persuasion, I suggest that the strengthening procedure is probably relevant for addressees as an explanation that makes verse 9 more comprehensible, rather than as confirming evidence convincing addressees of its truth. This corresponds with commentators' reading of this occurrence as explanatory. The material introduced by γάρ achieves relevance in relation to the information in verse 9. This makes sense of the intuition that the statement in verse 10 supports the claim in verse 9.

3.2.3. Romans 2:11

This third example occurs as part of a diatribe, beginning in 2:1, that is addressed to an imaginary interlocutor.[35] Whatever the specific identity of this conversation partner, the diatribe challenges self-righteous presumption and hypocrisy by demonstrating the inescapability and impartiality of God's eschatological judgment, at which time God will judge all human beings, Jews and gentiles alike, on the basis of their works. The statement in 2:6 that God will pay each person back according to that person's works is an accepted Jewish principle, which is then spelled out in verses 7–10 by means of two antithetical statements.[36] In verse 11 we find a Jewish theological axiom introduced by γάρ.[37]

---

35. The identity of the interlocutor in 2:1 is contested. See Barclay, *Paul and the Gift*, 464 n. 35. Some argue that Paul turns to address Jewish exceptionalism or pretension (though the Jewish identity of the interlocutor is explicitly identified only in 2:17). See Jonathan A. Linebaugh, "Announcing the Human: Rethinking the Relationship between Wisdom of Solomon 13–15 and Romans 1.18–2.11," *NTS* 57 (2011): 221; Dunn, *Romans 1–8*, 78. Others claim that he addresses the archetype of a hypocritical and judgmental person (e.g., Elliott, *Rhetoric of Romans*, 125–26; Jewett, *Romans*, 197), an arrogant gentile (see Stowers, *Rereading of Romans*, 101–4), or a judaizing gentile (see Thorsteinsson, Thiessen, and Rodríguez, "Paul's Interlocutor in Romans," 21).

36. For pay back as a Jewish principle, see Jewett, *Romans*, 209; Dunn, *Romans 1–8*, 78, 85; Ps 62:12; Prov 24:12. For verses 7–10 as two antithetical statements, see Cranfield, *Epistle to the Romans*, 146.

37. See Jouette M. Bassler, "Divine Impartiality in Paul's Letter to the Romans," *NovT* 26 (1984): 44; Deut 10:17; 2 Chr 19:7.

3. Consistent Yet Context-Sensitive: The Guidance γάρ Gives

2:6: ὃς ἀποδώσει ἑκάστῳ κατὰ τὰ ἔργα αὐτοῦ·
2:7: τοῖς μὲν καθ' ὑπομονὴν ἔργου ἀγαθοῦ δόξαν καὶ τιμὴν καὶ ἀφθαρσίαν ζητοῦσιν ζωὴν αἰώνιον,
2:8: τοῖς δὲ ἐξ ἐριθείας καὶ ἀπειθοῦσι τῇ ἀληθείᾳ πειθομένοις δὲ τῇ ἀδικίᾳ ὀργὴ καὶ θυμός.
2:9: θλῖψις καὶ στενοχωρία ἐπὶ πᾶσαν ψυχὴν ἀνθρώπου τοῦ κατεργαζομένου τὸ κακόν, Ἰουδαίου τε πρῶτον καὶ Ἕλληνος·
2:10: δόξα δὲ καὶ τιμὴ καὶ εἰρήνη παντὶ τῷ ἐργαζομένῳ τὸ ἀγαθόν, Ἰουδαίῳ τε πρῶτον καὶ Ἕλληνι·
2:11: οὐ γάρ ἐστιν προσωπολημψία παρὰ τῷ θεῷ.

Various commentators see the axiom introduced by γάρ in verse 11 as providing confirmation, grounds, or a conclusion for the statements in verses 6–10.[38] We can explain γάρ as a procedural indicator in verse 11 as follows. The connective triggers procedure G, and addressees' comprehension processes, following a relevance-guided heuristic, search for preceding claims that are not yet optimally relevant and that the statement following γάρ could potentially strengthen. The material immediately adjacent in verse 10 is considered. Since it does not stand alone as a statement, but is part of a complex of assumptions beginning in verse 6 (the statements in vv. 7–10 are grammatically dependent on the verb in v. 6), this complex is processed together as a single whole, and the information in verses 6–10 is identified as candidate for strengthening. We can summarize this information in a single statement P as follows: "God will pay back each person according to his/her works, Jews and gentiles alike: eternal life, glory, honor, and peace to those who do good, and wrath and distress to those who do evil." The information following the colon in this statement represents information in verses 7–10 that is in apposition with ἑκάστῳ in verse 6. It provides an elaboration of the basic proposition stated in verse 6.

I suggest that the following strengthening series may be constructed:

P (vv. 6–10): God will pay back to each person according to his/her works, Jews and gentiles alike (eternal life, glory, honor, and peace to those who do good, and wrath and distress to those who do evil).
Q introduced by γάρ (v. 11): There is no partiality with God.

---

38. E.g., Jewett, *Romans*, 195, 209; Cranfield, *Epistle to the Romans*, 150; Käsemann, *An die Römer*, 54.

IA: If there is no partiality with God, then God will recompense each person according to her deeds, Jews and gentiles alike.
C (confirming P in vv. 6, 9b, 10b): God will pay back to each person according to his/her works, Jews and gentiles alike.[39]

As a result of this inferential procedure triggered by γάρ, the validity of the assumptions communicated in verse 6 and verses 9b and 10b is confirmed. The main assertion that God will pay back each person according to his/her deeds, plus the claim that this means both Jews and gentiles, are adhered to more strongly. This underlines the argumentative salience of these claims. This example of γάρ is slightly less straightforward than the two previously discussed because addressees must infer that the assumptions to be strengthened stretch back to verse 6. Nevertheless, the strengthening relation is easily traceable and intuitively recognized by secondary interpreters. The γάρ clause in verse 11 achieves its relevance in relation to the information in verses 6–10 and thus can be viewed as supporting material in the argument. The fact that γάρ here introduces a theological axiom, presumably familiar to Paul's addressees and carrying the authority of accepted wisdom, adds additional ballast to the supporting premise. This powerful buttressing suggests that the γάρ clause may provide a response to implicit objections possibly raised by the preceding claims (in particular the claim that Jews and gentiles will receive the same recompense).[40] This is an example of strengthening that is probably relevant as confirmation, in which the strongly persuasive strategy of an authoritative axiom is employed as convincing proof. This may be because there is a higher risk that what is communicated here may not be accepted by addressees as valid. We see here that the type of persuasive material in which γάρ occurs influences the outworking of the strengthening procedure triggered.

In relevance theory terms, the axiom in verse 11 is an example of metarepresentation, that is, a re-representation of thoughts already represented in a different context.[41] Metarepresentations include citations

---

39. The information in vv. 7–10 that is not confirmed by this strengthening series does not appear here in C.

40. Rudolph argues that γάρ functions as a marker that alerts addressees that what follows is the communicator's "response to a perceived ... question or objection" that inhibits "receptivity to the intended message" (Rudolph, "Reclaiming ΓΑΡ," xx).

41. See glossary. In relevance theory terms, all verbal utterances are representations of thoughts.

and paraphrases from conventional wisdom, authoritative sources, and other individuals, as well as the communicator's own previous verbal representations of his thoughts. In as far as they represent material that is already accepted as valid, and sometimes as authoritative, by addressees, they bring additional weight to supporting material.[42] Consequently, we find that γάρ not infrequently introduces metarepresentations, including scriptural citations.

We can summarize our discussion of these three straightforward examples as follows: in expository material, γάρ can be accounted for as giving a set of procedural instructions that guides toward the inferential procedure of strengthening and thus reduces processing costs. In all cases, material introduced by γάρ can be viewed as strengthening or supporting preceding material. Strengthening works itself out as either the confirmation or explanation of previously communicated claims, increasing the strength with which addressees adhere to them as valid. The outworking of strengthening in different cotexts depends on the communicative aims of the passage. Rather than being relevant in its own right, material introduced by γάρ raises expectations of relevance in relation to preceding material, which it supports.

When we consider occurrences of γάρ in hortatory material, we need to bear in mind that the assumptions strengthened as a result of the procedural guidance γάρ gives are expressed as exhortations, often using imperatival forms, rather than as assertions or claims. These imperatives need to be disambiguated as propositional forms, that is, expressed as statements, before they can be used as input into inferential procedures. Relevance theory explains imperatives as expressing states of affairs that the communicator believes would be desirable if realized as real states of affairs. Thus all imperatives, whether requestive or advisory, can be stated as disambiguated propositional forms following the basic schema: "It is *desirable* to [do something]." In keeping with the relevance theory framework of this study, I will follow this schema here.[43]

---

42. Moyise discusses the role of citations from authoritative sources in ancient rhetoric (Moyise, "Quotations," 17–18). See also Perelman and Olbrechts-Tyteca's discussion of Aristotle's view of maxims: "the more [the form of a maxim] is traditionally known, the readier will be the acceptance of the statement and of the consequences it involves" (Perelman and Olbrechts-Tyteca, *New Rhetoric*, 166, referring to Aristotle, *Rhet.* 2.21, 1394a *et seq*).

43. Sperber and Wilson, *Relevance*, 250–51.

3.2.4. Romans 13:1

Romans 13:1-7 forms part of the major paraenetic section of the epistle that runs from 12:1 to 15:13. The pericope has generated fierce controversy because of its apparently quietist attitude toward political authority and endorsement of the ruling status quo, and some have sought to explain it as a non-Pauline interpolation.[44] This debate is not directly relevant to our examination of the role of γάρ as a procedural signal that guides exegesis, however. The paraenesis of chapters 12-13 is founded on the preceding theology of chapters 1-11, and there are various links between chapter 12 and 13:1-7.[45] Concepts such as τὸ ἀγαθόν and τὸ κακόν and the notion of "paying back" (ἀποδίδωμι), found in chapter 12, are picked up in 13:1-7 and thus reactivated in hearers' minds, along with associated contextual assumptions communicated in chapter 12. They form part of the nexus of highly accessible mutually manifest assumptions, that is, the shared cognitive environment, from which addressees draw inferences to arrive at a relevant interpretation of 13:1-7.

Despite the links with what precedes, Rom 13:1 marks the beginning of a new subsection in Paul's argument. Whereas 12:9-21 deals with what living as a sacrifice to God (12:1) means in terms of personal relationships guided by love, the exhortation in 13:1a signals a shift to a discussion of the implications of the new life in Christ for relationships with political and civic authorities.[46] This exhortation is often viewed as a thesis or "thematic exhortation" for the argument in verses 1b-7, which elaborates upon it.[47] There is agreement that γάρ in verse 1b introduces a rationale or

---

44. Jewett gives a brief overview of diverse interpretations of this passage (Jewett, *Romans*, 783-86). He notes various scholars who argue for an interpolation, among them Walter Schmithals, *Der Römerbrief: Ein Kommentar* (Gütersloh: Mohn, 1988). See also Neil Elliott, *Liberating Paul: The Justice of God and the Politics of the Apostle* (Sheffield: Sheffield Academic, 1994), 217-18; and Richard Burridge, *Imitating Jesus: An Inclusive Approach to New Testament Ethics* (Grand Rapids: Eerdmans, 2007), 117-21, who discusses examples of this passage being used to lend theological legitimation to oppressive governments.

45. Adams, *Constructing the World*, 199-200.

46. For 12:9-21 dealing with personal relationships, see Dunn, *Romans 9-16*, x; Jewett, *Romans*, 736.

47. Dunn, *Romans 9-16*, 176; Jewett, *Romans*, 781; Wilckens, *Der Brief an die Römer (Studienausgabe)*, 29.

justification for the exhortation in verse 1a.[48] This comes in the form of a theological statement from Jewish wisdom.[49]

13:1a: Πᾶσα ψυχὴ ἐξουσίαις ὑπερεχούσαις ὑποτασσέσθω.
13:1b: οὐ γὰρ ἔστιν ἐξουσία εἰ μὴ ὑπὸ θεοῦ,
13:1c: αἱ δὲ οὖσαι ὑπὸ θεοῦ τεταγμέναι εἰσίν.

We can explain this occurrence of γάρ in procedural terms, following the relevance-theoretic template, as follows. I propose that, on hearing 13:1a followed by 13:1b–c, procedure G is triggered by γάρ. Verse 1b and verse 1c are processed together as a complex of assumptions introduced by γάρ as strengthening premises, since verse 1c is the positive restatement of verse 1b. We can disambiguate and summarize this as Q: "All authority is from God." The assumption communicated by means of the exhortation in verse 1a is identified as a candidate for strengthening, and a disambiguated propositional form, P, is inferred from it: "It is desirable to submit to the governing authorities." A highly accessible background assumption is then activated to combine with Q. We can posit the following likely deductive series:

P (v. 1a): It is desirable to submit to the governing authorities.
Q introduced by γάρ (v. 1b): All authority is from God.
IA: If authority is from God, it is desirable/necessary to submit to it.
C (confirming and reiterating P): It is desirable to submit to the governing authorities.

As a result of this inferential series, the propositional form of the exhortation is confirmed as valid. Addressees are thus more strongly persuaded of the desirability of submitting to the authorities as a course of action to put into practice.[50] The statements in verse 1b–c increase the relevance of the exhortation in verse 1a, helping to underline its argumentative salience. The strengthening that γάρ guides toward here works itself out

---

48. Cranfield, *Epistle to the Romans*, 2:663; Jewett, *Romans*, 784; Wilckens, *Der Brief an die Römer (Studienausgabe)*, 29.
49. Dunn, *Romans 9–16*, 761, 770.
50. Blakemore shows how nonfactual desirable states of affairs such as imperatives can be strengthened by other communicated assumptions, just as truth conditional assertions can (Blakemore, *Semantic Constraints*, 80–81).

as relevant as a justification providing grounds for an exhortation. The fact that the material introduced by γάρ would have been a theological axiom to Paul's addressees, given their theocentric worldview, reinforces the support provided by the γάρ clause. This is another example of γάρ introducing an authoritative metarepresentation that adds to the persuasiveness of the argument.

3.2.5. Romans 13:8

After the discussion of the relationships of believers to public authorities in 13:1–7, which includes the exhortation in 13:6–7 to pay whatever is due, including taxes, in 13:8–10 the argument moves on to a summarizing exhortation to love others.

13:8a: Μηδενὶ μηδὲν ὀφείλετε
13:8b: εἰ μὴ τὸ ἀλλήλους ἀγαπᾶν·
13:8c: ὁ γὰρ ἀγαπῶν τὸν ἕτερον νόμον πεπλήρωκεν.
13:9:   τὸ γὰρ Οὐ μοιχεύσεις, Οὐ φονεύσεις, Οὐ κλέψεις, Οὐκ ἐπιθυμήσεις, καὶ εἴ τις ἑτέρα ἐντολή, ἐν τῷ λόγῳ τούτῳ ἀνακεφαλαιοῦται [ἐν τῷ] Ἀγαπήσεις τὸν πλησίον σου ὡς σεαυτόν.

We can analyze the occurrence of γάρ in 13:8c in a similar way to the example in verse 1a. The connective triggers procedure G, and the immediately preceding material in verse 8b is identified as candidate for strengthening. We can represent the assumptions that are likely involved in the deductive procedure as follows:

Exhortation (v. 8a–b): Do not owe anything to anyone except [the debt of][51] love for one another.

This command (and the metaphor of love as a debt) can be disambiguated and expressed as the following propositional form:

P (v. 8a–b): (It is desirable not to have anything that must be repaid to other people), and it is desirable to love other people.

---

51. In inferential series, I use square brackets around information that represents the explication of ellipsis.

Q introduced by γάρ (v. 8c): Anyone who loves other people fulfills [God's] law [by loving other people].
IA: If someone fulfills God's law by doing an action, it is desirable to do that action.
C (confirming the desirability of the exhortation in v. 8b): It is desirable to love one another.

The result of this deductive procedure, is that the communicated assumption "It is desirable ... to love one another" is adhered to more strongly, since its reasonableness and logical coherence have been independently verified. Here too, the result of the strengthening procedure is relevant as a justifying rationale. If, as some suggest, the statement in verse 8c is an allusion to the Jesus tradition and to Jesus's summing up of the law in the command of Lev 19:18, then this would be another example of γάρ introducing a metarepresentation as supporting material in order to bolster the persuasive punch of the exhortation it supports.[52]

Our discussion of these straightforward occurrences has demonstrated that a procedural strengthening account following a relevance-theoretic template provides a consistent explanation of the role of γάρ in various passages from different text types in Romans. We have discussed a variety of uncontroversial examples in order to establish, on the one hand, that γάρ is a procedural indicator that gives a core set of instructions guiding toward strengthening and, on the other, that this strengthening works itself out in diverse ways in different contexts. The connective raises expectations that what follows will be relevant as supporting material for previously communicated claims. The result is to reinforce previously communicated assumptions, in order to increase the persuasiveness and coherence of the argument.

Procedure G follows a relevance-guided heuristic in identifying which previously communicated information is to be strengthened, in accessing contextual assumptions, and in constructing strengthening series. The resulting strengthening effect is relevant in various ways in diverse cotexts and for different addressees. Sometimes it works itself out as confirming evidence increasing the plausibility of preceding claims, sometimes as an explanation increasing comprehensibility, sometimes as a rationale

---

52. For v. 8c as an allusion to Lev 19:18, see Sarah Whittle, *Covenant Renewal and the Consecration of the Gentiles in Romans*, SNTSMS 161 (Cambridge: Cambridge University Press, 2015), 115–16; Dunn, *Romans 9–16*, 782.

or grounds justifying the desirability of an exhortation, sometimes as convincing authoritative proof. For every occurrence, however, the core strengthening instructions are the same, allowing us to rely on γάρ as a consistent communicative signal that increases the relevance and argumentative salience of preceding assumptions. In this way, the connective constrains interpretation in a particular direction, reducing processing costs. In every case, the material γάρ introduces can be understood as supporting information in relation to the more salient preceding assumptions that it helps to strengthen.

3.3. Strengthening Guidance in More Complex Cases: Romans 7:7–20

Having established the validity of a procedural account of γάρ from a variety of straightforward occurrences, we will next consider how this account is also able to provide a consistent explanation of somewhat complex occurrences in Romans. I have chosen to discuss a series of examples within two texts, one expository, 7:7–20, and one hortatory, 14:1–11. I have selected these because both contain a high concentration of diverse occurrences, including various somewhat complex examples. As we examine these more complex occurrences, an awareness of the contextual assumptions highly accessible in the cotext becomes more important, since the strengthening inferential procedure sometimes involves assumptions that are not immediately adjacent to the γάρ clause in question. Examining these occurrences in their cotext allows us to pay closer attention to potential contextual assumptions at play, as well as to pertinent exegetical problems as necessary. In addition, a systematic discussion of cotext enables us to trace the role of γάρ within the wider argument. In particular, we can see not only how γάρ flags up supporting or background information, but also how this facilitates the identification of the argument's more salient points. Furthermore, it increases awareness of how material following γάρ may revisit and reactivate assumptions communicated further back in the argument, increasing their relevance.

As in the previous section, for each example I will demonstrate the procedural role of γάρ by constructing a probable strengthening series, assuming the likely cognitive environment of the letter's Roman addressees, as discussed under §2.4.1, above. I will do this by adapting and extending Blakemore and Blass's simple template of a deductive strengthening series in order to incorporate additional contextual assumptions.

3. Consistent Yet Context-Sensitive: The Guidance γάρ Gives   85

3.3.1. Cotext of Romans 7:7–20

The subsection 7:7–20 occurs as the second major section of the epistle, which a majority of modern commentators regard as running from 5:1 to 8:39.[53] This section might be summed up as a discussion of the new life in Christ that believers enjoy as God's children, liberated from sin and death, and enabled by the Spirit. The section is characterized by sharp antitheses between the old age and the new, between Adam and Christ (5:12–21), death and life, sin and righteousness (ch. 6), and life according to the flesh versus life according to the Spirit (ch. 8). The issue of the Jewish law, a recurrent theme in chapters 2–4, also resurfaces in 5:12–21, 8:1–11, and, most notably, in chapter 7.

Various interpreters understand 7:1–6 as a continuation of the discussion in chapter 6 of the antithesis between the old life of slavery to sin and death and the new life in Christ, with the Jewish law now in focus.[54] We can suppose that Paul's radical statement in 7:4 concerning the necessity of believers dying in relation to the law, and his assertion in 7:5 that sinful passions are somehow stimulated by the law, may have raised troubling questions for an audience that, according to 7:1, knows and respects the Jewish law.[55] We can suggest, following Dunn, that this issue would already have been raised by the argument of the previous chapters.[56] In 7:7–25, with the tensions in Paul's attitude toward the law fully exposed by 5:20 and 7:1–6, he turns to address these questions head on.[57] Scholars disagree as to how to break down 7:7–25 into subsections.

---

53. See the discussion under §4.2.1, below.
54. E.g., Cranfield, *Epistle to the Romans*, 331; Dunn, *Romans 1–8*, 358; Elliott, *Rhetoric of Romans*, 236–37.
55. Wolter views 7:7–25 as "unfolding" the statement in 7:5, and dealing with possible misunderstandings relating to what Paul has just said (Wolter, *Röm 1–8*, 425).
56. Dunn, *Romans 1–8*, 399. See also Werner G. Kümmel, *Römer 7 Und das Bild des Menschen im Neuen Testament*, TB 53 (Munich: Kaiser, 1974), 46.
57. Dunn reads 7:7–25 as a "defense of the law" demanded by Paul's prior discussion (Dunn, *Romans 1–8*, 376); and Wright as a discussion of where the law fits in God's purposes in the light of the new reality in Christ (Wright, *Paul and the Faithfulness of God*, 892). See also, e.g., Wolter, *Röm 1–8*, 425; Kümmel, *Römer 7*; Cranfield, *Epistle to the Romans*, 340. In contrast, Watson argues that Paul aims to evoke "a horror of life under the law" (Watson, *Paul, Judaism and the Gentiles*, 277–78); Charles K. Barrett regards 7:7–25 as a "digression" (Barrett, *A Commentary on the Epistle to the Romans*, BNTC [London: Black, 1971], 140); and Käsemann as a foil for the dis-

I will limit my discussion to verses 7–20.[58] Along with various commentators, I read the parallel rhetorical questions in verse 17 and verse 13 as marking the beginning of fresh stages in the argument and will thus treat verses 7–12 and verses 13–20 as separate subsections.[59]

The series of rhetorical questions followed by the emphatic denial, μὴ γένοιτο, in verse 7 and verse 13, is typical of a diatribal style. The second question in verse 7, "Is the law sin?," and the question in verse 13, "Has what is good become death to me?," suggest that Dunn is right in asserting that Paul is responding to potential objections concerning the role of the Jewish law, raised by his previous argument. Verses 7–25 are thus an essential part of Paul's main argument that is necessary to ensure continued receptivity toward his message. These verses have a clear persuasive intent, achieved by means of both logical argumentation and rhetorical devices such as questions and repetition.

Much ink has been spilled over the referent of the first-person singular pronoun in this passage. There is not space here to discuss the numerous differing interpretations.[60] The picture is complicated by the fact that some scholars detect a shift in the referent between 7:7–12 and 7:13–25.[61] I follow the view that 7:7–13 are to be interpreted in relation to 7:5, where Paul has referred to the passions aroused by the Jewish law in, it seems, both Jews and gentiles, given Paul's use of the first-person plural in 7:5.[62] Consequently, 7:7–12 may be understood as describing the role of God's law in creating consciousness of sin for all human beings who come into contact with it. Scholars note the possible allusions to Gen 2–3 in these verses.[63] Adam represents the human race, and Adam's experience in the face of God's commandments is the archetypal human response to God's

---

cussion of life in the Spirit in ch. 8 (Käsemann, *An die Römer*, 200). Stowers reads the subsection as a speech-in-character representing the dilemma of gentiles who look to the Jewish law for mastery of their passions (Stowers, *Rereading of Romans*, 202).

58. There is only one occurrence of γάρ in vv. 21–25, which falls into the category of problematic rather than somewhat complex.

59. E.g., Wolter, *Röm 1–8*, 425, 441; Jewett, *Romans*, 459; Wright, "Romans," 410; Wilckens, *Der Brief an die Römer*, 2:74.

60. See Wolter's overview of the debate (Wolter, *Röm 1–8*, 426–27), and Cranfield's summary of major interpretations of the *I* in 7:7–13 and 14–25 (Cranfield, *Epistle to the Romans*, 342–44).

61. See Cranfield, *Epistle to the Romans*, 344–47; Käsemann, *An die Römer*, 196.

62. See Kümmel, *Römer 7*, 46.

63. Wright, *Paul and the Faithfulness of God*, 893; Watson, *Paul, Judaism and the*

law. *I* thus refers to humankind's general experience (as Dunn puts it, "I = Adam = humankind = everyman") when confronted with God's command.[64] Paul describes the effect of God's commandment primarily in terms of an encounter with the Jewish law, but the probable allusion to Adam suggests that he also sees encompassed in its scope humanity's universal experience in response to God's commandments regarding right and wrong. If so, then Paul speaks autobiographically only in as far as general human experience is his experience too.[65] This interpretation makes good sense not only in relation to the previous cotext, but also given the predominantly gentile make-up of Paul's audience.

Closely related to the interpretation of the *I* is the interpretation of νόμος in this passage, which occurs some fifteen times. Although there is agreement that the referent is clearly the Jewish law in some instances (7:7, 12, 14, 22), others are much more ambiguous (e.g., 7:21, 23) and could potentially be read as referring to a more general universal law, or a principle. I will touch on this question only as it becomes directly relevant to the investigation of γάρ in particular verses.

3.3.2. Romans 7:7

7:7a: Τί οὖν ἐροῦμεν; ὁ νόμος ἁμαρτία; μὴ γένοιτο·
7:7b: ἀλλὰ τὴν ἁμαρτίαν οὐκ ἔγνων εἰ μὴ διὰ νόμου·
7:7c: τήν τε γὰρ ἐπιθυμίαν οὐκ ᾔδειν εἰ μὴ ὁ νόμος ἔλεγεν, Οὐκ ἐπιθυμήσεις.

By means of the second rhetorical question in 7:7a, Paul makes explicit a preposterous potential implication that could be drawn from his previous argument: the Jewish law can be equated with sin.[66] He immediately refutes this in the strongest terms: μὴ γένοιτο. In verse 7b we then find an assertion that qualifies this emphatic denial: while it is true that the law is absolutely

---

Gentiles, 281–85; Dunn, *Romans 1–8*, 383; Käsemann, *Römer*, 186. Wolter and Kümmel deny such an allusion, however (Wolter, *Röm 1–8*, 436; Kümmel, *Römer 7*, 86).

64. Dunn, *Romans 1–8*, 383.

65. See Dunn, *Romans 1–8*, 400; Cranfield, *Epistle to the Romans*, 342. For a contrasting view, see Wolter, *Röm 1–8*, 431–32; Wright, "Romans," 551–54; Douglas J. Moo, *The Epistle to the Romans*, NICNT 5 (Grand Rapids: Eerdmans, 1996), 431.

66. Commentators are agreed on reading νόμος in 7:7–12 as the Mosaic law. See, e.g., Wolter, *Röm 1–8*, 428; Moo, *Epistle to the Romans*, 431; Dunn, *Romans 1–8*, 378; Käsemann, *An die Römer*, 183.

not sin, there is nevertheless a relationship between the two.⁶⁷ This assertion begins Paul's complex response to the potential objection raised by 7:5. It is followed in 7:7c by a clause introduced by τε γάρ, which consists of a negative hypothetical conditional assertion completed by a quotation from the Decalogue, which is an abbreviation of the tenth commandment.

The combination τε γάρ is unusual in New Testament Greek. Although it is also found in Rom 1:26 and 14:8, it occurs nowhere else in the New Testament except Heb 2:11. Commentators broadly read the two connectives as introducing the rationale for the assertion in verse 7b. More specifically, Werner Kümmel interprets them as introducing a more precise fact ("Tatsache") giving grounds for the previous claim, while Marie-Joseph Lagrange maintains that the combination of connectives indicates that verse 7c is the proof of verse 7b.⁶⁸ Because of the rarity of the combination in the New Testament, it seems best to treat the two connectives separately and not as an expression with a single function. We can interpret τέ as meaning "and" or "also," though a number of commentators choose to leave it untranslated.⁶⁹

Following a procedural account, I propose that γάρ in verse 7c triggers procedure G and identifies the immediately adjacent claim in verse 7b as a candidate for strengthening. This claim may raise implicit questions for addressees, which would need to be answered in order for this claim to be optimally relevant to them. The procedure then searches for contextual assumptions made highly accessible by the material introduced by γάρ in verse 7c (premise Q), given the cotext of verse 7b. It combines these contextual assumptions with Q in a strengthening inferential series that may be along the following lines:

P (v. 7b, disambiguated): The *I* knew sin through the [Jewish] law.⁷⁰

---

67. Kümmel, *Römer 7*, 47.

68. Kümmel, *Römer 7*, 47; Marie-Joseph Lagrange, *Saint Paul, Épître aux Romains* (Paris: Lecoffre, 1916), 168.

69. For the meaning *and* or *also*, see Barclay M. Newman Jr., *A Concise Greek-English Dictionary of the New Testament* (Stuttgart: Deutsche Bibelgesellschaft; New York: United Bible Societies, 1993). For those leaving it untranslated, see, e.g., Dunn, *Romans 1–8*, 375; N. T. Wright, *Paul for Everyone: Romans, Part 1; Chapters 1–8* (London: SPCK, 2004), 122.

70. I will use the expression "the *I*" to disambiguate the referent of ἐγώ in this passage, to make clear that the referent is a generalized construct.

3. Consistent Yet Context-Sensitive: The Guidance γάρ Gives

Q introduced by γάρ (v. 7c, disambiguated): The *I* knew coveting because the [Jewish] law said, "Do not covet."
IA1: Coveting is sin. (Assumption accessible from encyclopedic knowledge of Jewish law).
IA2: To know coveting through the Jewish law is to know sin through the Jewish law.
C (confirming v. 7b): The *I* knew sin through the Jewish law.

The deduction triggered by γάρ in verse 7c makes use of a specific example, given in verse 7c, to confirm and thus strengthen the claim in verse 7b. This is an instance of γάρ introducing a specific example that backs up a general assertion.[71] Whether this procedure achieves relevance as confirming evidence, or as an explanation, depends on whether verse 7b raises implicit questions of plausibility or of comprehensibility for particular addressees. The claim in verse 7b becomes more comprehensible but also more plausible by means of the example given. The inferential series constructed is an extension of the simplest deductive template proposed by Blakemore, in that it involves accessing two contextual assumptions rather than one. This may thus be regarded as a slightly more complex occurrence of γάρ. Nevertheless, it has the same core procedural function as the occurrences we have previously discussed. It gives processing instructions that guide toward backward strengthening and signals that the information it introduces is relevant in relation to, and within the context of, this preceding claim for which it provides support.

In this instance, the information introduced by γάρ is at least partially well-known to Paul's addressees (the citation of the tenth commandment).[72] Here also, then, γάρ introduces information that is accepted by his addressees as authoritative, lending weight to the argument. The connective τέ can perhaps be analyzed as contributing further to the impact of the evidence presented in verse 7c. It may draw attention to this specific example introduced by γάρ as significant and indisputable evidence. At any rate, it does not appear to interfere with or modify the procedural instructions given by γάρ.

---

71. See Bauer, *Wörterbuch*, s.v. "γάρ," 1d.
72. Dunn argues that the idea that covetousness was the root of all sin was also an established part of Jewish thought (Dunn, *Romans 1–8*, 380).

3.3.3. Romans 7:8

7:8a: ἀφορμὴν δὲ λαβοῦσα ἡ ἁμαρτία διὰ τῆς ἐντολῆς κατειργάσατο ἐν ἐμοὶ πᾶσαν ἐπιθυμίαν·
7:8b: χωρὶς γὰρ νόμου ἁμαρτία νεκρά.

Romans 7:8a continues the explanation, begun in verse 7b, of how the law is in close relationship with sin. In this verse there is a shift in focus to the topic of sin, which is presented as a personified power that takes advantage of the commandment given by God and produces all kinds of covetous desires in the *I*. Kümmel and Dunn both take νόμος and ἐντολή as referring to a single reality in verses 7–12.[73] The commandment to which verse 8a refers is the one cited in verse 7c, which is an example that represents the whole Mosaic law. Some commentators read γάρ in verse 8b as introducing an explanation for the whole of verses 7–8a, an explanation that extends to the end of verse 10.[74]

We can explain γάρ in verse 8b as follows. Procedure G is triggered by the connective, and the preceding claim in verse 8a is identified as the most likely candidate for strengthening. This claim may raise implicit questions for addressees either regarding its validity, or relating to comprehension (e.g., "How is it that sin produced all kinds of covetous desires in the *I* through the commandment?"). The information introduced by γάρ in verse 8b makes accessible additional background assumptions, on the basis of which a deductive series is constructed:

> **P** (v. 8a): Sin seized the opportunity and produced all kinds of covetous desires in the *I* through the commandment.
> **Q introduced by γάρ** (v. 8b, disambiguated): In the absence of the law, sin is powerless/without effect.[75]
> **IA1**: By *the commandment* is meant the law, since the commandment is a specific instance of the law. (Highly accessible from encyclopedic knowledge of the Jewish law, and the citation of the tenth commandment in v. 7c.)
> **IA2**: If sin is powerless/without effect in the absence of the law, then sin is powerful/has an effect where the law is present.

---

73. Dunn, *Romans 1–8*, 380; Kümmel, *Römer 7*, 56.
74. Kümmel, *Römer 7*, 56; Wright, *Climax of the Covenant*, 21.
75. This is a disambiguation of the metaphorical use of νεκρά.

IA3: If sin has an effect where the law is present, then the commandment is an opportunity for sin to produce covetous desires in the *I*. (Inferable from background knowledge of what it means for sin to have an effect, made highly accessible by v. 8a.)

IA4: If the commandment is an opportunity for sin to produce covetous desires in the *I*, then sin will seize that opportunity and produce all kinds of covetous desires in the *I* through the commandment. (Inferable from common sense.)

C (confirming v. 8a): Sin seized the opportunity and produced all kinds of covetous desires in the *I* through the commandment.

As a result of this somewhat more complex inferential series, deduced automatically by subpersonal processes, the claim in verse 8a is strengthened. In effect, the inferential series provides an answer for possible implicit objections initially raised by verse 8a, with the result that the latter is adhered to more strongly.[76] Given these potential objections, it seems most likely that in this instance the result of the strengthening procedure is relevant as confirming evidence that strengthens a previous claim. This strengthening contributes to the persuasiveness of the argument. On this account, γάρ introduces a confirmation of the immediately preceding assertion rather than an explanation for the whole of verses 7–8a, as some commentators suggest. Nevertheless, the inference that "law" and "commandment" in verse 8a and b refer to the same reality in turn reinforces the association with the specific example of a commandment found in verse 7c, creating an impression of tight connection between verses 7–8 as a whole. The repetition of *law* throughout verses 7–8 also contributes to this coherence.

This series extends the basic strengthening template further in that it accesses a number of background assumptions and involves a number of inferential steps. I suggest that all of these assumptions would plausibly have been highly accessible to Paul's addressees, given the cotext, and the proposed reconstruction of their cognitive environment.

3.3.4. Romans 7:11

7:10a: ἐγὼ δὲ ἀπέθανον
7:10b: καὶ εὑρέθη μοι ἡ ἐντολὴ ἡ εἰς ζωήν, αὕτη εἰς θάνατον·

---

76. See Rudolph, "Reclaiming ΓΑΡ," xx.

7:11a: ἡ γὰρ ἁμαρτία ἀφορμὴν λαβοῦσα διὰ τῆς ἐντολῆς ἐξηπάτησέν με
7:11b: καὶ δι' αὐτῆς ἀπέκτεινεν.

In 7:9–10 we find the continuation of the mininarrative, begun in verse 8a, that describes the chain of events that follows from sin seizing the opportunity provided by the law and awakening all kinds of desires in the *I* (v. 8a). These events are expressed in sharply antithetical terms, highlighting the contrast between, on the one hand, life for the *I*, and lifeless sin, in the absence of the law and, on the other, sin springing to life, resulting in death for the *I*, in the presence of the law. In 7:11a the participial clause of verse 8a is repeated, this time introduced by γάρ, and with ἡ ἁμαρτία fronted.[77] The repetition draws attention to the main argumentative point of 7:7–11, namely, that it was sin that exploited the law in order to gain mastery over humanity. At the same time, the fronting further highlights sin's role as active subject, as does the use of the transitive verb ἀπέκτεινεν. Verse 11 summarizes the thought of verses 8–10, underlining the fact that the blame for the deathly fruit that comes from the law (7:5) is to be laid fairly and squarely at sin's door.

Commentators generally view the material introduced by γάρ in verse 11a as explanatory of what precedes, without specifying further which element it explains. Kümmel, however, reads verse 11 precisely as an explanation of the statement in verse 10b.[78] But the statement in verse 10a might equally well be read as part of the information that needs clarification by the γάρ clause in verse 11: the whole of verse 10 is an elaboration of the thought expressed in 7:5 regarding the sinful passions aroused by the law leading to death. Its starkness might well raise implicit questions for addressees, both of comprehension and of acceptability, meaning that verse 10 is not yet optimally relevant to them as it stands. Consequently, strengthening material is offered in verse 11a, introduced by γάρ.

On a procedural account, γάρ in verse 11a triggers procedure G, and verse 10 is identified as the most obvious candidate for strengthening. Verse 10a–b is taken as a single complex of assumptions for strengthening, because the statement in verse 10a is a presupposition of the claim in verse

---

77. Interestingly, when the participial clause occurs for the first time in v. 8, it is introduced by δέ as part of a set of assumptions relevant in their own right. In v. 11, in contrast, it is recycled and introduced by γάρ as part of a complex that addressees expect to be relevant in relation to previously communicated assumptions.

78. Kümmel, *Römer 7*, 53.

10b, and both clauses may raise implicit objections. Verse 11, meanwhile, introduced by γάρ, is also processed as a single complex of strengthening assumptions that belong very closely together conceptually. We can split verse 10 down into two claims that need strengthening:

P1 (v. 10a): The *I* died.
P2 (v. 10b): The commandment that was intended as a means to life was found to be a means of death for the *I*.
Complex Q introduced by γάρ (v. 11): Sin seized the opportunity to deceive the *I* through the commandment and killed the *I* through the commandment.

I suggest that either one strengthening series may be constructed for claims P1 and P2, or alternatively, two in parallel, depending on what is most relevant to particular addressees. Although I will lay these two series out one after the other, we can assume that both would be processed in parallel as part of the search for the most relevant interpretation that makes best sense of all the data in verse 11.

I propose a strengthening series for P1 (v. 10a) along the following lines:

P1 (v. 10a): The *I* died.
Q (v. 11b): Sin (seized the opportunity to deceive the *I* through the commandment and) killed the *I* through the commandment.
IA1: If sin ... killed the *I* through the commandment, then the *I* died.
C (confirming v. 10a): The *I* died.

As a result, the assertion in verse 10a is explained so that it becomes more comprehensible and plausible.

Meanwhile, in relation to P2 (v. 10b), the following background assumptions are likely made accessible by Q:

IA1: If sin deceived and killed the *I* through the commandment, then the commandment brought death instead of life for the *I*.
C (confirming v. 10b): The commandment brought death instead of life for the *I*.

As a result, an inferential series is derived in relation to verse 10b that is relevant either as an explanation or as a confirmation of that claim. This explanation/confirmation goes some way to answering possible questions raised by verse 10, making it either more comprehensible, or more plausible, or both.

Whether or not both these strengthening series are established will depend on whether a particular addressee finds that both verse 10a and verse 10b need strengthening in order to be optimally relevant, or only verse 10b. Thus the construction of these inferential series is determined by what best satisfies expectations of relevance for different addressees. As a result of the strengthening procedure, the claims in verse 10 become more argumentatively salient, and other implications that potentially follow from them may also be inferred and held as valid by addressees; for example, "God's law does not bring life as it was intended to," "God's law is powerless against sin," and "God's law is not to blame for death that comes as a consequence of sin." In sum, the occurrence of γάρ in 7:11 can be seen as a somewhat complex instance that can be well explained by our procedural account by extending Blass's basic strengthening template in order to posit two possible parallel series. The construction of these series is guided by considerations of relevance.

The subsection begun in 7:7 is rounded off by 7:12, which draws a conclusion from the preceding discussion in order to answer the question posed in verse 7a, "Is the law sin?" The emphatic implication of 7:7–11, spelled out here, is that the Mosaic law is holy, righteous, and good, a continuing part of the purposes of God, despite its manipulation by sin.

3.3.5. Romans 7:14

The subsection 7:13–20 begins in verse 13a, like the preceding subsection 7:7–12, with a rhetorical question. This expresses a possible false implication to be drawn from the previous argument (particularly in view of v. 12), which is immediately emphatically refuted.[79] A corrective to this false implication then follows in verse 13b, which spells out that it is not the law that brings death to the *I*, but sin, which manipulates the law. In addition, the two final ἵνα clauses in verse 13 can be read as stating the purpose behind the law and its role in bringing out and increasing sin.[80]

---

79. Wright notes that the fact that γάρ introduces v. 14 means that 7:14 must be taken together with 7:13, and a paragraph break inserted after v. 12, rather than after v. 13 (Wright, "Romans," 565, contra Dunn, *Romans 1–8*, 375, Käsemann, *An die Römer*, 189, and various English translations).

80. See Käsemann, *An die Römer*, 188; Wright, *Paul and the Faithfulness of God*, 895; Dunn, *Romans 1–8*, 387.

3. Consistent Yet Context-Sensitive: The Guidance γάρ Gives

The anacoluthon in verse 13b is ambiguous, but the overall sense is clear.[81] Supplying the phrase ἐμοὶ ἐγένετο θάνατος (from v. 13a) after ἡ ἁμαρτία seems the best way of disambiguating here.[82] The formula οἴδαμεν ὅτι that introduces verse 14 indicates that what follows is a generally accepted fact, already well known to Paul's audience.[83]

7:13a: Τὸ οὖν ἀγαθὸν ἐμοὶ ἐγένετο θάνατος; μὴ γένοιτο·
7:13b: ἀλλὰ ἡ ἁμαρτία, ἵνα φανῇ ἁμαρτία, διὰ τοῦ ἀγαθοῦ μοι κατεργαζομένη θάνατον,
7:13c: ἵνα γένηται καθ' ὑπερβολὴν ἁμαρτωλὸς ἡ ἁμαρτία διὰ τῆς ἐντολῆς.
7:14a: οἴδαμεν γὰρ ὅτι ὁ νόμος πνευματικός ἐστιν,
7:14b: ἐγὼ δὲ σάρκινός εἰμι πεπραμένος ὑπὸ τὴν ἁμαρτίαν.

Given the preceding cotext of 7:7–12, and the clear allusion to the Jewish law in 7:13, the majority of scholars interpret νόμος as referring to torah in 7:14.[84] Meanwhile γάρ in verse 14 is read in various ways, with the precise nature of the relationship between verse 13 and verse 14 understood differently. Some explain γάρ in general terms as introducing an explanation or support for verse 13 or providing grounds for verse 13b.[85] Kümmel is more precise: while verse 14a provides grounds for the denial in verse 13a that the law bears responsibility for the death of the *I*, verse 14b provides a rationale for the events described in 7:8–11 and verse 13b. Thus the two parts of verse 14 serve as a rationale for verse 13 by presenting the objective premises for what is described there.[86]

We can explain γάρ in verse 14 as follows. Procedure G is triggered by the connective. Since a potential strengthening relation is not obvious between the material following γάρ in verse 14 and the ἵνα clause in verse 13c, the disambiguated claim in verse 13b is considered next and

---

81. Dunn, *Romans 1–8*, 386.
82. Following Kümmel, *Römer 7*, 56. Wilckens provides a justification of the alternative reading (Wilckens, *Der Brief an die Römer*, 2:84).
83. Dunn, *Romans 1–8*, 80.
84. E.g., Wolter, *Röm 1–8*, 444; Wilckens, *Der Brief an die Römer (Studienausgabe)*, 86–87; Dunn, *Romans 1–8*, 387; Cranfield, *Epistle to the Romans*, 355; Kümmel, *Römer 7*, 57, 61.
85. See Cranfield, *Epistle to the Romans*, 355; Wilckens, *Der Brief an die Römer*, 2:85, who sees the "Begründung" extending from vv. 14–16.
86. Kümmel, *Römer 7*, 58.

identified as a candidate for strengthening. The double clause following γάρ in verse 14 is processed as a single complex of assumptions (Q).[87] As with the example in 7:11, we can split the information in verse 13 into two claims, one in verse 13a and one in verse 13b, that are strengthened by the information in verse 14a and verse 14b respectively. We can suggest that deductive series are constructed, using highly accessible contextual assumptions, something like the following:

P1 (v. 13a, disambiguated): The good [law] absolutely did not become death to the *I*.
P2 (v. 13b, disambiguated): Instead, sin, in order that it might be shown as sin, [became death to the *I*], working death to the *I* through the good [law].
Q introduced by γάρ (v. 14): The law is spiritual, but the *I* is fleshly, sold as a slave to sin.[88]

As with the example in 7:11, we can treat the two inferential series separately.

Strengthening series for P1 (v. 13a):
Q introduced by γάρ (v. 14a): The law is spiritual.
IA1: If the law is spiritual, the law is good and life-bringing. (Accessible from encyclopedic knowledge of Jewish teaching.)
IA2: If the good law is life-bringing, the law does not bring death to the *I*. (Inferable from common sense.)
C (confirming v. 13a): The good law absolutely did not become death to the *I*.

As a result of this series, the claim communicated in verse 13a via the rhetorical question and its emphatic answer is strengthened, so that addressees adhere to it more strongly. Meanwhile, the information in verse 14b, which makes highly accessible further contextual assumptions, is processed as strengthening evidence for the claim in verse 13b:

---

87. In v. 14b δέ introduces the second statement in an antithetical pair that belongs tightly together.
88. Literally, "sold under sin."

P2 (v. 13b, disambiguated): Instead, sin, in order that it might be shown as sin, [became death to the *I*], working death to the *I* through the good [law].
Q introduced by γάρ (v. 14b): The *I* is fleshly, sold as a slave to sin.
IA1: If the *I* is fleshly and sold as a slave to sin, sin is the *I*'s master. (Accessible from encyclopedic knowledge of the concept of slavery.)
IA2: If sin is the *I*'s master, the good law says that the wage the *I* receives from sin is death. (Accessible from previous cotext: 6:23.)
IA3: If the good law says that the wage the *I* receives from sin is death, then sin results in the good law pronouncing death for the *I*.
IA4: If sin results in the good law pronouncing death for the *I*, then sin becomes death to the *I*, working death through the good law.
C (confirming v. 13b): Sin became death to the *I*, working death to the *I* through the good law.[89]

In this way, the claim communicated in verse 13b is likewise strengthened, so that addressees adhere to it more strongly. The two parts of the antithetical statement introduced by γάρ in verse 14a and b are thus relevant in relation to the two assertions in verse 13a and verse 13b respectively, contributing to their argumentative salience.[90] The proposed inferential strengthening series for this instance of γάρ are more complex than those previously discussed. Not only do they involve splitting the assumptions in verse 14a–b into two parts and manipulating them as two separate pieces of input, but they also involve several contextual assumptions from background knowledge and the previous cotext. This is thus a somewhat complex instance of γάρ that a procedural strengthening explanation is nevertheless well able to account for.

This posited inferential series is only one possibility for establishing a strengthening connection between verse 14 and verse 13. Depending on contextual assumptions available to different addressees, and differing expectations of relevance, we can envisage that another briefer series might be constructed by some, requiring less processing effort. Moreover,

---

89. Since the subordinate clause ἵνα φανῇ ἁμαρτία is not confirmed by this strengthening series, it does not appear as part of C.
90. This analysis undermines Käsemann's view that v. 14 represents the beginning of a new subsection, with the second half of v. 14 salient as its theme (Käsemann, *An die Römer*, 189–90). I suggest instead that any main summarizing point is to be found in v. 13, particularly v. 13b.

the strengthening may be relevant as an explanation to some but as a validating confirmation or justification to others. This freedom to work out the strengthening in whatever way is most relevant accounts for the range of scholarly explanations of γάρ in this verse. Once again, γάρ guides in the direction of strengthening, constraining interpretation, but the details of this strengthening may be worked out in diverse ways.

3.3.6. Romans 7:15

7:15a: ὃ γὰρ κατεργάζομαι οὐ γινώσκω·
7:15b: οὐ γὰρ ὃ θέλω τοῦτο πράσσω, ἀλλ' ὃ μισῶ τοῦτο ποιῶ.

Various scholars read verse 15, introduced by γάρ, as the beginning of an explanation of what it means to be "sold under sin." Cranfield views γάρ in verse 15a as indicating the relation of the whole of verses 15–23 to verse 14, Jewett regards verses 15–16 as a clarification of verse 14, while Käsemann considers verses 15–20 to illustrate the theme he finds stated in the second half of verse 14.[91] Wright, on the other hand, takes verse 15a as the beginning of a further explanation of verse 13b, while Kümmel interprets verse 15 as demonstrating the validity of the claim that the *I* is fleshly and a slave to sin, a claim which is in turn part of the rationale for verse 13b.[92] In contrast, Wolter maintains that γάρ here introduces a conclusion.[93] Meanwhile commentators are broadly in agreement that γάρ in verse 15b explains, provides grounds for, or supports, verse 15a specifically. There is some discussion as to the interpretation of γινώσκω in verse 15a. Along with Kümmel and various English translations, I will follow the interpretation "understand."[94] This reading is most compatible with a procedural account of both occurrences of γάρ in verse 15, as we shall see.

The occurrence in verse 15a is somewhat complex in that the material it introduces does not achieve relevance as strengthening material on its own but needs to be completed by the following γάρ clause in verse 15b. This accounts for the observation by commentators that γάρ in verse 15a introduces more than the material in that clause alone. The occurrence

---

91. Cranfield, *Epistle to the Romans*, 358; Jewett, *Romans*, 462; Käsemann, *An die Römer*, 191.
92. Wright, *Climax of the Covenant*, 218; Kümmel, *Römer 7*, 59.
93. "Folgernd" (Wolter, *Röm 1–8*, 446).
94. E.g., Kümmel, *Römer 7*, 59; NET, NIV, ESV, RSV.

3. Consistent Yet Context-Sensitive: The Guidance γάρ Gives

can be explained as follows. Following procedure G, a strengthening series cannot be easily established between verse 15a and either verse 14, or verse 13, without unreasonable processing effort. That is, verse 15a on its own does not satisfy expectations of relevance. Consequently, γάρ in verse 15b then raises expectations that the material following it will achieve relevance by strengthening the statement in verse 15a in such a way that it in turn completes its own strengthening task. I suggest that something like the following double inferential series may be involved, in which verse 15b strengthens verse 15a and, in turn, verse 14b:

P1 for strengthening (v. 14b): The *I* is fleshly, sold as a slave to sin.
P2 for strengthening (v. 15a): The *I* does not understand what the *I* does.
Complex Q introduced by γάρ (v. 15b): The *I* does not do what the *I* wants to do. The *I* does what the *I* hates.
IA1: If the *I* does not do what the *I* wants to do but what the *I* hates, the *I* does not understand what the *I* does. (Inferable from common sense/encyclopedic knowledge of human experience.)
C1 (confirming v. 15a): The *I* does not understand what the *I* does.
IA1: If the *I* does what the *I* hates and does not understand what the *I* does, the *I* is not master of the *I*'s own actions, but something else is master of the *I*. (Inferable from common sense/human experience.)
IA2: If the *I* does what the *I* hates, the *I* does what is wrong. (Inferable from common sense/experience.)
IA3: If the *I* does what is wrong, and is not master of the *I*'s actions, sin is the *I*'s master and the *I* is a slave to sin. (Inferable from common sense, concept of sin/wrongdoing and concept of slavery.)
C2 (confirmation of v. 14b): The *I* is sold as a slave to sin.[95]

In this way, the statement in verse 15b increases the relevance of the statement in verse 15a, enabling background assumptions about wrongdoing to be accessed that provide an inferential bridge back to the statement in verse 14b that the *I* is sold as a slave to sin. The strengthening triggered by γάρ in both verse 15b and verse 15a seems most likely to be perceived as relevant as an explanation of previous information that raises ques-

---

95. Since the assertion in v. 14b that the *I* is fleshly is not reinforced by this strengthening series, it does not appear here in C.

tions of comprehension. As a result, the statement in verse 14b is in turn strengthened, and verse 15a becomes optimally relevant in a strengthening relation with this statement. We can say that the consolidating explanation of verse 14b, begun in verse 15a, is both completed and further supported by the second γάρ clause in verse 15b. Thus not only verse 15a, but also verse 14b, becomes more comprehensible and plausible for addressees. This makes sense of interpreters' analysis of verse 15b as belonging closely with verse 15a as part of a single explanation of what precedes. On the other hand, this analysis rules out Wolter's reading of γάρ in verse 15a as "folgernd." The occurrences in verse 15a and b, and also verse 14, form a short strengthening chain that results in the cumulative strengthening not only of the claim in verse 14b that the *I* is sold as a slave to sin, but also in the further strengthening of the claims in verse 13. This highlights the argumentative salience of the latter. We will come across other examples of such backward strengthening chains elsewhere in Romans and discuss their contribution to the coherence of the argument in more detail below.

Some commentators remark on the parallels between verse 15 and the thought of Greco-Roman writers and philosophers.[96] If Paul is indeed here alluding to an epigrammatic formula that may have been familiar to his Roman addressees, then this could be another instance of γάρ introducing a metarepresentation that adds authoritative weight to the support that it provides for preceding assumptions.

3.3.7. Romans 7:18–19

In 7:16 Paul draws a conclusion regarding the law, which rounds off his defense of the law given in answer to the rhetorical question of verse 13a. This is a restatement of the claim in verse 12 that the law is good, this time inferred from a different premise. In verse 17 a fresh argumentative point is made: it is indwelling sin that is to blame for the *I*'s wrongdoing. The argument in verses 13–16 has exonerated the law from responsibility for humanity's sin and death; now the statement in verse 17 claims that the *I* is

---

96. Stowers finds in v. 15 and vv. 19–20 a "virtually proverbial saying" derived originally from Euripides's *Medea* (Stowers, *Rereading of Romans*, 189), Käsemann sees an allusion to Ovid, *Metam.* 7.19–20 (Käsemann, *An die Römer*, 190), and Jewett notes parallels with Epictetus, *Disc.* 2.26.1–2 (Jewett, *Romans*, 463).

also not to blame.⁹⁷ Commentators are broadly agreed that verses 18–19, which contain a series of three γάρ clauses, together explain or provide supporting proof for the claim in verse 17.⁹⁸

7:17:   νυνὶ δὲ οὐκέτι ἐγὼ κατεργάζομαι αὐτὸ ἀλλὰ ἡ οἰκοῦσα ἐν ἐμοὶ ἁμαρτία.
7:18a: οἶδα γὰρ ὅτι οὐκ οἰκεῖ ἐν ἐμοί, τοῦτ᾽ ἔστιν ἐν τῇ σαρκί μου, ἀγαθόν·
7:18b: τὸ γὰρ θέλειν παράκειταί μοι, τὸ δὲ κατεργάζεσθαι τὸ καλὸν οὔ·
7:19:   οὐ γὰρ ὃ θέλω ποιῶ ἀγαθόν, ἀλλὰ ὃ οὐ θέλω κακὸν τοῦτο πράσσω.

Following a procedural account of γάρ in verse 18a, we can suggest that an inferential series may be constructed that leads to the strengthening of the assertions in verse 17:

> **P** (v. 17, disambiguated): It is not the *I* who does this [evil], but the sin living in the *I*.
> **Q introduced by** γάρ (v. 18a): (The *I* knows that) what is good is not living in the *I*, that is, in the *I*'s flesh.
> **IA1**: If what is good is not living in the *I*'s flesh, then sin is living in the *I*'s flesh. (Inferable from common sense and presupposition communicated in v. 17.)
> **IA2**: If sin is living in the *I*'s flesh, then sin makes the *I*'s flesh carry out evil actions. (Inferable from common sense, concept of sin, etc.)
> **C** (confirming v. 17): It is not the *I* who does this evil, but the sin living in the *I*.

The claim in verse 17 is thus strengthened, with the result that addressees hold it more strongly as valid. The strengthening procedure γάρ guides toward may achieve relevance as confirming evidence, or as an explanation that makes better sense of verse 17, grounding it in addressees' existing knowledge of the world. Either way, verse 18a achieves relevance in relation to verse 17, which it reinforces, adding to its argumentative salience.

The occurrence of γάρ in verse 18b is relatively straightforward. The statement it introduces in verse 18b is neatly paraphrased by Jewett as "the

---

97. See Barrett, *Epistle to the Romans*, 147.
98. E.g., Wilckens, *Der Brief an die Römer*, 2:87; Jewett, *Romans*, 467; Cranfield, *Epistle to the Romans*, 360.

I wants to perform the good but is unable to do so."[99] We can use this paraphrase in our reconstruction of the likely strengthening series involved:

> **P** (v. 18a): What is good does not live in the *I*, that is, in the *I*'s flesh.
> **Q introduced by** γάρ: The *I* wants to perform the good but is unable to do so.
> **IA**: If the *I* wants to perform the good but is unable to do so, then it is evidence that good does not live in the *I*, that is, in the *I*'s flesh.
> **C** (confirming v. 18a): What is good does not live in the *I*, that is, in the *I*'s flesh.

This strengthening procedure may be relevant to addressees either as a confirmation or an explanation. Since verse 18a in turn strengthens verse 17, the knock-on effect of this reinforcement of verse 18a is to further bolster the strength with which verse 17 is held by addressees, emphasizing the argumentative salience of the latter.

Romans 7:19 consists of a double, antithetical assertion introduced by γάρ, the content of which is similar to that of verse 15b. Here, however, it is explicitly stated that what the *I* wants and fails to do is ἀγαθόν, while what the *I* does not want, but does, is κακόν. Various commentators interpret verses 19–20 as recapitulating what has already been claimed, rather than advancing the line of thought.[100] Since the occurrence of γάρ in verse 19 is a straightforward case of strengthening, confirming the claims in verse 18b, we will not set out the inferential series in detail. Verse 19 is in effect a paraphrase of assumptions already communicated in verse 15b. It therefore seems likely that the strengthening procedure is relevant not as an explanation making sense of verse 18b but as persuasive confirmation of the validity of the claims in that verse. I suggest that here the core strengthening guidance that γάρ gives creates an impression or display of compelling supporting evidence, which is enough to satisfy addressees' expectations of relevance (that is, it is sufficient to persuade them to accept v. 18b more firmly). This is despite the fact that the strengthening procedure essentially repeats assumptions that are already strongly manifest and so does not provide compelling independent evidence from

---

99. Jewett, *Romans*, 458.
100. E.g., Wolter, *Röm 1–8*, 455; Dunn, *Romans 1–8*, 407; Käsemann, *An die Römer*, 195.

a logical point of view.[101] If, as with verse 15, the material in verse 19 is a metarepresentation of a well-known formula, this also adds to the persuasive rhetorical effect.

Since, by means of the backward strengthening chain of γάρ clauses, verse 18b supports verse 18a, which in turn reinforces verse 17, the overall effect of this persuasive supporting material is to increase the argumentative impact of verse 17 and its cognitive effects. Verse 17 is thereby highlighted as a prominent main point in the argumentation. We shall see that this phenomenon of chains of γάρ clauses with a cumulative, backward strengthening effect plays a significant role in the argument of the epistle, assisting us in tracing its argumentative thrust at various points.

To round off this subsection, Rom 7:20a communicates in a conditional construction an assumption already communicated in verses 15b, 16a, and 19b, while 7:20b states an implication already drawn in verse 17 and made more salient by the γάρ clauses in verses 18–19. The subsection thus concludes with the reassertion of the argumentative claim that it is not the *I* that is responsible for the evil that it does against its will, but instead indwelling sin.

3.3.8. Summary of Findings from Romans 7:7–20

Our examination of γάρ in the expository material of Rom 7:7–20 has demonstrated that a procedural account is able to explain somewhat more complex occurrences in terms of core procedural instructions guiding toward the inferential procedure of strengthening. In all cases, the connective guides addressees to expect that the material it introduces will be relevant as strengthening premises that, together with highly accessible contextual assumptions, increase the relevance of preceding material by providing independent support for it. In all cases, γάρ guides toward the cognitive effect of strengthening and serves as a communicative signal that reduces processing costs. The strengthening effect created contributes to the persuasiveness of the argument.

We have seen that the procedural strengthening hypothesis is able to make sense of these somewhat complex occurrences by incorporating a number of highly accessible contextual assumptions into strengthening series of inferences. As well as accounting for strengthening material

---

101. Cf. the discussion of rhetorical strengthening in 6:19–20 under §4.5, below.

that is relevant as a confirmation, an explanation, or a proof, a procedural account is also able to make sense of information that is relevant as a more specific example of a general claim (7:7b), of occurrences that by themselves do not achieve strengthening but need to be completed by a subsequent γάρ clause (7:15a), and of examples that may primarily create a strengthening impression (7:19) rather than guiding toward a complete logical strengthening series. This last case will be of significance when we come to investigate atypical examples of γάρ introducing rhetorical strengthening (see §4.5, below).

While the core procedural instructions given by γάρ remain constant, the strengthening effect it guides toward thus works itself out differently in various cotexts, according to the differing expectations of relevance that addressees may have. As a consequence, certain occurrences may be interpreted differently by diverse addressees and interpreters. Addressees choose whichever outworking of the inferential procedure best satisfies expectations of relevance for them, so we cannot say with certainty in what way particular addressees will find the strengthening procedure relevant. If a particular claim raises objections and leaves them unconvinced, they are likely to process supporting material introduced by γάρ as confirming evidence; if it leaves them asking questions of comprehension, on the other hand, they are likely to process it as an explanation. The account accommodates the fact that different addressees may not derive identical inferential series (see v. 11). It likewise accounts for the fact that some interpreters may invest more processing effort in establishing full logical series, while others may simply take on trust that the partial evidence supplied does indeed lead to strengthening as γάρ indicates.

I suggest that this procedural explanation throws light on the contours of the argument of this passage. Because γάρ flags up supporting information that consolidates and increases the relevance of preceding claims, it allows us to identify these strengthened claims as relatively important in the argument. Claims that are supported by a whole series of strengthening γάρ clauses leading back to them are particularly argumentatively salient. They give rise to many new cognitive effects and represent some of the key main points of the argument.

3.3.9. Implications for Tracing Paul's Argument in 7:7–20

In the light of this, it is useful to take stock of some argumentative implications of a procedural account of γάρ in 7:7–20. These will feed into our discussion in chapter 6 of the wider argument of the epistle. We have seen that information introduced by γάρ is relatively less salient, argumentatively speaking, than the preceding material it strengthens and represents supporting information that consolidates main argumentative claims. The latter, meanwhile, give rise to many new cognitive effects. By increasing the relevance of those main points, information introduced by γάρ helps to highlight what is most argumentatively significant.

On the basis of these insights, we can propose the following outline of salient claims that, backed up by γάρ clauses, are particularly relevant in 7:7–20, representing main points that advance the argument:

7:7: It is through the law that the *I* became aware of sin.
7:8: Sin produced all kinds of covetous desires in the *I* through the commandment (law).
7:10: The commandment that was intended to lead to life led to death for the *I*.

The explicit implication in verse 12 that is then drawn as a conclusion, introduced by ὥστε, is likewise salient in the argument:

7:12: The law is holy and the commandment is holy and righteous and good.
7:13: It was not the good [law], but sin that became death for the *I*, working death through the good [law] (so that sin might be shown as sin and so that sin might become exceedingly sinful through the commandment).
7:16b: The *I* agrees with the law that the law is good.[102]
7:17: It is not the *I* who produces this evil; it is the sin living in the *I*.[103]
7:20b: It is no longer the *I* who does what the *I* does not want to; it is the sin living in the *I*.[104]

---

102. The fresh conclusion drawn in the apodosis of the conditional construction in v. 16 also represents a salient interim summarizing argumentative point, although it is not backed up by a γάρ clause.

103. Both vv. 13 and 17 are supported by a cumulative strengthening chain of three γάρ clauses, providing powerful buttressing, and making both particularly argumentatively salient.

104. This restatement of the highly salient v. 17 further increases its salience.

This tracing of the main argumentative points in the subsection, based on the guidance given by γάρ, supports interpretations that read 7:7–20 as a defense of the Jewish law. In particular, this analysis is compatible in large part with Wright's reading of the contours of the argument in these verses.[105] Wright's discussion of this passage is noteworthy for the particular attention it pays to connectives as communicative signals that guide the development of the argument. In contrast, an analysis such as Käsemann's, which finds in verse 14b ("sold as a slave under sin") the subsection's theme and which splits verse 13 off from verses 14–20, seems incompatible with a procedural strengthening account of γάρ.[106]

3.4. Flagging Up Reinforcements: Romans 14:1–12

Having shown that a procedural account of γάρ is able to provide a consistent and unified explanation for somewhat complex occurrences in a stretch of expository material in Romans, in this section I will demonstrate how it is also able to account for similar examples in hortatory material. As with our examination of somewhat complex occurrences in expository material, for hortatory material, too, we will consider a string of instances within a stretch of text, 14:1–12. This will allow us first to build a richer understanding of the available cotext and the likely contextual assumptions at play in the processing of any given occurrence of γάρ. Second, it will give us greater insight into the overall effect of several occurrences of γάρ in a given subsection, and the role they play in distinguishing supporting information from the more salient claims that are reinforced in the section, which, I suggest, represent the main thrust of the argument.

3.4.1. Cotext of Romans 14:1–12

This subsection forms part of the paraenesis of the major section that runs from Rom 12:1–15:13 and discusses the ethical and practical implications of the new life in Christ. This life is summed up at the head of the sec-

---

105. Wright, *Climax of the Covenant*, 218. Wright identifies the assertions in v. 13b as the main point, or theme, of 7:13–20, while vv. 14–20 offer several explanations of this main point. His discussion accords more importance to the two purpose clauses in v. 13b–c than the above analysis, however.

106. Käsemann, *An die Römer*, 189–90, 195.

tion in the metaphor of believers presenting themselves to God in worship as living sacrifices (12:1–2). It works itself out particularly in terms of relationships both within and outside the Christian community (see the discussion under §3.2.4, above).

Within this paraenesis, 14:1–15:13 represents a switch from the more general ethical instructions of chapters 12–13 to a detailed and sustained discussion of the issue of mutual acceptance within the Christian community, regardless of differing convictions relating to certain practices and observances. Many scholars regard the instructions in 14:1–15:13 as directed toward real rather than hypothetical problems among Roman believers.[107] There have been diverse attempts to identify the weak and the strong.[108] A scholarly majority now argues that the weak are torah-observant Christ-believers, whether Jewish, or gentile but Jewish-orientated, while the strong are Christ-believers who do not observe torah, both gentile and Jewish.[109] The disagreements between them are best interpreted as differences over the observance of Jewish food laws and Sabbaths, which Paul discusses in deliberately nonspecific terms, perhaps so as not to exacerbate tensions, nor emphasize identities that are irrelevant from the perspective of the gospel.[110] In 14:1–15:13 as a whole Paul exhorts particularly the stronger in faith, among whom he counts himself, to accept those who are weaker (an evaluation based on their scruples about food and holy day observances). He also admonishes those who have such scruples not to judge those who do not.

---

107. E.g., Barclay, *Paul and the Gift*, 511; Watson, *Paul, Judaism and the Gentiles*, 175; Wright, "Romans," 732. Campbell traces the marked swing in recent scholarly opinion toward identification of a specific Roman situation behind Rom 14–15 (Campbell, "Addressees of Paul's Letter to the Romans," 171–72).

108. See Reasoner's overview of different positions (*Strong and the Weak*, 4–22).

109. E.g., Barclay, "Do We Undermine the Law?," 38–40; Watson, *Paul, Judaism and the Gentiles*, 175; Reasoner, *Strong and the Weak*, 200–201; Wilckens, *Der Brief an die Römer*, 3:79. Exceptions to this consensus include Das and Thorsteinsson, Thiessen, and Rodríguez, who argue that both the weak and the strong are exclusively gentile (Andrew A. Das, *Solving the Romans Debate* [Minneapolis: Fortress, 2007]; Thorsteinsson, Thiessen, and Rodríguez, "Paul's Interlocutor in Romans," 14), and Mark D. Nanos, who contends that the weak are non-Christ-believing Jews (Nanos, *The Mystery of Romans: The Jewish Context of Paul's Letter* [Minneapolis: Fortress, 1996], 155).

110. Wright suggests that Paul avoids referring directly to tensions between Jewish and gentile believers, so as not to exacerbate these ("Romans," 731). See also Barclay, *Paul and the Gift*, 511–12.

Romans 14:1–15:13 also raise questions related to the climax and purpose of the letter. I will not engage with the debate at this point but will revisit the question in chapter 6 below in order to show how a consistent procedural reading of γάρ is able to shed light on these questions.

3.4.2. Romans 14:3

14:3a: ὁ ἐσθίων τὸν μὴ ἐσθίοντα μὴ ἐξουθενείτω,
14:3b: ὁ δὲ μὴ ἐσθίων τὸν ἐσθίοντα μὴ κρινέτω,
14:3c: ὁ θεὸς γὰρ αὐτὸν προσελάβετο.

In 14:1 we find an imperative, προσλαμβάνεσθε, that is directed particularly at the "strong" among Paul's addressees, since those addressed are urged to accept the person who is weak in faith (τὸν ἀσθενοῦντα). This exhortation sums up the theme of the 14:1–15:13: mutual acceptance within the Christian community. Romans 14:2 elaborates on verse 1 by giving a specific example, in two contrasting parts, of the kind of situation that might provoke disputes and a lack of mutual acceptance among believers: one person has the faith to eat everything, while a weak person only eats vegetables.[111] Based on this double example, verse 3a and 3b then give two further exhortations that are more specific outworkings of the command in verse 1.

Commentators are divided as to whether the γάρ clause in verse 3c is to be understood in relation to verse 3b only or in relation to both verse 3b and verse 3a.[112] We can explain this instance of γάρ procedurally as follows. Procedure G, triggered by the connective, searches for a preceding communicated assumption in relation to which the γάρ clause is relevant as a strengthening premise. Following a relevance-guided heuristic, it considers the exhortation in verse 3b first. Despite the third-person singular pronoun in verse 3c, which might initially lead addressees to infer that verse 3c is relevant only in relation to verse 3b as Cranfield and Dunn

---

[111]. Barclay argues that the background to the abstinence in view is to be found in observance of Jewish food laws by the weak (Barclay, "Do We Undermine the Law?," 39). Reasoner provides a detailed investigation of the "consumptive asceticism" in evidence here (Reasoner, *Strong and the Weak*, 64–87).

[112]. For the former view, see Dunn, *Romans 9–16*, 803; Cranfield, *Epistle to the Romans*, 2:702, and for the latter, Käsemann, *An die Römer*, 353; Jewett, *Romans*, 843. Cranfield judges that Käsemann takes "an unjustifiable liberty with the text" by interpreting αὐτόν as referring to both the noneater of v. 3a and the eater of v. 3b.

suggest, several other clues in the cotext lead to the inference that verse 3c is also relevant in relation to verse 3a. First, verse 3b is the second of a balanced pair formed by verse 3a–b, as indicated by the syntactic parallelism in these clauses. Second, the repetition of the verb προσλαμβάνω in verse 3c means that the exhortation in verse 1 to accept the one who is weak in faith is very highly accessible. This leads addressees to infer that verse 3c must serve as support not just for the exhortation to accept the person who is strong in faith and eats (v. 3b), but also for the exhortation to accept the person who is weak in faith and does not (v. 3a). The strengthening of the exhortation in verse 3b would seem to demand more processing effort in the cotext. Verse 3a–b is thus selected as a single complex of assumptions for strengthening. I suggest that an inferential series may constructed along the following lines:

> **P** (propositional form of v. 3): It is desirable for the person who eats not to despise the person who does not eat, and it is desirable for the person who does not eat not to judge the person who eats.
> **Q introduced by** γάρ (v. 3c): God has accepted that person.
> **IA**: If God has accepted a person, it is desirable for other people not to despise or to judge that person.
> **C** (confirming v. 3): It is desirable for the person who eats not to despise the person who does not eat, and it is desirable for the person who does not eat not to judge the person who eats.

As a result of the procedure triggered by γάρ, the exhortations in verse 3 are confirmed by independent evidence, giving rise to the cognitive effect of strengthening. Since the aim of the exhortation is to persuade toward action, this strengthening is most likely to be relevant as a justification that convinces rather than as an explanation. We should note that γάρ here introduces a theological statement that may echo Psalms such as 26:10 in the LXX and that adds extra authoritative weight to the supporting material, grounding the exhortation in a theological framework.[113]

The procedural account thus makes sense of this occurrence that is somewhat complex because of the ambiguity regarding the reach of the assumptions strengthened by the γάρ clause. This account of γάρ supports Käsemann's reading rather than Cranfield's. The inferential procedure not

---

113. Dunn, *Romans 9–16*, 803.

only strengthens verse 3a and b but also contributes to the coherence of the argument by reactivating (and thus consolidating) the exhortation of verse 1.

In verse 4 Paul develops the topic of judging, using a rhetorical question posed in diatribal style, and the metaphor of household slaves, to challenge the presumptuousness of those who judge other believers. The statement in verse 4b explains why this is presumptuous: it is the business of a master alone to judge his slaves; the judgment of others is irrelevant.[114] The clear implication is that God is the master, and Lord, of believers, who are God's slaves (see 6:22); only God has the authority to judge them and approve them to continue in their position.[115] Verse 4c continues the metaphor, affirming that the slave (the believer) will stand, σταθήσεται δέ, approved by and acceptable to God, "upheld" in his presence.[116] Whether or not this verb has an eschatological dimension as some commentators suggest, I suggest that the declaration may raise implicit questions of plausibility for any addressees who feel justified in judging or despising other believers who have different convictions.[117]

Verse 4d is introduced by a straightforward instance of γάρ that results in the strengthening of the claim in verse 4c. We will not discuss this occurrence in detail. The effect of the strengthening it triggers is to draw attention to, and consolidate, the point in verse 4c that believers stand and are acceptable before God because of God himself.

3.4.3. Romans 14:5

14:5a: ὃς μὲν [γὰρ] κρίνει ἡμέραν παρ' ἡμέραν,
14:5b: ὃς δὲ κρίνει πᾶσαν ἡμέραν·
14:5c: ἕκαστος ἐν τῷ ἰδίῳ νοΐ πληροφορείσθω.

In 14:5a and b, Paul introduces a second paired example of a dispute that leads to a lack of mutual acceptance: the issue of observance of sacred

---

114. Dunn, *Romans 9–16*, 804.
115. See Moo, *Epistle to the Romans*, 840; Dunn, *Romans 9–16*, 804. Fitzmyer finds here the image of a judge's tribunal before which the slave stands. Joseph A. Fitzmyer, *Romans: A New Translation with Introduction and Commentary*, AB 33 (New York: Doubleday, 1993), 689–90.
116. Moo, *Epistle to the Romans*, 841; Porter, *Letter to the Romans*, 260.
117. For the eschatological interpretation, see Jewett, *Romans*, 843.

3. Consistent Yet Context-Sensitive: The Guidance γάρ Gives   111

days.[118] This example is syntactically parallel with the one in verse 2. The connective γάρ appears as a textual variant in certain manuscripts, notably Sinaiticus and Alexandrinus, but is omitted from P46, Vaticanus, Bezae, and the corrected version of Sinaiticus. Bruce Metzger recognizes that the external evidence for omission is slightly stronger than for inclusion. Nevertheless, the committee working on the UBS text has included γάρ in the fourth and fifth edition texts in square brackets.[119] This is because, in their judgment, copyists may not have appreciated the "Pauline usage" of γάρ according to which the connective is used to express "merely a continuation rather than a causal relationship." Consequently, copyists may have deleted the original connective.[120] Our account of γάρ challenges this: according to a procedural explanation, the connective does not in fact have a continuative function in Paul's writing, so a justification of its presence in the original text on this basis has no foundation. On the contrary, the fact that it is difficult to establish any kind of strengthening relationship between the double assertion in verse 5a–b and the claims in verse 4 supports the view that γάρ is not original in this verse and should be omitted, in keeping with the weight of external evidence. We see here that a procedural account of γάρ can, in some cases, contribute to textual criticism, providing support for certain variants, and undermining the case for others.

3.4.4. Romans 14:6

14:6a: ὁ φρονῶν τὴν ἡμέραν κυρίῳ φρονεῖ·
14:6b: καὶ ὁ ἐσθίων κυρίῳ ἐσθίει,
14:6c: εὐχαριστεῖ γὰρ τῷ θεῷ·
14:6d: καὶ ὁ μὴ ἐσθίων κυρίῳ οὐκ ἐσθίει καὶ εὐχαριστεῖ τῷ θεῷ.

---

118. Barclay explains this dispute in terms of Jewish Sabbath observance (Barclay, "Do We Undermine the Law?," 39, 53). Reasoner likewise finds Sabbath observance as the "nub" (Reasoner, *Strong and the Weak*, 139–58). Jewett gives an overview of various possible interpretations of the controversy (Jewett, *Romans*, 844–45).

119. NA[28] also includes γάρ in square brackets.

120. Bruce Metzger, *A Textual Commentary on the Greek New Testament: A Companion Volume to the United Bible Societies' Greek New Testament (4th rev. ed.)*, 2nd ed. (Stuttgart: Deutsche Bibelgesellschaft; New York: United Bible Societies, 1994), 468.

In verse 5c, a further exhortation expresses a guiding principle for believers in such matters of conduct where freedom of opinion is permitted: each believer must follow her own conscience. In verse 6 Paul then presents three specific examples of Christian conduct to show how all are equally acceptable to God if carried out κυρίῳ, "to/for the Lord," that is, to honor the Lord. The second of these examples (v. 6b) alone is followed by a γάρ clause in verse 6c. This is another straightforward example of γάρ that leads to the strengthening of the claim in verse 6b. It seems likely that addressees will find this strengthening effect relevant as confirmation that increases the plausibility of the claim in verse 6b and answers implicit questions it may raise in addressees' minds. The fact that only the second of three examples is supported by a strengthening γάρ clause may suggest that Paul perceives the statement in verse 6b as more controversial, with his Roman addressees potentially skeptical about the claim that eating all kinds of foods honors God, while accepting the examples he gives of abstinence and the observance of sabbaths. We note that in this example, the strengthening premise introduced by γάρ, while not a theological statement as such, is nevertheless rooted in a theological framework.

3.4.5. Romans 14:7–9

14:7: οὐδεὶς γὰρ ἡμῶν ἑαυτῷ ζῇ καὶ οὐδεὶς ἑαυτῷ ἀποθνῄσκει·
14:8a: ἐάν τε γὰρ ζῶμεν, τῷ κυρίῳ ζῶμεν,
14:8b: ἐάν τε ἀποθνῄσκωμεν, τῷ κυρίῳ ἀποθνῄσκομεν.
14:8c: ἐάν τε οὖν ζῶμεν ἐάν τε ἀποθνῄσκωμεν, τοῦ κυρίου ἐσμέν.
14:9a: εἰς τοῦτο γὰρ Χριστὸς ἀπέθανεν καὶ ἔζησεν
14:9b: ἵνα καὶ νεκρῶν καὶ ζώντων κυριεύσῃ.

Various commentators interpret verses 7–9 as belonging tightly together as an explanation or rationale. Cranfield, for example, asserts that γάρ in verse 7 indicates that verses 7–9 are to be read as support for what has been said in verse 6.[121] Käsemann views verses 7–9 as providing a rationale for the preceding example, while Wright reads the verses together as "explaining the argument so far by grounding it in the very heart of the gospel."[122]

---

121. Cranfield, *Epistle to the Romans*, 707.
122. Käsemann, *An die Römer*, 356. Käsemann appears to mean the three examples in v. 6. Wright, "Romans," 737.

3. Consistent Yet Context-Sensitive: The Guidance γάρ Gives

Some scholars suggest that in verses 7–9 Paul may be using material already familiar to his audience, either a Christian confessional statement, Paul's own teaching (see 2 Cor 5:15), Jewish teaching, or the thought of other ancient writers.[123] If this is the case, this is another example of γάρ introducing a metarepresentation already known and accepted by addressees.

The occurrence of γάρ in verse 7 is somewhat complex because a strengthening relation between the statement introduced by γάρ and the immediately preceding statement in verse 6c is difficult to establish. We can suggest the following procedural explanation. Procedure G finds that the immediately preceding statement in verse 6c does not satisfy expectations of relevance when taken alone as a candidate for strengthening. Following a relevance-guided heuristic, it next tests out the information in verse 6a–b and finds expectations of relevance satisfied by processing verse 6a–c together as a set of three examples. This set gives rise to the implication (also inferred from v. 5c) that whatever believers do when fully convinced of the rightness of an action, they do for the Lord, honoring him. This implied principle may not be immediately accepted, given the disagreements in view among Paul's addressees, and thus needs strengthening by the information introduced by γάρ in verse 7. The construction of an inferential strengthening series is then attempted but a logical gap remains, so that it is not possible to confirm independently the claim that believers do everything *for the Lord* on the basis of verse 7 alone. As a result, verse 7 is not yet optimally relevant to addressees. By the end of verse 7 we therefore have two claims that are not yet optimally relevant, one in verse 6 and one in verse 7.

The double statement in verse 8a–b is closely parallel to the double statement of verse 7. Verse 8 recalls Rom 6:10–11 and may well reactivate for addressees the assumptions communicated there. The occurrence of γάρ in verse 8a triggers procedure G, which identifies the statement in verse 7 as a candidate for strengthening by verse 8, since it is not yet optimally relevant. In a similar way to the double series we traced in 7:15, I suggest that something along the lines of the following double inferential series may be constructed, in which verse 8 strengthens verse 7, and in turn, the implication drawn from verse 6:

---

123. Dunn points out that the idea in v. 8 of living for *God* is typical of Jewish and Christian thought (*Romans 9–16*, 799, 807). See also Jewett, *Romans*, 847–48; Käsemann, *An die Römer*, 356.

P1 (implication drawn from v. 6): All that believers do when fully convinced of the rightness of an action,[124] they do for the Lord to honor him.
P2 (v. 7, disambiguated): No [believer] lives for herself or dies for herself.
Q introduced by γάρ (v. 8, disambiguated): Whether believers live or die, believers live or die for the Lord.
IA: If, whether believers live or die, believers live or die for the Lord, then no believer lives or dies for herself.
C1 (confirming P2, v. 7): No believer lives or dies for herself.
IA1: Living and dying encompasses all of life and all that believers do. (Inferred from common sense.)
IA2: If no believer lives for herself or dies for herself, but believers live and die for the Lord, then all that believers do when fully convinced of the rightness of an action, they do for the Lord to honor him.
C2 (confirming contextual implication P1, drawn from v. 6): All that believers do when fully convinced of the rightness of an action, they do for the Lord to honor him.

The procedural guidance given by γάρ in verse 8 leads to the strengthening of verse 7, enabling background assumptions to be accessed relating to the fact that everything believers do is done for the Lord. These provide an inferential bridge back to the contextual implication drawn from the examples in verse 6, resulting in turn in the independent confirmation of this implication. Thus the supporting evidence for the principle communicated in verse 6, support for which is partially provided in verse 7, is both completed and further bolstered by the material in verse 8. As a result, both the claim in verse 7 and the examples in verse 6 are held more strongly as valid by addressees, contributing to the persuasiveness of the argument, and the coherence of the cotext. The close dependence of verse 7 on verse 8a–b in order to achieve optimal relevance makes sense of commentators' analysis of verses 7–8 as a single chunk that explains or supports verse 6. If verses 7–8 contain metarepresented material as scholars suggest, then this lends extra weight to this supporting evidence, bringing additional backup behind Paul's claims and adding to their persuasive punch.

---

124. Inferred from 14:5c.

The occurrence of γάρ in verse 7, then, is somewhat complex in more than one respect. Unusually, it is a contextual implication in the form of a general principle drawn from the three examples in verse 6 that is strengthened, rather than an explicitly communicated claim. Moreover, the γάρ clause in verse 7 needs to be completed by a second γάρ clause in verse 8 in order to achieve optimal relevance. Nevertheless, we have once again been able to account for this occurrence as a procedural indicator guiding toward backward strengthening, by adapting and extending the basic procedural strengthening template proposed by Blakemore and Blass.

In 14:8c, Paul draws an explicit implication from the assumptions in verses 7–8b: "Whether we [believers] live or die, we are the Lord's." This conclusion is then backed up further in verse 9, which consists of a theological statement that expresses the purpose behind Christ's death and resurrection in terms of the establishment of his Lordship. The occurrence of γάρ in verse 9 is straightforward, so I will not discuss the likely strengthening series involved. As a result of the strengthening procedure triggered, addressees are persuaded to accept the conclusion in verse 8c more firmly as valid. The fact that this occurrence of γάρ introduces an axiomatic theological statement about Christ's death, resurrection, and Lordship that some suggest may be a confessional statement means that weighty material is brought to bear in support of the statement in verse 8c. As a consequence, the strengthening that γάρ guides toward in verse 9 is in all likelihood primarily relevant neither as further explanation nor as evidence providing logical confirmation of verse 8c, but rather as authoritative theological proof that backs up the conclusion in verse 8c and lends it particular prominence. In this case, it is the weight of accepted authority that helps to convince, rather than the construction of an independent, logical series. As Wright argues, the theological statement in verse 9 does not stand on its own but forms part of the explanation of verses 7–9, which grounds the exhortations and argument of verses 1–6 in "the very heart of the gospel."[125] Within this explanation, the conclusion of verse 8c is made salient by the following γάρ clause. We should note that the theological statement in verse 9, weighty and authoritative as it is, plays a supporting role, argumentatively speaking. We will return to this point.

---

125. Wright, "Romans," 737.

3.4.6. Romans 14:10–11

14:10a: σὺ δὲ τί κρίνεις τὸν ἀδελφόν σου;
14:10b: ἢ καὶ σὺ τί ἐξουθενεῖς τὸν ἀδελφόν σου;
14:10c: πάντες γὰρ παραστησόμεθα τῷ βήματι τοῦ θεοῦ,
14:11: γέγραπται γάρ, Ζῶ ἐγώ, λέγει κύριος, ὅτι ἐμοὶ κάμψει πᾶν γόνυ καὶ πᾶσα γλῶσσα ἐξομολογήσεται τῷ θεῷ.

Verse 10a–b consists of two rhetorical questions, addressed in second-person singular form to an imaginary interlocutor, as in verse 4. After the explanatory material of verses 7–9, Paul here recapitulates the main line of argument found in verses 3–4a, challenging the presumption of those who judge and despise their fellow believers. The implication to be drawn from the questions is that they have no right to do so. According to Dunn, the diatribal style has an "emotional impact."[126] The occurrence of γάρ in verse 10c introduces another accepted truth from Jewish (and Christian) teaching and is a paraphrase of the thought communicated in 2:1–16.

We can explain γάρ in verse 10c as a procedural indicator as follows. Procedure G is triggered, and the contextual implication drawn from the rhetorical questions in verse 10a–b, "Believers have no right to judge or despise fellow believers," is identified as candidate for strengthening by the following γάρ clause. I propose that something like the following assumptions may be involved in the construction of a strengthening series:

P (implication drawn from v. 10a–b): Believers have no right to judge or despise fellow believers.
Q introduced by γάρ (v. 10c, disambiguated): All [believers][127] will be judged by God.
IA1: If all believers will be judged by God, all believers are equal before God and God is their judge. (This reactivates assumptions communicated in 2:6–11.)
IA2: If all believers are equal before God and God is their judge, no believer has the higher status or authority over other believers to judge them.

---

126. Dunn, *Romans 9–16*, 797.
127. Here the first-person plural of the verb, and the cotext, lead addressees to infer that believers are in view.

IA3: If no believer has the higher status or the authority over other believers to judge them, then believers have no right to judge or despise fellow believers.
C (confirming v. 10a–b): Believers have no right to judge or despise fellow believers.

This is a somewhat complex instance of γάρ because several deductive steps are necessary in order to establish a supporting relation between the γάρ clause and preceding assumptions. As a result of the inferential guidance γάρ gives, the implication drawn from the preceding rhetorical questions is strengthened by a compelling theological justification. Given the sharp challenge to arrogance and presumptuousness issued by the rhetorical questions, I suggest that this γάρ clause is relevant as an authoritative justification that, if necessary, counters indignation on the part of addressees and unwillingness to accept the rebuke communicated in verse 10a–b. It thereby increases addressees' acceptance of the less than palatable truth indirectly expressed by means of the questions. Once again, we see that the metarepresentation of a theological statement is wielded as powerful support for hortatory material.

In verse 11, γάρ, together with the authoritative introductory formula γέγραπται, introduces a scriptural citation that blends the expression, "As I live, says the Lord," with a citation from the LXX of Isa 45:23.[128] Here the material following γάρ is a clear example of an authoritative metarepresentation that lends further weight to the statement it supports in verse 10c, which in turn provides backing for the challenge issued in the rhetorical questions. This is a straightforward example of γάρ and a typical example of the connective introducing a scriptural citation that functions as proof in support of a preceding statement.

As a result of the strengthening procedure, which leads to the independent confirmation of the statement in verse 10c, the latter is reinforced for addressees. In this case, the strengthening γάρ guides toward is hardly relevant as a convincing confirmation, since verse 10c is itself an accepted theological axiom. Instead, the strengthening achieved here seems relevant as authoritative proof that brings added weight to bear behind verse 10c, which in turn buttresses the uncompromising challenge issued in verse 10a–b. Together the two authoritative γάρ clauses in verses 10c–11 contribute to the punch

---

128. See, e.g., Num 14:28; Isa 49:18; Jer 22:24; Ezek 5:11.

and argumentative salience of the rhetorical questions, that is, to their cognitive effects. Dunn notes the persuasive effect of the material introduced by γάρ here: "the citation of one of the most powerful monotheistic passages in the scriptures (Isa 45:23) would have a powerful effect particularly on those seeking to be loyal to Jewish traditional beliefs."[129] I suggest that it is the authoritative character of the material introduced by γάρ, together with the way that it is combined with other known background assumptions as a result of procedure G, that creates a potent persuasive effect.

In 14:12 we find a conclusion that is drawn from, and sums up, the preceding material: "Each of us must give an account of ourselves to God." It rounds off the theological support provided for the rebuke communicated in verse 10, an admonition that in turn reiterates the main points of Paul's argument from verses 3–4.

3.4.7. Summary of Findings from Romans 14:1–12

From this examination of γάρ in the hortatory material of Rom 14:1–12, I have demonstrated that a range of somewhat complex occurrences can all be accounted for in terms of procedural instructions guiding toward the inferential procedure of backward strengthening. This includes examples where several contextual assumptions must be accessed in order to complete the inferential series and an occurrence where the strengthening is completed by a second subsequent γάρ clause (vv. 7–8). It also explains occurrences where the preceding assumptions that are strengthened are not simply those immediately adjacent to the γάρ clause (v. 3) or are not explicitly communicated (vv. 7, 10c).

In all cases, the core instructions given by the connective are the same: γάρ triggers a procedure whereby the information it introduces is processed as premises that are relevant in relation to, and as support for, previously communicated assumptions, with the result that addressees adhere more firmly to these previous claims. In each case, γάρ guides toward the cognitive effect of strengthening. It serves as a consistent communicative signal, reducing processing costs. By strengthening previous claims (often expressed in the form of exhortations), the procedure γάρ triggers, together with the supporting material it introduces, contribute

---

129. Dunn, *Romans 9–16*, 815.

to the persuasiveness of the argument. They thus play a part in motivating addressees to act upon the advice or warnings given.

As with other occurrences already discussed, the core procedural instructions guiding toward strengthening work themselves out in diverse ways in different contexts according to what is most relevant to particular addressees. This accounts for the fact that commentators explain the function or meaning of γάρ in diverse ways. Thus in 14:1–12 we find examples where the strengthening procedure may be perceived as relevant as a justifying rationale for an exhortation (v. 3c), as a convincing confirmation that may counter implicit objections (v. 4c and v. 6b), as a further explanation (v. 8a), and as a weighty and authoritative theological proof, where strengthening is achieved by acceptance of what is authoritative rather than by logic (vv. 9–11).

3.4.8. Implications for Tracing Paul's Argument in 14:1–12

As with 7:7–20, it is useful at this point to note some implications of this procedural strengthening account of γάρ for tracing the contours and thrust of the argument in this subsection. By identifying the assumptions strengthened by γάρ clauses, we can track some of the most salient points of the argument and start to outline its main thrust. In hortatory material such as chapter 14, we find that the salient argumentative points are most often exhortations. These are frequently supported by grounding theological statements introduced by γάρ, which represent an accepted theological framework and bring powerful persuasive backing behind the exhortations. Rhetorical questions are also salient, potentially giving rise to many cognitive effects in the form of contextual implications.

On the basis of the guidance given by γάρ and the supporting material it flags up, I suggest that the more salient argumentative points in 14:1–12 are the following:

14:1:   Accept the weaker believer.
14:3a: The person who eats everything should not despise the person who does not.
14:3b: The person who does not eat everything should not judge the person who does.
14:4a,c: Believers have no right to judge another person's slave. The Lord's slaves will stand.

14:5–6: Some believers observe sacred days, while others consider them all to be the same. Each believer should be convinced in her own mind. All that believers do [when fully convinced], they do for the Lord, to honor him.
14:10a,b: Believers have no right to judge a fellow believer.
14:12: Each believer will give an account to God.

This suggested highlighting of particularly salient points is not intended to imply a structural analysis that identifies a hierarchy of different levels and units of information. Instead, it simply offers a fresh look at the line of argument in light of the guidance given by γάρ. Paying attention to γάρ as a procedural signpost does not automatically enable us to identify all the main points of Paul's argument, since not all are followed by γάρ clauses and some that are form part of an extended supporting explanation (see v. 8c). We also need to be aware of other connectives, such as δέ, οὖν, and ἄρα, which indicate new implications or conclusions, as well as other textual clues. But our analysis of γάρ does help to flag up which statements are more salient in relation to others and which may be particularly argumentatively significant. It compels us to take seriously the cotext and the close relationship between information introduced by γάρ and previously communicated information, reinforcing the coherence of the argument.

By way of example: having examined γάρ in 14:7–9, we see that there is a clear consolidating relationship between verse 6 and these verses, indicated by γάρ in verse 7 and verse 8a. As a result, the insertion of a paragraph break between verse 6 and verse 7, such as we find in the NRSV, is misplaced and misleading.[130] It appears that the translators have allowed the weighty but supporting theological statement in verse 9 to distract them from the main argumentative point, which is the exhortation to addressees to accept one another as fellow slaves of the Lord. By paying attention to γάρ as an indicator of consolidating material, we are able to focus better on the direction and contours of the main line of Paul's thought and pay attention to what is being reinforced in the previous cotext. We can see that verses 7–9 are neither a "digression," nor the "central statement of the passage from which all else naturally flows."[131] Instead, these verses pro-

---

130. See Wright, "Romans," 737. Wright, in fact, erroneously cites the NIV as inserting a break at this point.

131. Käsemann cites Adolf Jülicher as representing the former view, while Käsemann himself argues for the latter. See Adolf Jülicher, "Der Brief an die Römer," in *Die*

vide the necessary theological grounding for Paul's exhortation to radical mutual acceptance.¹³² That is, γάρ here points to background material that provides an accepted theological frame of reference, connecting the main points of the argument back to an understanding of reality grounded in faith in Christ, which provides a motivating rationale for them. Thus a procedural account of γάρ enables us to interpret verses 7–9 in their proper place within the argument as a whole.

To summarize, in this chapter I have demonstrated from representative examples how a procedural strengthening hypothesis for γάρ is able to provide a unified and consistent explanation for a variety of straightforward and somewhat complex occurrences of the connective in Romans. All occurrences, in both expository and hortatory material, can be explained in terms of core procedural instructions that guide toward the inferential procedure of strengthening of preceding assumptions. The connective raises expectations that the material that follows it will be relevant as strengthening material in relation to previous assumptions. The connective constrains interpretation, thus reducing processing costs, and can be relied upon as a communicative signal in exegesis. This is especially useful for modern interpreters who have no access to the cognitive environment of the author or the first addressees and no certainty regarding the contextual assumptions manifest to them.

The procedure triggered by γάρ uses a relevance-guided heuristic to infer which preceding claim is to be strengthened and in what way. The result of the procedure is the consolidation of preceding claims or exhortations. This gives rise to the cognitive effect of strengthening, increasing addressees' adherence to these assumptions. The strengthening procedure may be relevant to addressees in different ways, according to the type of persuasive material, the communicator's persuasive aims, the cotext, and the perspective, knowledge, and attitudes of addressees. Thus in material that aims to convince skeptical addressees, it may work itself out as independent confirming evidence that convinces by rational argument, whereas in material where the validity of claims is not at stake it is more likely to work itself out as an explanation that increases comprehension. In passages where Paul perhaps seeks to challenge or persuade addressees regarding

---

Schriften Des Neuen Testaments, ed. Wilhelm Bousset and Wilhelm Heitmüller, 3rd ed. (Göttingen: Vandenhoeck & Ruprecht, 1917), 2:223–335, cited by Käsemann, *An die Römer*, 356.

132. Wright, "Romans," 737.

the desirability of an unpopular course of action, strengthening may work itself out as an authoritative proof that persuades because of trust in the source. Occasionally the strengthening may be relevant as a rhetorical display that creates a convincing impression of compelling evidence.

The assumptions that are strengthened as a result of the procedure are argumentatively salient, very often representing the main thrust of the argument, while the material introduced by γάρ can be seen as supporting or background information. In particular, a chain of consecutive γάρ clauses has a cumulative strengthening effect, leading back to the claim at the head of the chain, which is highly salient in the argument as a result. The connective thus helps us to distinguish between material that moves the argument forward and material that may be theologically important, representing an accepted theological framework, but that, in argumentative terms, serves as buttressing. The connective and the inferential procedure it triggers contribute both to the coherence and to the persuasiveness of the argument.

This procedural account of γάρ is enlightening in various ways. Reading γάρ as a consistent communicative signal allows us on occasion to make decisions about textual variants (14:5) and confirms certain lines of exegesis, while undermining others (a point that will be explored more fully in ch. 5, below). It helps us to pay attention to the coherence of whole subsections. It encourages us to recognize the relationship not only between γάρ clauses and immediately preceding assumptions, but also how material introduced by γάρ may reactivate, consolidate, and underline assumptions communicated further back in the cotext. Finally, it assists us in tracing the contours of the argument. In particular, γάρ flags up supporting information that bolsters the most salient argumentative points, points that give rise to many fresh cognitive effects. This buttressing material frequently takes the form of accepted and authoritative theological statements, which are often metarepresentations of sayings and ideas, probably well known to Paul's addressees, attributable to Jewish and early Christian teaching, to generally accepted wisdom, and sometimes to Paul himself.

4
What Kind of Strengthening? Problematic Examples

In this chapter I will extend the demonstration of the relevance-theoretic, procedural account of γάρ in Romans begun in chapter 3 in order to show how it is able to provide a unified and consistent explanation for occurrences that might be judged problematic. We will consider a representative sample of problematic instances that have been selected to represent the range of difficulties encountered in the interpretation of γάρ in the epistle. These are taken from both expository and hortatory material and from passages that achieve persuasion primarily by means of rhetorical features, as well as from passages that employ more logical argumentation, based on claims and substantiating evidence.[1] I will briefly discuss the surrounding cotext of each example in order to provide an orientation to some of the most obvious contextual assumptions that may be at play in interpretation. The chapter will finish with some general observations and conclusions to be drawn from the procedural account of γάρ presented and their implications for the interpretation of Romans. These conclusions will serve as a foundation for the discussion in chapters 5 and 6, which will illustrate from some specific examples how this account can throw fresh light on some disputed aspects of the interpretation of the epistle.

As outlined in chapter 3, by problematic occurrences of γάρ I mean those atypical examples for which an obvious supporting relationship with preceding material is, on the face of it, difficult to identify, leading to a lack of consensus regarding their interpretation. From the point of view

---

1. Rhetorical features are emphatic repetition, metaphor, rhetorical questions, antithetical parallelism, irony, etc. These have a persuasive effect based not primarily on the rational substantiation of claims, but on the creation of an impression that affects emotions.

of a procedural account, such occurrences might be seen as problematic because a simple strengthening inferential series may be difficult to construct with preceding claims, and the contextual assumptions involved may not be easily identifiable to modern interpreters. In addition, these occurrences are frequently found in passages of considerable exegetical ambiguity and complexity. The difficulties of interpreting these cases of γάρ in turn compound the interpretative uncertainties of their cotexts. Some of these examples occur at pivotal points in the letter's argument and in passages that have been made to bear much theological freight (other such examples will form the focus of chs. 5 and 6, below).

Rather than discussing these occurrences in epistolary order, I will consider them in two broad groups. Those in the first group, 2:25; 5:6–7; and 9:11, broadly represent more complex cases of logical strengthening. By this I mean the cognitive effect of strengthening that occurs as the result of a full logical series of inferences providing supporting evidence that rationally and independently confirms a claim.[2] Those in the second group, 7:1; 6:19–20; and 15:24, involve strengthening that is influenced by rhetorical as well as logical factors. By rhetorical strengthening I mean the cognitive effect of strengthening achieved as the result of rhetorical features that create an impression of strengthening that is enough to satisfy expectations of relevance, even if a full logical series is not constructed.[3] As we shall see, both kinds of strengthening may be in evidence in some cotexts, depending on what is relevant to particular addressees, so this division is somewhat artificial but useful for ease of discussion.

I will discuss the examples of rhetorical strengthening in order of atypicality rather than in epistolary order. Thus 7:1 is an example of logical strengthening that is also exploited for rhetorical purposes, and 6:19 and 6:20 are examples of rhetorical strengthening where the construction of a full logical series is not required, although some inferencing is involved. Romans 15:24, meanwhile, is an example of the core function of γάρ being exploited in an unusual way with a very specific rhetorical purpose.

---

2. The occurrences discussed hitherto have been examples of logical strengthening.

3. Hellholm's identification of two main types of argumentation is along these lines (Hellholm, "Enthymemic Argumentation in Paul," 119–20 n.7). See §3.1.1 n. 5, above.

4. What Kind of Strengthening? Problematic Examples

4.1. Romans 2:25: Questions of Coherence

2:23: ὃς ἐν νόμῳ καυχᾶσαι, διὰ τῆς παραβάσεως τοῦ νόμου τὸν θεὸν ἀτιμάζεις·
2:24: τὸ γὰρ ὄνομα τοῦ θεοῦ δι' ὑμᾶς βλασφημεῖται ἐν τοῖς ἔθνεσιν, καθὼς γέγραπται.
2:25a: περιτομὴ μὲν γὰρ ὠφελεῖ ἐὰν νόμον πράσσῃς·
2:25b: ἐὰν δὲ παραβάτης νόμου ᾖς, ἡ περιτομή σου ἀκροβυστία γέγονεν.

The occurrence of γάρ in 2:25 is problematic because a supporting relationship with what immediately precedes in verse 24 is, at first sight, not obvious. The apparent difficulty of this occurrence is illustrated by BDAG's categorization under the subheading, "the thought to be supported is not expressed, but must be supplied from the context."[4] Consequently, scholars disagree as to whether the statement introduced by γάρ in verse 25 represents the beginning of a fresh line of thought (see below). A majority of translations insert a paragraph break before verse 25.

4.1.1. Cotext

In 2:17 the diatribal style of 2:1–5 resumes with a fresh speech directed toward an imaginary interlocutor. As in 2:1, the identity of the interlocutor here is fiercely contested. Some understand the same addressee to be in view as in 2:1, with the addressee's identity now explicit: σὺ Ἰουδαῖος ἐπονομάζῃ.[5] Others argue that in 2:17 Paul makes a shift from the more general address of 2:1 to engage a hypothetical Jew, or a representative of a certain expression of Judaism.[6] Without entering into the details of this

---

4. BDAG, s.v. "γάρ," 1e.
5. E.g., Dunn, takes the addressee to represent a "typical" Jew (Dunn, *Romans 1–8*, 108). See also Cranfield, *Epistle to the Romans*, 138. Watson argues that in 2:1 and 2:17 Paul is criticizing the leaders, or teachers, of the Jewish community (Watson, *Paul, Judaism and the Gentiles*, 198–203). For Campbell, the figure in 2:17 and 2:1 is "representative of an elite group of literate Jewish males ... learned in the law and ... Jewish traditions, into which [Paul's opponent] falls" (Campbell, *Deliverance of God*, 559–60). In contrast, Rodríguez and Thiessen identify the interlocutor of 2:1 and 2:17 as a judaizing gentile (Rodríguez and Thiessen, *So-Called Jew in Paul's Letter to the Romans*).
6. See discussion under §3.2.3 n. 35, above, and Barrett, *Epistle to the Romans*, 43; Elliott, *Rhetoric of Romans*, 127; Jewett, *Romans*, 221. Stowers argues that 2:17–29

debate, it is evident that in verses 17–24 Paul criticizes a certain kind of presumptuous and hypocritical attitude, which gains a sense of superiority and moral security from the Jewish law, while failing to put the law into practice. In verses 21–22 a series of four rhetorical questions exposes the fundamental hypocrisy of this stance, summarized in the hard-hitting accusation of verse 23: "You who boast in the law, you dishonor God by transgressing the law." In verse 24, γάρ introduces a slightly altered version of Isa 52:5 (LXX), which contains a probable echo of Ezek 36:20–21.[7] The strengthening triggered by this occurrence of γάρ is relevant as an authoritative proof that buttresses the statement in verse 23.

Although 2:25–29 is viewed by some as the beginning of a fresh subsection, most scholars see at least a general connection between these verses and what precedes in 2:17–24.[8] Dunn finds in verses 25–29 a new subsection that abruptly introduces the subject of circumcision, while also paralleling the thought of verses 12–16.[9] In his view, the verses represent the climax of the indictment of Jewish presumption begun in 2:1. Cranfield interprets γάρ as indicating a connection between the whole of verses 25–29 and "what precedes." In his view, verses 25–29 confirm and clarify what Paul has previously asserted by answering "an obvious objection from the Jewish side" regarding circumcision as one of the chief grounds of Jewish confidence.[10] Similarly, Barrett argues that in verse 25 Paul invokes a particular commandment, circumcision, in response to a Jewish objector.[11] This reading overlaps with BDAG's analysis that the thought to be supported by the γάρ clause in verse 25 is not expressed. It assumes that certain other background assumptions must also be highly accessible to addressees, in

---

is a type of *prosōpopoiia* presenting a characterization of "the pretentious teacher" (Stowers, *Rereading of Romans*, 150–53, 159). The addressee is an imaginary Jewish moral teacher, who aims to "transform the gentiles by getting them to do works from the law."

7. Cranfield, *Epistle to the Romans*, 171.

8. Käsemann maintains that γάρ in v. 25 "introduces a new round of discussion," characterizing this use of γάρ as "argumentative" (Käsemann, *An die Römer*, 67). Ziesler takes vv. 25–29 as a new pericope (Ziesler, *Paul's Letter to the Romans*, 92). Moo views vv. 17–24 and vv. 25–29 as separate subsections (Moo, *Epistle to the Romans*, 158, 166).

9. Dunn, *Romans 1–8*, 125, 119. See also Wilckens, *Der Brief an die Römer*, 1:154.

10. Cranfield does not specify which element of the preceding material the verses confirm (Cranfield, *Epistle to the Romans*, 171).

11. Barrett, *Epistle to the Romans*, 57.

particular, the claim that circumcision is the sign of God's covenant with the Jewish people, Israel's special status among the nations, and a reason for Jewish confidence.[12] It also presupposes that circumcision is the example par excellence of Jewish law-keeping, which brings honor to God.[13] On this interpretation, Paul assumes that such background assumptions will be uppermost in the minds of his audience and thus passes seamlessly from questions of boasting in and keeping the Jewish law (vv. 17–24) to the question of circumcision (vv. 25–29), without explaining further the relevance of circumcision in this context.[14]

Others view 2:17–29 as a more closely knit pericope.[15] Barclay, for instance, reads 2:17–29 as an address to "the Jew" that deals with the question of how Jewish identity is "received and recognized" in God's sight.[16] Wright interprets verses 25–29 as the second paragraph of the subsection 2:17–29, which as a whole outlines the fact that ethnic Israel, resting on its special vocation as God's people, has not lived up to this vocation. Within this, verses 25–29 present a "stronger and more detailed form" of the argument in verses 13–15 regarding the torah. Verse 25 can be viewed as an "initial statement" from which the rest of the paragraph "emerges."[17] Stowers, meanwhile, finds a symmetry between the role of 2:25–29 in relation to 2:17–24, and 2:6–16 in relation to 2:1–5. In both cases, "a characterization of the interlocutor through censorious apostrophe (2:1–5, 17–24)" is followed by an explanation about "how doers of the law, whether Jew or gentile, will be justified by God" (2:6–16, 25–29).[18]

---

12. See Wolter, *Röm 1–8*, 200, and Watson, commenting on Jub. 15:25–28: "Circumcision is the indispensable sign that one is a member of Israel, the holy people, and that one therefore belongs to the Lord" (Watson, *Paul and the Hermeneutics of Faith*, 231; see also Cranfield, *Epistle to the Romans*, 171).

13. See Dunn, *Romans 1–8*, 120; John M. G. Barclay, "Paul and Philo on Cirumcision: Romans 2.25–9 in Social and Cultural Context," *NTS* 44 (1998): 544. Cf., however, Wolter, who argues that no Jew would have claimed that circumcision alone was enough to stay in the covenant without law-keeping (Wolter, *Röm 1–8*, 200).

14. See Wright, *Paul for Everyone*, 39–40.

15. E.g., Wolter, *Röm 1–8*, 190; Jewett, *Romans*, 219–21, 231. Both take 2:17–29 as a single pericope in two subsections, vv. 17–24 and vv. 25–29. Jewett nevertheless regards 2:25 as a thesis statement from which further inferences are drawn.

16. Barclay, *Paul and the Gift*, 469.

17. Wright, "Romans," 448.

18. Stowers, *Rereading of Romans*, 154.

4.1.2. Analysis of γάρ

Using the framework of relevance theory, we can propose the following procedural account of γάρ in verse 25. Procedure G is triggered by γάρ. Given that the material in verse 25a–b is held together as a balanced antithetical whole by the connectives μέν ... δέ, it is inferred that verse 25a and verse 25b are to be processed together as a single strengthening complex of assumptions.[19] Within this the material in verse 25a represents an accepted presupposition and functions as a concessive clause, while the main strengthening statement lies in verse 25b.[20]

Following a relevance-guided heuristic, addressees' comprehension processes attempt to construct a deductive series that strengthens the immediately preceding statement in verse 24 but this not possible without unreasonable processing effort. Since the material in verse 24 functions as a scriptural proof, we can suggest that this statement is in fact already optimally relevant and does not need further strengthening. The repetition in verse 25 of the vocabulary of law-breaking (παραβάτης νόμου) from verse 23, on the other hand, makes the claim in verse 23 particularly highly accessible for strengthening by verse 25. Moreover, despite the scriptural support provided in verse 24, the claim in verse 23 may still raise objections, as various scholars suggest, and may thus not yet be optimally relevant.[21] A deductive series is thus inferred that strengthens verse 23, along the following lines:

> **P (v. 23):** You, the one who boasts in the [Jewish] law, dishonor God by transgressing the law.
> **Implicit objections raised by P:** How do those who boast in the Jewish law (i.e., circumcised Jews) dishonor God? Does circumcision not count?
> **Q introduced by γάρ (v. 25):** Circumcision is of value if you [who boast in the Jewish law] put the law into practice. But if you are a transgressor of the law, your circumcision has become uncircumcision.

---

19. Jewett, *Romans*, 231, citing Otto Michel, *Der Brief an die Römer*, KEK 4 (Göttingen: Vandenhoeck & Ruprecht, 1978), 132.
20. Dunn, *Romans 1–8*, 121.
21. E.g., "How can you claim that Jews dishonor God by boasting in the law yet transgressing the law, since Jews are circumcised? Does circumcision count for nothing?"

4. What Kind of Strengthening? Problematic Examples 129

IA1: The interlocutor who boasts in the law is a Jew. (Inferable from verse 17.)[22]

IA2: If the interlocutor who boasts in the law is a Jew, then the interlocutor who boasts in the law is circumcised.

IA3: Circumcision is of value because it is the outward sign that a person is a member of God's holy covenant people. (Inferable from encyclopedic knowledge of Jewish teaching.)[23]

IA4: If, because of transgression of the law, the interlocutor's circumcision has become uncircumcision, then the outward sign that the interlocutor is a member of God's holy people has become a contradiction and a sign of hypocrisy. (Inferable from previous cotext of vv. 17–22, knowledge of Jewish teaching, the concepts of circumcision/uncircumcision, etc. Previously communicated assumptions from 2:12–13 may also be reactivated here.)

IA5: If, because of transgression of the law, the outward sign that the interlocutor is a member of God's holy people has become a sign of hypocrisy, then God is dishonored by the interlocutor. (Inferable from knowledge of Jewish teaching, concept of hypocrisy, etc.)

(**IA6**: If God is dishonored by the interlocutor who carries the outward sign of a member of God's holy people but who transgresses the law, then the name of God is blasphemed among the gentiles/nations.)[24]

IA7: If, because of transgression of the law, God is dishonored by the interlocutor who carries the outward sign of a member of God's holy people, then the interlocutor that boasts in the law dishonors God by transgressing the law.

C (confirming verse 23): You, the one who boasts in the Jewish law, dishonor God by transgressing the law.

As a result of this strengthening series, the claim in verse 23 is independently confirmed. The accessing of highly accessible contextual assumptions helps to ground this claim in knowledge already accepted by addressees, making it more compelling, and overturning potential objections raised by it. Consequently, addressees are persuaded to adhere to it

---

22. Following the standard interpretation of 2:17. See nn. 5 and 6, above.

23. See Wolter, *Röm 1–8*, 200; Barclay, "Paul and Philo on Cirumcision," 545; Dunn, *Romans 1–8*, 119–20.

24. This confirms the statement in v. 24, even though this citation is already optimally relevant.

more strongly and its relevance is increased. Thus the antithetical statement in verse 25 serves to back up the point made in verse 23.

The proposed strengthening series here is relatively complex. It represents a hypothesis based on our inferences regarding the probable cognitive environment of Paul's audience. It posits strengthening in response to implicit objections that themselves assume other contextual knowledge (e.g., a close link between boasting in the law, law-keeping, circumcision, and honoring God).[25] Different addressees may find this strengthening procedure relevant either as a confirming and justifying rationale or as a further explanation of the way in which the one that boasts in the law dishonors God. Addressees will choose to construct different inferential series according to the contextual information most easily accessible to them and to what produces most strengthening effects for least effort. For those who have serious objections to the statement of verse 23, the effort invested in constructing a full logical series such as the one above will be necessary and worthwhile.[26] For those who are already convinced of Paul's viewpoint, on the other hand, expectations of relevance will be satisfied by the general impression of strengthening created by the presence of γάρ as a strengthening signal. Consequently, they will not invest processing effort in constructing a full logical series.

Notwithstanding the relative complexity of the strengthening series proposed, it makes sense of this occurrence of γάρ as guiding addressees toward the cognitive effect of strengthening. Addressees are encouraged to find the relevance of the material in verse 25 in relation to preceding material, rather than as a fresh argumentative point relevant in its own right or as a statement that primarily looks forward to and serves as a foundation for the statement in verse 26. This procedural explanation of γάρ in verse 25 supports interpretations such as Stowers's, which view verses 25–29 as part of a single subsection with verses 17–24. Moreover, it provides a cognitively grounded explanation for Cranfield's view that the material in verse 25 answers an implicit objection raised by the preceding material. Because of the contextual assumptions activated by verse 23 in the form of these objections, the subject of circumcision is not introduced as abruptly as Dunn claims. The reactivation of previ-

---

25. Dunn assumes a close association in Jewish thought between the law, law-keeping, circumcision, and Jewish confidence in God's favor and salvation (Dunn, *Romans 1–8*, 125–26).

26. E.g., torah-observant Christ-believers. See Stowers, *Rereading of Romans*, 158.

ously communicated assumptions from verses 12–13 as part of the inferential series also accounts for the observation that the thought of verses 25–27 parallels that of verses 12–14. In sum, reading γάρ in this way encourages interpreters to look backward in order to understand the relevance of verse 25, rather than reading it as the beginning of a fresh line of thought. This highlights the coherence of the argument of the wider subsection.

At the same time, this analysis of γάρ is compatible with the view that the material in verse 25 also serves as a platform for the subsequent discussion of circumcision and Jewish identity in verses 26–29.[27] Though γάρ itself guides only toward a strengthening procedure, the information it introduces as strengthening premises may subsequently be processed as a foundation upon which verses 26–29 build further. This relationship with the following claims is inferred by addressees from the subsequent cotext, but is not signaled by a procedural indicator. In this way, the information in verse 25 serves a dual purpose in the argument, looking both backward and forward, even though γάρ only indicates the former function.

4.2. Romans 5:6–7: Parenthesis or Adjustment?

5:5:	ἡ δὲ ἐλπὶς οὐ καταισχύνει, ὅτι ἡ ἀγάπη τοῦ θεοῦ ἐκκέχυται ἐν ταῖς καρδίαις ἡμῶν διὰ πνεύματος ἁγίου τοῦ δοθέντος ἡμῖν.
5:6:	ἔτι γὰρ Χριστὸς ὄντων ἡμῶν ἀσθενῶν ἔτι κατὰ καιρὸν ὑπὲρ ἀσεβῶν ἀπέθανεν.
5:7a:	μόλις γὰρ ὑπὲρ δικαίου τις ἀποθανεῖται·
5:7b:	ὑπὲρ γὰρ τοῦ ἀγαθοῦ τάχα τις καὶ τολμᾷ ἀποθανεῖν·
5:8:	συνίστησιν δὲ τὴν ἑαυτοῦ ἀγάπην εἰς ἡμᾶς ὁ θεός, ὅτι ἔτι ἁμαρτωλῶν ὄντων ἡμῶν Χριστὸς ὑπὲρ ἡμῶν ἀπέθανεν.

Romans 5:6–7 contains three problematic instances of γάρ, the interpretation of which is bound up with various exegetical difficulties.[28] Scholars disagree regarding the relationship of verse 6 with what precedes, since it is

---

27. See Jewett, *Romans*, 221; Wright, "Romans," 448; Barclay, *Paul and the Gift*, 469.
28. Leander Keck provides a detailed discussion of the exegetical problems. Leander Keck, "The Post-Pauline Interpretation of Jesus' Death in Rom 5,6–7," in *Theologia Crucis—Signum Crucis: Festschrift für Erich Dinkler zum 70. Geburtstag*, ed. C. Andersen and Günther Klein (Tübingen: Mohr Siebeck, 1979), 237–48.

difficult to identify an obvious supporting, causal, or explanatory relationship with verse 5. Meanwhile the interpretation of both occurrences in verse 7 is affected by the opacity of the logic of the two statements in this verse.[29] The relationship between verse 7a and verse 6 is disputed, while the occurrence in verse 7b introduces a statement that is taken by some as a correction, albeit awkward and ambiguous, of the claim in verse 7a, and by others as a parenthesis.[30] Some have attempted to resolve the difficulties by proposing that verses 6–7 represent a post-Pauline interpolation.[31] Given the fact that the verses are also often considered to be of crucial doctrinal significance, these occurrences of γάρ are prime examples of the problematic category.

4.2.1. Cotext

Romans 5:1–11 may be analyzed either as belonging with the first major section of the letter (chs. 1–4) or as opening the second major section of the letter, running to the end of chapter 8.[32] The themes, vocabulary, and style of chapters 5–8 are noticeably different from chapters 1–4, and chapters 5–8 are punctuated by the refrain του κυρίου ἡμῶν Ἰησοῦ Χριστοῦ that occurs some six times, at opening and concluding points in the argument.[33] At the same time, the use in 5:1–11 of the vocabulary of justification, faith, and boasting, all of which play a key role in the first major section of the letter, leads many to recognize the transitional quality of these verses.[34]

Romans 5:1–5 states the consequences of justification ἐκ πίστεως for believers in Christ: peace with God, grace, and the hope of the glory of

---

29. Michael Wolter views v. 7 as an anacoluthon interrupting the line of thought. Michael Wolter, *Rechtfertigung und Zukünftiges Heil: Untersuchungen zu Röm 5, 1–11*, BZNW 43 (Berlin: de Gruyter, 1979), 167.

30. E.g., Jewett, *Romans*, 360; Zerwick, *Grammatical Analysis*, 470.

31. E.g., Keck, "Post-Pauline Interpretation," 237–48.

32. Wolter, Wilckens, and Dunn regard 3:21–5:21 and 6:1–8:39 as distinct sections (Wolter, *Röm 1–8*, xiii; Wilckens, *Der Brief an die Römer*, 1:181, 286; Dunn, *Romans 1–8*, 242). Stowers reads 4:23–5:11 as a "hortatory conclusion" to chs. 1–4 (Stowers, *Rereading of Romans*, 247). Those who take 5:1–11 with what follows include Käsemann, *An die Römer*, 122, Cranfield, *Epistle to the Romans*, 253–54, Wright, "Romans," 508 and Campbell, *Deliverance of God*.

33. See Campbell, *Deliverance of God*, 62–73; Cranfield, *Epistle to the Romans*, 254.

34. E.g., Barclay, *Paul and the Gift*, 494 n. 1; Simon Gathercole, *Where Is Boasting? Early Jewish Soteriology and Paul's Response in Romans 1–5* (Grand Rapids: Eerdmans, 2002), 252–55.

4. What Kind of Strengthening? Problematic Examples 133

God. In contrast to 2:17, 23 and 3:27, the notion of boasting in verses 2–3 now has a positive sense. Verses 3–4 consist of a chain sequence of key terms that builds to a small climax in verse 5a, the salience of which is increased by the repetition of the term ἐλπίς. This leads various interpreters to identify Christian hope as the theme of 5:1–11.[35] This climax rounds off the statement of the present implications of justification and makes use of the vocabulary of shame (οὐ καταισχύνει), the reverse side of boasting and honor, in order to underline the theme of boasting in the hope of the glory of God.[36] Verse 5b is introduced by the marker ὅτι, which most scholars read as "because" but can also be translated "in that." Thus the fact that God's Spirit has poured out the love of God in believers' hearts is viewed as the proof or ground for the confident claim that hope does not put them to shame.[37] This is the first mention of ἡ ἀγάπη in the epistle, a key concept in the climactic conclusion of chapters 5–8, 8:31–39, and in chapter 13. The ambiguous genitive construction ἡ ἀγάπη τοῦ θεοῦ has historically occasioned much debate.[38] A majority of modern commentators opt for the subjective reading, "God's love (for believers)," rather than the objective, "(believers') love for God."[39]

Opinions differ as to whether to take 5:1–11 as a single pericope or to treat 5:6–11 as a separate subsection.[40] Most are agreed, however, that 5:6–8 belong closely together. Verse 8b can be viewed as a restatement of the claim of verse 6. Wolter sees verse 8a as picking up the thought of verse 5b-c and verse 8b taking up verse 6.[41] For Wright, verse 6 states a basic

---

35. Watson, *Paul, Judaism and the Gentiles*, 271; Gathercole, *Where Is Boasting?*, 257–58; Wright, *Paul and the Faithfulness of God*, 885. See also Wolter, *Rechtfertigung und Zukünftiges Heil*, 218–20.

36. Wolter, *Röm 1–8*, 326.

37. Cranfield, *Epistle to the Romans*, 262; Dunn, *Romans 1–8*, 252. Wolter argues that the love of God shown in Christ's death for the ungodly is the ground of eschatological hope (Wolter, *Rechtfertigung und Zukünftiges Heil*, 159–76).

38. Wilckens provides a history of the debate (Wilckens, *Der Brief an die Römer*, 1:300–305).

39. Though Wright follows the Augustinian reading, "love for God" (Wright, "Romans," 517).

40. Those who see it as a single pericope are, e.g., Käsemann, *An die Römer*; Wilckens, *Der Brief an die Römer*; Jewett, *Romans*. Wright views it as a separate subsection (Wright, *Paul and the Faithfulness of God*, 1:410). He nevertheless reads 5:6–11 as "explaining and grounding" the themes set out in 5:1–5 (Wright, "Romans," 514).

41. Wolter, *Röm 1–8*, 328.

premise, verse 7 comments on this, and verse 8 draws the conclusion.[42] Jewett finds in verses 6–8 a "chiastic argument" that uses "traditional creedal formulations interspersed with rhetorical comments."[43] The fourfold repetition of ἀποθανεῖν in verses 6–8 emphasizes the cohesiveness of the thought, as well as the focus on Christ's death.[44] The chain of three consecutive γάρ clauses in verses 6–7 also contributes to the impression of a close-knit complex of thought. I will thus discuss these three occurrences in conjunction with each other.

Many commentators interpret verses 6–8 as explaining, or providing grounds for, what precedes but disagree as to whether the verses primarily explain further the hope referred to in verse 5a or the love of God in verse 5b. Wright reads γάρ in verse 6 as indicating that the whole of verses 6–11 explains the previous summary of the argument in verses 1–5, grounding the hope referred to in verses 2–5 in something that has happened.[45] Likewise, Dunn interprets verses 6–8 as providing "further justification for the hope of verses 3–5."[46] Gathercole, meanwhile, regards eschatological hope as the subject of verses 5–10, within which verses 6–8 explain the love of God in the past, which guarantees the future hope. In his view, γάρ in verse 6 indicates that these verses explain verse 5.[47] In a similar vein, Wolter argues that while verse 5b provides grounds for the thesis about confident hope in verse 5a, the aim of the argumentation in verses 6–8 is to "fill in the content" of ἡ ἀγάπη τοῦ θεοῦ (v. 5b), in which the hope is grounded.[48] Others place the emphasis still more firmly on the love of God as the element explained by verses 6–8. For Barrett, the material following γάρ in verse 6 represents a proof for the love of God, while for Cranfield verses 6–8 "describe the nature of the divine love" referred to in verse 5.[49] Käsemann, for his part, understands verse 5b to raise the question, "How can one become certain of God's love through the Spirit?," to which verses 6–8 then provide an answer by referring to Jesus's death.[50]

---

42. Wright, "Romans," 518.
43. Jewett, *Romans*, 357.
44. Dunn, *Romans 1–8*, 246.
45. Wright, *Paul and the Faithfulness of God*, 886.
46. Dunn, *Romans 1–8*, 254.
47. Gathercole, *Where Is Boasting?*, 258.
48. Wolter, *Rechtfertigung und Zukünftiges Heil*, 167, 170.
49. Barrett, *Epistle to the Romans*, 105; Cranfield, *Epistle to the Romans*, 263. See also Wilckens, *Der Brief an die Römer*, 1:288.
50. Käsemann, *An die Römer*, 127.

4.2.2. Analysis of γάρ

The syntax of verse 6, and the repetition of ἔτι, is awkward, and a range of textual variants exists, among them some that omit γάρ, such as εἴ γε ... ἔτι.[51] There is a consensus that the difficult combination ἔτι γάρ ... ἔτι, which is supported by the best external evidence, is original.[52] The occurrence of γάρ in verse 6 can be explained within a relevance-theoretic framework as a procedural indicator in the following way. The connective triggers procedure G and the material in verse 6 is taken as a strengthening premise that should achieve relevance in relation to a preceding assumption. Following a relevance-guided heuristic, the immediately preceding complex of assumptions communicated in verse 5 is identified as the most obvious candidate for strengthening. The claims in verse 5 may raise implicit questions for some addressees, for instance, "How does God's love poured out in our hearts by the Holy Spirit provide grounds for confidence that hope (in the glory of God) will not disappoint us?" Highly accessible contextual assumptions are searched for to combine in an inferential series that will address these questions. We can propose the following strengthening series:

> **Complex P for strengthening** (v. 5): This hope does not put us [Paul and his addressees, believers in Christ] to shame because the love of God has been poured into our hearts by means of the Holy Spirit given to us.
> **Q introduced by γάρ** (v. 6): While we [believers] were still weak/helpless, Christ at that time died for the ungodly.[53]
> **IA1**: We believers are the ungodly Christ died for. (Inferred from verse 6a and verse 6b.)
> **IA2**: The weak/helpless and ungodly are without merit and honor. (Inferable from encyclopedic knowledge of Greco-Roman cultural norms.)[54]

---

51. Attested by Vaticanus.

52. See, e.g., Jewett, *Romans*, 345; Metzger, *Textual Commentary on the Greek New Testament*, 453; Wilckens, *Der Brief an die Römer*, 1:294.

53. Jewett provides a discussion of the theological problems associated with the use of ἀσθενής and κατὰ καιρόν here (Jewett, *Romans*, 358).

54. Reasoner, *Strong and the Weak*, 59–61. Cf. 1 Cor 1:26–27.

IA3: If the weak/helpless and ungodly are without merit and honor, then Paul's addressees, believers, the weak/helpless and ungodly, did nothing to merit Christ's help (death) on their behalf.

IA4: If Paul's addressees did nothing to merit Christ's death on their behalf, Christ's death on their behalf was an unexpected and incongruous act of mercy in their favor.[55] (Inferable from common sense and knowledge of concept of mercy.)

This series of inferences is logically incomplete, however. It fails to lead to a conclusion that strengthens the claims in verse 5. Given the information in verse 6, it does not seem possible to establish a complete inferential series without unreasonable processing effort: the connection between Christ's death for the ungodly and God's love is not yet highly accessible nor easily inferable in the cotext. As a result, the statement in verse 6, which γάρ indicates is relevant in relation to preceding claims, has not yet achieved optimal relevance.[56] It may raise implicit questions, such as: "What does Christ's death for the ungodly have to do with the love of God poured out in our hearts as grounds for confident hope?" I suggest that this then raises expectations that what follows in verse 7 will complete the strengthening that γάρ in verse 6 has led addressees to expect.

Moving on to γάρ in verse 7a, I suggest that the connective reinforces the expectations of strengthening material that will give rise to adequate cognitive effects from verse 6 and, in its turn, verse 5, so that both become optimally relevant. Procedure G, triggered by γάρ in verse 7, identifies the statement in verse 6 as candidate for strengthening. Addressees' subpersonal comprehension processes attempt to read the statement following γάρ in verse 7a as a strengthening premise and to combine it with background assumptions in a logical series. But again, the establishment of a complete inferential series is problematic. I propose that something like the following contextual assumptions may be accessed:

P (v. 6): While we [Paul's addressees, believers] were still helpless/weak, at that time Christ died for the ungodly [Paul's addressees, believers].

---

55. See Wolter, *Rechtfertigung und Zukünftiges Heil*, 171, and Barclay's use of the term "incongruous" (Barclay, *Paul and the Gift*, 490).

56. See 7:15a and 14:7 for similar examples where a subsequent γάρ clause is needed in order to complete the strengthening and achieve relevance.

Q introduced by γάρ (v. 7a): Someone will scarcely die for a righteous person.[57]
IA1: A righteous person has merit and honor, but the antithesis, an ungodly person, has no merit or honor. (Accessible from 2:7 and 2:10 and inferable from knowledge of Jewish teaching and of Greco-Roman cultural norms.)[58]
IA2: If someone will scarcely die even for a righteous person, then it is unheard of/incongruous/shocking that someone will die for an ungodly person.[59] (Inferable from common sense and knowledge of Jewish teaching and Greco-Roman norms.)[60]

Although it is possible to draw certain inferences in the direction of a strengthening relation between verse 6 and verse 7a, a logical gap remains and a complete inferential series cannot be established without unreasonable processing effort. As a result, verse 7a, verse 6, and verse 5 are all not yet optimally relevant. Moreover, the claim in verse 7a itself potentially raises further questions, for example, "Is it true that someone will scarcely die for a righteous person?" or, "Is it not well known that someone may sometimes die for a righteous person?"[61] As a result, the statement in verse 7a may not initially be accepted as valid. In short, the clause introduced by γάρ in verse 7a does not yet satisfy expectations of relevance as strengthening material. Consequently, I suggest that there is a heightened

---

57. See, e.g., Cranfield, *Epistle to the Romans*, 256; Jewett, *Romans*, 344. The term μόλις can also be read as "rarely" (Dunn, *Romans 1–8*, 245) or "hardly" (Stuhlmacher, *Paul's Letter to the Romans*, 78).
58. Gathercole argues that in Greco-Roman culture it would be "unthinkable to lay down one's life for the impious," who "endanger the gods' approval of the nation." Simon Gathercole, *Defending Substitution: An Essay on Atonement in Paul* (Grand Rapids: Baker Academic, 2015), 105.
59. See Dunn, *Romans 1–8*, 255.
60. Wolter sees the LXX version of Prov 11:31 providing a background to Paul's thought here: εἰ ὁ μὲν δίκαιος μόλις σώζεται, ὁ ἀσεβὴς καὶ ἁμαρτωλὸς που φανεῖται; (Wolter, *Rechtfertigung und Zukünftiges Heil*, 172).
61. Wolter notes that the Hellenistic idea of dying for a beloved friend, family member, or native country, may provide a background to v. 7b (Wolter, *Rechtfertigung und Zukünftiges Heil*, 171–72). If so, it may raise implicit questions about the claim in v. 7a. Gathercole discusses examples of vicarious deaths in the classical tradition, which provide a background here (Gathercole, *Defending Substitution*, 90–103).

expectation that further strengthening material in the form of an explanation will follow.

The example of γάρ that introduces verse 7b seems to confirm this expectation. Procedure G is triggered and verse 7b is processed as a strengthening premise, identifying the immediately preceding claim in verse 7a as the candidate for strengthening. I suggest that the following strengthening series may be constructed:

P (v. 7a): Someone will scarcely die for a righteous person.
Implicit question raised by P: Is it true that someone will scarcely die for a righteous person?
Q introduced by γάρ (v. 7b): Someone may possibly indeed dare to die for a good person.
IA1: *Good person* and *righteous person* are roughly synonymous.[62] (Inferable from encyclopedic knowledge and from the cotext of verse 6.)
IA2: If someone may possibly dare to die for a good person, then with daring and courage a person will sometimes die for a good person.[63]
IA3: If with daring and courage someone will indeed sometimes die for a good person, then it is possible, even if difficult and exceptional, to die for a good/righteous person.

---

62. In the cotext, both are in basic antithesis with ἀσεβῶν in v. 6. Wolter asserts that in contemporary literature there is no evidence of the "good" person being valued more highly than the "just" person; instead, the two terms complete each other (Wolter, *Rechtfertigung und Zukünftiges Heil*, 174). See also Jewett, *Romans*, 360; Gathercole, *Defending Substitution*, 89. Jewett, however, notes that, "many efforts have been made to distinguish between [δικαίου and τοῦ ἀγαθοῦ] so as to rescue some semblance of logical development." Some read τοῦ ἀγαθοῦ as referring to the category of the truly good person (e.g., Barrett, *Epistle to the Romans*, 106) or to a person's "benefactor" (e.g., Cranfield, *Epistle to the Romans*, 264). Wolter himself interprets τοῦ ἀγαθοῦ as a neuter noun, meaning "the (public) good," to salvage the logic of v. 7b (Wolter, *Rechtfertigung und Zukünftiges Heil*, 175). But a procedural reading of γάρ allows us to read both δικαίου and τοῦ ἀγαθοῦ as masculine without interpreting them in contrast with each other.

63. Wolter argues that in Hellenistic culture there is a widespread association between the concepts τολμᾶν and ἀποθνήσκειν ὑπέρ. Together they highlight the idea of dying for another person, one's country, or for an ideal, as very exceptional, and proof of great courage (Wolter, *Röm 1–8*, 331; Wolter, *Rechtfertigung und Zukünftiges Heil*, 172).

IA4: If it is possible, even if difficult and exceptional, to die for a righteous person, then someone will indeed on rare occasions die for a righteous person.

C (confirming a modified understanding of verse 7a that communicates that dying for a righteous person is possible but exceptional):[64] Someone will on rare occasions die for a righteous person.

As a result of this inferential series, the statement in verse 7a is strengthened. The strengthening procedure draws in extra contextual assumptions that answer implicit objections by making connections with addressees' existing background knowledge, helping to convince addressees of the validity of verse 7a. In this particular case, we might say that the strengthening procedure is relevant as an adjustment to addressees' previous understanding of verse 7a.[65] It increases the comprehensibility of verse 7b in the cotext by underlining the fact that the death of someone for a righteous person is both exceptional and possible. This strengthening account is able to accommodate commentators' readings of verse 7b as a correction or clarification of verse 7a, or indeed as parenthetical. In all these cases, the material introduced by γάρ in verse 7b achieves relevance in relation to verse 7a, which it strengthens.

Although the inferential series triggered by γάρ in verse 7b leads to the strengthening of verse 7a, this does not in turn clarify the strengthening relationship between verse 7a and verse 6, nor between verse 6 and verse 5. For the moment, the coherence of these verses remains opaque, and expectations raised by γάρ in verse 6 and verse 7a that the preceding claims will be strengthened are not yet satisfied. Moving on to verse 8, however, the connective δέ, in conjunction with the content of verse 8, guides addressees to infer that verse 8 as a whole is to be processed as the second half of the antithetical pair of statements begun in verse 7a: "Someone will scarcely and very exceptionally die for a righteous person (v. 7a),

---

64. This reading fits with Keck's explanation that v. 7b paraphrases the point of v. 7a, expressing "in a more positive way the point of μόλις in v. 7a. The couplet acknowledges that voluntary death for the sake of someone/something worthy is possible, though rare" (Keck, "Post-Pauline Interpretation," 243). This makes good sense of the sequence of v. 7a and v. 7b without requiring us to follow Keck's view of vv. 6–7 as an interpolation.

65. See Wolter, *Röm 1–8*, 330: "Mit v. 7b will Paul den in v. 7a ausgesprochenen Gedanken nicht korrigieren, sondern … zuspitzen."

but (God demonstrates his own love toward us in that) Christ died for us while we were still sinners." Thus verse 8b completes the antithesis begun in verse 7a, while verse 8a makes explicit the implication to be drawn from Christ's death in terms of God's love. This goes some way to answering the implicit question raised by verse 6: "What does Christ's death for us the ungodly have to do with the love of God poured out in our hearts as grounds for confident hope?" I suggest that verse 8 triggers the following inferences in relation to verse 6, or something similar:

> **P for strengthening** (v. 6): While we [believers] were still weak/helpless, Christ at that time died for the ungodly.
> **Q introduced by γάρ** (vv. 7–8, disambiguated): Someone will scarcely and very exceptionally die for a righteous person, but God demonstrates his love for us [Paul's addressees, believers] in that Christ died for us while we were still sinners.
> **IA**: If someone will scarcely and very exceptionally die for a righteous person, but God demonstrates his love for believers in that Christ died for believers while believers were still sinners, then Christ's death for believers, at the time we were weak/helpless as ungodly sinners, demonstrates God's exceptionally great love for us.
> **C** (strengthening verse 6 by increasing its cognitive effects): Christ's death for us ungodly believers, at the time we were weak/helpless, demonstrates God's exceptionally great love for us.

This new inference drawn from verse 6 is then taken as input into a strengthening series that results in the strengthening of verse 5:

> **Complex P for strengthening** (v. 5): This hope does not put us [Paul's addressees, believers] to shame, in that the love of God has been poured into our hearts by means of the Holy Spirit given to us.
> **Implicit question raised by verse 5**: How does God's love poured out in our hearts by the Holy Spirit provide grounds for confidence that this hope (in the glory of God) will not disappoint believers?
> **Q** (inferred from strengthened version of verse 6): Christ's death for us ungodly believers, at the time we were weak/helpless, demonstrates God's exceptional love for us.
> **IA**: If Christ's death for ungodly believers at the time we were weak/helpless demonstrates the exceptionally great nature of God's love for us, then the fact that this exceptionally great love of God has been

4. What Kind of Strengthening? Problematic Examples 141

poured out into the hearts of believers by means of the eschatological Holy Spirit is grounds for confident boasting in the eschatological hope of the glory of God, which will not put believers to shame.[66]

C (strengthening verse 5): This eschatological hope will not put us believers to shame, because the exceptionally great love of God for us who were weak/helpless and ungodly has been poured out in our hearts by means of the eschatological Holy Spirit given to us.

As a result of the strengthening of verse 6, made possible by the completion in verse 8 of the thought begun in verse 7, the claims of verse 5 are also strengthened, answering the implicit questions raised by them. Consequently, verse 5 is likewise adhered to more strongly by addressees and achieves optimal relevance. The overall effect of the series of strengthening γάρ clauses in verses 6–8 is to increase the argumentative salience of the claims in verse 5, to which it leads back. This fits with the analysis of various scholars that the theme of the whole of verses 5–10, and indeed of verses 1–11, is eschatological hope. The outcome of this backward strengthening series accommodates both the view that verses 6–8 further explain God's love, and the view that verses 6–8 further explain the eschatological hope referred to in verse 5a. Because it is the love of God poured out in the heart of believers by the Spirit that provides grounds for the confident hope, the further explanation of the love of God in verses 6–8 ultimately leads to an increased understanding of the hope. We see here how the strengthening procedure triggered by a chain of γάρ clauses contributes to the coherence of the subsection, making the theme of hope highly salient as a lynchpin for the whole of 5:1–11 (cf. 5:2, 4, 9, 10, etc.).

I suggest that, because of the core strengthening guidance that γάρ gives, the chain of occurrences in verses 6–7 creates an impression of strengthening or supporting material that backs up what precedes in verse 5. For addressees for whom Paul's claims do not raise substantial questions or objections, expectations of relevance may be satisfied by this impression of support, without the extra effort of constructing several inferential strengthening series in order to find logical confirmation for the claims in verses 5–7. This impression of strengthening is sufficient to increase their adherence to the claims communicated. Thus, for some addressees,

---

66. Cf. Wolter's explanation of the relationship between God's love shown in Christ's death, God's love poured out by the Spirit in believers' hearts, and eschatological hope (Wolter, *Rechtfertigung und Zukünftiges Heil*, 159–76).

expectations of relevance may be achieved here by rhetorical strengthening (for clearer examples of rhetorical strengthening, see §§4.4, 4.5, and 4.6, below). For those, on the other hand, who may find Paul's claims perplexing or controversial, the instances of γάρ in these verses will trigger the search for complete logical strengthening series. This requires more processing effort but results in the full set of strengthening inferences being relevant as a rational confirmation or explanation.

In sum, the three occurrences of γάρ in 5:6–7 can all be explained in terms of the core function of guidance toward backward strengthening. These occurrences are atypical and, according to our classification, problematic. The examples in verse 6 and verse 7a do not achieve strengthening on their own but need to be completed by verse 7a and verse 8. The occurrence in verse 7b, meanwhile, is unusual in that it introduces material that has the effect of clarifying addressees' understanding by adjusting the focus of the claim in verse 7a. Moreover, this adjustment is inserted in the middle of the strengthening antithetical pair of statements in verse 7a and verse 8b, delaying the completion of the strengthening begun in verse 7a. Nevertheless, a procedural strengthening account within a relevance-theoretic framework accounts for them all.

We should note that the material that γάρ introduces in these verses represents information that is already familiar to Paul's audience, both from commonplaces or accepted truths and from the preceding cotext of the epistle. Various previously communicated assumptions are reactivated by verse 6 and by the search for a strengthening relationship between verse 6 and verse 5 and the preceding cotext. For instance, the concept ἀσεβῶν in verse 6 recalls the argument of 4:5, with its reference to the one who justifies the ungodly. In conjunction with this, the vocabulary of hope and of glory reactivates assumptions also communicated in chapter 4 regarding Abraham, who hoped against hope (4:18) and trusted in God, giving glory to him (4:20). Verse 6 also reactivates the assumption that Christ was handed over to death for the transgressions of believers (who are ungodly like Abraham: 4:25). Meanwhile the concept in verse 8 of Christ's death for sinners reactivates the thought of 3:21–26. Thus information introduced by γάρ consolidates the coherence of the wider cotext by the (re)activation of highly accessible contextual assumptions, which has the effect of reminding addressees of, and reinforcing, previous points made. I suggest that the backward strengthening procedure triggered by γάρ and the search for relevant contextual assumptions contributes further to this reactivation.

4.3. Romans 9:11–12: Complex Syntax

9:10: οὐ μόνον δέ, ἀλλὰ καὶ Ῥεβέκκα ἐξ ἑνὸς κοίτην ἔχουσα, Ἰσαὰκ τοῦ πατρὸς ἡμῶν·
9:11a: μήπω γὰρ γεννηθέντων μηδὲ πραξάντων τι ἀγαθὸν ἢ φαῦλον,
9:11b: ἵνα ἡ κατ' ἐκλογὴν πρόθεσις τοῦ θεοῦ μένῃ,
9:12a: οὐκ ἐξ ἔργων ἀλλ' ἐκ τοῦ καλοῦντος,
9:12b: ἐρρέθη αὐτῇ ὅτι Ὁ μείζων δουλεύσει τῷ ἐλάσσονι,
9:13: καθὼς γέγραπται, Τὸν Ἰακὼβ ἠγάπησα, τὸν δὲ Ἠσαῦ ἐμίσησα.

The occurrence of γάρ in 9:11 is problematic because of the syntactical complexities of the thought in 9:10–12. Commentators are divided as to the main verb of these verses. The unusual order in which the information is presented in this sentence also complicates matters, with a purpose clause intervening in verse 11b before the completion of the summary of the narrative events (which begins in verse 10 but finishes only in verse 12). As a result, it is not easy to trace an obvious supporting relationship between the material introduced by γάρ and what precedes it. Commentators disagree in their analysis of the connection indicated.

4.3.1. Cotext

This example occurs toward the beginning of the sustained argumentation of chapters 9–11, the third major section of the epistle. After a very personal expression of sorrow over ethnic Israel's current situation in relation to the gospel (9:1–5), in 9:6 Paul begins a fresh line of argument with the statement, "It is not as though the word of God has failed." This claim, which can be seen as a negative response to the question implicitly raised by chapters 1–8, "Has God been unfaithful to his promises to Israel?," drives the argument of chapters 9–11.[67] In 9:6–29, using scriptural examples and citations, Paul emphasizes God's sovereignty and freedom in election, demonstrating how God's choice and call is not based on human criteria or worth.[68] The material in 9:6–29 is a complex

---

67. Barclay describes the claim in 9:6a as a "headline statement" for 9:6–29 (Barclay, *Paul and the Gift*, 526).
68. See Barclay, *Paul and the Gift*, 531–36.

interweaving of narrative sequence, midrashic exposition, and diatribal elements.[69]

In 9:6–13 Paul presents two scriptural examples of election from the point of view of the matriarchs involved: Sarah, mother of Isaac (vv. 7–9), and Rebekah, mother of Jacob (vv. 10–12). In the first example, God's promise made regarding Isaac (vv. 8–9) is highlighted as the decisive guarantee of election. In verse 10, Paul moves on to the second case, which is introduced by οὐ μόνον δέ, ἀλλὰ καί, indicating that a similar point is to be made about Rebekah as was made about Sarah.[70] The problematic syntax in this verse leads to various readings. Some argue that the verb is elliptical, and that a verbal phrase or verb must be supplied in verse 10, for instance, "[There is] also [the case of] Rebekah," or, drawing an inference from the point made about Sarah in verse 9, "Rebekah also [received a promise.]."[71] This latter reading helps to highlight the fact that the citation in verse 12 represents the promise made to Rebekah regarding Jacob. Others read the passive ἐρρέθη in verse 12b as the independent verb upon which the rest of the long sentence in verses 10–12 depends.[72] The idiom ἐξ ἑνὸς κοίτην ἔχουσα can be interpreted as, "as a result of intercourse with one man," or, alternatively, and more pertinently in the context, "as a result of one act of intercourse."[73] Either way, the implication is clear: Jacob and Esau had the same father and mother, and thus God's election of Jacob rather than Esau cannot be attributed to different parentage or different circumstances surrounding their conception (as might be possible in the case of Isaac's election).

---

69. See Jewett, *Romans*, 570–71, 581, 588; Käsemann, *An die Römer*, 255. Wright argues that Israel's "story of election" underlies chs. 9–11 and that Paul's telling of it in 9:6–29 would have been familiar to devout contemporary Jews (Wright, *Paul and the Faithfulness of God*, 1182–83). In contrast, Watson argues that in 9:6–29 Paul, while preserving the scriptural narrative sequence, engages in scriptural reinterpretation (Watson, *Paul, Judaism and the Gentiles*, 308–9).

70. Jewett, *Romans*, 577.

71. For the first option, see Cranfield, *Epistle to the Romans*, 470; see also, e.g., Lagrange, *Saint Paul, Épître aux Romains*, 230; Käsemann, *An die Römer*, 248. For the latter, see Watson, *Paul, Judaism and the Gentiles*, 577.

72. Barrett, *Epistle to the Romans*, 182; Wilckens, *Der Brief an die Römer*, 2:194.

73. For the first option, see, e.g., Jewett, *Romans*, 570. For the second, see Dunn, *Romans 9–16*, 538; Moo, *Epistle to the Romans*, 579.

4.3.2. Analysis of γάρ

Various scholars interpret γάρ in verse 11 as marking a connection with an unexpressed thought. For Dunn, the connective indicates that "Paul's thought is fuller than has so far been expressed," confirming that what follows in verses 11–12a is a "further but closely related point" that is "brought in as a kind of parenthesis."[74] Cranfield, too, suggests that γάρ indicates a connection with an implicit thought, which consists in the recognition that the example of Rebekah demonstrates a fresh characteristic of divine election, namely, independence from all human merit. On Cranfield's reading, it is this unexpressed thought that forms a kind of parenthesis, continued and explained in verses 11–13.[75]

We can explain γάρ in verse 11 as a procedural indicator as follows. Verse 10 is disambiguated by addressees to fill in the ellipsis thus: "Not only this, but Rebekah, who conceived both her sons at one time by one man, our father Isaac, is also another case of God's election of the children of the promise." This disambiguated statement is not yet optimally relevant, however, because it raises an implicit question: in what way is Rebekah another example of God's election of the children of the promise? Consequently, the statement in verse 10 is identified as the candidate for strengthening. The material following γάρ in verses 11–12 is processed as a single complex of strengthening assumptions that forms a grammatical unit: the genitive absolute construction in verse 11, and the ἵνα clause that modifies it, are all dependent on ἐρρέθη. An inferential series is then constructed that increases the relevance of the statement in verse 10.

Much of the difficulty with this particular case of γάρ lies in the unusual order of the strengthening information it introduces. We might expect the independent verb ἐρρέθη, and the citation from Gen 25:23, to follow γάρ immediately in verse 11a, since this is the minimum information needed for the establishment of a strengthening series that increases the relevance of verse 10. Verses 11b–12a communicate additional background assumptions that are not strictly necessary for the completion of this logical series but that instead represent further explanation and theological grounding

---

74. Dunn, *Romans 9–16*, 542, 538. Wilckens and Käsemann do not comment on γάρ, regarding vv. 11–12a as a parenthesis following on from the anacoluthon in v. 10, before the grammatical subject of v. 10 is picked up again, in the dative, in v. 12b (Wilckens, *Der Brief an die Römer*, 2:194; Käsemann, *An die Römer*, 251).

75. Cranfield, *Epistle to the Romans*, 477.

for the example of Rebekah.[76] In the inferential series below, I have put these additional assumptions in brackets.

We can suggest a strengthening inferential series along the following lines:

P (v. 10, disambiguated): Rebekah, who conceived [both her sons] at one time by one man, our father Isaac, is another case of God's election of the children of promise.

Q introduced by γάρ (vv. 11–12b, disambiguated): It was said to Rebekah, "The older will serve the younger," when the sons were not yet born and had not yet done anything good or bad, so that God's purposes in election might stand, based not on works but on him who calls.

IA1: "The older will serve the younger" was a promise made by God to Rebekah about her twin sons Esau and Jacob before their birth. (Inferable from encyclopedic knowledge of Jewish scripture.)

IA2: The promise "The older will serve the younger" is evidence that the younger, Jacob, was chosen before birth by God, not the older, Esau. (Inferable from knowledge of Jewish teaching and from the previous cotext.)

IA3: The promise "The older will serve the younger" is evidence that Jacob, who was chosen by God before his birth, is one of the children of the promise.

IA4: If Jacob, the younger, was chosen by God before birth when the twins had not yet done anything good or bad, then this is evidence that God's election is based not on human birth or merit but on God's purpose, promise, and call. (Inferable from the previous cotext, and from verses 11b–12a.)

(Additional implication IA5 inferable from verses 11b–12a: If God's election is not based on human birth or merit, and his purposes in election are fulfilled in choosing Jacob, then God's election depends on God's sovereign will.)

IA6: Since there is evidence that Jacob was chosen by God not because of human birth or merit but because of God's promise and call, so that God's purposes in election might stand, based not on works but on

---

76. These additional assumptions are, of course, of considerable theological import: see discussion below.

him who calls, then the case of Rebekah and her sons is an example of God's election of the children of the promise.
C (strengthening verse 10): Rebekah who conceived both her sons at one time from one man, our father Isaac, is also another case of God's election of the children of promise.

As a result of this strengthening series, the implicit question raised by verse 10 is answered, and the statement in verse 10 becomes more comprehensible. The material introduced by γάρ in verses 11-12 is relevant in relation to verse 10, which it helps to explain further, rather than giving rise to fresh cognitive effects in its own right. The information introduced by ἵνα in verse 11b-12a represents additional assumptions that make explicit the theological import of the example. These additional assumptions ultimately contribute to the increased argumentative salience of the statement in verse 10 by connecting this example with a theological framework, thus bolstering and underlining this second example of God's election as a main point in Paul's argument. The sandwiching of these additional assumptions between the statement of verse 10 and the main supporting statement in verse 12b makes sense of the fact that various scholars interpret verses 11-12a as parenthetical.

In this way, a relevance-theoretic, procedural explanation is able to account for γάρ in 9:11, as for other occurrences, in terms of the core function of guidance toward strengthening. Although elliptical thought and complex syntax make the strengthening relationship with preceding material relatively complex to trace here, γάρ nevertheless gives instructions to treat what follows as strengthening premises, which are to be processed in an inferential series involving background assumptions. In this instance, the strengthening procedure is most likely to work itself out as an explanation of the statement in verse 10. The material introduced by γάρ includes within it theological statements (vv. 11b-12a) which, while weighty, serve as background or supporting information for the strengthened preceding point, namely, that the promise made to Rebekah represents a second example of God's sovereign election of the children of the promise.[77]

---

77. *Pace* Wright, who argues that "the weight of the short paragraph" lies in vv. 11b-12a, despite their apparently parenthetical character (Wright, "Romans," 637), and Käsemann (*An die Römer*, 251-52).

The strengthening material introduced by γάρ in verses 11–12b is followed in verse 13 by a further scriptural citation from Mal 1:2. Although this is not introduced by γάρ, it can be read as introducing additional scriptural proof that further bolsters the strengthening explanation found in verses 11–12, increasing its cognitive effects. The overall effect of verse 13, following verses 11–12, is to contribute to the highlighting of the case of Rebekah as a second example of the nature of election, which is based on God's will and not human criteria.[78] The citation shows that the example of Rebekah, like that of Sarah in verses 7–9, has all the authority of scripture behind it. Both examples ultimately serve as supporting evidence for Paul's statement in verse 6b: "Not all who are descended from Israel are Israel." This statement, introduced by γάρ, in turn confirms and clarifies the main claim of the subsection in verse 6a, namely, that God's promises in election are reliable, despite ethnic Israel's current rejection of the gospel.[79] Thus the strengthening effect leads all the way back, via γάρ clauses in verses 6b, 9, and 11, to the statement in verse 6a, which is underlined as highly salient in the argument. Once again, we see that the strengthening triggered by γάρ consolidates the coherence of the subsection.

4.4. Romans 7:1: An Aside

7:1a: Ἢ ἀγνοεῖτε, ἀδελφοί,
7:1b: γινώσκουσιν γὰρ νόμον λαλῶ,
7:1c: ὅτι ὁ νόμος κυριεύει τοῦ ἀνθρώπου ἐφ' ὅσον χρόνον ζῇ;

Most scholars do not comment on this instance of γάρ, apparently reading it as introducing a parenthetical comment that interrupts the rhetorical question expressed in this verse. The parenthetical nature of the comment is clear from the syntax without γάρ, however, since the remark of verse 1b is embedded within the question, which is completed by the ὅτι clause in verse 1c. Thus the function of γάρ cannot simply be to introduce a parenthesis. This occurrence is potentially problematic, however, from the point of view of a procedural account. At first glance, it does not seem possible to identify a strengthening relationship between the statement introduced

---

78. This challenges Dunn's interpretation of v. 13 as the "proof text" that is the "final clincher in the argument," carrying more argumentative weight than the Genesis citation in v. 12b (Dunn, *Romans 9–16*, 544).

79. See Jewett, *Romans*, 580.

by γάρ in verse 1b and preceding communicated assumptions. Instead, the material introduced by γάρ appears to support what follows, that is, the completion, in 7:1c, of the rhetorical question. Can this occurrence be accommodated within a procedural account?

4.4.1. Cotext

As noted under §3.3.1, above, 7:1-6 is recognized by a majority of scholars as a continuation of the discussion of chapter 6. The metaphor of lordship, which runs throughout chapter 6 and is picked up in 7:1 (κυριεύω), helps to highlight the continuity between chapters 6 and 7. Some scholars see a close association between the statement in 6:14 that believers are not under law but under grace, and 7:1-6, which develops or elucidates this.[80] At the same time, as Dunn argues, a "new phase" in Paul's argument begins with 7:1, in which the subject of the Jewish law takes center stage.[81]

The rhetorical question in 7:1 begins with a direct address to Paul's audience, Ἦ ἀγνοεῖτε, ἀδελφοί. The formula ἦ ἀγνοεῖτε is typical of a diatribal style and communicates the assumption that Paul's addressees know what he is about to assert: it represents common knowledge for them.[82] The term of address ἀδελφοί implies a relationship of trust between communicator and addressees. The rhetorical question form underlines that the principle that is articulated in 7:1c is indisputable, namely, that the law only has authority over a person as long as that person is alive. It thus communicates an attitude of conviction on the part of the author, lending particular force to what is asserted by the implied answer, and has a persuasive goal.[83] We can disambiguate the interrogative form in propositional form as follows: "You are certainly not ignorant that (i.e., surely you know very well that) the law has authority over a person only as long as that person is alive."

---

80. E.g., Jewett, *Romans*, 428; Cranfield, *Epistle to the Romans*, 331.

81. Dunn, *Romans 1–8*, 367. There is disagreement as to whether νόμος in 7:1b-c refers to the Jewish law (Dunn, *Romans 1–8*, 359; Jewett, *Romans*, 430–31; Wilckens, *Der Brief an die Römer*, 2:66), or to a more general law (Wolter, *Röm 1–8*, 410; Käsemann, *An die Römer*, 177), or Roman law (Jülicher, "Der Brief an die Römer," 269). Given the wider cotext, the former seems most likely: the torah has been hitherto "the exclusive reference of ... [νόμος]" (Dunn, *Romans 1–8*, 368).

82. Wolter, *Röm 1–8*, 409; Jewett, *Romans*, 430; Cranfield, *Epistle to the Romans*, 332.

83. As Jewett notes, "the rhetorical question is intended to elicit the answer, 'Of course!'" (Jewett, *Romans*, 430).

4.4.2. Analysis of γάρ

In 7:1b Paul interrupts his rhetorical question with a statement, introduced by γάρ, that makes explicit that he is speaking to people who know the Jewish law. Jewett suggests that γάρ here introduces a "specification of the audience as adept in the law."[84] Käsemann, meanwhile, maintains that γάρ here does not so much indicate a rationale, as simply introduce what follows in 7:1c.[85] This observation points to the atypical character of this occurrence, which parallels certain examples of the connective in Classical Greek, sometimes categorized as "anticipatory."[86] The fact that the γάρ clause interrupts an incomplete communicated thought, which is then finished in 7:1c, suggests that Paul may be anticipating a possible objection on the part of his addressees and wants to preempt this by responding to it before addressees have a chance to formulate it. In this case, γάρ may here provide advance guidance that the premise it introduces contributes to the increased relevance of assumptions that have yet to be communicated in full.

I propose the following procedural account of this occurrence. The connective in verse 1b triggers procedure G. The incomplete clause in verse 1a is identified as the only possible candidate for strengthening. Despite the fact that the content of the principle that Paul assumes that his audience knows has not yet been articulated, it is possible to construct an inferential series on the basis of the fragmentary linguistic clues given by Ἢ ἀγνοεῖτε in verse 1a. I suggest that, because of the grammatically incomplete nature of verse 1a and the fact that it is interrupted, it is inferred that the γάρ clause is relevant in relation to the completed claim toward which verse 1a points. We can suggest the following inferential series:

P (v. 1a, disambiguated propositional form): You [Paul's Romans addressees] know the following information very well.

---

84. Jewett, *Romans*, 429.

85. "Das γάρ begründet nicht so sehr, wie es einleitet" (Käsemann, *An die Römer*, 177).

86. Denniston describes this anticipatory use: "Here the γάρ clause, instead of following the clause which it explains, precedes it, or is inserted parenthetically within it … the early position of the γάρ clause is to be explained … on stylistic and rhetorical grounds" (Denniston, *Greek Particles*, 68).

4. What Kind of Strengthening? Problematic Examples   151

Q introduced by γάρ (v. 1b): I [Paul] am speaking to those who know the Jewish law.
IA: If Paul is speaking to those who know the Jewish law, then Paul's addressees know the following information very well from their knowledge of the Jewish law.
C (confirming verse 1a): Paul's addressees know the following information very well.

As a result of this series, the claim is strengthened that Paul's addressees know the information (the principle) communicated in verse 1c, with the result that potential objections are dealt with. As a consequence, addressees are, I suggest, more disposed to accept this claim about their knowledge as valid even before hearing the content of the information in question. Thus the statement introduced by γάρ in verse 1b is relevant in relation to verse 1a and 1c combined, strengthening the claim made in verse 1a and c together, increasing the cognitive effects that arise from it, and underlining its salience. Once the information in verse 1c is also communicated, the details of the claim of verse 1a and c are accepted firmly by addressees as valid, since the claim is backed up by the appeal in verse 1b to their knowledge of the Jewish law. The statement in verse 1b, an assumption already accepted by addressees, serves as supporting or background information. In this instance, the strengthening procedure triggered by γάρ is most likely to be relevant as confirming proof that convinces addressees of the validity of a claim. Both the fact that the strengthening premise is embedded in the middle of the claim it strengthens and the fact that this premise consists of metatextual information about the addressees themselves lead to the perception that the strengthening information is parenthetical.[87]

The unusual positioning of this γάρ clause before the completion of the claim that it strengthens can be attributed to rhetorical or persuasive goals, as Denniston suggests.[88] The statement in verse 1b is not essential for comprehension of the rhetorical question and could equally well have been communicated at the end of 7:1c. The insertion of this γάρ clause in the middle of the main claim of verse 1 creates extra processing effort. Given that optimal relevance consists of a balance between cognitive effects and processing effort, the extra processing effort involved here

---

87. Metatextual information is representation that represents another representation; for a fuller description, see glossary.
88. Denniston, *Greek Particles*, 68.

must be offset by extra cognitive effects in order for this γάρ clause to be relevant as a strengthening premise. I propose that Paul's swift countering of a potential objection to his claim in verse 1 before this claim has even been fully articulated creates an impression of unassailable logic and deft argumentative skills. This gives rise to extra effects in the form of trust in Paul's reliability and skill as a teacher and orator, able to formulate a well-crafted logical argument and deal with objections. This parenthetical comment can thus be explained as a rapid and rhetorically strategic afterthought that contributes to the persuasiveness of the argument and counters epistemic vigilance targeting both the reliability of the communicator and the coherence of the argument.[89] In addition, the γάρ clause may have the extra rhetorical effect of winning over the audience by praise, by drawing attention to the fact that they are not ignorant with regard to the Jewish faith and law.[90]

It is the content and the positioning of this γάρ clause that achieves these extra rhetorical effects rather than γάρ itself. The connective, meanwhile, as in other more typical instances, gives procedural instructions toward strengthening, constraining the potential range of inferences that might be drawn from the information in verse 1b, thus reducing processing effort. Its core procedural function is the same as with all the other occurrences examined. In addition to this, however, its core strengthening function is exploited to create a secondary rhetorical effect, by means of the strategic placement of the γάρ clause. Thus a relevance-theoretic framework enables us both to make sense of γάρ here in terms of core strengthening guidance and to explain its unusual character in terms of extra cognitive effects.

We can conclude, then, that this atypical example involves a combination of logical strengthening and rhetorical strengthening effect. Inferential strengthening is achieved, and a logical series constructed, despite the fact that the assumptions strengthened are only partially communicated prior to the strengthening premise and do not achieve their relevance as strengthened assumptions until they are fully communicated in verse 1c.[91]

---

89. Epistemic vigilance is a cognitive capacity, posited by cognitive scientists and assumed by relevance theory, that evaluates the reliability of a piece of communication in terms of rational coherence, and trustworthiness of source. See glossary.

90. Wolter reads v. 1b as a *captatio benevolentiae* that flatters addressees, strengthening the impact of the rhetorical question (Wolter, *Röm 1–8*, 409–10).

91. Blass's phrase "backward strengthening" may not be entirely appropriate here,

As with other occurrences, the information introduced by γάρ is relevant in relation to other, more salient, communicated assumptions and can be viewed as background or supporting information, rather than giving rise to new argumentative implications in its own right. This makes sense of scholars' intuition that the information in verse 1b is parenthetical. The fact that the γάρ clause interrupts the assumptions it strengthens, and is, as a result, bracketed by them, is to be attributed to the rhetorical goal of creating an impression of convincing argumentation.

4.5. Romans 6:19–20: A Supporting Exhortation?

6:17:   χάρις δὲ τῷ θεῷ ὅτι ἦτε δοῦλοι τῆς ἁμαρτίας ὑπηκούσατε δὲ ἐκ καρδίας εἰς ὃν παρεδόθητε τύπον διδαχῆς,
6:18a: ἐλευθερωθέντες δὲ ἀπὸ τῆς ἁμαρτίας
6:18b: ἐδουλώθητε τῇ δικαιοσύνῃ
6:19a: ἀνθρώπινον λέγω διὰ τὴν ἀσθένειαν τῆς σαρκὸς ὑμῶν.
6:19b: ὥσπερ γὰρ παρεστήσατε τὰ μέλη ὑμῶν δοῦλα τῇ ἀκαθαρσίᾳ καὶ τῇ ἀνομίᾳ εἰς τὴν ἀνομίαν,
6:19c: οὕτως νῦν παραστήσατε τὰ μέλη ὑμῶν δοῦλα τῇ δικαιοσύνῃ εἰς ἁγιασμόν.
6:20a: ὅτε γὰρ δοῦλοι ἦτε τῆς ἁμαρτίας,
6:20b: ἐλεύθεροι ἦτε τῇ δικαιοσύνῃ.
6:21a: τίνα οὖν καρπὸν εἴχετε τότε;
6:21b: ἐφ' οἷς νῦν ἐπαισχύνεσθε,
6:21c: τὸ γὰρ τέλος ἐκείνων θάνατος.
6:22a: νυνὶ δὲ ἐλευθερωθέντες ἀπὸ τῆς ἁμαρτίας δουλωθέντες δὲ τῷ θεῷ ἔχετε τὸν καρπὸν ὑμῶν εἰς ἁγιασμόν,
6:22b: τὸ δὲ τέλος ζωὴν αἰώνιον.

The two occurrences of γάρ in 6:19b and 6:20a can be regarded as problematic examples for several reasons. With regard to verse 19b, there is disagreement among scholars regarding the relationship between the aside in verse 19a and the immediately preceding and subsequent cotext. It is difficult to identify an obvious logical strengthening relationship between the material following γάρ in verse 19b-c and preceding assumptions.

---

though the kernel of the assumption to be strengthened has in fact already been communicated in v. 7:1a.

In addition, the main verb of the complex of assumptions introduced by γάρ in verse 19b is an imperative, παραστήσατε (v. 19c). This is unusual: a γάρ clause usually consists of a statement, often representing familiar or accepted information, as we have seen. Third, the cotext (6:15–23) achieves its persuasive effect not by tight logical argumentation consisting of claims and supporting evidence, but rather by the use of rhetorical devices, in particular, repetition and extended metaphor. We should be alert to the possibility that the primarily rhetorical rather than logical character of the argumentation in 6:15–23 may have an influence on the use of the connective here. With regard to γάρ in verse 20, meanwhile, there is a divergence of opinion concerning the relation of the statement in verse 20 with what precedes and regarding the extent of the material introduced by the connective.

4.5.1. Cotext

As part of the epistle's second major section, Rom 6 discusses the implications for believers of the reign of grace, brought about by the obedience of Jesus Christ (5:12–21). There are obvious continuities between chapters 5 and 6. Both are dominated by the fundamental antithesis between the old life, or age, in Adam and the new life in Christ. Both, using the vocabulary of rule and mastery, characterize sin and death as powers that reign in opposition to the reign of God (expressed in terms of righteousness, grace, and life). But while 5:12–21 takes a bird's eye view of the broad sweep of the human story, focusing on Adam and Christ and the vastly asymmetrical effects of their contrasting acts for the whole of humanity, chapter 6 homes in on the present implications of this for believers. Both 5:12–21 and 6:15–23 make use of primarily rhetorical rather than closely reasoned logical argumentation in order to persuade addressees of the utter antithesis between the old age and the new.[92]

In 6:1–14 Paul discusses believers' identification with Christ's death and resurrection through baptism, and the implications for Christian living. Romans 6:12–14 contains antithetical exhortations to believers to

---

92. See Hellholm, "Enthymemic Argumentation in Paul," 178; Käsemann, *An die Römer*, 169–70. The subsection makes use of the rhetorical features of repetition, vivid metaphor, and antithetical parallelism, among others. Dunn refers to the "series of antitheses and balances" in 6:13–23 (Dunn, *Romans 1–8*, 335). See also Jewett, *Romans*, 414.

4. What Kind of Strengthening? Problematic Examples 155

present their bodies, not to their old master, sin, but to God, as instruments of righteousness. Some scholars regard the imperatives of verses 12-14 as the beginning of a fresh subsection, while others read them as the continuation of the previous pericope.[93] The diatribal style of 6:1-3, with its pattern of rhetorical questions followed by answers, is resumed in verse 15. Verses 15-23 are dominated by the antithesis between slavery to sin and slavery to righteousness.[94] This is initially stated in verse 15 in terms of existence, ὑπὸ νόμον versus ὑπὸ χάριν, and is emphasized rhetorically by the use of repetition and of antithetical paired statements (v. 18a/v. 18b, v. 19b/v. 19c, v. 20a/v. 20b, v. 20/v. 22a, v. 21c/v. 22b).

Verse 19a consists of a metatextual remark in which Paul comments on his use of the graphic metaphor of slavery. Various commentators interpret this comment as parenthetical but disagree as to whether the parenthesis looks backward or forward.[95] Douglas Moo argues that it is not necessary to choose between these two alternatives: since the metaphor of slavery is employed both in verse 18 and verse 19b–c, the comment in verse 19a can be read as a parenthetical explanation of Paul's use of the imagery of slavery in both.[96]

4.5.2. Analysis of γάρ

The occurrence of γάρ in 6:19b introduces a complex clause that is held together by the conjunctions ὥσπερ (v. 19b) and οὕτως (v. 19c) and continues to the end of verse 19c. This clause, which takes the form of an exhortation, expressed by παραστήσατε in verse 19c, communicates an antithetical comparison between believers' old way of life as slaves of sin and their new life as slaves of righteousness. It is, in effect, a restatement of the thought of verse 13. Most commentators make no comment on this occurrence. A number, however, read verses 19b–c as providing an expla-

---

93. Among those seeing it as a fresh section are, e.g., Dunn, *Romans 1-8*, 334; Käsemann, *An die Römer*, 151. Those viewing it as a continuation of the previous section are, e.g., Jewett, *Romans*, 413; Wright, "Romans," 536. Wright sees the parallel questions in v. 1 and v. 15 as structuring ch. 6.

94. Käsemann, *An die Römer*, 168-71.

95. E.g., Dunn, *Romans 1-8*, 354, and Cranfield, *Epistle to the Romans*, 325, in contrast to Barrett, *Epistle to the Romans*, 132, respectively.

96. Moo, *Epistle to the Romans*, 403. See also Wolter, *Röm 1-8*, 399.

nation for the statements in verses 17–18.[97] More specifically, Lagrange claims that verse 19b–c explains what slavery, or service, to justice means (v. 18).[98] In contrast, Jewett argues that verse 19b–c provides an explanation of why Paul must speak in "human terms" (v. 19a).[99] Barrett, meanwhile, translates γάρ as "the point of the matter is this," suggesting that what follows should be processed as a new or summarizing point.[100] The absence of logical development in the subsection has been noted and criticized by some, but as Käsemann points out, Paul is here concerned not so much with moving the argument forward, as with underlining and emphasizing, by means of various rhetorical devices, the dialectic that constantly demands an either-or from believers.[101]

I suggest that the guidance that γάρ gives here is affected by the rhetorical quality of the argumentation in this subsection. I propose that we can make sense of γάρ as a procedural indicator in the following way. On the basis of the grammar of verse 19b–c, the whole of this complex clause is processed as strengthening premises introduced by γάρ. But it does not seem possible (without unreasonable processing effort) to construct a strengthening inferential series between verse 19b–c and either the metatextual aside in verse 19a, or the statements of verse 18, or verse 17, as some propose. Instead, I propose that the strengthening guidance given by γάρ has a rhetorical rather than strictly inferential character. I suggest that addressees automatically associate a strengthening role with γάρ because of its core function in more logically argumentative contexts. Its presence thus automatically raises expectations that what follows it will be relevant as strengthening information. Given the primarily rhetorical rather than logical quality of the persuasion in this subsection, addressees' expectations of relevance are satisfied with the impression of strengthen-

---

97. E.g., Stuhlmacher, *Paul's Letter to the Romans*, 95 and Wright, who states: "it is not clear how much a command can actually explain something"; nevertheless, Paul "is explaining the balance of the two 'slaveries,' further unpacking the paradox of being 'liberated' into a different 'slavery'" (Wright, "Romans," 546).

98. Lagrange, *Saint Paul, Épître aux Romains*, 157.

99. Jewett, *Romans*, 420.

100. Barrett, *Epistle to the Romans*, 132. Barrett also notes, however: "This verse adds little fresh substance to what has already been said two or three times in this chapter."

101. Käsemann criticizes Jülicher's judgment that "nirgendwo im Briefe würden ohne erkennbaren Fortschritt des Gedankens so viel Worte um die gleiche Sache gemacht" (Käsemann, *An die Römer*, 169–70).

ing created by γάρ together with the rhetorical repetition of previously communicated assumptions. As a result, a full logical series that rationally confirms preceding assumptions is not constructed, since it is not necessary and would lead to undue processing effort.

Paul's metatextual comment in verse 19a suggests that he anticipates that his statements in verses 16–18 regarding slavery to righteousness may raise objections and need reinforcement in order to be optimally relevant. The material γάρ introduces in verses 19b–c is an exhortation that has already been communicated, and strengthened for optimal relevance, in verses 13–14. Addressees have therefore already accepted it firmly as valid. The exhortation in verse 19c, however, differs from verse 13b in one respect: the vocabulary of slavery, δοῦλα, is substituted for the vocabulary of tools or weapons, ὅπλα. I suggest that this unusual reuse and adaptation of an exhortation so that it functions as strengthening material introduced by γάρ, rather than as a main argumentative point, contributes to the persuasive effect. While using accepted assumptions from verse 13, it presents the metaphor of slavery, previously communicated in verses 16–18, in a new guise. This is presumably in order to persuade addressees of the validity of the metaphor. The combination in verse 19b–c of assumptions from verse 13 plus this metaphor of slavery, creates a convincing impression that the metaphor is a valid one. The main point of the assertions in verses 16–18 is to communicate, by means of this metaphor, the totality of the antithesis between the old life dominated by sin versus the new life dominated by righteousness. The strengthening complex introduced by γάρ in verse 19b–c thus serves as confirmation and reinforcement of this antithesis.

Although a detailed logical series is not constructed between verse 19b–c and verses 17–18, I suggest that inferences are nevertheless involved in the processing of verse 19b–c, along the following lines:

> **P** (vv. 17–18, summarized in propositional form): You [Paul's addressees] were slaves of sin, but you obeyed the pattern of teaching you were taught. Having been freed from sin, you were enslaved to righteousness.
> (**Implicit objection raised**: Is the metaphor of slavery an appropriate way to describe believers' experience?)
> **Q introduced by** γάρ (v. 19b–c): Just as once you [Paul's addressees] presented your members as slaves to uncleanness and lawlessness, in the same way now present your members as slaves of righteousness for sanctification.

IA1: "You were slaves of sin, but you obeyed the pattern of teaching you were taught. Having been freed from sin, you were enslaved to righteousness" means that addressees' past life, totally controlled by sin, and present life, totally controlled by righteousness, are two antithetical states.

IA2: "It is not desirable to present your members as slaves of unrighteousness, but it is desirable to present your members as slaves of righteousness for sanctification" are accepted assumptions (v. 13).

IA3: These accepted assumptions (v. 13) reinforce the claim in verses 17–18 that addressees' past life and addressees' present life are two antithetical states.

IA4: This accepted material supports the validity of the metaphor of slavery to describe Paul's addressees' experience.

C (confirming verses 17–18): Addressees' past and present lives are in total antithesis to each other, and the metaphor in verses 17–18 of slavery to different masters is a valid one to describe this experience.

As a result of such inferences, the metaphor of slavery applied to the experience of believers in verses 17–18 is validated. Addressees adhere more strongly to the claim that their experience can be described as slavery, and it becomes optimally relevant for them. The antithesis between the old life and the new life of believers is buttressed and highlighted and its argumentative salience heightened. The overall effect of the rhetorical display of strengthening created by γάρ in verse 19b, together with the repetition of familiar material in verses 19b–c, is to increase the cognitive effects derived from verses 17–18.

Thus the connective here contributes to a rhetorical display that emphasizes the complete antithesis between the old life and the new, which is sufficient in itself to satisfy expectations of relevance, without the construction of a complete logical strengthening series.[102] The acceptance of verse 19b–c as strengthening material nevertheless triggers inferences of its own. Thus even rhetorical strengthening involves the drawing of inferences.

Here, as elsewhere, γάρ can be said to give procedural guidance toward backward strengthening. The result of this strengthening seems relevant not so much as an explanation as some commentators suggest but

---

102. This is not dissimilar from examples in which γάρ introduces scriptural citations relevant as authoritative proof, where the supporting material is automatically accepted as backup for preceding claims without the construction of a full logical series.

4. What Kind of Strengthening? Problematic Examples 159

as backup for potentially controversial claims related to the metaphor of slavery. Since the overall point of the subsection is the rhetorical underscoring of a basic antithesis rather than a logical development in thought, addressees' expectations of relevance are satisfied by a general impression of strengthening or reinforcement. As with other examples, the connective in 6:19b gives guidance that limits processing costs by indicating that the information in verses 20–22 is to be taken as strengthening material rather than representing fresh implications. The guidance, however, leads to primarily rhetorical rather than logical strengthening, contributing to a strengthening display that underscores an emphatic contrast. Like 7:1b, then, the core strengthening function of γάρ in 6:19b interacts with, and is adapted to, the rhetorical quality of its cotext.

Moving on to 6:20, the statement introduced by γάρ is a virtual reverse mirror of verse 18 (repeated once more in verse 22a). There is a wide variety of opinion as to how to interpret γάρ and the relationship between what follows and the preceding cotext. The pair of temporal adverbs ὅτε (v. 20) and νυνί (v. 22a), as well as the mirroring in verse 22 of the vocabulary of verse 20, structures the thought of verses 20–22 as a single antithetical whole. This expresses again the dominating antithesis in terms of slavery to sin and slavery to righteousness. Wolter asserts that γάρ in verse 20 has simply a "connecting and continuative" function.[103] Cranfield takes verses 20–21 together, interpreting them as supporting and "reinforcing [the] urgency" of the command given in verse 19.[104] Wright reads γάρ as introducing verses 20–22, which provide a "yet further explanation."[105] Moo, meanwhile, suggests that the whole of verses 20–23 provides "the ground of the command in verse 19b."[106] Others, however, limit the supporting statement introduced by γάρ in verse 20a to verse 20 alone, since verse 21a is introduced by the connective οὖν.[107] Dunn reads verse 20 as a "more concise formulation" of verses 17–18 that "drives home the contrast" already stated; similarly, Käsemann interprets verse 20 as presenting the antithesis from the other side.[108]

---

103. Wolter, *Röm 1–8*, 401.
104. Cranfield, *Epistle to the Romans*, 327.
105. Wright, "Romans," 546.
106. Moo, *Epistle to the Romans*, 405.
107. Jewett, *Romans*, 421, citing Otto Kuss, *Der Römerbrief übersetzt und erklärt* (Regensburg: Pustet, 1957–1978), 2:392.
108. Dunn, *Romans 1–8*, 347; Käsemann, *An die Römer*, 175.

As with the occurrence in 6:19, I propose that this occurrence of γάρ may be explained in terms of a core strengthening function that is influenced by the rhetorical character of the cotext. Addressees automatically associate a strengthening role with γάρ because of its core function in more logically argumentative contexts. Expectations of relevance are satisfied with the impression of strengthening created by γάρ, and effort is not expended in the search for a logical strengthening series that rationally confirms a preceding claim.

Given the antithetical parallelism between verse 20 and verse 22, the whole of verses 20–22 is processed as a complex of strengthening assumptions introduced by γάρ. The rhetorical question and answer in verse 21a–b, and the information introduced by a further instance of γάρ in verse 21c, are all processed as belonging within the larger complex of assumptions in verses 20–22, making accessible further relevant background information within it.[109] We have already seen that the immediately preceding material in verse 19b–c is essentially a repetition of the exhortations in verse 13, themselves reinforced by a confirming rationale in verse 14. Thus in verse 19b–c this material is employed rhetorically in order to emphasize the dominating antithesis rather than as a genuine exhortation to action at this point. In verse 20 γάρ then guides toward the further reinforcement of the antithesis by continuing the display of strengthening material (vv. 20–22) that consists largely of a repetition of the statements of verses 17–18. Expectations that the material in verses 20–22 will be relevant as strengthening material are satisfied by this rhetorically powerful repetition of the total contrast between allegiance to sin and allegiance to righteousness presented in verses 16–19. In this way, verses 20–22 bolster the statements of verses 16–19 by further underscoring their main idea. The overall effect of the impression created by the γάρ clauses in verse 19b–c and verses 20–22 is to emphasize the total, mutually exclusive antithesis between the old life with sin as master and the new life in Christ, with God as Lord. This account fits with the views of scholars who identify verses 20–22 as a whole as a reinforcing explanation of what precedes.

---

109. This background information further increases the implications to be drawn from the antithesis that dominates the subsection. The fact that verse 21c forms an antithetical parallel to verse 22c is further evidence that vv. 20–22 belong together as a single complex of thought. Verse 22 completes the contrast between the fruit of slavery to sin (v. 21) and the fruit of slavery to God.

In sum, as with other examples of γάρ discussed, γάρ in 6:19 and 6:20 can both be explained as procedural indicators, with a core function of guidance toward the strengthening of preceding information, helping to reduce processing costs. Both indicate that the information introduced is relevant in relation to previously communicated assumptions, leading to the increase of their cognitive effects and argumentative salience. Instead of guiding toward the construction of complete logical strengthening series, however, in both instances γάρ helps to create a rhetorical impression of powerful buttressing and consolidation. This is in keeping with the primarily rhetorical rather than logical character of the cotext. A relevance-theoretic, procedural explanation is able to account for these atypical examples of the connective by recognizing the interaction between the core function of the connective and the type of argumentation in this subsection.

4.6. Romans 15:24: A Delicate Request

15:23: νυνὶ δὲ μηκέτι τόπον ἔχων ἐν τοῖς κλίμασι τούτοις, ἐπιποθίαν δὲ ἔχων τοῦ ἐλθεῖν πρὸς ὑμᾶς ἀπὸ πολλῶν ἐτῶν,
15:24a: ὡς ἂν πορεύωμαι εἰς τὴν Σπανίαν
15:24b: ἐλπίζω γὰρ διαπορευόμενος θεάσασθαι ὑμᾶς
15:24c: καὶ ὑφ᾽ ὑμῶν προπεμφθῆναι ἐκεῖ
15:24d: ἐὰν ὑμῶν πρῶτον ἀπὸ μέρους ἐμπλησθῶ.

This occurrence of γάρ is problematic because of the elliptical syntax of verses 23–24a and the absence of an explicit preceding statement, with an independent verb, which is obviously strengthened by the γάρ clause. This has been chosen as a further atypical example of γάρ because here, too, the connective's core strengthening function is exploited for rhetorical effect.

4.6.1. Cotext

Romans 15:14–33 is generally regarded as the first part of the epistle's closing section, in which Paul turns from the argumentation of the main body of the letter to the matter of his relationship with his addressees and his apostolic calling to the gentiles (vv. 14–21) and to a discussion of his future plans (vv. 22–33).[110] This is then followed by the concluding greet-

---

110. E.g., Jewett, *Romans*, 900; Dunn, *Romans 9–16*, 855; Stuhlmacher, *Paul's*

ings of chapter 16. Scholars draw attention to the parallels between the content of 15:14–33 and the opening section of the epistle. Dunn identifies a "bracketing effect" created by 1:8–15 and 15:14–33, arguing that the themes of the former are restated in the latter, including the subject of the hindrance Paul has experienced hitherto in coming to Rome (1:13a and 15:22), and his desire to see the Romans for their mutual benefit (1:11–12 and 15:23-24, 28-29).[111] Various scholars note the *captatio benevolentiae* of 15:14-15, by means of which Paul seeks to win the goodwill of his addressees.[112] In 15:16–21 Paul sets forth his unique calling as apostle to the gentiles, expressed in terms of priestly service.[113] In verses 17-19 he presents his apostolic credentials and in verse 20 makes explicit the focus of his ministry, namely, the evangelization of regions that have not previously heard the gospel.

In 15:22 Paul moves on to a discussion of his travel plans and revisits the thought of 1:13a: he has been prevented numerous times from coming to Rome. In verse 23 he reaffirms his long-held desire to visit the capital. In verses 23-24a we find a series of dependent verbal forms, but no main verb, before the thought is interrupted by the γάρ clause of verse 24b. Some later manuscripts have attempted to resolve the anacoluthon by the insertion of the phrase ἐλεύσομαι πρὸς ὑμᾶς at the end of verse 24a.[114]

4.6.2. Analysis of γάρ

Scholars explain the γάρ clause in 15:24b in various ways. Cranfield reads it in relationship with the implicit claim that Paul will in the future come to Rome, communicated by means of the incomplete statement of verses 23-24a. Thus the γάρ clause is "explanatory of the substance of the preceding incomplete sentence" and has a parenthetical role.[115] Similarly, Moo reads γάρ as explanatory, introducing an elaboration on what Paul has

---

Letter to the Romans, 235. Ben Witherington regards 15:14-21 as the *peroratio*, and 15:22-33 as a reference to Paul's travel plans. Ben Witherington III, *Paul's Letter to the Romans: A Socio-rhetorical Commentary* (Grand Rapids: Eerdmans, 2004), 16.

111. Dunn, *Romans 9–16*, 857.

112. E.g., Jewett, *Romans*, 903; Käsemann, *An die Römer*, 373; Barrett, *Epistle to the Romans*, 274.

113. Whittle and Jewett both discuss the links between the cultic language of 15:16 and 12:1 (Whittle, *Covenant Renewal*, 182–83; Jewett, *Romans*, 907).

114. See Dunn, *Romans 9–16*, 870.

115. Cranfield, *Epistle to the Romans*, 769, 750.

"hinted at in verses 23–24a," namely, that he hopes to fulfill his desire to visit the Romans as part of his journey to Spain.[116] Dunn takes the whole of verses 24–27 as a "sidetracking parenthesis" in which Paul's words are carefully chosen to avoid offense and argues that the unfinished sentence begun in verse 23 is only finally completed at the end of verse 28: "I will go by way of you to Spain."[117]

Along similar lines, various scholars suggest that the γάρ clause of verse 24 may function rhetorically, contributing to an impression of indirect or diplomatic communication. Jewett, for instance, argues that the anacoluthon of verses 23–24a may be intentional, functioning as part of Paul's "diplomatic strategy" of leaving his missionary plans open to the response of his Roman addressees.[118] He draws attention to the expression προπεμφθῆναι in verse 24c, which, in the majority of its New Testament uses, functions as a quasitechnical term for provision or support for missionary work.[119] Thus in verse 24b Paul can be understood to be indirectly requesting help from his addressees for his planned mission to Spain. Similarly, Käsemann suggests that Paul expresses his wish for assistance in verse 24b–d by means of dependent clauses because he dares not speak more freely to the Roman believers.[120]

Following our relevance-theoretic approach, the occurrence of γάρ in verse 24 can be explained procedurally as follows. The connective triggers procedure G and verse 24b–d is processed as a complex of strengthening premises that is dependent on ἐλπίζω. Addressees' comprehension processes then search for the nearest preceding claim that needs strengthening. Despite the anacoluthon, the implicit claim "I plan to come to Rome" is communicated strongly by verses 23–24a, as various scholars suggest.[121] This claim may raise implicit questions for addressees, however. Since Paul has not succeeding in visiting Rome for so many years, they may be skeptical about his commitment or ability to carry out this

---

116. Moo, *Epistle to the Romans*, 901. See also Käsemann, *An die Römer*, 380.
117. Dunn, *Romans 9–16*, 871.
118. Jewett, *Romans*, 924–26. Lagrange likewise suggests that the anacoluthon serves a communicative function, allowing Paul to express feelings of frustration that he cannot come to Rome immediately (Lagrange, *Saint Paul, Épître aux Romains*, 357).
119. On the latter point, see, e.g., 1 Cor 16:6; 2 Cor 1:16; Acts 15:3; Moo, *Epistle to the Romans*, 901; Dunn, *Romans 9–16*, 872.
120. Käsemann, *An die Römer*, 380.
121. I.e., it is easily inferable from vv. 23b–24a.

plan in the future. Or questions may be raised for them regarding the specifics of his visit. This implicit claim thus needs further strengthening. An inferential series is thus constructed involving verse 24b–d that results in the confirmation of the implicit claim in verses 23–24a. I propose that the following assumptions may be involved:

> **P** (implicit claim communicated by verses 23–24a): I [Paul] plan to come to Rome.
> **Q introduced by** γάρ (v. 24b–d): I [Paul] hope to visit you when passing through and to be sent on my way there [to Spain] by you [Paul's Roman addressees] once I have had the pleasure of your company a little.
> **IA**: If Paul plans to visit his Roman addressees when passing through Rome and to be sent on his way to Spain from Rome, then Paul has specific future plans to come to Rome.
> **C** (strengthening implicit claim communicated by verses 24b–d): Paul plans to come to Rome.

In this way, the implicit assumption in verses 23–24a is strengthened with the help of additional assumptions that give more detail regarding how Paul envisages coming to Rome. This explanatory detail strengthens the validity of the claim that Paul does indeed have a firm intention to come to Rome, after so many years when he has not succeeded in doing so. The strengthening procedure may be relevant as an explanation for some, and as confirming evidence for others, depending on the particular questions or objections raised for them by verses 23–24a. The material introduced by γάρ serves as supporting, or background detail, that increases the relevance of the preceding claim.

At the same time, I suggest that γάρ also has a secondary rhetorical function here, where Paul is presenting a delicate request for assistance to an audience that he does not know personally. As mentioned above, the request is expressed indirectly by means of the expression ὑφ' ὑμῶν προπεμφθῆναι. It is included as part of the background or supporting information indicated by γάρ, rather than presented as a direct request, which we might expect to be introduced by δέ.[122] The connective here seems to be used in a similar way to the English *you see*, which might be used to

---

122. Cf. Paul's request for prayer in 15:30.

introduce a delicate request presented via an explanation: "Now, since I no longer have a role in these regions and since I've been wanting to visit you for years, when I go to Spain.... You see, I hope to visit you while passing through and to be sent on my way there by you."

If this is so, then a by-product of the core function of γάρ, namely, the flagging up of information introduced by γάρ as relatively less salient in argumentative terms, is here exploited by the writer for rhetorical ends. Because it is included as part of the background strengthening information γάρ introduces, the request for assistance in verse 24c is presented as nonsalient and therefore nonthreatening information. In this case, γάρ contributes to the rhetorical effect of the communication, not by introducing a convincing and authoritative metarepresentation, nor by creating a strengthening impression, but instead by helping to attenuate information that might initially be unpalatable. Thus the procedural guidance given by γάρ is exploited for a secondary rhetorical purpose. As always, the connective guides toward the strengthening of the previously communicated information, but its function as a flag for supporting information is also used as a cover for Paul's request for assistance. By communicating this request indirectly as part of the complex of assumptions in verse 24b–d, Paul leaves the question of the Romans' potential support for his mission open and dependent on their response.[123] Here, then, we have not so much a parenthetical remark (which implies purely background and possibly optional information), as an intentionally indirect presentation of information that is in fact communicatively salient and that gives rise to various fresh cognitive effects in the form of implications.

In sum, this atypical occurrence of γάρ can be explained by a procedural account. As with all other cases discussed, the connective gives procedural guidance toward backward strengthening, increasing adherence to a previous claim. It helps to reduce processing costs by indicating that what follows it is relevant in relation to previously communicated information. At the same time, because it is associated in addressees' minds with background information, γάρ in this case secondarily contributes to a rhetorical effect that softens the directness of a request requiring tact in order to achieve its desired effect.

---

123. This reading of the γάρ clause of v. 24b–d also fits with the view that the anacoluthon of vv. 23–24a is to be attributed to the delicacy of the request.

The preceding discussion of representative problematic instances of γάρ in Romans has demonstrated that a procedural account that makes use of the cognitive framework of relevance theory is able to explain these occurrences consistently in terms of a core strengthening function. The occurrences discussed above are problematic for conventional readings of γάρ in a variety of ways. In some cases, the difficulty lies in identifying a strengthening relationship with the immediately preceding cotext (2:25; 5:6–7; 9:11; 6:19–20). In some instances, it is because of exegetical disagreement about immediately preceding or subsequent information (5:6–7). In certain cases, the difficulties arise as a result of complex syntax (5:6; 9:11; 15:24), the unusual placement of the γάρ clause (7:1b), or the apparent interruption of main argumentative points (5:7b; 9:11). In 6:19 γάρ introduces an exhortation, which would typically not function as supporting information and which does not trigger a full logical series of strengthening inferences (6:19, 20). In several examples, the strengthening γάρ guides toward has a rhetorical aspect (6:19, 7:1, 15:24). In all these cases, however, the connective can be explained as a consistent procedural indicator or signpost that reduces processing effort. It does this by signaling that the information that it introduces is to be processed as strengthening or supporting information, relevant in relation to other previously communicated assumptions, rather than leading to fresh implications. As a result of the strengthening procedure triggered by γάρ, these preceding assumptions are adhered to more strongly by addressees.

This relevance-theoretic, procedural account is able to provide a unified and cognitively grounded account of various intuitions and observations offered by more traditional accounts of γάρ. The strengthening guidance indicated by γάρ achieves relevance in different ways in diverse cotexts. Thus in 5:7b addressees are likely to find it relevant as an adjustment or further specification dealing with potential objections. In 7:1b it is relevant as a rhetorical parenthesis that interrupts the main thought for persuasive effect. In 6:19b–20 the strengthening works itself out as an emphatic repetition. Moreover, the way in which the cognitive effect of strengthening is achieved is influenced by the type of argumentation, whether primarily the closely argued logical development of thought, or argumentation that makes its point by means of rhetorical display and effect. In cotexts where addressees require additional confirming evidence, rationale, or explanation in order to be fully convinced of the validity of claims, the strengthening procedure results in previously communicated assumptions

4. What Kind of Strengthening? Problematic Examples 167

being adhered to more strongly.[124] In cotexts where the persuasiveness of the argumentation consists primarily in the use of rhetorical effect, on the other hand, the strengthening effect may be achieved by an impression of strengthening, rather than by the construction of a complete logical series.[125] I suggest that this is because the connective is automatically associated in addressees' minds with a strengthening effect, as a consequence of the inferential strengthening it most typically triggers. In rhetorical cotexts, the presence of γάρ, in combination with other rhetorical features, creates a display of reinforcing material that is enough to satisfy addressees' expectations of relevance without the construction of an inferential series. In this way the strengthening that γάρ helps to achieve is influenced by different argumentative strategies. Moreover, a secondary effect of the connective's core procedural guidance is to flag up that the material it introduces is supporting information that is less argumentatively salient than the assumptions it strengthens.[126] This secondary effect may be exploited for rhetorical purposes in certain instances. Thus in 7:1b the background information introduced by γάρ is strategically and preemptively positioned in order to create an impression of skillful argumentation that deals with objections before they arise. In 15:24, meanwhile, the connective and its associations with background information are used as a cover for the communication of salient but sensitive information.

4.7. The Procedural Guidance γάρ Gives: A Summary

In chapters 3 and 4 I have demonstrated, using a relevance-theoretic framework and from a representative range of examples in Romans, the validity of a strengthening procedural hypothesis for γάρ. These examples have included not only straightforward and somewhat complex instances, but also occurrences that might be perceived as problematic on a traditional reading of the connective. My analysis has considered γάρ in different

---

124. In this case, the rational coherence of claims and supporting evidence counters addressees' epistemic vigilance mechanisms targeted at the coherence of the argument.

125. In this case, addressees' epistemic vigilance mechanisms are countered by impressive rhetorical display that may have an impact on addressees' emotions.

126. This background material may be presented as a main argumentative point at other places in the argument (e.g., the same information that in 6:13b is presented as a salient exhortation, giving rise to many fresh cognitive effects, is presented in 6:19b as supporting information).

types of argumentation in the epistle, both expository and hortatory, and both closely argued logical subsections and passages where persuasion is achieved primarily by means of rhetorical display. This demonstration of a procedural account has involved the extension of the basic template for an inferential strengthening series proposed by Blakemore and Blass in order to explain less straightforward occurrences. Its most significant findings can be summarized under the four points below.

1. A procedural explanation of γάρ provides a fresh, unified, and consistent account of all occurrences in Romans, which is cognitively grounded and built on the firm theoretical foundation of relevance theory. It explains γάρ in terms of a core function of guidance toward the inferential procedure of strengthening. Consequently, the connective can be considered to be a consistent communicative signal. In every case, γάρ indicates that the information that it introduces is to be processed as relevant in relation to previously communicated assumptions, rather than as relevant in its own right. It raises expectations that the material it introduces, the exact extent of which is inferred from the cotext, will be relevant as strengthening or supporting information. In each case, γάρ triggers a strengthening procedure, which results in stronger adherence to preceding assumptions, that is, the cognitive effect of strengthening. The procedural instructions γάρ gives help to constrain interpretation, reducing ambiguity, acting as a signpost for the direction of the argument, and thus diminishing processing costs.

2. The procedural account is flexible: the core procedural instructions given by γάρ toward strengthening work themselves out in diverse ways in different cotexts. The strengthening procedure may be relevant as confirming evidence, a grounding rationale, a further explanation, authoritative proof, a further specification, a parenthetical remark, an adjustment to a previous claim to make it more precise, and so on. The identification of strengthened assumptions, and of strengthening premises, is in all cases guided by the search for relevance. This provides an explanation for the fact that strengthened assumptions do not always immediately precede the γάρ clause and that implicitly communicated information may be strengthened.

The strengthening procedure may achieve relevance in various ways for different addressees, depending on their perspectives, encyclopedic knowledge and attitudes of skepticism or trust. Thus information introduced by γάρ may be relevant to some as confirming evidence, but to others as an explanation. Complex inferential series will only be fully constructed by addressees who need further convincing of the validity of

4. What Kind of Strengthening? Problematic Examples 169

Paul's claims. Those who adopt a stance of basic acceptance of the communicator's trustworthiness may have their expectations of relevance satisfied by the construction of a briefer inferential series or accept the impression of confirming evidence that the presence of γάρ creates. The procedural account thus accommodates the fact that different addressees may derive differing deductive series, or indeed, none, and for the fact that addressees will invest varying degrees of effort in processing, depending on what they hope to gain from the communication.

The strengthening procedure is also affected by the type of argumentation in which a particular example of γάρ occurs, whether expository or hortatory, and whether tightly argued logic or rhetorical display. Thus in closely argued expository passages where the argument is developed logically by means of the presentation of claims and supporting premises, the strengthening procedure is most likely to achieve relevance by means of a complete inferential series. In passages where the main points of the argument are backed up by various scriptural citations, the procedure is likely to achieve relevance as an authoritative proof that convinces as much by virtue of the authoritative source quoted as by the rational quality of the supporting evidence presented. Meanwhile in highly rhetorical passages, strengthening is achieved by means of a rhetorical display of impressive reinforcement. This rhetorical strengthening may take various forms: emphatic repetition of previously communicated assumptions, vivid metaphor, an authoritative metarepresentation, rhetorical questions, and so on. In such rhetorical contexts, in which the main points of the argument are reinforced not so much by supporting premises as by an appeal to the emotions and the senses, the connective itself can be understood to contribute to the compelling rhetorical display simply by virtue of association in addressees' minds with persuasive evidence and buttressing, as a result of its core strengthening function. On occasion, the core procedural function of γάρ, and its outworkings, is also exploited with the secondary aim of creating a particular rhetorical effect.

Because of its flexibility, the procedural strengthening account is able to accommodate a range of explanations proposed by scholars for specific occurrences, without treating γάρ as a bland or loose connective that simply takes its meaning from the cotext in which it occurs. In brief, the connective functions as a broad interpretative constraint within which different addressees and interpreters work, using contextual information, to infer an interpretation that is relevant to them, bringing them adequate cognitive effects.

3. The core procedural guidance given by γάρ contributes to the coherence of the argument of particular subsections, and indeed, of the wider epistle. The search for a consolidating inferential series between material introduced by γάρ and preceding material makes obvious the close relationship between γάρ clauses and the previous cotext. In addition, the search for accessible contextual assumptions to be combined in the strengthening series of inferences frequently leads to the reactivation of assumptions that have already been communicated further back in the preceding cotext. This reactivation makes such assumptions more memorable, and the whole argument more comprehensible and coherent.

In addition, chains of γάρ clauses such as those in 5:6–8; 7:14–15; and 7:18–19 contribute to the coherence of their cotexts. The effect of such chains is a cumulative backward strengthening effect, as each γάρ clause in turn functions as a strengthening premise for the previous one, increasing the cognitive effects derived from it. The end result of this cumulative strengthening is the highlighting of the claim at the beginning of the chain, to which the whole chain leads back. The argumentative salience of this claim is thereby underlined, as is its significance for the direction of the wider argument.

Although material introduced by γάρ achieves relevance in relation to preceding assumptions, information introduced by the connective may also subsequently serve as a springboard for further development of the argument, as in 2:25. In such a case the content of the γάρ clause is processed first in relation to preceding information and is then picked up and built or elaborated upon in the subsequent argument. While this material might be viewed as looking in two directions, backward in support and forward in order to provide a foundation for the following claims, this double role is to be distinguished from the function of γάρ. The latter purely provides guidance toward strengthening and does not guide toward the drawing of inferences in relation to the subsequent argument.

4. The demonstration of a procedural account shows that information introduced by γάρ is to be processed as supporting background material that bolsters preceding claims or exhortations, increasing their relevance and salience. As buttressing material, assumptions introduced by γάρ play second fiddle, in argumentative terms, to the claims they strengthen. But because their role is to strengthen the validity of these claims, increasing their acceptability to addressees, these strengthening assumptions often take the form of metarepresentations of authoritative or generally accepted truths. These include scriptural citations and theological statements as

well as familiar axioms from the ancient world, or metarepresentations of Paul's own thought. Such metarepresentations bring the additional weight of accepted authority behind the claims that are strengthened, lending powerful persuasive punch to the supporting information. In some cases (e.g., 2:11; 13:8-9; 14:7-11), these metarepresentations represent an accepted theological framework that provides grounding for the main points of the argument.

The procedural account of γάρ has significant implications for the interpretation of Romans. Once we assume a core procedural function for γάρ, it can be relied upon as a consistent communicative signal that contributes to exegesis by lessening ambiguity and guiding interpretation in a particular direction. Consequently, γάρ should not be dismissed as a bland or loose connective, the meaning of which is discerned once the interpretation of the cotext is already decided upon. Instead, it needs to be paid attention from the outset as an important interpretative signpost that helps interpreters find their way through the thickets of exegetical detail and to get a view of the whole shape of the argumentative wood rather than becoming lost in the trees. As a significant linguistic clue, γάρ can help to confirm certain interpretations and rule out others. This guidance is particularly valuable for modern interpreters, who find themselves in a secondary communication situation in which the contextual assumptions available to the first addressees are no longer accessible. It is to these interpretative implications of the procedural account of γάρ that we now turn in chapters 5 and 6.

5
γάρ as Exegetical Signpost: Pointing a Path through the Undergrowth

In chapters 3 and 4 we saw how a relevance-theoretic, procedural account of γάρ in Romans make sense of the connective as a consistent communicative clue that guides interpretation in a particular direction. As a consequence, it can be relied upon in exegesis as an important interpretative signpost. In this chapter, I will demonstrate, from two passages in the epistle where much is at stake exegetically, how a procedural account of γάρ provides significant guidance in deciding between major interpretative options. My particular aim here is to show how a procedural account can serve as a tool for finding a way through interpretative impasses at the microlevel of individual verses and their contested ambiguities. I will consider various scholarly views in relation to the exegetical problems under discussion and show how a procedural account of γάρ provides support for certain interpretations, but undermines others. Of course, the exegesis of individual verses cannot be separated from the interpretation of the wider cotext, as we have already seen. The guidance that γάρ provides more widely toward identifying the contours, direction, and thrust of whole sections of the argument, however, will be more particularly the subject of chapter 6.

For this discussion we will consider two passages containing instances of γάρ, 4:1–2 and 10:4–5. These occur at points where there is major scholarly disagreement over a particular ambiguous phrase or clause. These disputed phrases play a key role in the development and direction of the argument. In each case, there is a choice between several major interpretative options that have been made to bear considerable argumentative weight and that feed into significantly different readings of the wider cotext and of the letter as a whole. The exegesis of 4:1–2 has implications for whether the theme of justification by faith is to be understood primarily in terms of universal human experience or in relation to the question of Jews and gentiles as members of God's people. The interpretation of 10:4–5 is crucial for different views of the role of the Jewish law in God's purposes and of the issue of Israel's stumbling in relation to the gospel. These questions are fundamental to very different scholarly perspectives regarding the center of Romans, and of Paul's theology. Despite the fact that the passages in which these examples occur are highly contested, the occurrences of γάρ are themselves relatively little discussed by commentators. As a result, a vital clue to interpretation is overlooked at points where its guidance is potentially highly valuable.

5.1. Romans 4:1–2: Testing Interpretations

4:1: Τί οὖν ἐροῦμεν εὑρηκέναι Ἀβραὰμ τὸν προπάτορα ἡμῶν κατὰ σάρκα;
4:2a: εἰ γὰρ Ἀβραὰμ ἐξ ἔργων ἐδικαιώθη,
4:2b: ἔχει καύχημα,
4:2c: ἀλλ' οὐ πρὸς θεόν.

5.1.1. Cotext

The relationship between Rom 4 and the preceding argument in chapter 3 is vigorously disputed, leading to a whole range of diverse readings.[1] This is, in part, because of the "notorious unclarity" of 4:1.[2] The discussion of Abraham in Rom 4 is often interpreted as an example or proof from scripture (specifically, from the torah itself) that supports the thesis about justification by faith in 3:21–31.[3] Some scholars argue that 4:1 and the subsequent discussion in chapter 4 belongs closely with Paul's specific claim in 3:31 that he does not annul but upholds the Jewish law.[4] Others regard the reference to Abraham in 4:1 as the expression of an objection raised by the

---

1. For a succinct overview, see N. T. Wright, "Paul and the Patriarch: The Role of Abraham in Romans 4," *JSNT* 35 (2013): 208.

2. Hays, "Have We Found Abraham to Be Our Forefather," 77.

3. E.g., Porter, *Letter to the Romans*, 102; Wilckens, *Der Brief an die Römer*, 1:257; Käsemann, *An die Römer*, 98. See also Wolter, *Röm 1–8*, 275.

4. Clyde Thomas Rhyne, *Faith Establishes the Law: A Study on the Continuity between Judaism and Christianity, Romans 3.31*, SBLDS 55 (Missoula, MT: Scholars Press, 1981), 76; Kümmel, *Römer 7*, 5–6; Lagrange views the statement in 3:31 as a heading for the following discussion in ch. 4 (Lagrange, *Saint Paul, Épître aux Romains*, 80).

statement in 3:27 that boasting has been excluded.[5] This objection is then dealt with in the subsequent discussion in chapter 4.

Following Stowers, some interpreters emphasize the close-knit continuity of the diatribal exchange, begun in 3:27, that continues into 4:1–2.[6] On this view, Paul uses a sequence of questions and answers to bring his Jewish interlocutor round to his point of view. Thus Campbell reads 4:1 as the voice of Paul's opponent, who, after enumerating in 3:27–31 three challenges to Paul's gospel as presented in 3:21–26, introduces Abraham as a "star witness" from the Pentateuch to support his challenge.[7]

A range of readings of the relationship between chapter 3 and chapter 4 also exists among those who approach Romans from the so-called New Perspective.[8] Dunn regards chapter 4 as an exposition of the theme of the epistle's basic argument so far, namely, that God justifies both gentile and Jew through faith, for which Abraham represents a "crucial test case."[9] Richard Hays, on the other hand, argues that, following the claim in 3:27–31 that the one God deals with Jews and gentiles alike, Paul puts forward a straw man position in 4:1. This expresses a particular ethnocentric Jewish view claiming a special status for the circumcised, which Paul then knocks down in the subsequent discussion.[10] Both Hays and Wright follow a minority reading of 4:1: "What then shall we say? Have we found … that Abraham is our forefather according to the flesh?" (see §5.1.2, below).[11] For his part, Wright, who argues that 3:21–4:25 must be viewed as a whole, finds in chapter 4 an exposition of Gen 15 "in relation to the covenantal promise of a single worldwide family," which is part of Paul's demonstration of God's faithfulness to the covenant with Israel.[12] This follows on from the redefinition of election that Wright claims is outlined in

---

5. Cranfield, *Epistle to the Romans*, 224–26.
6. Stowers, *Rereading of Romans*, 231–37.
7. Campbell translates 4:1 as follows: "What then shall we say that we have found in relation to Abraham…?" (Campbell, *Deliverance of God*, 724).
8. See §1.1.2 n. 34, above.
9. Dunn, *Romans 1–8*, 196.
10. Hays, "Have We Found Abraham to Be Our Forefather," 87.
11. Hays, "Have We Found Abraham to Be Our Forefather," 82, following Theodor Zahn, *Der Brief des Paulus an die Römer*, KNT 6 (Leipzig: Deichart, 1910), 215.
12. Wright, *Paul and the Faithfulness of God*, 996; Wright, "Paul and the Patriarch," 207.

3:29–30 and shows that God's people, Abraham's family, consists of all who are characterized by faith as Abraham was, gentiles as well as Jews.[13]

Watson, who, while not embracing the New Perspective, takes a sociological approach to Romans, regards chapter 4 as a reinterpretation of the figure of Abraham. This opposes the Jewish view of Abraham as a model of the law-observant Jew and presents him as a model of faith in the divine promise.[14] Barclay, meanwhile, affirming aspects of both Lutheran and New Perspective readings, brings out "Paul's dual portrayal of Abraham, as both *believer* in God and *father* of a multinational family." He interprets 3:27–31, with its insistence that boasting is excluded, that is, that all "human capital" counts for nothing and that a person is justified through faith, as the "thematic introduction" to the discussion of Abraham in chapter 4. Romans 4:1–12 thus unpacks and grounds the claims of 3:27–30.[15]

5.1.2. Exegetical Issues in 4:1

The connective οὖν in 4:1 indicates that what follows is an implication that may be drawn from what has just been said. This inference is communicated in the form of a question. Debate over 4:1 centers on the ambiguous infinitive construction εὑρηκέναι Ἀβραάμ. The textual variant that places this infinitive before the noun Abraham is best attested. Other variants that place it after ἡμῶν, or omit it altogether, can be explained as attempts to resolve the grammatical incompleteness of the phrase.[16] A majority of scholars take the infinitive construction together with the formula Τί οὖν ἐροῦμεν, and Abraham as subject of εὑρηκέναι, translating variously as "What … are we to say that Abraham … found?," "What did Abraham find to be the case?," "What … shall we say that Abraham … has discovered?"[17] On such a reading, however, the formula Τί οὖν ἐροῦμεν does not follow the pattern of its use elsewhere in Romans, where it functions as a self-standing rhetorical question, which is then followed by another independent rhetorical question or an independent state-

---

13. Wright, *Paul and the Faithfulness of God*, 1002.
14. Watson, *Paul, Judaism and the Gentiles*, 261.
15. Barclay, *Paul and the Gift*, 480–82. See in particular n. 87.
16. See Cranfield's discussion (Cranfield, *Epistle to the Romans*, 226).
17. Cranfield, *Epistle to the Romans*, 225; Dunn, *Romans 1–8*, 198; Barclay, *Paul and the Gift*, 483.

ment.¹⁸ This leads Hays to propose his alternative interpretation, which is followed in a modified form by Wright and others. This interpretation takes the formula in 4:1 as a stand-alone question, followed by a second question: "What then shall we say? Have we found Abraham to be our forefather (only) according to the flesh?"¹⁹ Here Abraham is taken as the object of the infinitive construction and its implied subject as "we," by analogy with the preceding rhetorical question.

A further difficulty is posed by the use of the first-person plural in 4:1. In other passages in Romans ἐροῦμεν is used deliberatively and inclusively, encompassing both communicator and addressees (who are predominantly gentile).²⁰ Some, however, argue, on the basis of the expression τὸν προπάτορα ἡμῶν κατὰ σάρκα, that in 4:1 Paul is speaking exclusively as a Jew, addressing questions raised by an imaginary Jewish conversation partner or answering a hypothetical question from Jewish Christ-believers.²¹ Still others argue that here it is not Paul's voice speaking, but the voice of the imaginary Jewish interlocutor of 2:17–24, with whom Paul continues to argue.²²

The prepositional phrase κατὰ σάρκα is also ambiguous in this verse, both syntactically and conceptually. Most commentators view this as modifying the noun phrase Ἀβραὰμ τὸν προπάτορα ἡμῶν. Jewett is in a minority in taking it together with the infinitive, so that the question is "what Abraham [our forefather] found on the basis of his fleshly capacities," the latter expression translating κατὰ σάρκα and referring to "the competitive ... propensity of human beings to boast in fleshly achievements."²³ Others detect different nuances in κατὰ σάρκα. As Hays notes, the expression is theologically loaded for Paul. Most obviously, it refers simply to natural physical descent (see 1:3; 9:3, 5), denoting Abraham as physical progeni-

---

18. See 6:1; 7:7; 8:31; 9:14, 30.
19. Hays, "Have We Found Abraham to Be Our Forefather," 81. See Wright, "Paul and the Patriarch," 227: "What shall we say, then? Have we found Abraham to be our ancestor in a human, fleshly sense?"; Campbell, *Deliverance of God*, 724; Stowers, *Rereading of Romans*, 234; Elliott, *Rhetoric of Romans*, 158–59.
20. Elliott, *Rhetoric of Romans*, 158.
21. Wilckens, *Der Brief an die Römer*, 1:244; Hays, "Have We Found Abraham to Be Our Forefather," 79 n. 13; Watson, *Paul, Judaism and the Gentiles*, 261–62.
22. E.g., Stowers, *Rereading of Romans*, 233–34; Campbell, *Deliverance of God*, 716–18.
23. Jewett, *Romans*, 308.

tor of the Jews.²⁴ Hays identifies at least two other dimensions of meaning in Paul's usage, however: an allusion to circumcision and to "the mode of human existence apart from God." Hays finds a "complex interweaving" of these nuances in 4:1.²⁵ Dunn argues that the expression here has somewhat negative overtones, bringing to mind circumcision and associated notions of boasting in the works of the law.²⁶

I propose that a procedural reading of γάρ in 4:2 has the potential to illuminate these exegetical disagreements, providing support for certain of these interpretations and undermining others.

5.1.3. A Procedural Reading of γάρ in 4:2

In 4:2a–b γάρ introduces a conditional statement that contains several of the epistle's key concepts and terms: ἐξ ἔργων, ἐδικαιώθη, and καύχημα. For the purposes of this discussion, I will simply use the standard translations "works," "justified," and "boast" (except when examining the particular interpretation of a scholar who uses an alternative translation). Wolter's reading of verse 1 as an introductory question functioning as a heading, and verse 2 as a thesis statement, disregards the clear guidance given by γάρ in verse 2.²⁷ Other scholars pay the connective more attention. For Cranfield, γάρ indicates that what follows it "explains the relevance" of the question in verse 1 to the claim in 3:27 that boasting has been excluded.²⁸ Wright, too, takes verse 2a–b to explain the question in verse 1 but in very different terms: if Abraham's covenant membership was defined in terms of "works of torah," then he would have an ethnic boast, and gentiles joining Abraham's family would have to become ethnic Jews.²⁹ Jewett, meanwhile, argues from the γάρ clause that the majority reading of κατὰ σάρκα is untenable and incompatible with the preceding cotext.³⁰ In his view, the γάρ clause provides the reason for the "negative answer" that

---

24. Hays, "Have We Found Abraham to Be Our Forefather," 87–88 n. 37. See Barclay, *Paul and the Gift*, 483.
25. Hays, "Have We Found Abraham to Be Our Forefather," 87–88 n. 37.
26. Dunn, *Romans 1–8*, 199.
27. Wolter, *Röm 1–8*, 278–81.
28. Cranfield, *Epistle to the Romans*, 227. See also Käsemann, *An die Römer*, 98.
29. Wright, "Paul and the Patriarch," 230.
30. Jewett, *Romans*, 307, 309.

5. γάρ as Exegetical Signpost: Pointing a Path through the Undergrowth   179

Paul's audience must supply in answer to the question, "What shall we say our forefather Abraham found according to the flesh?"[31]

The protasis of the conditional statement in verse 2a can be understood as counterfactual, and the apodosis in verse 2b similarly so.[32] Some commentators, however, read the latter as a concession to the idea that Abraham may indeed have had a boast in the sphere of the flesh.[33] Given the claim in 3:27 that boasting is excluded, it seems best to read verse 2c as swiftly denying both the assumption communicated in verse 2a that Abraham was justified because of works, and the statement in verse 2b that he has a boast, that is, grounds for God's reward or favor.[34] Verse 2c is then followed in verse 3 by a scriptural citation, introduced by γάρ plus an introductory formula expressed as a rhetorical question. This citation provides strengthening, in the form of authoritative scriptural support, for the claim in verse 2c that Abraham does not have a boast before God, which in turn further increases the relevance of the question in verse 1.

From the point of view of a procedural account, the occurrence of γάρ in 4:2 can be explained as a straightforward example of guidance toward strengthening.[35] Procedure G is triggered and the conditional clause in verse 2a–b is processed as a strengthening premise. The preceding material in verse 1 is identified as the most obvious and accessible candidate for strengthening.

Since there are several possible interpretations of verse 1, I will examine each in turn for its compatibility with a procedural strengthening reading. We begin with the majority reading that takes Abraham as subject of εὑρηκέναι. The following assumptions, or similar, may be involved in the construction of a strengthening series:

---

31. Jewett does not make explicit what this negative answer is (Jewett, *Romans*, 307).

32. Wolter, *Röm 1–8*, 281; Wright, *Paul and the Faithfulness of God*, 1003; Jewett, *Romans*, 310.

33. Ulrich Wilckens, "Die Rechtfertigung Abrahams nach Römer 4," in *Rechtfertigung als Freiheit: Paulusstudien* (Neukirchen-Vluyn: Neukirchener Verlag, 1974), 261; Gathercole, *Where Is Boasting?*, 241.

34. See Moo, *Epistle to the Romans*, 260–61; Cranfield, *Epistle to the Romans*, 228; Barclay, *Paul and the Gift*, 484.

35. Because of the exegetical ambiguity of the cotext, however, this occurrence is categorized as somewhat complex in the table of occurrences.

P (disambiguated propositional form of v. 1): "It is relevant/important to know what Abraham, our [we Jews'] forefather according to the flesh, found (in this matter)."
Q introduced by γάρ (v. 2a–b): If Abraham was justified by works, he has a boast.
IA1: If Abraham has a boast if he was justified by works, then the figure of Abraham invalidates the previous claim in 3:27–28 that boasting is excluded because a person is justified by faith without works of the law.[36]
IA2: If the figure of Abraham invalidates the claim in 3:27–28, then it is relevant/important to the argument to know what Abraham our forefather according to the flesh found in this matter.
C (strengthening assumptions communicated by v. 1): It is relevant/important to know what Abraham our forefather according to the flesh found in this matter.

On this reading, as a result of the strengthening indicated by γάρ, the relevance of the rhetorical question in 4:1 is increased, making it more comprehensible within the flow of the argument. The strengthening procedure is thus relevant as an explanation. This explanation is then immediately followed in verse 2c by a denial of the assumptions communicated in it. The procedural instructions given by γάρ in verse 2a, combined with the information it introduces, which picks up the vocabulary of 3:27–28, encourage addressees to make sense of the question in verse 1 in relation to the claims in 3:27–28 regarding boasting and justification by faith without works of the law. The question is thus explained as a highly accessible inference to be drawn from 3:27–28. As a result, the argumentative pertinence and salience of this question is strengthened, leading to raised expectations of significant cognitive effects that will be derived from its answer that follows in 4:3–25. A procedural reading of γάρ in 4:2a is thus compatible with the majority reading of 4:1, the relevance of which is increased by verse 2a–b when interpreted in relation to the assumptions communicated in 3:27–28.

Following the majority reading of 4:1, then, the strengthening procedure triggered by γάρ consolidates the coherence of 3:27–4:1. Addressees

---

36. The repetition of the vocabulary of boasting in 4:2b reactivates the assumptions communicated in 3:27–28.

5. γάρ as Exegetical Signpost: Pointing a Path through the Undergrowth 181

are directed to process 4:1–2 and what follows as a continuation of the discussion of the exclusion of boasting for all who are justified by faith. We can suggest that this previous discussion would naturally bring Abraham to mind for Paul's addressees, familiar as they were with Jewish teaching and the perception of Abraham as the highly regarded model of an obedient, faithful Jew, whose circumcision was a sign of obedience to the covenant with Yahweh.[37]

Second, let us consider Hays's minority reading of 4:1. Is a procedural account of γάρ compatible with this? Once again, I propose that γάρ in 4:2a triggers procedure G, and the information in verse 2a is processed as a strengthening premise. Addressees' comprehension processes search for a strengthening series to construct in support of the material in 4:1:

P (v. 1, disambiguated propositional form): It is relevant/important to know whether Abraham is our [we Jews'] forefather [only] according to the flesh.
Q introduced by γάρ (v. 2a–b): If Abraham was justified by works, he has an [ethnic] boast.

It is difficult, without undue processing effort, to construct any strengthening inferential series between verse 2a–b and verse 1 as construed by Hays. Any attempt involves accessing contextual assumptions that are not readily accessible in the cotext, which would require much effort and which are speculative, such as the assumption that the expression "forefather according to the flesh" implies an ethnic boast. Additionally, any such series would be considerably more complex than the series proposed for the majority interpretation. On Hays's reading, then, the information introduced by γάρ in verse 2a does not make easily accessible any contextual assumptions from the preceding cotext that would help to increase the relevance of the question in 4:1.

Hays himself acknowledges that his reading of 4:1 introduces Abraham somewhat abruptly into the argument and is thus problematic in terms of

---

37. Wolter suggests that it is the theme of the removal of the difference between Jews and gentiles (Rom 3:22, 28, 30) that inevitably leads to the question of Abraham (Wolter, *Röm 1–8*, 277). For Abraham as a model, see Watson, *Paul and the Hermeneutics of Faith*, 277. Jewett cites 1 Macc 2:52 in this regard: Αβρααμ οὐχὶ ἐν πειρασμῷ εὑρέθη πιστός, καὶ ἐλογίσθη αὐτῷ εἰς δικαιοσύνην; (Jewett, *Romans*, 308–9). See also Gen 17:9–14.

its preceding flow.[38] His solution is to argue that the inference drawn in 4:1, that "Abraham is our forefather κατὰ σάρκα," is developed from the false suggestion in the rhetorical question of 3:29a that "God is the God of the Jews only."[39] Both statements (4:1 and 3:29a) represent a type of "inappropriately ethnocentric" Judaism that Paul wants to demonstrate as false. For Hays, the relevance of the refutation of the false inference in 4:1 will only become fully clear as Paul continues his argument in chapter 4. He will go on to show that Judaism itself, rightly understood, does not claim its relation to Abraham by virtue of physical descent, but by virtue of sharing Abraham's trust in God's promises (vv. 10–17).[40] But Hays's interpretation ignores the guidance that γάρ gives that the information in 4:2a–b must be processed as increasing the relevance of preceding assumptions. Even if we take the claim communicated in 3:29a as a highly accessible contextual assumption, as Hays suggests, it is difficult to make sense of verse 2a as supporting or explanatory information for the question in verse 1 as Hays construes it.[41] In short, a procedural account of γάρ in verse 2 is not compatible with this reading.

Third, does a procedural reading of γάρ in 4:2 throw any light on Wright's variation on Hays's reading? Wright argues that the link between the counterfactual statement in 4:2a–b and 4:1 is to be understood in terms of the association that Paul has made between "works of torah" and "Jews only" in 3:28–29 and of the redefinition of covenant membership of

---

38. Hays, "Have We Found Abraham to Be Our Forefather," 86.

39. Hays regards this as an assumption against which Paul is arguing. But the rhetorical questions of 3:29a–b imply that Paul regards the answer ("Of course God is not only the God of the Jews, but also of the gentiles!") as an accepted truth for his addressees that emphatically denies the false assumption expressed by the question. See Nils A. Dahl, "The One God of Jews and Gentiles," in *Studies in Paul: Theology for the Early Christian Mission* (Minneapolis: Augsburg, 1977), 189. Paul uses this axiom of Jewish belief (see Stowers, *Rereading of Romans*, 216) to bolster his statement in v. 28, which in turn strengthens the salient claim of v. 27. *Pace* Hays, the information in vv. 29–30 thus does not represent a main argumentative point, but a strengthening theological framework. Dunn notes a tension in Paul's thought here (Dunn, *Romans 1–8*, 188).

40. Hays, "Have We Found Abraham to Be Our Forefather," 87–88.

41. As Jewett notes, Hays's interpretation "requires an overly subtle argument that must insert the word 'only' to make a link between the rhetorical question and the more immediate context of 4:2–10" (Jewett, *Romans*, 307).

God's family found in 3:21–31.[42] This reading depends on Wright's understanding of justification in terms of believers being declared righteous as members of God's covenant people, Abraham's family.[43] Thus verse 2a explains the question of verse 1 in terms of whether Abraham's covenant membership is defined in terms of "works of torah," which would mean that he and his family had a valid ethnic boast. Consequently, any gentiles wanting to belong to this family would have to consider themselves ethnic Jews.[44]

Testing out the compatibility of Wright's reading with a procedural account of γάρ, we can posit that the connective in 4:2 triggers procedure G. Addressees' comprehension processes search for an inferential series to construct that strengthens the assumptions behind the question in verse 1:

P (v. 1): Have we [gentile and Jewish Christians[45]] found Abraham to be our ancestor in a human, fleshly sense?
Q introduced by γάρ (v. 2a): If Abraham became a member of the covenant family by works [of torah], he has an [ethnic] boast.[46]
?IA1: If Abraham can boast ethnically because of works of torah, gentiles need to become members of Abraham's physical family (based on ethnic descent) by circumcision to become members of God's covenant people. (But this inference is both speculative and a non sequitur: it is not highly accessible in the cotext and assumes several other presuppositions that are not obvious.)[47]
IA2: If gentiles must be circumcised to become members of God's covenant people, then the claim in verse 30 is invalidated that both Jews and gentiles become members of God's covenant people by faith.
IA3: If the claim in verse 30 is invalidated if Abraham is the ancestor of gentile and Jewish believers in a human, fleshly sense, then it is argumentatively relevant to know if Abraham is the forefather of gentile and Jewish believers according to the flesh.

---

42. Wright, *Paul and the Faithfulness of God*, 1000.
43. Wright, *Paul and the Faithfulness of God*, 957–59.
44. Wright, "Romans," 490.
45. Wright, "Romans," 489.
46. Wright, "Romans," 490.
47. E.g., that Abraham can boast ethnically because of works of the law and that a legitimate ethnic boast for Abraham necessitates gentile circumcision.

C (strengthening v. 1): It is relevant to know if Abraham is the ancestor of gentile and Jewish believers in a human, fleshly sense.

The result of this inferential strengthening series is not sound, however, because it involves non sequiturs, and speculative contextual assumptions. As with Hays's interpretation, it is difficult here to establish a valid strengthening inferential series between verse 2 and verse 1 without undue processing effort.

Moreover, even if we allow that *works of the law* and *Jews only* are closely associated concepts in the preceding argument and understand justification in terms of membership of God's people as Wright does, there remains a fundamental problem with his interpretation.[48] It is this: the direction of Paul's argument in 3:27–31 leads *away* from the conclusion that gentiles must embrace works of the law, including circumcision (see 3:30), and become part of Abraham's ethnic family, in order to be justified. Consequently, it seems most unlikely that Paul's addressees would infer from 3:27–31 that ethnic descent from Abraham is, after all, essential for inclusion in the community of those who are justified by faith and be led to raise the question in 4:1 of whether Abraham is their ancestor in a human, fleshly sense.[49] The thrust of the preceding argument leads in precisely the opposite direction. The fact that a procedural strengthening account of γάρ in 4:2 is not easily compatible with this reading of 4:1 helps to expose this lack of argumentative coherence, which seems the major weakness of this interpretation. While Wright's interpretation looks back to the preceding cotext in its interpretation of 4:1–2, it does so in a way that creates extra processing effort, neglecting the obvious conceptual links between 4:2 and 3:27–28, which make a strengthening interpretation in terms of the claims in 3:27–28 most easily inferable and thus most relevant. Given the preceding cotext, Wright's interpretation is less than optimally relevant.

In sum, the procedural instructions given by γάρ in 4:2 help us to rule out both Hays's and Wright's reading of 4:1 as something of an argumenta-

---

48. Wright's reading is not obvious from a prima facie reading of 3:21–31.

49. Barclay comments on the improbability of gentile believers asking themselves whether they were descended from Abraham's "fleshly family": "as far as we know, no one in Paul's day considered that Gentiles, even proselytes, could claim physical ancestry from Abraham; circumcision would not mean discovering Abraham to be their 'physical father'" (Barclay, *Paul and the Gift*, 483 n. 88).

5. γάρ as Exegetical Signpost: Pointing a Path through the Undergrowth   185

tive tangent. If we take seriously the strengthening guidance given by γάρ, we must interpret 4:1 as relevant in relation to the question of whether anyone can be said to be justified by works of the law and therefore to have a valid boast or merit in God's eyes based on their obedience and faithfulness in keeping the Jewish law.

Finally, we should consider how a procedural account of γάρ in 4:2 may illuminate Jewett's interpretation of 4:1. Following this interpretation, we can suggest that something akin to the following assumptions may be involved in the attempted construction of a strengthening series that increases the relevance of verse 1:

> **P** (v. 1, disambiguated propositional form): It is important/relevant to know what our [we believers'] forefather Abraham found according to his fleshly capacities/achievements.[50]
>
> **Q introduced by γάρ** (v. 2a–b): If Abraham was set right through works, he has a boast.[51]
>
> **?IA1**: The expression Abraham's "fleshly capacities/achievements" alludes to circumcision and other acts of obedience to God's commands. (?Inferable from background Jewish assumptions and 3:29.)[52]
>
> **?IA2**: Abraham's circumcision and other acts of obedience are to be understood as "works of the law." (Inferable from background knowledge of Jewish teaching.)[53]
>
> **IA3**: If Abraham has a boast if he is set right through circumcision and other acts of law obedience (works), then this invalidates the claim in 3:27–28 that boasting is excluded because a person is set right by faith without works of the law.

---

50. Jewett, *Romans*, 307–8.
51. Jewett, *Romans*, 304.
52. Jewett suggests that this assumption would have been readily accessible to Paul's audience, but does not cite clear evidence for it (Jewett, *Romans*, 308, particularly n. 20). A passage such as Sir 44:19–20 might possibly be understood to make highly accessible the link between flesh, circumcision, and faithfulness/obedience to God's commandments. See also, e.g., Dunn, *Romans 1–8*, 199; Phil 3:1–11; Gal 6:12–13.
53. Watson shows that the author of Jubilees regards Abraham as a torah-observant Jew, faithful to the law "even before the law's full revelation," while Philo regards Abraham as conforming to the unwritten laws of the created order, an earlier articulation of the Mosaic law (Watson, *Paul and the Hermeneutics of Faith*, 230–42). Dunn, meanwhile, draws particular attention to Sir 44:19–21 (Dunn, *Romans 1–8*, 200–201).

IA4: If what Abraham found in relation to his fleshly capacities/achievements invalidates the claim in 3:27-28, then it is relevant to the argument to know what Abraham our forefather found in relation to his fleshly capacities.

C (strengthening assumptions communicated by v. 1): It is relevant to know what Abraham our forefather found in relation to his fleshly capacities/achievements.

As a result of this series, the relevance of the question in verse 1 is increased via access to assumptions associated with Paul's claims in 3:27-28. As in the case of the majority reading, so also following Jewett's interpretation, γάρ guides addressees to make sense of verse 1 in relation to the preceding claims that boasting is excluded because a person is justified not by works of the law but by faith. But the above attempt to construct a deductive series involves background assumptions that are not the most immediately accessible given the cotext, in particular the assumption that κατὰ σάρκα in 4:1 would be understood in terms of "fleshly achievements," especially circumcision. So although Jewett's interpretation is logically compatible with a procedural reading of γάρ, the proposed series requires more processing effort and is thus less relevant than the one based on the majority reading.

In sum, a relevance-theoretic, procedural account of γάρ in 4:2a, which treats the connective as a consistent communicative signal guiding addressees toward inferencing and the use of contextual information, provides valuable illumination for different construals of 4:1. A procedural account supports the majority interpretation, allowing us to see more clearly how the γάρ clause in 4:2a contributes to the coherence of the cotext. Within this interpretation, κατὰ σάρκα is best understood, as Barclay suggests, as a "standard recognition" of Abraham as the physical ancestor of the Jews used by Paul for the purposes of argument before he redefines Abraham's fatherhood in the subsequent argument in terms of father of all, Jews and gentiles, who are ungodly and who trust in God who raises the dead.[54] Paul can then also be understood to be using "we" in 4:1 as an exclusive first-person plural ("we the Jews"), while addressing an audience that is predominantly non-Jewish. In contrast, a procedural account of γάρ rules out Hays's and Wright's alternative readings as tangential to the argumentative thrust in 3:27-4:25 and provides only weak

---

54. Barclay, *Paul and the Gift*, 483.

5. γάρ as Exegetical Signpost: Pointing a Path through the Undergrowth   187

support for Jewett's interpretation. Our account of γάρ thus leads us to conclude that in 4:1 Paul is voicing a possible question raised by the previous argument of 3:27–31 that can be paraphrased thus: "What about Abraham our [Jewish] physical forefather? What has he found as far as boasting is concerned? Doesn't he, the model of obedience and faithfulness, at least have some merit or worth before God because of his obedient acts?"

5.2. Romans 10:4–5: Respecting Coherence

The exegesis of both 10:4 and 10:5–6 is the source of major scholarly disagreement and has an important bearing on the interpretation of the wider cotext of 9:30–10:13.[55] Romans 10:4 is a notorious *crux interpretum*. Because of its perceived theological importance, it has sometimes been considered in isolation from its cotext.[56] The occurrences of γάρ in 10:4–5, however, are the last two in a strengthening chain of four (10:2–5).[57] Badenas draws attention to these occurrences of γάρ as implying "a continuous explanation within the development of Paul's flow of thought." Consequently, both 10:4 and 10:5 should be interpreted in close connection with the cotext, and verses 1–13 taken together as a subsection.[58]

---

55. Meyer and Badenas both discuss 10:4 as a *crux interpretum* (Meyer, "Romans 10:4," 80; Badenas, *Christ the End of the Law*, 2). On 10:5, see, e.g., the contrasting views of Whittle and Watson (Whittle, *Covenant Renewal*, 52–56; Watson, *Paul and the Hermeneutics of Faith*, 331–41), as well as those of Badenas in contrast to Käsemann (Badenas, *Christ the End of the Law*, 121–25; Käsemann, *An die Römer*, 271).

56. Romans 10:4 read in a particular way encapsulates the perspective that there is a sharp discontinuity in God's purposes between Israel and the church, law and gospel, etc. In Rhyne's words: "Rom 10.4 has become the *locus classicus* for expressing the discontinuity between the Church and the Old Testament" (Rhyne, *Faith Establishes the Law*, 8). Alain Gignac displays this tendency to accord 10:4 a special role, likening it to "un rocher solidement ancré au milieu du courant tumultueux d'une rivière." Alain Gignac, "Le Christ, τέλος de la Loi [Rm 10,4], une lecture en termes de continuité et de discontinuité dans le cadre du paradigme paulinien de l'élection," *ScEs* 46 (1994): 16. Wilckens, despite viewing v. 4 as providing a rationale for v. 2, also regards the former as a "thesis" (Wilckens, *Der Brief an die Römer [Studienausgabe]*, 221, 224).

57. Meyer, "Romans 10:4," 86.

58. Badenas, *Christ the End of the Law*, 112. See also Wright, "Romans," 652; Wilckens, *Der Brief an die Römer (Studienausgabe)*, 218. In contrast, Jewett, Moo, Dunn, Käsemann, and most English translations treat 10:5–13 as a separate paragraph (Jewett, *Romans*, 622; Moo, *Epistle to the Romans*, 643; Dunn, *Romans 9–16*, 599–600; Käsemann, *An die Römer*, 271).

10:1: Ἀδελφοί, ἡ μὲν εὐδοκία τῆς ἐμῆς καρδίας καὶ ἡ δέησις πρὸς τὸν θεὸν ὑπὲρ αὐτῶν εἰς σωτηρίαν.
10:2: μαρτυρῶ γὰρ αὐτοῖς ὅτι ζῆλον θεοῦ ἔχουσιν ἀλλ' οὐ κατ' ἐπίγνωσιν·
10:3a: ἀγνοοῦντες γὰρ τὴν τοῦ θεοῦ δικαιοσύνην καὶ τὴν ἰδίαν [δικαιοσύνην] ζητοῦντες στῆσαι,
10:3b: τῇ δικαιοσύνῃ τοῦ θεοῦ οὐχ ὑπετάγησαν·
10:4: τέλος γὰρ νόμου Χριστὸς εἰς δικαιοσύνην παντὶ τῷ πιστεύοντι.
10:5: Μωϋσῆς γὰρ γράφει τὴν δικαιοσύνην τὴν ἐκ [τοῦ] νόμου ὅτι ὁ ποιήσας αὐτὰ ἄνθρωπος ζήσεται ἐν αὐτοῖς.
10:6: ἡ δὲ ἐκ πίστεως δικαιοσύνη οὕτως λέγει, Μὴ εἴπῃς ἐν τῇ καρδίᾳ σου, Τίς ἀναβήσεται εἰς τὸν οὐρανόν; τοῦτ' ἔστιν Χριστὸν καταγαγεῖν

5.2.1. Cotext

This passage occurs in the middle of the third major section of the letter, chapters 9–11 (see §3.2.2, above). These form a close-knit argumentative unit and address the question of the continuing role of ethnic Israel in God's purposes, and the nature of God's election, in the light of God's righteousness and mercy revealed in the gospel of Christ to Jew and gentile alike.[59] As Friedrich Avemarie notes, while past generations of scholars tended to read in Rom 10 a presentation of unbelieving Israel's guilt, recent scholarship focuses instead on Israel's failure of knowledge, its missing of the goal, or its misstep.[60] Many scholars regard the line of argument of chapter 10 as beginning in 9:30–33, where the metaphor of a race is used for Israel's zealous but unsuccessful pursuit of "the law of righteousness" (9:31), which contrasts with the gentiles' unlooked for attainment of righteousness.[61] In 9:33 a blended citation from Isa 28:16 and 8:14 refers to the stone of stumbling placed in Zion, which is partially repeated in 10:11.[62] Although Paul's earnest expression of his desire for the salvation of Israel

---

59. For chs. 9–11 as a close-knit unit, see Wilk, "Rahmen und Aufbau."

60. Friedrich Avemarie, "Israels rätselhafter Ungehorsam (Röm 10) als Anatomie eines von Gott provozierten Unglaubens," in Wilk and Wagner, *Between Gospel and Election*, 302–3. Examples of the traditional reading are Cranfield and Käsemann (Cranfield, *Epistle to the Romans*, 2:505; Käsemann, *An die Römer*, 267). For missed goal and misstep readings, see Barclay, *Paul and the Gift*, 537–38 and Campbell, *Deliverance of God*, 786.

61. E.g., Barclay, *Paul and the Gift*, 537; Meyer, "Romans 10:4," 81; Dunn, *Romans 9–16*, 579; Badenas, *Christ the End of the Law*, 108.

62. See Dunn, *Romans 9–16*, 583.

in 10:1 is regarded by some as a break in the flow of thought, in 10:2–4 his discussion of Israel's misdirected zeal continues.[63] As Meyer points out, verse 2, introduced by γάρ, gives the grounds for Paul's expression of concern for Israel in verse 1 "by characterizing his people both positively and negatively," while verse 3, also introduced by γάρ, "in turn explains verse 2 by elaborating on both aspects of the analysis."[64]

The claim in 10:3 that Israel has sought to establish its own righteousness, and has not understood or submitted to God's righteousness, is introduced by γάρ. It is relevant as a further explanation of the claim in verse 2 that Israel's zeal for God is without knowledge. Verse 3 is dominated by the contrast between τὴν τοῦ θεοῦ δικαιοσύνην and τὴν ἰδίαν [δικαιοσύνην]. The references in the preceding cotext of 9:30–31 to gentiles' attainment of δικαοσύνην ... τὴν ἐκ πίστεως, and in 9:32 to Israel's pursuit of righteousness ὡς ἐξ ἔργων, throw light on verse 3.[65] Israel's striving to establish its own righteousness is to be understood in terms of the latter, while God's righteousness is associated with the former. Scholars' differing interpretations of the concept δικαιοσύνη throughout the letter are determinative for their reading of these terms in this passage.[66]

5.2.2. Exegetical Issues in 10:4

The exegetical difficulties of this verse stem primarily from the ambiguity of the expression τέλος ... νόμου Χριστός. In addition, there is a question regarding the relationship of the prepositional phrase εἰς δικαιοσύνην to

---

63. See Avemarie, "Israels rätselhafter Ungehorsam," 300; Dunn, *Romans 9–16*, 587.
64. Meyer, "Romans 10:4," 86.
65. Barclay, *Paul and the Gift*, 539.
66. Thus, for Cranfield, God's righteousness is "God's ... gift of a status of righteousness," while Israel's own righteousness is "a righteous status of their own earning" (Cranfield, *Epistle to the Romans*, 2:515). For Käsemann, the former is God's power as Lord and Creator, which is contrasted with Israel's "Leistungsfrömmigkeit" through works of the law (Käsemann, *An die Römer*, 268–69). For Dunn, Israel's own righteousness is "Israel's claim to a righteousness which was theirs exclusively" (Dunn, *Romans 9–16*, 595). For Wright, God's righteousness is "God's equitable covenant faithfulness" and Israel's own, the attempt to set up "a status of 'covenant membership' which would be for Jews and Jews only" (Wright, "Romans," 654–55; Wright, *Paul and the Faithfulness of God*, 1169). For Barclay, Israel does not submit to "the righteousness of God that has been enacted in Christ," but seeks instead to validate its own torah-based righteousness as worthy of God's favor (Barclay, *Paul and the Gift*, 238–41).

the rest of the sentence. The noun τέλος has a wide semantic range in Greek and in 10:4 could be interpreted as *termination/cessation* ("Christ has abolished the law": the temporal interpretation), *goal* ("the law points to Christ": the teleological interpretation), or *fulfillment* ("Christ fulfills the law": the completive interpretation).[67] These different options potentially lead to polarized views of Christ's role in relation to the Mosaic law, although there is also overlap between aspects of these meanings.[68] In the twentieth century the temporal interpretation was dominant and continues to be advocated by some.[69] Others, while embracing the temporal interpretation, have argued for a more nuanced reading that includes other aspects of the sense of τέλος.[70] In more recent scholarship, the teleological and completive views have enjoyed something of a resurgence.[71]

The phrase εἰς δικαιοσύνην is understood variously as expressing purpose or goal, means, accusative of respect, or as consecutive.[72] The expression can either be read as modifying τέλος ... νόμου Χριστός ("Christ

---

67. Badenas, *Christ the End of the Law*, 4. For a detailed study of the semantic range of τέλος in extrabiblical and biblical Greek, see Badenas, *Christ the End of the Law*, 38–78.

68. See Badenas's overview of the history of interpretation of the expression (Badenas, *Christ the End of the Law*, 7–34). Dunn cautions against insisting on one sense to the exclusion of the others (Dunn, *Romans 9–16*, 589). Given the focus on Israel in the cotext, there is agreement that the referent of νόμος is the Mosaic law.

69. E.g., Lagrange, *Saint Paul, Épître aux Romains*, 253; Dunn, *Romans 9–16*, 596; Käsemann, *An die Römer*, 270; Stuhlmacher, *Paul's Letter to the Romans*, 155–56; Watson, *Paul and the Hermeneutics of Faith*, 335. Avemarie provides an overview of different ways in which "Christ is the end of the law" is understood (Avemarie, "Israels rätselhafter Ungehorsam," 310–13).

70. See Wilckens, *Der Brief an die Römer (Studienausgabe)*, 223: "Im Sinn von 8,2 kann man sogar sagen: Christus ist das Ziel des Gesetzes, sofern in Christus Jesus die Tora zum 'Gesetz des Geistes des Lebens' geworden ist."

71. See Barclay, *Paul and the Gift*, 540: "What God has given in Christ ... is the fulfilment of what was envisaged by the torah"; and Avemarie, "Israels rätselhafter Ungehorsam," 313. Campbell argues that Christ is the "end" of the law in the sense of "finishing line" or "goal" that brings the race to an end (Campbell, *Deliverance of God*, 790–91). Wright, William S. Campbell, Badenas, and Rhyne follow the teleogical reading, while Jewett argues for goal and fulfillment (Wright, "Romans," 657; William S. Campbell, *Paul's Gospel in an Intercultural Context: Jew and Gentile in the Letter to the Romans*, SIGC 69 [Frankfurt am Mainz: Lang, 1992], 62–63; Badenas, *Christ the End of the Law*, 147; Rhyne, *Faith Establishes the Law*, 104; Jewett, *Romans*, 620).

72. See, respectively, Meyer, "Romans 10:4," 86, and Wright, "Romans," 657; Dunn, *Romans 9–16*, 596; Stuhlmacher, *Paul's Letter to the Romans*, 153; Cranfield,

5. γάρ as Exegetical Signpost: Pointing a Path through the Undergrowth 191

is the τέλος of the law as a means of righteousness") or as modifying παντὶ τῷ πιστεύοντι (e.g., "to bring righteousness" to everyone who believes, "to righteousness for everyone who believes," or "so that there might be righteousness for all who have faith").[73]

Various scholars comment on the occurrence of γάρ in this verse, acknowledging that the close relationship that it indicates between 10:4 and what precedes it must be taken into account in interpretation.[74] Wilckens regards γάρ here as indicating that verse 4 provides grounds for the critique found in verse 3, while Cranfield reads it as indicating that verse 4 is an explanation of verse 3b. Meyer, too, recognizes that γάρ signals that verse 4 is an explanation of verse 3 and uses this signal as a key to deciding between "Christ the termination of the torah" and "Christ the goal and intent of the torah."[75] What light can a procedural reading of γάρ in 10:4 shed on the interpretation of both τέλος ... νόμου Χριστός and εἰς δικαιοσύνην in this verse?

5.2.3. A Procedural Reading of γάρ in 10:4

Let us begin with the "termination/cessation" reading of τέλος ... νόμου Χριστός. Is a procedural strengthening account of γάρ compatible with this? Here, following Dunn's interpretation, I will also read εἰς δικαιοσύνην as expressing means. Procedure G is triggered by γάρ, and the information that follows in verse 4 is processed as a complex of strengthening premises. Following a relevance-guided heuristic, addressees' comprehension processes search for preceding material, the relevance of which would be increased by verse 4. As no strengthening series can be constructed between verse 4 and verse 3b alone without undue effort, the whole of verse 3 is selected as a complex of assumptions for strengthening, and an attempt is made to construct a strengthening series such as the following:

Epistle to the Romans, 519. Cranfield states: "If Christ is the goal of the law, it follows that a status of righteousness is available to everyone who believes."

73. Respectively: Dunn, *Romans 9–16*, 596; Zerwick, *Grammatical Analysis*, 482; Käsemann, *An die Römer*, 267, 270 ("Christus ist des Gesetzes Ende zur Gerechtigkeit für jeden, der glaubt"); Wright, "Romans," 656–57.

74. See Meyer, "Romans 10:4," 86; Jewett, *Romans*, 619. Dunn argues that failure to take it into account has "marred" discussion of the verse (Dunn, *Romans 9–16*, 589). This is an instance of γάρ that Dunn deems to be significant as a communicative signal, in contrast to some others (see discussion of 1:16–17 under §6.2.3, below).

75. Meyer, "Romans 10:4," 86.

P (v. 3): Not knowing God's righteousness, and seeking to establish their own righteousness, [the people of Israel] did not submit to God's righteousness.

Q introduced by γάρ (v. 4): Christ is the termination of the law as a means to righteousness for all who believe.

IA1: If Christ is the termination of the law as a means to righteousness for all who believe, then the law is obsolete as a means of righteousness.

IA2: By *establishing their own righteousness* is meant that Israel pursued the law of righteousness by accomplishing works of the law. (Possibly inferable from 9:31–32.)

IA3: If Israel pursued the law of righteousness by accomplishing works of the law, but the law is obsolete as a means of righteousness, then Israel pursued the law of righteousness in vain. (Inferable from common sense.)

?IA4: If Israel pursued the law of righteousness in vain, then Israel did not submit to God's righteousness. (This inference is a non sequitur, however: the fact that Israel pursued the law of righteousness in vain does not necessarily imply that Israel did not submit to God's righteousness.)

?C: Not knowing God's righteousness, and seeking to establish their own righteousness, the people of Israel did not submit to God's righteousness.

Although on this interpretation it is possible to draw a certain number of inferences from information made accessible by verse 4 in relation to verse 3, we are left with a logical gap, and the series is unsound, because of the presence of a non sequitur. It is difficult without undue effort to construct a complete logical series between the claim that Christ is the termination of the law, and the claim in verse 3 that Israel did not know or submit to God's righteousness but sought to establish its own. This interpretation raises further questions for addressees in relation to the statement in verse 3, in particular, "What is the link between Christ terminating the law and God's righteousness?" and "What is the righteousness of God to which Israel did not submit?"[76] (The answer to this second question is available

---

76. As Meyer points out, if we read τέλος as termination, then v. 4 does not provide any explanation for the main clause of v. 3, "Israel did not submit to God's righteousness" (Meyer, "Romans 10:4," 86). Meyer also argues that reading εἰς δικαιοσύνην

5. γάρ as Exegetical Signpost: Pointing a Path through the Undergrowth   193

from what has been said in 3:21–26, but it may take considerable processing effort at this point to access assumptions communicated in chapter 3, as they are not made highly accessible here.) As a result, the claim in verse 3 remains less than optimally relevant. In this way, a procedural reading of γάρ in verse 4 does not support Dunn's interpretation, "Christ is the termination of the law as a means of righteousness for all who have faith."

Second, is a procedural account of γάρ compatible with the interpretation of τέλος ... νόμου Χριστός as Christ is the goal or fulfilled intention of the Mosaic law?[77] Since a majority of interpreters who follow this teleological interpretation also read εἰς δικαιοσύνην as communicating purpose or result, I will follow this reading of the expression here. Following a procedural reading of γάρ, procedure G identifies the statement in verse 3b as a candidate for strengthening. We can suggest the following likely strengthening series:

P (v. 3b): [The people of Israel] did not submit to God's righteousness.
Q introduced by γάρ (v. 4): Christ is the goal [fulfilled intention] of the law, bringing righteousness to all who have faith.
IA1: The goal of the law is to bring righteousness and life to God's people. (Inferable from encyclopedic knowledge of Jewish teaching and from 7:10, 12–14.)[78]
IA2: If Christ is the goal of the law, bringing righteousness to all who have faith, this means Christ fulfills the intention of the law to bring righteousness and life to God's people by bringing righteousness to all who have faith. (Inferable from IA1 and from assumptions reactivated from 8:1–4.)
IA3: The people of Israel do not have faith in Christ. (Inferable from 9:1–3, 9:30–10:1, etc.)

---

as "as a means to," as Dunn does (Dunn, *Romans 9–16*, 589), is an unwarranted filling in of the ellipsis.

77. Although Badenas begins by distinguishing between "teleological" and "completive" interpretations, he later suggests that the two can be collapsed into one, as there is much overlap between them, providing that *goal* is not understood simultaneously as *termination* (Badenas, *Christ the End of the Law*, 147). See also Barclay, *Paul and the Gift*, 537; Meyer, "Romans 10:4," 86.

78. Wilckens, *Der Brief an die Römer (Studienausgabe)*, 223; Wright, *Paul and the Faithfulness of God*, 1037.

IA4: If Israel does not have faith in Christ, and Christ fulfills the intention of the law to bring righteousness and life … by bringing righteousness to all who have faith, then Israel has not submitted to God's righteousness.

C (strengthening v. 3b): (Not knowing God's righteousness and seeking to establish their own) the people of Israel did not submit to God's righteousness.

As a result of the construction of this logical series, the claim in verse 3b becomes more comprehensible and plausible. The statement in verse 4 is relevant as a strengthening explanation of the claim that Israel has not submitted to God's righteousness. In particular, this strengthening makes immediately accessible the link between Christ as τέλος νόμου and God's righteousness to which Israel did not submit (v. 3): Christ, as goal and fulfilled intention of the law, is the one who brings/realizes God's righteousness and life, so Israel's failure to trust in him means a failure to submit to God's righteousness.[79] A procedural strengthening reading of γάρ thus supports a goal/fulfillment interpretation of τέλος … νόμου Χριστός.

Third, does a procedural account of γάρ support or undermine a reading such as Wilckens's, which combines the termination and goal senses of τέλος? Wilckens takes εἰς δικαιοσύνην as communicating purpose or result.[80] On this interpretation, I suggest that the following strengthening series may be constructed between the statement in verse 4 and the material in verse 3:

P (v. 3): Not knowing God's righteousness, and seeking to establish their own, [Israel] did not submit to God's righteousness.

Q introduced by γάρ (v. 4): The goal and termination of the law is Christ, bringing righteousness to all who believe [in him].

IA1: The goal of the law is to bring righteousness and life to God's people.

IA2: If Christ is the goal and termination of the law, bringing righteousness to all who believe in him, it is Christ who brings God's righteousness to God's people through their belief in him. (Inferable from IA1 and assumptions reactivated from 8:1–4.)

---

79. Meyer, "Romans 10:4," 86.

80. Wilckens translates by: "das Endziel des Gesetzes ist Christus zur Gerechtigkeit" (Wilckens, *Der Brief an die Römer [Studienausgabe]*, 217).

(IA3: If Christ is the termination of the law, the law is obsolete as a way to righteousness.)
(?IA4: By *establishing their own righteousness* is meant that the people of Israel pursued the law of righteousness by accomplishing works of the law.)
(IA5: If Israel pursued the law of righteousness by accomplishing works of the law, but the law is obsolete as a way to righteousness, then Israel pursued the law of righteousness in vain.)
(?IA6: If Israel pursued the law of righteousness in vain, then Israel did not submit to God's righteousness.)
IA7: Israel has not believed in Christ.
IA8: If Israel has not believed in Christ, Israel has not known or submitted to God's righteousness.
C: Israel did not submit to God's righteousness.

From the above series, we see that it possible to construct a logical strengthening sequence between verse 4 and verse 3 in terms of the concept of Christ as goal of the law, but not in terms of Christ as termination of the law. For the latter, we encounter the same difficulties as with Dunn's interpretation. The attempt to process this concept as a strengthening premise for the claim in verse 3 creates undue processing effort and thus leads to a less than optimally relevant interpretation.

In sum, if we take seriously the procedural guidance γάρ gives in verse 4, the interpretation "termination" for τέλος is indefensible, leading to an obscuring of the coherence of 10:2–4, whether or not it is combined with the sense "goal." This throws into question Dunn's reading of this subsection, and the wider argument, as asserting that, "Christ is the end of the old epoch and of Israel's exclusive privileges with it."[81] Furthermore, the interpretation of εἰς δικαιοσύνην as indicating purpose or result is compatible with our procedural account of γάρ (fitting logically, as it does, with the concept of Christ as goal/fulfillment of the law), whereas the interpretation "as a means to righteousness" is irrelevant in the cotext, creating extra processing effort.

---

81. Dunn, *Romans 9–16*, 590–91, 596.

5.2.4. Exegetical Issues in 10:5–6

As mentioned above, the presence of γάρ in 10:5 is an indication that this verse is to be processed in close relation to verse 4, rather than as the beginning of a new paragraph.[82] Moreover, there is a parallelism, structural, verbal, and conceptual, between verse 5 and verse 6, created in particular by the noun phrases τὴν δικαιοσύνην τὴν ἐκ [τοῦ] νόμου and ἡ ... ἐκ πίστεως δικαιοσύνη, both of which introduce scriptural citations. The two verses are thus most naturally interpreted together as a single block of explanatory material introduced by γάρ, with δέ in verse 6 introducing the second half of the parallel. Furthermore, since the speech of the personified righteousness by faith (plus interpretations in the style of a pesher, introduced by τοῦτ' ἔστιν) continues into verse 8, the whole of verses 5–8 can be read as explanatory material introduced by γάρ in 10:5.[83]

Romans 10:5 and 10:6 contain, respectively, citations from the Torah, from Lev 18:5, and a composite citation from Deut 8:17; 9:4; and 30:12.[84] The relationship between verse 5 and verses 6–8 in Paul's argument is much contested: Are they in sharp contrast, or are they complementary, the citations from Deuteronomy reinterpreting and bringing out the full sense of the Leviticus quotation? Depending on their view of this relationship, some scholars find in these verses clear support for either a termination reading of τέλος ... νόμου Χριστός or for a goal/fulfillment reading.[85]

---

82. For Wright, vv. 5–9 "explain and undergird" vv. 1–4, forming the "exegetical heart of the passage" (Wright, "Romans," 652). For Dunn, vv. 5–10 provide the "scriptural underpinning" for the whole of 9:30–10:4, though he treats 10:5–13 as a separate paragraph (Dunn, *Romans 9–16*, 599).

83. For the description of it as a pesher, see Jewett, *Romans*, 662; Richard B. Hays, *Echoes of Scripture in the Letters of Paul* (New Haven: Yale University Press, 1989), 79–80.

84. Whittle gives a detailed discussion of Paul's adaptation in vv. 6–8 of the citations from Deuteronomy (Whittle, *Covenant Renewal*, 47–50).

85. For the termination reading, see Watson, *Paul and the Hermeneutics of Faith*, 332: "The initial function of the Leviticus citation ... is to confirm the assertion ... that 'Christ is the end of the law'"; Käsemann, *An die Römer*, 272; Dunn, *Romans 9–16*, 602. For the goal/fulfillment reading, see Cranfield's discussion, for whom vv. 5–13 explain not just τέλος ... νόμου Χριστός but also εἰς δικαιοσύνην παντὶ τῷ πιστεύοντι (Cranfield, *Epistle to the Romans*, 2:522).

The apparent contrast between the citations in verse 5 and verse 6 is potentially problematic for a goal reading of τέλος in verse 4.[86] The parallel between ἡ δικαιοσύνη ἡ ἐκ [τοῦ] νόμου, which introduces the quotation from Lev 18:5, and ἡ ἐκ πίστεως δικαιοσύνη, which introduces the citation from Deut 30:11–14, is frequently read as antithetical. On this reading, Lev 18:5, communicated by Moses the lawgiver, represents righteousness as conceived of within the old epoch of the law, which promises life only to those who keep the law.[87] The adapted version of Deut 30, on the other hand, is spoken by the personified righteousness by faith, who speaks in opposition to Moses and represents the new epoch of righteousness through faith in Christ.[88] Käsemann notes that all references to law and works are left out of this adapted version of Deuteronomy.[89]

Avemarie, however, argues for a concessive reading of 10:5 in relation to 10:6, which is compatible with the interpretation "Christ is the goal of the law." This reading recognizes the validity of torah, and keeping its commandments, but the righteousness that comes by faith surpasses this, alone enabling the recognition of Christ as the object of the torah.[90] Badenas, meanwhile, questions the interpretation of δέ in verse 6 as introducing a contrast, arguing that the γάρ-δέ construction (in vv. 5–6) is used conjunctively here rather than adversatively (as in 3:21–22).[91] He regards verse 5 as a scriptural explanation of the statement in 10:4 that the goal of the law for

---

86. Avemarie, "Israels rätselhafter Ungehorsam," 310. Barclay is unusual in arguing for a goal/fulfillment interpretation of 10:4 but for a clear contrast between righteousness ἐκ τοῦ νόμου and righteousness ἐκ πίστεως in 10:5–6 (Barclay, *Paul and the Gift*, 542).

87. Käsemann, *An die Römer*, 273. Similarly, Watson, *Paul and the Hermeneutics of Faith*, 331–40.

88. See, however, Meyer's critique of this reading, since it implies that the law is alien to God, and "law" and "Christ" are in opposition (Meyer, "Romans 10:4," 89).

89. Käsemann, *An die Römer*, 271. Whittle also draws attention to the absence in the citation of the reference to hearing and doing the commandment, which is found in Deut 30:12 (Whittle, *Covenant Renewal*, 49).

90. Avemarie, "Israels rätselhafter Ungehorsam," 314. See also Whittle, *Covenant Renewal*, 50: "Indeed, law promised life to those doing it …, but, in the hermeneutical move of Righteousness by Faith, law's promise of life finds its goal not in those who do it, but in those who trust in Christ."

91. Badenas, *Christ the End of the Law*, 123 n. 282. See also Campbell, *Paul's Gospel in an Intercultural Context*, 64–65; Hays, *Echoes of Scripture*, 76.

righteousness is Christ, which then serves as an introductory statement for the citation of Deut 30:12–14. By bringing these two citations together, Paul equates "the righteousness taught by the law" and "righteousness by faith," showing that "doing the righteousness taught by the law is coming to Christ for salvation, and thus, receiving life." The speech of righteousness by faith in verses 6–8 can thus be understood as an explanation of verse 5, that is, as an interpretation of "what the text means" from the perspective of righteousness by faith.[92]

5.2.5. A Procedural Reading of γάρ in 10:5

Let us explore how a procedural reading of γάρ in 10:5 illuminates the question of the argumentative relationship between the citations in verse 5 and verses 6–8. First, does a procedural account provide support for an interpretation such as Käsemann's that takes verse 5 and verse 6 in antithesis? I will call this interpretation A. On this reading, γάρ triggers procedure G and the entirety of verses 5–8 is processed as strengthening premises. Following a relevance-guided heuristic, the statement in verse 4 is identified for strengthening. I suggest that the following strengthening series, or something similar, may be constructed:

> **P (v. 4):** Christ is the termination of the law bringing/resulting in righteousness ("zur Gerechtigkeit") to everyone who believes.
>
> **Q introduced by γάρ** (vv. 5–8): Moses writes about the righteousness that is from the law, "The one doing these things will live by them." In contrast, the righteousness by faith says this: "Do not say in your heart, 'Who will ascend into heaven?,' that is, to bring Christ down, or 'Who will descend into the abyss?' that is, to bring Christ up from the dead." But what does it say? "The word is near you, in your mouth and in your heart," that is, the word of faith we preach.

---

92. Badenas, *Christ the End of the Law*, 124, 129. See also Wright, "Romans," 660, 662; Jewett (*Romans*, 625), who views the citation of Lev 18:5 in v. 5 as "the premise required for the reinterpretation of Deut. 30 in vv. 6–7"; and Elliott (*Rhetoric of Romans*, 267 n. 2): "What Moses writes about 'the righteousness that comes from the Law' ... is given its content through the messianic exegesis of Deut 30.12–14: faith in Jesus Christ is what Torah itself requires."

IA1: If the righteousness that is from the law says, "The one doing these things will live by them," then righteousness and life from the law is attained by doing/keeping the law.
IA2: If righteousness by faith says …[93] "The word is near you, in your mouth and in your heart," that is, the word of faith we preach, then righteousness by faith involves an internal response of believing in Christ.
IA3: If righteousness and life from the law are attained by doing the law, but righteousness by faith involves an internal response of believing in Christ, then Christ represents the termination of the law bringing righteousness to everyone who believes in Christ.
C (confirming v. 4): Christ is the termination of the law bringing righteousness to everyone who believes.

As a result of this inferential series, the statement in 10:4 is strengthened. The strengthening procedure is relevant as a further explanation of this claim. A procedural account of γάρ in verse 5 is thus compatible with interpretation A of 10:4 and with Watson and Käsemann's contention that the contrast in verses 5–6 confirms the assertion in verse 4 that Christ is the termination of the law.

Second, does a procedural reading of γάρ in 10:5 fit with a view such as Badenas's, that verses 6–8 are not in antithesis with verse 5, but rather in continuity, reinterpreting it and bringing out its fuller meaning, in the light of Christ? I will call this interpretation B. On this reading, too, the entirety of verses 5–8 is processed as strengthening premises, and the statement in verse 4 is identified for strengthening. On this interpretation, the following strengthening series, or something similar, may be constructed:

P (v. 4): Christ is the goal/fulfilled intention of the law, bringing righteousness to everyone who has faith.
Q introduced by γάρ (vv. 5–8): Moses writes about the righteousness that is from the law, "The one doing these things will live by them"; and the righteousness by faith says this: "Do not say in your heart, 'Who will ascend into heaven?,' that is, to bring Christ down, or 'Who will descend into the abyss?' that is, to bring Christ up from the dead." But what does it say? "The word is near you, in your mouth and in your heart," that is, the word of faith we preach.

---

93. Abbreviated for reasons of space.

IA1: If the righteousness that is from the law says, "The one doing these things will live by them," then the goal/intention/result of the righteousness that comes from obeying the law is life.

IA2: If righteousness by faith says … "The word is near you, in your mouth and in your heart," that is, the word of faith we preach, then the divine word/command to be faithful and obey is near in the gospel message about faith in Christ.[94]

IA3: If the goal of the righteousness that comes from obeying the law is life, and the divine word to be faithful and obey is near in the gospel of Christ, then the way to obey the law and have life is through faith in Christ.[95]

IA4: If the way to obey the law and have life is through faith in Christ, then Christ is the goal/fulfilled intention of the law, bringing righteousness to everyone who has faith.

C (strengthening v. 4): Christ is the goal/fulfilled intention of the law, bringing righteousness to everyone who has faith.

This series strengthens the claim in verse 4 by means of the authoritative scriptural citations in verses 5–8, which are not set in antithesis, but interpret one another. The strengthening procedure may be relevant as a further explanation or as validating confirmation, depending on what achieves the most cognitive effects for different addressees. On this interpretation, the claim that the goal or fulfilled intention of the law is Christ is supported from two different passages from the torah itself. Together these bring out the life-giving intention of the law and its fulfillment through faith in Christ, which is effectively obedience to God's command to choose life.[96] A procedural reading of γάρ in 10:5 is thus fully compatible with interpretation B of verses 5–8.

Although a procedural account of γάρ in 10:5 fits with both interpretation A and interpretation B above, in deciding between these, we need to take into account the whole chain of γάρ clauses in 10:2–5 and the guidance that this gives toward the coherence of the subsection. While the

---

94. For word/command, see Wright, *Paul and the Faithfulness of God*, 1174. See Whittle, *Covenant Renewal*, 50.

95. See Whittle, *Covenant Renewal*, 50, 56.

96. See Deut 30:15, 19. This reading illuminates the statement in 9:31 that Israel pursued the law of righteousness but did not achieve the law: it did not achieve the law's life-giving intention, though it pursued works of the law.

5. γάρ as Exegetical Signpost: Pointing a Path through the Undergrowth   201

contrastive reading of verses 5–8 is compatible with procedural γάρ, the termination reading of verse 4, which the contrastive reading confirms, is not: we have seen that the termination reading cannot be understood to strengthen what precedes it in verse 3, without undue processing effort. Ultimately the termination reading of τέλος in verse 4, supported by the contrastive reading of verses 5–8, is undermined by a procedural account of γάρ. Similarly, a teleological reading of verse 4, followed by a contrastive reading of verses 5–6, is undermined by a procedural explanation of the connective, since it does not pay attention to the strengthening guidance given by γάρ in verse 5, which indicates that what follows should be interpreted in close conjunction with the immediately preceding statement, providing support for it.[97] On the other hand, a teleological or completive interpretation of verse 4, supported by a continuative reading of verses 5–8, is confirmed by procedural γάρ, encouraging a reading of 10:1–13 as a seamless whole and cementing the coherence of the whole argument back to 10:1 (and behind that, 9:30–33).

In this chapter we have explored the interpretative impact of a procedural account of γάρ at the microlevel of exegesis. Reading γάρ as a procedural indicator enables us to rely on it as a consistent communicative clue and significant exegetical signpost. Its strengthening guidance allows us to choose between major interpretative options in some highly contested passages, clearing a way through certain exegetical thickets and making a real contribution to exegesis. This procedural account of γάρ has provided significant illumination for two important *cruces interpreti* in Rom 4:1–2 and 10:4–5. In the former, it confirms a standard reading of 4:1, undermining Hays's alternative construal. In the latter, it renders less plausible a termination or cessation interpretation of τέλος ... νόμου Χριστός, while supporting the interpretation *goal* or *fulfilled intention*. In addition, it suggests that 10:5 and 10:6–8 are best read, not in antithesis, but in continuity with each other, with 10:6–8 interpreting 10:5 in the light of 10:4 and the preceding cotext, to which it leads back via the strengthening chain of γάρ clauses (10:2–5).

In each case, the procedural indicator γάρ serves as a crucial piece of exegetical evidence to be taken into consideration from the outset of exegesis. Interpretations that do not allow for a strengthening relationship

---

97. For a teleological reading of v. 4, followed by a contrastive reading of vv. 5–6, see Barclay, *Paul and the Gift*, 542 n. 47.

between the γάρ clause and preceding claims are ruled out. In addition, the procedure helps to bind the γάρ clause and the strengthened claims with the preceding cotext, since the strengthening toward which γάρ guides involves the accessing of previously communicated contextual assumptions. The procedural reading of γάρ thus supports interpretations that recognize this cotextual coherence but throws into question those that neglect the close inferential and argumentative links with the wider preceding cotext.

It is to questions of the coherence, direction, and thrust of Paul's argument that we now turn in chapter 6. In what way is this small procedural signpost relevant not only at the microlevel of exegesis, but also on the macroplane of the wider argument?

6
γάρ as Communicative Signpost: Guidance in Tracing Paul's Argument

In the previous chapter, we saw how a relevance-theoretic, procedural account of γάρ can throw light on the interpretation of Romans at the microlevel of exegesis. In this chapter, we will explore the implications of this procedural account at the macrolevel of the epistle's wider argument. I will make use of the insight that γάρ helps us distinguish between strengthening information and more salient argumentative points. I suggest that this allows us at various points to trace more clearly the thrust of Paul's argument, seeing the argumentative woods for the trees, thus avoiding the pitfall of being sidetracked by theological questions that are not Paul's primary focus. I will show how reading γάρ as a communicative signpost assists us in finding a path through the exegetical maze at two pivotal points in the letter's argument. As a result, we are able to rule out certain interpretations as cul-de-sacs. Furthermore, it is my claim that this procedural guidance sheds light on the major interpretative questions of the purpose of the letter and the center and direction of its argument. In addition, we will see how γάρ contributes to the coherence of whole subsections and sections, compelling us to pay careful attention to the wider cotext of the epistle in our interpretation of particular passages.

I will discuss in detail one passage from the opening of the letter's argument, 1:15–18, and one from its close, 15:7–13. Both are arguably determinative for the contested issues of the letter's purpose, and the thrust of its argument. Both are the source of ongoing scholarly debate and give rise to an array of alternative interpretations. Our discussion will focus on recent readings of these passages that are illuminated in different ways by a procedural reading of γάρ. We will consider how this procedural analysis takes us forward in our understanding of the letter's purpose, audience, and argumentative path.

6.1. Direction and Center of the Argument of Romans

In chapter 2 I gave an overview of the unresolved question of the purpose of Romans. Closely associated with this is the much debated issue of the coherence, center, and thrust of Paul's argument.[1] While most commentators divide the body of the letter into four major sections based on its content and themes, there is disagreement as to where its argumentative center of gravity lies.[2] Many scholars broadly following a traditional Lutheran interpretation regard the exposition of justification by faith in chapters 1–4 as the centerpiece of Paul's argument.[3] Those who argue for an apocalyptic reading, on the other hand, find its center of gravity in chapters 5–8.[4] Others see the discussion of Israel within God's purposes in chapters 9–11 as the climax of the argumentation.[5] Some have focused on Rom 12:1-2 as central, while others again have identified chapters 14–15 as the key to understanding the letter's argument and purpose.[6] Finally,

---

1. See Longenecker, *Introducing Romans*, 128.

2. This fourfold division falls roughly along the lines of chs. 1–4; 5–8; 9–11; 12–15, though there is variation in relation to ch. 5 (Campbell, *Deliverance of God*, 471).

3. Moo cites Luther, who reads 3:21-26 as "the chief point, and the very central place of the Epistle, and of the whole Bible" (Moo, *Epistle to the Romans*, 218). See also, e.g., Mark A. Seifrid, "Unrighteous by Faith: Apostolic Proclamation in Romans 1:18–3:20," in *The Paradoxes of Paul*, vol. 2 of *Justification and Variegated Nomism*, ed. D. A. Carson, Peter T. O'Brien, and Mark A. Seifrid, WUNT 2/181 (Tübingen: Mohr Siebeck, 2004), 107; Cranfield, *Epistle to the Romans*, 199; Käsemann, *An die Römer*, 85.

4. E.g., Campbell, *Deliverance of God*; Richard N. Longenecker, "The Focus of Romans: The Central Role of 5:1–8:39 in the Argument of the Letter," in *Romans and the People of God: Essays in Honor of Gordon D. Fee on the Occasion of His Sixty-Fifth Birthday*, ed. Sven Soderlund and N. T. Wright (Grand Rapids: Eerdmans, 1999), 49–69. Porter, while following a more traditional reading, nevertheless finds in 5:1–21 the "climax" of Paul's argument (Porter, *Letter to the Romans*, 112).

5. E.g., Baur, *Apostle of Jesus Christ*, 327–28; Krister Stendahl, *Paul among Jews and Gentiles* (Philadelphia: Fortress, 1976), 4, 28; Dunn, *Romans 1–8*, lxii; Fitzmyer, *Romans*, 541. Elliott identifies 11:17-24 as "the climax of Paul's rhetoric" (Elliott, *Rhetoric of Romans*, 271).

6. For 12:1-2 as central, see Runar M. Thorsteinsson, *Paul's Interlocutor in Romans 2: Function and Identity in the Context of Ancient Epistolography*, ConBNT 40 (Stockholm: Almqvist & Wicksell, 2003), 53–54, cited in Thorsteinsson, Thiessen, and Rodríguez, "Paul's Interlocutor in Romans," 12: "the hortatory request in 12:1-2 constitutes the structural center" of Romans. For chs. 14–15 as key, see, e.g., Watson, *Paul, Judaism and the Gentiles*; Jewett, *Romans*; Minear, *Obedience of Faith*.

some who pay particular attention to the relationship between Jews and gentiles in Paul's argument argue that its climactic conclusion is found in 15:7–13.[7]

Related to this issue is the role of 1:16–17 in the epistle's argument and its relationship with the surrounding cotext.[8] A standard reading interprets these verses as a thesis statement for the whole epistle that summarizes its theme, though this is understood in diverse ways.[9] The thesis introduces the exposition of the letter body, beginning at 1:18. Many commentators and translators set these verses apart from the surrounding cotext in a subsection all of their own with a separate heading.[10] Indeed the verses have sometimes been read as a doctrinal summary not only of Romans but of Pauline theology.[11] Following a traditional reading, the thesis is developed in more detail in 3:21–26, after an extended demonstration in 1:18–3:20 of humanity's universal sinfulness, showing the necessity of justification by faith apart from works of the law.[12] Romans 4 then provides a scriptural proof of the validity of the thesis in the example of Abraham.[13] By the end of chapter 4, the thesis has essentially been proved.[14]

Various scholars, however, find this analysis of 1:16–17 and chapters 1–4 problematic. For a start, large chunks of the epistle's later argument arguably bear little obvious relation to the so-called theme in 1:16–17 (for

---

7. Whittle, e.g., finds the climax of Paul's discussion in 15:7–13 (Whittle, *Covenant Renewal*, 134). Bird regards 15:8–9 as the "pinnacle of the letter" (Bird, "Letter to the Romans," 198).

8. See Jewett, *Romans*, 135.

9. E.g., Antony C. Thistleton, *Discovering Romans: Content, Interpretation, Reception* (London: SPCK, 2016), 75; Tobin, *Paul's Rhetoric in Its Contexts*, 104; Wright, "Romans," 423; Moo, *Epistle to the Romans*, 63; Fitzmyer, *Romans*, 253; Käsemann, *An die Römer*, 18; Dunn, *Romans 1–8*, 36. In a variation, Cranfield identifies 1:16b–17 as the thesis (Cranfield, *Epistle to the Romans*, 87).

10. E.g., Jewett, *Romans*, 135; Wright, "Romans," 410; Dunn, *Romans 1–8*, 36–37; Käsemann, *An die Römer*, 18; NRSV; ESV; NET; NBS; FC; Semeur; GN.

11. E.g., Barrett, *Epistle to the Romans*, 21.

12. Cranfield, e.g., reads 3:21–26 is "the center and heart" not only of 1:18–4:25, but of Rom 1:16b–15:13 (Cranfield, *Epistle to the Romans*, 199).

13. E.g., Käsemann, *An die Römer*; Cranfield, *Epistle to the Romans*, vol. 1; Dunn, *Romans 1–8*. See Campbell's critique of this construal, which he summarizes as: "(1) a statement of the problem: 1:18–3:20; (2) a description of the solution in thesis form: 1:16–17; 3:21–31…; and (3) an authoritative scriptural attestation to that solution: 4:1–25" (Campbell, *Deliverance of God*, 315).

14. See Seifrid, "Unrighteous by Faith," 107.

instance, ch. 7 and chs. 12–15).[15] Chief among opponents of the standard reading is Campbell, who is highly critical of the prior assumption that 1:16–17 and 3:21–31 represent thesis statements, which are then used as an interpretative grid into which the rest of the argument of the epistle is forced, in a "vicious interpretative circle." Campbell argues that, while the material in 1:16–17 can be seen in retrospect to summarize the epistle's later discussion, there is nothing in the text that indicates its thematic status for addressees encountering the letter for the first time.[16] Campbell is particularly concerned to counter a foundationalist reading of 1:18–3:20, which he contends is the bedrock of the citadel of the justification theory he aims to deconstruct. In his view, such a reading regards 1:18–3:20 as a preparatory argument for the thesis announced in 1:16–17.[17] On such a prospective reading, the consciousness of the universal culpability of sinful humanity becomes a prerequisite for the arrival of the gospel in 3:21–31.[18] For Campbell, this reading is fundamentally anthropocentric, requiring rational individuals to recognize their sinful plight before the gospel provides them with a solution.[19]

Others question the validity of underlining 1:16–17 as a thesis divorced from its cotext by pointing to its close connection with the surrounding cotext, as signaled by the chain of four γάρ clauses in 1:15–18. As we have seen in §1.1.3, above, Elliott argues that these verses should be read as a single unit of thought that belongs tightly together. He is sharply critical of the approach commonly adopted by translators and commentators that breaks these connections; such a treatment of the text is "grammatically indefensible," though "useful to a particular theological reading" of the epistle.[20] Elliott argues that the theme essays composed in Paul's day had clear indications of their genre, but such indications are missing from

---

15. See Moo, *Epistle to the Romans*, 65 n. 9.

16. Campbell, *Deliverance of God*, 350.

17. This grid assumes that vv. 16–17 look forward only, summarizing the whole epistle *in nuce*, and that what follows begins a proof of this thesis. See Seifrid, "Unrighteous by Faith," 107.

18. Campbell, *Deliverance of God*, 316, 341, 1021 n. 7. Campbell is concerned to counter a Western, rationalistic, individualistic construal of the Pauline gospel.

19. Douglas A. Campbell, "Rereading Romans 1–3," in *Beyond Old and New Perspectives on Paul: Reflections on the Work of Douglas Campbell*, ed. Chris Tilling (Eugene, OR: Cascade, 2014), 139 n. 6.

20. Elliott, *Arrogance of Nations*, 75; Elliott, *Rhetoric of Romans*, 82.

Romans.²¹ The epistle should therefore be read, not as a theme essay, but according to its "clear epistolary signs."

In short, the question of the direction, center, and thrust of Paul's argument is far from settled. It has an important bearing on wider questions of the interpretation of the apostle's theology, and is integrally linked to the issue of the letter's purpose. It is my claim that a procedural reading of γάρ in the pivotal passages of 1:15–18 and 15:7–13 can throw light on the argumentative direction and emphases of Romans, and on its purpose.

6.2. Romans 1:15–18: Which Way Lies Relevance?

As the above discussion shows, Rom 1:15–18 occurs at a hotly debated hinge point at the opening of the epistle's argument. Although there is general agreement that these verses contain some of the epistle's main concepts and themes, there is much debate about their relationship with the preceding epistolary frame, and the ensuing argument. These verses contain a tight-knit fourfold chain of γάρ clauses and include, in 1:18, the most notorious occurrence of γάρ in the letter. The passage is thus a prime candidate for demonstrating how a procedural account of γάρ sheds significant light on contested issues relating to the wider argument.

6.2.1. Cotext

Romans 1:15–18 straddles the transition between the letter's opening epistolary frame (identified variously as vv. 1–15, vv. 1–16a, and vv. 1–17) and the main body of its argument.²² The frame consists of (1) an extended prescript (vv. 1–7) that includes Paul's summary of the gospel, (2) a thanksgiving and prayer section that is a modified version of a conventional Jewish liturgical εὐχαριστῶ formula (vv. 8–12), bringing into focus Paul's desired visit to Rome, and (3) a brief narrative account that provides the

---

21. E.g., a title introducing the subject, and a description of one's method (Elliott, *Arrogance of Nations*, 75). This is in contrast to Tobin, who maintains that in 1:16–17 Paul begins "by setting out the basic proposition he wants to argue," just as Epictetus does in most of his diatribes (Tobin, *Paul's Rhetoric in Its Contexts*, 104 n. 1). Tobin does not mention that Epictetus's propositions are not introduced by γάρ.

22. See, respectively, Wihelm Wuellner, "Paul's Rhetoric of Argumentation in Romans," in Donfried, *Romans Debate*, 133; Cranfield, *Epistle to the Romans*, 28; Wolter, *Röm 1–8*, xii.

background for this delayed visit (vv. 13–15).²³ In verse 13 Paul insists on the sincerity of his desire, explaining the delay in the fulfillment of his wish. His explicitly stated motivation for his eagerness to have spiritual fruit among the Roman believers (v. 13) is found in verse 14: he is a debtor to Greeks and barbarians, wise and foolish alike, that is, to all gentiles, because of his apostolic calling (v. 5).²⁴ The implication is that the Roman believers are among those toward whom Paul has an apostolic responsibility and that he is thus motivated by a strong sense of commitment to them. In verse 15 Paul rounds off this striking emphasis on his eagerness to visit the Roman believers with a further articulation of his strong desire to preach the gospel (εὐαγγελίσασθαι) to his addressees in Rome. This statement in verse 15 effectively summarizes the main point and focus of verses 8–15.

The interpretation of εὐαγγελίσασθαι is problematic. Elsewhere Paul uses the verb to refer exclusively to the preaching of the gospel that aims at the conversion of the unevangelized, but ὑμῖν in verse 15 indicates that his desire is to preach to his addressees, who are, however, already believers in Christ, as 1:6–7 indicates.²⁵ Furthermore, this reading of εὐαγγελίσασθαι contradicts 15:20, where the apostle refers to his principle of not proclaiming the gospel where Christ has already "been named," so as not to build on another's foundation.²⁶ In view of this, the verb is best understood not as proclaiming the gospel to the unconverted, but as referring to the preaching and teaching of Paul's distinctive version of the gospel to the Roman believers, a version that is particularly relevant to the situation in Rome (see below).²⁷ This reading fits with Paul's expressed desire in verse 11 to impart a spiritual gift for his addressees' strengthening, and his hope of having "fruit" among them (v. 13), which need not be understood in the

---

23. For (1), see Hans-Josef Klauck and Daniel P. Bailey, *Ancient Letters and the New Testament: A Guide to Context and Exegesis* (Waco, TX: Baylor University Press, 2006), 300. For the liturgical formula, see Elliott, *Rhetoric of Romans*, 79. For Paul's desire to visit Rome, see Wilckens, *Der Brief an die Römer*, 1:90. For (3), see Jewett, *Romans*, 127.

24. Wolter argues that by means of these two merisms, Paul designates the whole of non-Jewish humanity (Wolter, *Röm 1–8*, 111–12).

25. Wolter, *Röm 1–8*, 110.

26. Günther Klein's explanation of this contradiction seems unconvincing: there is little evidence in the letter that Paul is intending to found a church in Rome because the believers there lack "the authentic apostolic stamp" (Günther Klein, "Paul's Purpose in Writing the Epistle to the Romans," in Donfried, *Romans Debate*, 40). Instead, he regards them as a model of faith and maturity (1:8; 15:14).

27. See Jewett, *Romans*, 134; Dunn, *Romans 1–8*, 34; Fitzmyer, *Romans*, 251.

narrow sense of converts.[28] This reinforces the view that Paul's claim in verse 15 is in fact a summary of the thrust of the whole of 1:8–15.

6.2.2. Romans 1:16–18: Transitional Tension and Questions Raised

The ambiguity regarding the argumentative role of 1:16–18 is due partly to a tension between the conceptual content and communicative signals of these verses. While the content to some extent suggests a turn in verse 16 from the formalities and conventions of the letter opening to the subject of Paul's argument, the occurrences of γάρ suggest a close backward connection with the material in verse 15 (and preceding verses).

Four key questions for these verses are:

1. How should we interpret verses 16–17 in relation to the preceding and subsequent cotext?
2. What is the argumentative status of verses 16–17?
3. How should we interpret verse 18 in relation to the preceding and subsequent cotext?
4. What bearing do the answers to these questions have on discerning the purpose of the letter?

In seeking to answer these, I will first consider some scholarly attempts to make sense of 1:16–17, and 1:18, in the surrounding cotext, paying particular attention to their reading of γάρ. Using the framework of relevance theory once again, I will offer a procedural account of γάρ in these verses and show how this throws light on our questions, helping us to decide in favor of particular interpretations. For ease of presentation and analysis, I will discuss the three occurrences in 1:16–17, and the one in 1:18, in two different subsections.[29]

6.2.3. Romans 1:16–17: Different Readings of Communicative Signals, Content, and Cotext

1:13: οὐ θέλω δὲ ὑμᾶς ἀγνοεῖν, ἀδελφοί, ὅτι πολλάκις προεθέμην ἐλθεῖν πρὸς ὑμᾶς, καὶ ἐκωλύθην ἄχρι τοῦ δεῦρο, ἵνα τινὰ καρπὸν σχῶ καὶ ἐν ὑμῖν καθὼς καὶ ἐν τοῖς λοιποῖς ἔθνεσιν.

---

28. See Wilckens, *Der Brief an die Römer (Studienausgabe)*, 79 n. 85.
29. This is not because I view 1:18 as belonging to a separate section from 1:16–17; I hope to show precisely the opposite.

1:14: Ἕλλησίν τε καὶ βαρβάροις, σοφοῖς τε καὶ ἀνοήτοις ὀφειλέτης εἰμί,
1:15: οὕτως τὸ κατ' ἐμὲ πρόθυμον καὶ ὑμῖν τοῖς ἐν Ῥώμῃ εὐαγγελίσασθαι.
1:16a: Οὐ γὰρ ἐπαισχύνομαι τὸ εὐαγγέλιον,
1:16b: δύναμις γὰρ θεοῦ ἐστιν εἰς σωτηρίαν παντὶ τῷ πιστεύοντι, Ἰουδαίῳ τε πρῶτον καὶ Ἕλληνι.
1:17a: δικαιοσύνη γὰρ θεοῦ ἐν αὐτῷ ἀποκαλύπτεται ἐκ πίστεως εἰς πίστιν, καθὼς γέγραπται, Ὁ δὲ δίκαιος ἐκ πίστεως ζήσεται.
1:18: Ἀποκαλύπτεται γὰρ ὀργὴ θεοῦ ἀπ' οὐρανοῦ ἐπὶ πᾶσαν ἀσέβειαν καὶ ἀδικίαν ἀνθρώπων τῶν τὴν ἀλήθειαν ἐν ἀδικίᾳ κατεχόντων,

Various scholars seem unwilling to accord γάρ weight as a communicative clue in these verses. Dunn, for instance, dismisses Paul Achtemeier's analysis of 1:14–2:16 as a complete unit in which 1:16, 17, and 18 and following are all grammatically subordinate to 1:15, because, for Dunn, this is to "overload the significance of γάρ."[30] Campbell, too, dismisses the communicative role of γάρ. He regards the occurrence in verse 16a as an example of the "blander" use of the connective and maintains that Paul's eagerness to preach in Rome is probably not related to the "absence of shame" mentioned in verse 16a.[31] Here Campbell effectively makes a prior decision about the relationship between verses 14–15 and verse 16 based on his own wider reading of the letter's opening, leading him to discount the communicative clue given by γάρ because it does not fit.

Other commentators pay more attention to γάρ in verse 16a and the relationship it signals with what precedes. Moo recognizes that from the point of view of syntax, Paul's claim in verse 15 that he desires to preach the gospel in Rome is the "main statement in the sequence." Nevertheless, the language of verse 16a suggests "a shift in focus" away from Paul's own ministry to the gospel itself. So although verses 16–17 are technically part of the *proem* or introduction, they represent the transition into the letter body by stating the epistle's theme.[32] Cranfield, acknowledging that verses 16–17 belong formally with verses 8–15, breaks up verse 16, taking verse 16a with the preceding subsection but regarding verses 16b–17 as

---

30. Dunn, *Romans 1–8*, 38, citing Paul J. Achtemeier, *Romans*, IBC (Atlanta: John Knox, 1985), 35–36. (Dunn gives an erroneous reference [*IDB* 4:80–85, 91–99 sic] to Achtemeier's Romans commentary.)
31. Campbell, *Deliverance of God*, 340 and 1021 n. 6.
32. Moo, *Epistle to the Romans*, 64.

the statement of the letter's "theological theme."³³ Wilckens, however, criticizes both Cranfield's insertion of a break before verse 16b, and also Käsemann's before verse 16a, arguing that both destroy the coherence of verses 14–17, arising in turn out of verses 8–13.³⁴ Wilckens keeps verses 14–17 as a single paragraph, while recognizing the difficulties inherent in dividing up this text because of the fluidity of the transition from opening section to main letter body. Meanwhile R. Dean Anderson argues that formally speaking, Paul's statement in verse 15 might be considered to be the *propositio* for the entire epistle, because of the series of "causal conjunctions [γάρ]" in verses 16–18.³⁵ Nevertheless, for Anderson, 1:16–17 represents the real theme of Paul's argument.

Certain scholars, guided by γάρ in verse 16a, are more willing to accord the relationship between verse 15 and verse 16 real argumentative significance.³⁶ Wedderburn argues that there is no clear-cut division between verses 16–17 and either what precedes or what follows.³⁷ Influenced by Nils Dahl, he does not limit the thesis statement to verses 16–17.³⁸ Instead, he identifies *three* thematic statements in verses 16b–18, each of which is "logically connected" to what precedes by means of γάρ, so that all three "serve as a warrant" for what precedes.³⁹ In order to make sense of the connection between verse 16 and verse 15, Wedderburn turns to the letter's possible social setting. While some commentators interpret verse 16a, "I am not ashamed of the gospel," as an introductory confessional formula

---

33. Cranfield, *Epistle to the Romans*, 87.

34. Wilckens, *Der Brief an die Römer*, 1:77.

35. R. Dean Anderson Jr., *Ancient Rhetorical Theory and Paul*, CBET 18 (Kampen: Kok Pharos, 1996), 185. Witherington explains the *propositio* as that part of a rhetorical discourse that sets forth "the basic theme or proposition which the author will then advance by a series of arguments" (Witherington, *Paul's Letter to the Romans*, 47).

36. E.g., Elliott, *Arrogance of Nations*, 75–77; Elliott, *Rhetoric of Romans*, 82–83; Wedderburn, *Reasons for Romans*, 103–4; Achtemeier, *Romans*, 35–36; Minear, *Obedience of Faith*, 39.

37. Wedderburn, *Reasons for Romans*, 103.

38. Dahl, "Missionary Theology in the Epistle to the Romans," 79.

39. Wedderburn, *Reasons for Romans*, 124. Dahl argues that the question of whether a statement belongs with what precedes or follows is anachronistic, given that the text would have been read aloud and that the original handwriting would have had no paragraph markings (Dahl, "Missionary Theology in the Epistle to the Romans," 79).

for the thesis statement, Wedderburn reads it quite differently.[40] He argues that the connection indicated by γάρ in verse 16a with Paul's expressed desire in verse 15 makes best sense if there was some situational reason why Paul might potentially be ashamed of preaching the gospel in Rome. He proposes that Paul's gospel may have been discredited in Rome in some way. Romans 1–11 can then be read as a "defense of Paul's message and ministry" against charges in Rome that Paul's gospel is shameful because it portrays God as acting unrighteously in relation to his promises to Israel and as encouraging believers also to act unrighteously.[41]

Peter Stuhlmacher, though less interested in the connection between verse 16 and verse 15, also reads verse 16a as a response to a specific "problematic situation" in Rome. Following Carl Weizsäcker, he argues that Paul has judaizing critics in Rome, as elsewhere, who are at work among the Roman believers. Paul wants to allay their arguments and their slanderous rumors before he arrives.[42] Paul Minear also emphasizes the Roman situation in understanding the connection that γάρ indicates between verse 16 and what precedes but explains this in terms of conflict among believers in Rome. Paul's statement that he is not ashamed of the gospel (v. 16a) must be understood in terms of his intention to preach

---

40. For v. 16a as an introductory formula, see, for example, Käsemann, *An die Römer*, 19.

41. Wedderburn, *Reasons for Romans*, 103–4, 112–16. See also Reasoner, *Strong and the Weak*, 234–39. Reasoner argues that the fact that the gospel is not shameful is the primary topos of Romans, occasioned by the situation in Rome where the gospel is in danger of being shamed. The gospel is without shame because it "contains the truth of the righteousness of God..., is in continuity with Judaism (9–11; 15.8-12) and teach[es] the essence of torah (3.27-31; 13.8-10) and the purpose of torah (10.4)."

42. Stuhlmacher, *Paul's Letter to the Romans*, 5–6, 28; Stuhlmacher, "The Purpose of Romans," in Donfried, *Romans Debate*, 236. See also Tobin, *Paul's Rhetoric in Its Contexts*, 74–77. Tobin argues that most believers in Rome would have been troubled, even scandalized, by Paul's stance vis-à-vis the Jewish law expressed in the Galatian controversy and that Paul therefore writes to persuade them of the correctness of his gospel. Cf. Barclay, who argues that "Paul's special sensitivities regarding Torah and Israel ... may reflect anxieties about his own reputation," and that his stance on circumcision and torah "made it easy for Gentile believers to hail him (and for Jewish believers to distrust ... him) as leading the Jesus-movement away from its Jewish roots." For Barclay, however, this is not a significant factor for the letter's purpose (Barclay, *Paul and the Gift*, 458).

in Rome (v. 15), an intention that is "shaped" by the Roman situation, as described in chapters 14–15.[43]

Others, too, taking account of γάρ in verse 16a, agree that a specific situation in Rome provokes the bold statement in that verse but claim that the problem addressed is Roman imperial ideology, which the gospel confronts.[44] Wright has argued that the whole of 1:1–17 is shaped by the fact that Paul is writing to believers in Rome, the center of Roman imperial pretension.[45] It is against this political background that Paul is not ashamed of the gospel. Going further, in his 2008 monograph, Elliott takes an ideological-critical approach to the entire epistle, making an anti-imperial reading the key to its interpretation. He claims that Paul invokes "recognizable themes from imperial propaganda," thereby implicitly challenging them.[46] Elliott interprets 1:16a as a refusal to be "put to shame" by the Roman imperial "social and political order in which shame is constructed." Paul is "not ashamed of the proclamation of God's triumph" (v. 16a), because in it "the justice of God" is found. Romans 1:16–17 is thus a "declaration of confidence in God's saving justice," which is directly connected, by means of γάρ, both to Paul's "statement of purpose" in 1:13–15 and to the statement in 1:18 regarding the manifestation of God's wrath.[47]

Turning to verse 16b, this has traditionally been regarded as the beginning of the content of the thesis about the gospel, after the introductory formula of verse 16a. Commentators, while paying little attention to this occurrence of γάρ, read the statement it introduces in verse 16b as a theological rationale for Paul's lack of shame in proclaiming the gospel: the gospel is the power of God himself and effects salvation for all who have faith, first Jews and also Greeks.[48]

---

43. Minear insists that γάρ "should not be overlooked. It links these verses to the preceding statements in which the apostle presented his hopes in sending the letter." Minear suggests placing a comma after v. 15 to bring out more clearly this close connection between vv. 16–17 and v. 15 (Minear, *Obedience of Faith*, 39).

44. E.g., Jewett, *Romans*, 137–39.

45. Wright, "Romans," 404, 426; Wright, "Paul's Gospel and Caesar's Empire," in *Paul and Politics: Ekklesia, Israel, Imperium, Interpretation; Essays in Honor of Krister Stendahl*, ed. Richard A. Horsley (Harrisburg, PA: Trinity Press International, 2000), 172–73.

46. Elliott, *Arrogance of Nations*, 14.

47. Elliott, *Arrogance of Nations*, 51, 74.

48. For v. 16b as a theological rationale, see, e.g., Cranfield, *Epistle to the Romans*, 87; Moo, *Epistle to the Romans*, 66. For the gospel as the power of God, see Karl Barth,

214   Textual Signposts in the Argument of Romans

Verse 17a is introduced by a third occurrence of γάρ. For many interpreters, this verse represents the heart of the thesis of verses 16–17.[49] At the same time, most also recognize that it explains and confirms verse 16b, providing a justification or grounds for it and "undergirding" it.[50] Wedderburn is atypical in reading verse 17 not as the heart but as the second part of the threefold thematic statement of verses 16b–18.[51] This verse contains the key expressions δικαιοσύνη θεοῦ and ἐκ πίστεως εἰς πίστιν, which generate enormous debate in Pauline interpretation.[52] I will engage with these

---

A Shorter Commentary on Romans (London: SCM, 1959), 20. On σωτηρία, see Dunn's discussion; he sums up the concept as "deliverance from peril and restoration to wholeness" (Dunn, *Romans 1–8*, 39). See also Käsemann, *An die Römer*, 19. On the semantic range of the πίστις word group, encompassing the senses "belief," "trust," "faithfulness," fidelity and faith, see Campbell, *Deliverance of God*, 384–86, 610. Teresa Morgan also argues for the multivalency of πίστις, within which "trustworthiness and faithfulness are always implicit." Teresa Morgan, *Roman Faith and Christian Faith: Pistis and Fides in the Early Roman Empire and Early Church* (New York: Oxford University Press, 2015), 273. In an attempt to communicate this, I will translate πίστις as "faith" but πιστεύω henceforward as "be faith-full." Regarding *Greeks*, Paul here uses the standard Greco-Roman term, but the contrast "Jew and Greek" is a Jewish categorization. See Dunn, *Romans 1–8*, 40.

49. Wright, "Romans," 424.

50. E.g., Cranfield, *Epistle to the Romans*, 91; Dunn, *Romans 1–8*, 37; Wilckens, *Der Brief an die Römer*, 1:86. For undergirding, see Wright, "Romans," 424.

51. Wedderburn, *Reasons for Romans*, 124. See also Barth, *Romans*, 25.

52. The debate regarding δικαιοσύνη θεοῦ has sometimes been polarized, with the objective sense of a righteous status imputed forensically to believers (e.g., Martin Luther, *Lectures on Romans*, trans. Wilhelm Pauck, LCC 15 [London: SCM, 1961], 18; Cranfield, *Epistle to the Romans*, 97) set against the subjective sense of a characteristic or action of God (e.g., Campbell, *Deliverance of God*, 699–702). In the latter case, δικαιοσύνη θεοῦ is often understood as God's saving power or deliverance. Others argue that the two understandings should not be sharply separated (e.g., Käsemann, *An die Römer*, 27–29; Dunn, *Romans 1–8*, 41–42; Wolter, *Röm 1–8*, 123).

The interpretation of πίστις in v. 17 is closely bound up with the interpretation of δικαιοσύνη θεοῦ. Does it mean faith in the sense of belief, trust, or faithfulness, whether God's, Christ's, or believers'? Wolter represents a traditional reading of ἐκ πίστεως εἰς πίστιν: "Glaube und nichts als Glaube überall, vom Anfang bis Ende" (Wolter, *Röm 1–8*, 126). For πίστις with reference to the faithfulness of Christ, see Campbell, *Deliverance of God*, 613–16. Against this, see Francis B. Watson, "By Faith (of Christ): An Exegetical Dilemma and Its Scriptural Solution," in *The Faith of Jesus Christ: Exegetical, Biblical and Theological Studies*, ed. Michael F. Bird and Preston M. Sprinkle (Milton Keynes: Paternoster, 2009), 147–63; Watson, *Paul and the Hermeneutics of Faith*, 50–53. Wright, arguing against Watson, translates δικαιοσύνη θεοῦ as

debates in the following discussion in as far as they are pertinent to the guidance that γάρ gives toward the coherence of Paul's argument. For now I will use standard literal translations of these expressions, "righteousness of God" and "from faith to faith," though I will modify my translation of the latter as necessary in the light of my analysis. Many commentators see the citation from Hab 2:4 in verse 17b as scriptural proof for the claim in verse 17a.[53] The debate regarding the referent of ὁ δίκαιος is not directly relevant to the analysis of γάρ, but it seems best, with Teresa Morgan, to read the referent as the "righted" human being.[54] Meanwhile, as Morgan suggests, Paul may be deliberately exploiting the ambiguity of ἐκ πίστεως, in order to allude to the role of the faithfulness of God, Christ, and human beings in "the economy of salvation."[55]

6.2.4. Romans 1:16–17: A Procedural Account

Let us now turn to a procedural reading of γάρ and explore how it helps us trace a path through the exegetical undergrowth of verses 16–17. I propose that it can assist us in finding answers to the questions of the relationship between verses 16–17 and what precedes, and of the argumentative status of verses 16–17, as well as potentially shedding light on the letter's purpose.

We can suggest that Paul's claim in verse 15 (which summarizes the main implication of vv. 8–15) may not be optimally relevant as it stands. It may raise implicit questions as to whether the apostle is really so eager to preach in the capital, given his past failure to do so, alluded to in verses 10–14. The presence of the chain of strengthening γάρ clauses in verses

---

"God's covenant justice," i.e., God's faithfulness to the covenant, and ἐκ πίστεως εἰς πίστιν as "from [God's] faithfulness to [human] faithfulness" (Wright, *Paul and the Faithfulness of God*, 1466–69). Morgan argues that πίστις in 1:17b has a relational sense encompassing trust and faithfulness, and that Paul uses the term ambiguously, referring simultaneously to the faithfulness of God, Christ, and human beings (Morgan, *Roman Faith and Christian Faith*, 283–87).

53. Jewett, *Romans*, 136; Cranfield, *Epistle to the Romans*, 100. Watson takes an opposing view: the citation is not a "secondary confirmation," but the "matrix from which Paul's own assertion [about the righteousness of God] derives" (Watson, *Paul and the Hermeneutics of Faith*, 43).

54. Campbell argues for the christological reading of Hab 2:4 (Campbell, *Deliverance of God*, 613–16). In contrast, Watson represents the reading, "the one who is righteous by faith shall live" (Watson, "By Faith [of Christ]").

55. Morgan, *Roman Faith and Christian Faith*, 286.

16–18 contributes to the impression that Paul anticipates potential questions raised by his statement in verse 15, which he accordingly addresses by means of the information communicated in the γάρ clauses. According to our analysis of γάρ, this material provides bolstering evidence that helps convince addressees of the validity of his claim in verse 15.

The occurrence in verse 16a represents a relatively straightforward case of strengthening from the point of view of a procedural account of γάρ.[56] We can explain it as follows. Procedure G is triggered by γάρ and the immediately preceding assumptions communicated in verse 15 are identified as needing strengthening in order to be optimally relevant. I propose that something like the following inferential series may be constructed:

P (v. 15): I am eager to preach the gospel to you [believers] who are in Rome also.
Q introduced by γάρ (v. 16a): I [Paul] am not ashamed of the gospel.
IA1: If Paul is not ashamed of the gospel, Paul is confident in/boasts in/glories in the gospel.
IA2: If Paul is confident in/boasts in/glories in the gospel, then Paul is motivated/eager to preach the gospel to those who are in Rome. (Inferable from common sense.)
C (strengthening v. 15): Paul is eager to preach the gospel to the believers who are in Rome.

As a result of this strengthening series, verse 15 is confirmed by means of independent evidence, with the result that the claim in verse 15 may be accepted somewhat more firmly as valid by addressees. But it seems that Paul perceives that the statement in verse 16a is itself not yet optimally relevant as it stands, and so provides additional strengthening evidence, introduced by γάρ in verse 16b, in order to bolster the claim of verse 16a. Perhaps he anticipates that his statement in verse 16a will lead to further implicit questions for some addressees, such as: "Is it really true that Paul is not ashamed of preaching his gospel in Rome? Are there not aspects of his gospel for him to be ashamed of in Rome?"

Moving on, then, to verse 16b: I have argued that the close strengthening link between verse 16 and verse 15 indicated by γάρ in verse 16a

---

56. I have, however, categorized this occurrence as somewhat complex in the table of occurrences because of the interpretative complexity of the cotext and because relatively few interpreters acknowledge the supporting relation between v. 16a and v. 15.

strongly suggests that this clause is to be understood specifically in relation to Paul's desire to preach in Rome. Since verse 16b is also introduced by γάρ, indicating that it likewise reinforces what precedes, it too must be read as strengthening support for verse 16a and so, in turn, for the claim in verse 15. As we have seen in §6.2.3, above, various Rome-specific explanations have been proposed for Paul's mention in verse 16a of potential shame regarding the gospel. We will consider two different construals of these verses that pay attention to the close relationship between verse 16 and verse 15 to see what light a procedural reading of γάρ sheds on them. The first is the suggestion by Wedderburn that Paul is countering the perception among some Roman believers that he does not value the Mosaic law or the Jewish roots of their faith in Christ, which threatens to bring his gospel into disrepute and undermine unity among believers.[57] Following a construal such as this, Paul would be concerned, perhaps in the wake of the Galatian controversy, to address the misgivings of Jewish-influenced and torah-observant believers in Rome, modifying the presentation of his gospel to emphasize the role of Israel in relation to faith in Christ.[58]

Following this construal, then, we can propose the following series:

Series A (countering suspicions of anti-Jewish tendencies):
P (v. 16a): I [Paul] am not ashamed of the gospel.
Q introduced by γάρ (v. 16b): [The gospel] is the power of God for salvation for all who are faith-full, Jew first and also Greek.
IA1: There are a number of Jewish-orientated, torah-observant Christ-believers in Rome.[59] (Inference dependent on a reconstruction

---

57. Wedderburn, *Reasons for Romans*, 104, 141. See also Tobin, *Paul's Rhetoric in Its Contexts*, 70–78. This proposal follows elements of Stuhlmacher's reconstruction, without accepting his contention that throughout the letter Paul is arguing with Jewish opponents (Stuhlmacher, "Purpose of Romans," 240).

58. See Wilckens, "Über Abfassungszweck und Aufbau des Römerbriefes," 142–43, 167: "der Römerbrief [ist] eine apologetisch-reflektierte Wiederholung des Galaterbriefes." Cf. also Barclay, *Paul and the Gift*, 458–59; Tobin, *Paul's Rhetoric in Its Contexts*, 12, 70. Elliott, in his earlier work, construes Romans as a prophylactic attempt to prevent the kind of gentile boasting against Israel that has occurred elsewhere (Elliott, *Rhetoric of Romans*, 56, 260).

59. Whether Jewish, or gentile proselytes. Zetterholm talks in terms of "non-Jews ... [who] were Torah-observant to some extent" (Zetterholm, "Non-Jewish Interlocutor," 55–56). See also, e.g., Wolter, *Röm 1–8*, 38–39; Stuhlmacher, "Purpose of Romans," 238; Watson, *Paul, Judaism and the Gentiles*, 173–74; Schmithals, *Römerbrief*, 38–40.

of the Roman situation based on historical clues such as Ambrosiaster's statement regarding the Jewish origins of Roman Christianity, and evidence that some gentiles were attracted to Judaism in the first century.)[60]

IA2: Some in Rome are claiming that Paul's gospel has antinomian, anti-Jewish, and supersessionist tendencies. (Inference based on a particular reconstruction of the situation in Rome.)[61]

IA3: If the gospel Paul proclaims is the power of God for salvation for all who are faith-full, Jew *first* and also Greek, then Paul's gospel does not have anti-Jewish, supersessionist tendencies.

IA4: If Paul's gospel does not have anti-Jewish, supersessionist tendencies, then Paul does not need to be ashamed of it in Rome where there are many Jewish-orientated Christ-believers.

C (confirming v. 16a): Paul is not ashamed of the gospel.

As a result of this inferential series, Paul's claim in verse 16a is strengthened and its validity more firmly accepted, which in turn leads to the further reinforcement of the claim in verse 15. This suggested construal of the situation in Rome is thus supported by a procedural explanation of γάρ. The proposed strengthening series is compatible with the view that there are those who claim that Paul's gospel has anti-Jewish tendencies, who are influencing or could potentially influence the Roman believers, many of whom hold the Jewish faith in high regard and may be torah-observant, if they are not Jewish themselves. In response, Paul reinforces his claim that he is not ashamed to preach the gospel to those in Rome by emphasizing that his gospel of salvation, while being for *all* who are faith-full, respects Jewish priority.[62]

Second, let us consider an anti-imperial construal of these verses. Following this reading, it is possible to propose a different set of background

---

60. For Ambrosiaster, see Campbell, "Addressees of Paul's Letter to the Romans," 178, 194–95; Lane, "Social Perspectives," 202, citing Ambrosiaster, *Ad Romanos*: 4–7. For gentiles being attracted to Judaism, see Zetterholm, "Non-Jewish Interlocutor," 55, citing Josephus, *B.J.* 7.45; *C. Ap.* 2.282; Seneca, *Ep.* 108.22.

61. See Wedderburn, *Reasons for Romans*, 140–41, and Stuhlmacher, "Purpose of Romans," 240. The reconstructions of both are compatible with this series. Cf. also Wiefel's hypothesis that posits anti-Jewish sentiment in Rome rather than Paul himself countering an anti-Jewish charge (Wiefel, "Jewish Community," 85–101).

62. Tobin, *Paul's Rhetoric in Its Contexts*, 104.

assumptions that may be made highly accessible for addressees, and combined in a different strengthening series (B). This would be constructed along the following lines:

Series B: (anti-imperial reading):
    P (v. 16a): I [Paul] am not ashamed of the gospel.
    Q introduced by γάρ (v. 16b): [The gospel] is the power of God for salvation for all who are faith-full, Jew first and also Greek.
    IA1: Roman imperial ideology claims that the Roman emperor has the power to save people. (Inferred from encyclopedic knowledge of Roman culture.)[63]
    IA2: If the gospel is the power of God for salvation for all who are faith-full, then the gospel is powerful enough to challenge Roman imperial ideology.
    IA3: If the gospel is powerful enough to challenge Roman imperial ideology, then the gospel is something to boast in/glory in.
    IA4: If the gospel is something to boast in/glory in, then Paul is not ashamed of the gospel.
    C (confirming v. 16a): Paul is not ashamed of the gospel.

Series B also strengthens Paul's claim in verse 16a, so that addressees adhere to it more strongly, and it becomes more relevant for them. But here the strengthening comes from assumptions related to the issue of the clash between the gospel and imperial ideology. The fact that such a strengthening series is logically possible provides support for Elliott's construal of Romans. In an environment where the Roman emperor is lauded as savior of the world, Paul reinforces the validity of his claim that he is truly eager to preach the gospel in Rome by drawing attention to the saving power of the gospel.

Series A and B are, then, both logically possible and compatible with the procedural guidance given by γάρ in verse 16b. I suggest that addressees could construct one or other of these strengthening series, depending on what background assumptions are highly accessible to them, given their particular perspective and concerns. It remains to be seen, however, how compatible these two reconstructions are with other data in the epistle,

---

63. See, e.g., Dieter Georgi, "God Turned Upside Down," in Horsley, *Paul and Empire*, 148–49, 152; Elliott, *Arrogance of Nations*, 73.

both from the immediate subsequent cotext and from the wider argument of Romans.

Turning to γάρ in verse 17, from the point of view of a procedural account, this is another straightforward example of guidance toward strengthening.[64] The information it introduces is a complex of strengthening premises that backs up the statement of verse 16b and that is relevant as a further explanation. Whichever of the major interpretations we follow, it is possible to construct a strengthening inferential series between verse 17a and verse 16b without undue processing effort, with the result that the claim in verse 16b is strengthened. The theological statement of verse 17a is followed by a scriptural citation in verse 17b that in turn provides authoritative support for the claim in verse 17a. I will examine possible inferential series triggered by γάρ in verse 17 in more detail as part of the discussion of 1:18.

6.2.5. Romans 1:16–17: Argumentative Implications

A procedural reading of γάρ in verse 16a–b supports both a construal of the letter's purpose that includes a concern on Paul's part to show that his gospel is not anti-Jewish (series A) and an anti-imperial construal (series B). In both cases, the strengthened claim that Paul is not ashamed of the gospel is closely connected by means of γάρ with the immediately preceding claim in verse 15 that Paul is keen to preach the gospel to those *in Rome*. Whichever strengthening series is constructed, the knock-on effect of the strengthening of verse 16a is to bolster further this claim, increasing its argumentative salience. Verse 16b, which in turn strengthens verse 16a, is likewise to be understood in relation to verse 15. The occurrences of γάρ in verse 16a and verse 16b indicate that verse 16 cannot be understood as a self-standing, contextless distillation of the gospel that Paul is about to present. Instead, the particular articulation of relevant aspects of Paul's gospel in verse 16 is shaped by the fact that Paul aims to show the specific relevance of his gospel for his Roman addressees in their particular situation.

As far as verse 17 is concerned, the strengthening material introduced by γάρ is to be viewed as supporting information that is argumentatively less salient (producing fewer fresh implications) than the preceding

---

64. This occurrence, like the one in v. 16a, is listed in the table of occurrences as somewhat complex because of the contested character of the immediate cotext.

claims it strengthens. This is despite the fact that it contains information of great theological weight. Wright characterizes the statement in verse 17 as "the deepest thing Paul wishes to say" and the "foundation" of the whole sequence of explanatory clauses in verses 16–17.[65] This analysis, however, seems to confuse the theological freight of the statement in verse 17 with its argumentative role. According to a procedural analysis of γάρ, the latter is consolidating, as γάρ in verse 17a indicates, rather than spearheading.[66]

To sum up our discussion of verses 16–17, a relevance-theoretic, procedural reading of γάρ throws new light on the interpretation of these verses, providing support for readings that throw into question a thematic reading of these verses. The close relationship with verse 15 suggests that these verses do not represent a timeless, universal summary of Paul's gospel but rather a tailored, context-dependent extract, shaped by the contingencies of his communication with the Romans, as verse 15 indicates.[67] Paul aims to convince his addressees that his gospel is relevant to them in Rome, that it is good news that he can announce to them with confidence, and he thus communicates here particular elements of his gospel that support that aim. At the same time, the supporting material in verses 16–17 gives snatches of what is to come in the development of Paul's argument in Romans, rather like melodies in an overture to an opera. This is to be expected, given that verses 16–17 represent selected aspects of the tailored gospel that Paul will unfold in the rest of the epistle. Wedderburn's description of verses 16b–18 as "programmatic" or introductory allows us to take a step away from the interpretative grid imposed by the notion of a thesis statement that Campbell warns against.[68]

---

65. Wright, "Romans," 423. Wright regards the whole of the epistle as effectively "unpacking" the "dense statement" of 1:16–17.

66. Cf. Elliott, *Arrogance of Nations*, 275. Wright does recognize the dual argumentative function of vv. 16–17, noting that Paul offers the thematic statement as "the further explanation of his desire to come to Rome and announce the gospel there" (Wright, "Romans," 423) but does not exploit the implications of this.

67. Paul's expressed desire to strengthen the Roman believers (v. 11) is evidence that he is concerned with their specific situation.

68. Campbell, *Deliverance of God*, 602. Campbell himself characterizes 1:16–17 as an "argumentative wedge" of "traditional material that Paul and the Roman Christians share." This fits with a reading of vv. 16–17 as material that consolidates rather than spearheads.

Let us pause to take stock of our findings in relation to our four initial questions (6.2.2).

Partial answers to three of the four questions have emerged. (1) On the basis of a procedural analysis of γάρ, verses 16–17 should be interpreted in a close inferential strengthening relationship with Paul's claim in verse 15. Verse 17 strengthens the statement in verse 16b, verse 16b the assertion in verse 16a, and verse 16a the statement in verse 15, in a cumulative backward strengthening chain. It remains to be seen how these verses relate to what follows in verse 18 (question 3). (2) The information in verses 16–17 thus looks backward, argumentatively speaking, to the claim in verse 15, supporting it and lending it persuasive punch. Verses 16–17 can be understood as shaped and tailored by the contingencies of this claim, and should not be regarded as a contextless, summarizing thesis that heralds the exposition of Paul's gospel from verse 18 onward. As for our question (4), answers (1) and (2) point to a purpose that is Rome-directed. Paul writes because, as apostle to the gentiles, he wants to share his gospel with the Roman believers, and the glimpses we have of that gospel in verses 16–17 are uniquely expressed in Rome-relevant, Jewish-rooted yet multiethnic terms. The proposal that Paul shares his gospel with his Roman addressees at this time specifically in order to address a particular situation among addressees in Rome remains an open question that needs further evidence for its corrobation. We will return to it in the light of our discussion of 15:7–13.

6.2.6. Romans 1:18: Different Readings of Communicative Signals, Content, and Cotext

1:17a: δικαιοσύνη γὰρ θεοῦ ἐν αὐτῷ ἀποκαλύπτεται ἐκ πίστεως εἰς πίστιν, καθὼς γέγραπται, Ὁ δὲ δίκαιος ἐκ πίστεως ζήσεται.

1:18: Ἀποκαλύπτεται γὰρ ὀργὴ θεοῦ ἀπ' οὐρανοῦ ἐπὶ πᾶσαν ἀσέβειαν καὶ ἀδικίαν ἀνθρώπων τῶν τὴν ἀλήθειαν ἐν ἀδικίᾳ κατεχόντων,

In this section I will address question (3) in particular and also consider how this throws further light on questions (1), (2), and (4). We have already noted that the occurrence of γάρ in 1:18 is the last in the chain of γάρ clauses beginning in 1:16 and have suggested that it therefore cannot simply be divorced from what precedes, however we interpret the relationship. Scholars privilege this occurrence with an unusual amount of attention. This is not only because of its strategic argumentative loca-

6. γάρ as Communicative Signpost: Guidance in Tracing Paul's Argument   223

tion and crucial significance as a macroargumentative signpost, but also because of the incompatibility of a traditional causal reading of γάρ with a reading of 1:18 as the beginning of a major section.[69]

We have already noted the problem of the relationship between the supposed thesis of 1:16–17 and the statement concerning the revelation of God's wrath in 1:18.[70] A standard reading of Rom 1 views 1:18 as the beginning of the epistle's first major section, and yet verse 18 is introduced by γάρ.[71] Furthermore, this signal of close backward connection is corroborated by the striking parallelism created by the repetition in verse 18 of the present passive ἀποκαλύπτεται from verse 17a and the repetition in verse 18 of terms from the δικαι- word group.[72] The verb ἀποκαλύπτεται has strikingly different subjects in the two verses: righteousness of God in verse 17 and wrath of God in verse 18. Various scholars argue that the verb implies a background of Jewish apocalyptic and eschatological thought that expected the definitive revelation of the righteousness/justice of God as eschatological judge at the end of the present age.[73] This would take the form of the vindication of God's righteous people on the one hand and the visitation of God's wrath against the injustice and wickedness of their enemies on the other.[74] The present tense in verses 17 and 18 suggests that Paul conceives of this revelation as already taking place. Many scholars understand this to be whenever the gospel is announced.[75]

---

69. Wright sums up its significance: "The problem posed by the opening main section of Romans ... can be sharpened to an extremely fine point. Why does Paul say *gar* at the start of 1:18?" (Wright, *Paul and the Faithfulness of God*, 764).

70. For discussions of the problem, see Wright, *Paul and the Faithfulness of God*, 764–67; Wedderburn, *Reasons for Romans*, 108; Cranfield, *Epistle to the Romans*, 106–10.

71. For verse 1:18 as the beginning of the first major section, see, e.g., Jewett, *Romans*; Wright, "Romans"; Moo, *Epistle to the Romans*, 90; Dunn, *Romans 1–8*, 36; Käsemann, *An die Römer*, 18; Wilckens, *Der Brief an die Römer*, 1:93.

72. The parallelism of ἀποκαλύπτεται is pointed out by Günther Bornkamm, "Revelation," in *Early Christian Experience* (New York: Harper & Row, 1969), 46; Cranfield, *Epistle to the Romans*, 109–10. The double use of ἀδικία in v. 18 contrasts with δικαιοσύνη and δίκαιος in v. 17. See Dunn, *Romans 1–8*, 56; Jewett, *Romans*, 152.

73. E.g., Wilckens, *Der Brief an die Römer*, 1:100–103; Dunn, *Romans 1–8*, 43; Wedderburn, *Reasons for Romans*, 104; Wright, "Romans," 431–32; Wright, *Paul and the Faithfulness of God*, 767.

74. See Wedderburn, *Reasons for Romans*, 119.

75. E.g., Cranfield, *Epistle to the Romans*, 91–92; Wilckens, *Der Brief an die Römer*, 1:102–4. See also Wright, *Paul and the Faithfulness of God*, 767–68.

Against this apocalyptic background, Wilckens emphasizes the antithetical nature of the parallelism between verse 17 and verse 18: God's righteousness and God's wrath are in sharp contrast, even while being part of the same eschatological event.[76] Wedderburn, in contrast, regards the parallelism as complementary: the statement concerning God's wrath in verse 18 represents a dimension of the eschatological revelation of God's righteousness.[77] Thus verse 17 and verse 18 present two complementary aspects of God's saving activity, setting right what is wrong: if one is taking place, the other is also taking place.[78] God's righteousness and God's wrath throw light on each other as two aspects of the saving power of God (v. 16b), newly revealed in the gospel. In contrast, other scholars, among them Campbell, are reluctant to associate the notion of the wrath of God in any way with God's righteousness or with the gospel announcement that God saves.[79]

The way interpreters choose to read (or ignore) γάρ in verse 18 seems often to follow from their prior interpretation of the parallelism or otherwise between verse 17 and verse 18. Wright catalogues five different explanations offered by different interpreters for γάρ in verse 18 before presenting his own.[80] I suggest that these can be reduced to three broad categories: a loose approach, in which γάρ essentially plays no guiding or constraining role; a traditional account, which attempts to take γάρ seriously as an exegetical signal by reading it as causal or explanatory, and a third approach that treats the connective as a communicative signal and pays attention to it within its preceding cotext.

Representatives of the first approach effectively deny that the connective functions as a communicative signal (see §1.1.2, above). The role of γάρ is determined by the cotext. This approach leads some commentators to view γάρ in 1:18 as transitional or indicating continuation, while others interpret it as adversative or as introducing grounds for the preceding claim, depending on the particular construal of 1:18–32, or indeed,

---

76. Wilckens, *Der Brief an die Römer*, 1:101.
77. Wedderburn, *Reasons for Romans*, 119.
78. See Linebaugh, "Announcing the Human," 226; Elliott, *Arrogance of Nations*, 74; Wedderburn, *Reasons for Romans*, 119–20, 125–27. Wedderburn explains this Jewish conception of the revelation of God's righteousness as "two-edged," entailing God's simultaneous deliverance of the faithful, and judgment on their wicked oppressors.
79. E.g., Campbell, *Deliverance of God*, 706–7.
80. Wright, *Paul and the Faithfulness of God*, 764–67.

1:18–3:20 or 1:18–4:25, already chosen.[81] This approach is advocated by BDAG, which asserts that the occurrence in 1:18 is an instance in which the connective "appears to be used adverbially like our 'now.'"[82] The loose approach admits of a diversity of interpretations of 1:18 in its cotext. These range from traditional readings of 1:18 and the material that follows as a counterpoint or antithesis to the gospel, with 1:18 as a heading, through Dunn's New Perspective interpretation, to Campbell's provocative rereading of 1:18–32 as spoken in the voice of Paul's opponent.[83] Many interpretations adopting this approach are incompatible with a procedural view of γάρ. This approach effectively deprives itself of the communicative guidance offered by the connective.

A key claim of Campbell's is that although there are no explicit textual signals indicating a switch in voice from Paul to his opponent in 1:18, Paul's addressees would have detected this by the nonverbal performative signals that Phoebe, the letter carrier and reader, would have given as she read.[84] This is an argument from silence and thus on one level unassailable. But in fact the text itself carries a vital and explicit communicative clue as to how it should be interpreted in its surrounding cotext: γάρ. This clue points in precisely the opposite direction from Campbell's interpretation.[85] According to our analysis, γάρ indicates that the material in verse 18 is to be interpreted as strengthening or bolstering what has just been claimed in verse 17 and not as presenting an antithetical parallel to it. Campbell

---

81. For the transitional reading, see Porter, *Letter to the Romans*, 63, and Zerwick, *Grammatical Analysis*, 459: "γάρ normally explanatory, here merely continues what goes before." A majority of translations adopt this approach, leaving γάρ untranslated here (e.g., NIV; REB; FC; Semeur). For the adversative reading, see C. H. Dodd, *The Epistle of Paul to the Romans*, MNTC (London: Hodder & Stoughton, 1932), 18. Lagrange likewise asserts that γάρ indicates "une légère opposition" (Lagrange, *Saint Paul, Épître aux Romains*, 21). NLT translates with the adversative "but." For reading γάρ as introducing the grounds for the preceding claim, see Wolter, *Röm 1–8*, 130–31.

82. BDAG, s.v. "γάρ," 2.

83. For the counterpoint reading, see Fitzmyer, *Romans*, 277; Anderson, *Ancient Rhetorical Theory and Paul*, 187; Dodd, *Epistle of Paul to the Romans*, 18. For 1:18 as a heading, see Stuhlmacher, *Paul's Letter to the Romans*, 34. Dunn, *Romans 1–8*, 51; Campbell, *Deliverance of God*, 542–43.

84. Campbell, *Deliverance of God*, 530–32.

85. See Barclay, *Paul and the Gift*, 462 n. 29; Griffith-Jones, "Beyond Reasonable Hope of Recognition," 170: "Why ... did Paul not ... simply introduce the change of direction and tone with an adversative ἀλλά (instead of the quite misleading γάρ), [and] flag up the change of speaker and place ὀργὴ θεοῦ emphatically?"

and others point to the fact that in certain cases in Classical Greek and the LXX γάρ occurs in dialogue where there is a switch in speaker.[86] But on closer analysis of the examples given, γάρ can be understood in each case as introducing information that further strengthens preceding communicated assumptions (usually by means of explanation), whether these have been communicated by a previous speaker or the current interlocutor. In no case does γάρ itself introduce information that represents fresh information relevant in its own right as a new implication, and that requires a switch to a completely new communicative context. Nor in any case does γάρ itself indicate a switch in speaker.

Campbell's loose approach to γάρ is based on the premise that it is the wider argument of the cotext that must be determinative for the interpretation of the connective, rather than vice versa. While acknowledging the importance of finding an explanation for γάρ in 1:18, he shies away from stating explicitly how he does read the connective, beyond the suggestion that it is probably an example of "blander" use.[87] He implies, however, that γάρ is used adversatively. In an attempt to find support for this reading, he misrepresents Cranfield's reference to a view from which Cranfield in fact distances himself, namely, that 1:18 is an instance of "an adversative γάρ" that "signals an unexpressed 'no' in a dialogical text."[88] Campbell's treatment of γάρ allows him to argue for a fundamental discontinuity between 1:16–17, on the one hand, and 1:18, on the other. He argues that the "stylistic parallel" between verse 17 and verse 18 in fact denotes a "deliberate contrast" between "two quite different theological programs." Romans 1:18 states the Teacher's "programmatic theological claim" that can in no way be understood as a development of the statement concerning God's righteousness in 1:17. Instead, in 1:17 and 1:18 is found "a fundamentally incompatible juxtaposition denoting two irreconcilable gospels and interpretations of the Christ event."[89]

---

86. See Campbell, "Douglas Campbell's Response to Robin Griffith-Jones," 180 n. 25; Daniel Rodriguez, "On Γαp'd: Dialogue in LXX Isaiah and Romans," *Modula Aggregation of Principles for Bible Translation* (2014), https://map.bloomfire.com/posts/2237610-on-d.

87. Campbell, *Deliverance of God*, 340, 1021 n. 6. See also 1082 n. 61, where Campbell talks of a "muted link," a "pleonastic use" and a "clarifying or emphatic reading," as diverse examples of bland uses.

88. Campbell, *Deliverance of God*, 1021 n. 6, citing Cranfield, *Epistle to the Romans*, 106.

89. Campbell, *Deliverance of God*, 707.

On Campbell's reading, then, 1:18 cannot in any way be interpreted as strengthening or supporting Paul's statement in 1:17. Consequently, a procedural strengthening account of γάρ undermines Campbell's construal at this crucial point to the extent that his whole edifice is in danger of coming crashing down. In this way, a procedural account of γάρ has fundamental implications for an influential interpretation of the wider argument of Romans. It establishes the connective as a key communicative signpost that, when found at a major argumentative crossroads such as 1:18, is ignored by interpreters at their peril.

The second approach to γάρ in 1:18 is more briefly dealt with. Various scholars attempt to take the connective seriously following the traditional causal reading, but simultaneously regard 1:18 as the beginning of a major section in Paul's argument, despite the connection with the preceding argument that γάρ indicates. On this reading, γάρ introduces a supporting rationale for the thematic statement of verses 16–17, which is nevertheless set apart as a result of the section break. The major section begun in verse 18, however, provides support for, rather than a radical contrast to, the notion of God's righteousness that is revealed in the gospel (v. 17). As a result, there is closer continuity than on a radically antithetical reading such as Campbell's. Interpreters taking this approach tend to emphasize the parallelism between verse 17 and verse 18 and to view God's righteousness and God's wrath as two closely related sides of one revelation.[90]

This approach to γάρ is adopted not only by some who follow a traditional "plight-solution" interpretation of chapters 1–4, but also by more recent interpreters proposing a variety of interpretations.[91] Most share in common the reading of verses 16–17 as a *de facto* thematic statement. Among these is Wright. He reads γάρ as causal at "each point in the sequence" of verses 16–18, arguing that if the passage was read in reverse,

---

90. E.g., Bornkamm, "Revelation," 63–64; Linebaugh, "Announcing the Human," 225–26.

91. For the plight-solution interpretation, see, e.g., William Sanday and Arthur C. Headlam, *A Critical and Exegetical Commentary on the Epistle to the Romans*, ICC (Edinburgh: T&T Clark, 1902), 40; Barrett, *Epistle to the Romans*, 34. Cranfield follows a modified version, arguing that γάρ indicates that the whole of 1:18–3:20 supports the specific claim that in the gospel the righteousness of God is being revealed *from faith to faith* (Cranfield, *Epistle to the Romans*, 108). For other interpretations, see, e.g., Barclay, *Paul and the Gift*, 462; Jewett, *Romans*, 150–52; Linebaugh, "Announcing the Human," 216, 223. Linebaugh's interpretation is, however, atypical, in that he takes vv. 16–18 together as the "kerygmatic proclamation": see §6.2.9, below.

"therefore" could be substituted for each "for."[92] Romans 1:18–3:20 explains and unpacks the dense thematic statement of 1:16–17, and 1:17 balances 1:18 in a presentation of divine saving purposes and divine justice.[93] Romans 1:18–2:16 then explain the "depth and universal impartiality" both of sin, and of judgment against wickedness, which are revealed in the gospel of Jesus the Messiah. The gospel reveals that the human disease of sin demands "drastic divine surgery" within Israel itself.[94] If unpacking is understood in terms of explanation, Wright's reading of γάρ in verse 18 is broadly compatible with a procedural reading.[95] This interpretation of γάρ leads him to regard the material in 1:18–3:20 as, on the one hand, supporting the thematic statement, while, on the other, unfolding a new and radical understanding of the depth of human sin.[96] But this reading of γάρ does not explain the strengthening connection indicated by the series of γάρ clauses from verse 18 all the way back to verse 15. This is despite the fact that Wright acknowledges that Paul offers the statement in verses 16–17 as the further explanation of his desire to preach the gospel in Rome and argues that Paul's gospel confronts Roman imperial ideology.[97]

In general, this second approach to γάρ, though broadly compatible with a strengthening procedural explanation, does not fully exploit the communicative guidance given by the connective. In particular, it does not encourage us to pay attention to the role played by previously communicated assumptions from the preceding cotext in establishing a strengthening relationship. As a result, it does not emphasize the way in which γάρ contributes to the coherence of wider subsections. Consequently, this approach misses the significance of the tight chain of γάρ clauses leading all the way back to verse 15 and does not seek to integrate this into an explanation of verse 18 and verses 16–17.

The third scholarly approach to γάρ in 1:18 is most compatible with a procedural reading. It not only takes the connective seriously as a communicative signal but also pays close attention to the fourfold chain of γάρ clauses in verses 16–18. Runge, who applies insights from discourse

---

92. Wright, *Paul and the Faithfulness of God*, 765.
93. Wright, "Romans," 428; *Paul and the Faithfulness of God*, 769.
94. Wright, *Paul and the Faithfulness of God*, 768–69.
95. Throughout his discussions of Romans, Wright consistently reads γάρ as introducing explanations that unpack preceding statements.
96. Wright, *Paul and the Faithfulness of God*, 768–69.
97. Wright, "Romans," 423.

6. γάρ as Communicative Signpost: Guidance in Tracing Paul's Argument   229

analysis to Romans, is one example of this approach. Runge views γάρ as a discourse marker or structural signal that indicates that the material that follows it functions as supporting information or "motivational material" and represents a "digression" from the main argument. Information introduced by γάρ is "embedded" within the higher level of the argument of the information that it supports. Each γάρ clause in verses 16–18 thus represents an argumentative digression that "sidestep[s] onto an embedded argument line," taking Paul further away from his "big idea" in 1:8–10, which is his desire to visit Rome. Despite recognizing the structural significance of this desire to visit Rome, however, Runge's interpretation of the epistle's argument seems unaffected by it.[98] He maintains that Paul does not return to the structural level of this initial "big idea" until 15:22. His analysis of γάρ is helpful to the extent that it recognizes that each chunk of motivating material introduced by the connective "looks backward rather than forward." Ultimately, however, Runge gives more attention to the hierarchical structure of the text than to Paul's communicative intentions. Thus for Runge, 1:18–4:25 represents "one giant digression in Paul's overall argument."[99] His perspective prevents him from considering Paul's desire to visit Rome, and the situation there, as a key to tracing the coherence of Paul's thought in verses 15–18.

In contrast, other representatives of this approach give close consideration to the coherence of the assumptions communicated in the preceding cotext of verse 18, viewing verses 15–18 as a single complex of thought that should not be broken up by the imposition of a section heading.[100] Dahl, for instance, finds in 1:16 "the encompassing theme for the whole main body of the letter" and in verses 17 and 18 two antithetical subthemes. He recognizes the close link between the "thematic statement" of verses 16–18 and Paul's "travel plans" in verses 14–15 and makes sense of this in terms of Paul's missionary concerns, which are behind the purpose of the letter. The thematic statement about the gospel as God's power for salvation provides a motivation for why Paul is not ashamed of the gospel but wants to "confess it boldly to all people everywhere, even *in Rome*" (emphasis

---

98. Runge views this mismatch between structure and argument as problematic but does not attempt to resolve it (Runge, *Romans*, 19).

99. Runge, *Romans*, 5, 19.

100. See Dahl, "Missionary Theology in the Epistle to the Romans," 78; Wedderburn, *Reasons for Romans*, 124; Elliott, *Arrogance of Nations*, 83–85.

added).[101] Wedderburn, on the other hand, also views the statement in verse 18 as the third part of the programmatic statements of verses 16b–18 but construes the letter's purpose quite differently. God's wrath is part of the "two-edged quality" of God's righteousness.[102] The statement in verse 18 thus provides a rationale for the claim in verse 17: "God's righteousness is being revealed [in the gospel], since, for a start, this aspect of it, God's wrath, is being revealed [in the preaching of Paul's gospel]." The triple programmatic statement gives a threefold reason why Paul is not ashamed of the gospel. This claim in turn provides a rationale for why Paul is keen to preach the good news to those in Rome, specifically related to the situation there, where there is a danger that Paul's gospel may be viewed as shameful (see §6.2.3, above).[103]

Elliott, meanwhile, uses his anti-imperial reading to explain the relationship between 1:15 (and preceding) and 1:16–18. He argues that in order to make sense of the series of γάρ clauses we must answer the question, "How is God's justice revealed through the revelation of God's wrath?" The answer is that God's justice is being demonstrated in the gospel in a publicly manifest way in the current situation in Rome, in the execution of God's wrath against the wicked and unjust.[104] Elliott contends that the statement in verse 18 is an allusion to the notorious depravity and savagery of the imperial house and, further, that the whole of 1:18–32 can be read as a "catalog of misdeeds ... of the Julio-Claudian dynasty," against whom God's wrath is being demonstrated in the spectacular deaths of emperors such as Gaius.[105] Thus in Romans Paul declares a message of God's sovereignty and justice in the Messiah and an imminent day of reckoning, which challenges imperial injustice.

In sum, this third approach to γάρ in 1:18 comes closest to paying full attention to the connective's communicative guidance, though it does not recognize the inferential guidance that γάρ gives. Dahl, Wedderburn, and Elliott all effectively treat γάρ as a communicative signpost, respecting the integrity of the sequence of γάρ clauses in verses 15–18. As a result, all take into careful account the preceding cotext all the way back to verse 15. But these three interpreters arrive at three quite different construals

---

101. Dahl, "Missionary Theology in the Epistle to the Romans," 82, 78.
102. Wedderburn, *Reasons for Romans*, 119.
103. Wedderburn, *Reasons for Romans*, 124–25.
104. Elliott, *Arrogance of Nations*, 76–77.
105. Elliott, *Arrogance of Nations*, 82.

of these verses in relation to the letter's main argument and purpose. Can the application of a procedural account of γάρ help us to decide between them?

6.2.7. Romans 1:18: Applying a Procedural Account

Let us consider first Dahl's interpretation (D). Dahl translates 1:16b as follows: "The gospel is God's power for salvation, for Greeks as well as for Jews."[106] Verse 17, "In the gospel God's righteousness is being revealed, 'from faith to faith,'" and verse 18, "The wrath of God is revealed from heaven against all ungodliness and wickedness of the human race," are read as two antithetical subthemes that are dealt with "in reverse order," in 1:18–3:20 and 3:21–4:25 respectively.[107] On a procedural reading of γάρ, verse 18 represents a complex of strengthening premises and the statement in verse 17 a claim that needs strengthening. Following Dahl's antithetical reading, however, no strengthening inferential series between verse 18 and verse 17 obviously suggests itself without undue processing effort. The connection between verse 17 and verse 18 can only be understood in the light of the subsequent argument in chapters 1–4, not immediately established inferentially in the light of the preceding cotext. It is equally difficult to establish an inferential strengthening series between verse 18 and the whole of verse 16b–17:

Series D:
   P (v. 16b–17): The gospel is God's power for salvation, for Greeks as well as for Jews. In the gospel God's righteousness is being revealed, "from faith to faith."[108]
   Q introduced by γάρ (v. 18): The wrath of God is revealed from heaven against all ungodliness and wickedness of the human race.
   IA: If the wrath of God is revealed from heaven against all ungodliness and wickedness of the human race, then all humanity needs saving.

We are left here with a logical gap: it does not follow from the fact that all humanity needs saving that the gospel is therefore God's power for salva-

---

106. Dahl, "Missionary Theology in the Epistle to the Romans," 78. Dahl reverses the order of "the Jew … and also the Greek" and leaves out "for all who believe."
107. Dahl, "Missionary Theology in the Epistle to the Romans," 82.
108. Dahl is silent regarding the citation in v. 17b.

tion. Despite Dahl's recognition that verses 16–18 must be understood as closely connected, a procedural reading of γάρ does not support his interpretation.

Second, we consider Elliott's interpretation (E). Following a procedural account of γάρ in verse 18, verse 17 is identified as needing strengthening and verse 18 as a complex of strengthening premises. Is it possible to construct a strengthening series between the two?

Series E:

P (v. 17): In the proclamation of God's imminent triumph[109] the justice of God is revealed, through faithfulness, to faithfulness; as it is written, "The one who is just will live by faithfulness."

Q introduced by γάρ (v. 18): The wrath of God is revealed from heaven against all impiety and injustice of those who by their injustice suppress the truth.[110]

IA1: The injustice and ungodliness in question are the injustice and ungodliness of the Roman emperors and imperial house. (Highly accessible in the social setting of Rome, according to Elliott's construal.)[111]

?IA2: God's wrath against Roman imperial injustice is revealed publicly in the spectacular deaths of the emperors. (Elliott contends that this would have been easily inferable for Paul's addressees, but this seems speculative.)

IA3: The gospel is the proclamation of the triumph of Jesus's/God's alternative, counterimperial lordship. (Highly accessible in the social setting of Rome, according to Elliott.)[112]

?IA4: If God's wrath is revealed publicly against imperial injustice in the deaths of the emperors, it demonstrates that God's justice is being revealed in the proclamation of the triumph of God's lordship. (But this is based on the speculative IA2, and is also a non sequitur.)[113]

---

109. Elliott's translation of "in the gospel" (Elliott, *Arrogance of Nations*, 74).

110. Elliott, *Arrogance of Nations*, 74.

111. This view is challenged by John M. G. Barclay, "Why the Roman Empire Was Insignificant to Paul," in *Pauline Churches*, 363–89.

112. E.g., Elliott, *Arrogance of Nations*, 51, 74. See also Wright, "Romans," 404; Jewett, *Romans*, 138–39; Georgi, "God Turned Upside Down."

113. It is not possible, without undue effort, to infer a logical connection between the deaths of the emperors and the proclamation of the gospel.

?C: (strengthening v. 17a): In the proclamation of God's imminent triumph, the justice of God is revealed.

Series E is problematic in two ways. First it depends on accessing speculative background assumptions, particularly those concerning the deaths of the emperors as a demonstration of God's justice. Second, it involves a non sequitur and so is not a complete series. In addition, while the series reinforces the first part of verse 17a, it does not lead to the strengthening of the expression ἐκ πίστεως εἰς πίστιν. So a strengthening procedural account of γάρ in verse 18 is not fully compatible with Elliott's anti-imperial reading of verses 15–18, despite the noteworthy attention Elliott pays to Paul's claim in verse 15 in his construal of verses 16–18.

Third, we turn to Wedderburn's interpretation of verses 15–18 (F).[114] In relevance-theoretic terms, this reading acknowledges that assumptions communicated in verses 15–17 are all highly accessible as part of the comprehension of verse 18. Applying a procedural analysis, the information in verse 18 is identified as strengthening premises and the statement in verse 17 as needing strengthening. I suggest that the following strengthening series might be constructed, triggered by γάρ in verse 18:

Series F:
    P (v. 17a): In the gospel [that Paul preaches] God's righteousness is being revealed, "from faith to faith."[115]
    Q introduced by γάρ (v. 18): The wrath of God is revealed from heaven against all ungodliness and wickedness of the human race.
    IA1: God's wrath is the negative side of the eschatological revelation of God's righteousness.[116] (Accessible from encyclopedic knowledge of Jewish teaching.)[117]
    IA2: The wrath of God is revealed from heaven against all ungodliness and wickedness of the human race in the preaching of Paul's gospel.[118] (Inferable from the fact that the gospel is the topic of v. 16 and salient in the preceding cotext: vv. 1–5, 9, 15.)

---

114. Wedderburn, *Reasons for Romans*, 124–25.
115. Wedderburn is silent regarding the citation in v. 17b.
116. Wedderburn *Reasons for Romans*, 119. See Rom 2:5 for the eschatological character of God's wrath.
117. E.g., Isa 13:6–14:8; 59:15–18; Zeph 1:14–2:3; 3; Mal 4:1–5.
118. Wedderburn, *Reasons for Romans*, 120.

IA3: If God's wrath against ungodliness and wickedness of the human race is the negative side of the revelation of God's righteousness and is revealed in the preaching of the gospel, then the gospel reveals God's righteousness.

C (strengthening v. 17a): In the gospel that Paul preaches, God's righteousness is being revealed.

This inferential series leads to the strengthening of the statement in verse 17a, with the result that it is held more firmly as valid by addressees. Wedderburn's interpretation is, then, compatible with a procedural reading of γάρ. Moreover, IA4 and IA5 below, although logically superfluous to the strengthening of verse 17a, are, on Wedderburn's analysis, made highly accessible following on from IA3 of this series and contribute to the further strengthening of verse 16a, via the chain of γάρ clauses:

IA4: If the gospel reveals God's righteousness, it demonstrates that God is righteous.
IA5: If the gospel demonstrates that God is righteous, then the gospel is not shameful.

Wedderburn's reading of verse 18 is thus supported by a procedural reading of γάρ both in verse 18 and in the whole strengthening chain of verses 16–18. But it has a weakness: while contributing to the strengthening of the claim that God's righteousness is being revealed in the gospel, it does not provide further support for the assumption communicated in verse 17a that this revelation happens ἐκ πίστεως εἰς πίστιν. In focusing on an explanation of verse 18 in terms of the previous statements about God's righteousness and the claim that the gospel is not shameful, Wedderburn neglects the equally significant claims regarding the relationship between πίστις and the gospel in verse 16b and verse 17a. Since these claims are not further strengthened by verse 18 on his construal, they become less argumentatively salient than the claim regarding God's righteousness.

Is it possible to find an interpretation that recognizes the strengthening role of verse 18 in relation to what precedes *and* respects the chain of γάρ clauses in 1:16–18, as Wedderburn does, and at the same time accords argumentative significance to all of 1:17a, including the phrase ἐκ πίστεως εἰς πίστιν? The scriptural citation from Habakkuk in 1:17b brings weight behind this expression, highlighting its argumentative importance (as does the repetition of the πιστ- root four times in vv. 16b–17).

I propose that a solution is possible if we follow a reading of πίστις as faithfulness in verse 17, along the lines of Wright, Morgan, and others.[119] On such an interpretation, πίστις can be understood both in relation to God's righteousness in verse 17a and God's wrath in verse 18, as God demonstrates his righteousness through his faithfulness to his faithful people in saving them from unrighteousness and injustice, and in setting the world to rights. In this way, we can make sense of verse 18 as strengthening material for the claim that God's righteousness is revealed ἐκ πίστεως εἰς πίστιν. Following Wright's interpretation, I propose the strengthening series below (G). The citation from Hab 2:4 is omitted from this because the series increases the relevance of verse 17a rather than verse 17b. I suggest that the citation, as authoritative scripture, is already optimally relevant as it stands and does not need further strengthening. Addressees' comprehension processes therefore jump over verse 17b and select the statement in verse 17a as the candidate for strengthening.

Series G:
   P (v. 17a): In the gospel the righteousness of God is being revealed from [God's] faithfulness to [human] faith-fullness.
   Q introduced by γάρ (v. 18): The wrath of God is being revealed from heaven against all ungodliness and unrighteousness of human beings who suppress the truth in unrighteousness.
   IA1: The wrath of God is being revealed from heaven against all ungodliness and unrighteousness ... in the preaching of Paul's gospel.
   (**IA2**: Paul's gospel is about Jesus as Messiah and eschatological Lord. [Inferable from 1:3–4.])
   IA3: God's wrath against unrighteousness, revealed in the gospel, is the negative side of the eschatological revelation of God's righteousness and part of his salvation of his faith-full people.
   IA4: If God's wrath against unrighteousness, revealed in the gospel, is part of his salvation of his faith-full people, then God's wrath is an expression of God's faithfulness toward his faith-full people.
   IA5: If God's wrath, revealed in the gospel, is an expression of God's faithfulness toward his faith-full people, then in the gospel God's righ-

---

119. Wright, *Paul and the Faithfulness of God*, 1001, 1466–71; Morgan, *Roman Faith and Christian Faith*, 286. Wright understands the πίστις of believers as a complex concept in which faith/trust in God and faithfulness as God's people merge.

teousness is revealed out of God's faithfulness toward those who are faith-full.
C (strengthening v. 17a): In the gospel the righteousness of God is being revealed out of God's faithfulness to human faith-fullness.

Unlike series F, this proposed inferential series leads not only to the strengthening of the claim that God's righteousness is being revealed in the gospel, but also to the strengthening of the information that this is revealed ἐκ πίστεως εἰς πίστιν. It thus increases the comprehensibility of the whole statement in verse 17a so that it is held more strongly as valid, thereby augmenting its argumentative relevance and salience. As with Wedderburn's interpretation, this series is able to make sense of verse 18 both in the immediately preceding cotext of verse 17 and the wider cotext of verses 15–18. Backed up in this way by verse 18, verse 17 in turn provides further strengthening for the claim in verse 16b:

P (v. 16b): The gospel is the power of God for salvation for all who are faith-full, Jews first and also Greeks.
Q introduced by γάρ (v. 17a): In the gospel God's righteousness is being revealed out of God's faithfulness toward those who are faith-full.
IA: If, in the gospel, God's righteousness is being revealed out of God's faithfulness toward those who are faith-full, shown in his wrath against unrighteousness, then the gospel is the power of God for salvation for all who are faith-full, Jews first and also Greeks.
C (strengthening v. 16b): The gospel is the power of God for salvation for all who are faith-full, Jews first and also Greeks.

As a result of this series, verse 16b is also strengthened so that addressees hold it more firmly as valid and it produces increased cognitive effects for them. These include the strengthening of various potential implications relating both to the priority of the Jews in God's purposes and to the fundamental parity of Jews and gentiles in the light of the gospel.[120] Such implications hint at a unifying purpose for the letter among Jewish-orientated and gentile-orientated Roman believers.[121] We can suggest that

---

120. See Barclay, *Paul and the Gift*, 454, 461.
121. See Watson, *Paul, Judaism and the Gentiles*, 190.

the perception that Paul's gospel has anti-Jewish tendencies may have threatened to destabilize relations and exacerbate tensions between torah-observant and non-torah-observant believers in Rome.¹²² In response, Paul backs up his claim that he is not ashamed to preach the gospel to those in Rome, using the striking expression Ἰουδαίῳ τε πρῶτον καὶ Ἕλληνι, in order to emphasize both that his gospel of salvation respects the special role of Israel in God's purposes and that it is for *all* who are faith-full, Jews and gentiles alike.¹²³ We must wait for our discussion of 15:7–13 to explore whether such a construal is supported by data from other parts of the letter.

The strengthening of the claims in verse 16b, guided by γάρ in verse 17a, leads in turn to the further reinforcement of verse 16a, persuading skeptical addressees of the validity of the claim that Paul is not ashamed of the gospel (as good news to be proclaimed in Rome). If we revisit series A (countering suspicions of anti-Jewish tendencies) proposed above for the strengthening of verse 16a, we find that the proposed strengthening series G for verses 17–18 fits well with it. Series G provides an extra inference (+IA) gained from verse 17 and 18 that can be inserted into series A and functions as further bolstering support for the claim that Paul's gospel does not have anti-Jewish tendencies:

P (v. 16a): I [Paul] am not ashamed of the gospel.
Q (v. 16b, introduced by γάρ): [The gospel] is the power of God for salvation for all who are faith-full, Jew first and also Greek.
IA1: There are many Jewish-orientated Christ-believers in Rome.
IA2: Some in Rome are claiming that Paul's gospel is anti-Jewish.
IA3: If the gospel Paul proclaims is the power of God for salvation for all who are faith-full, Jews first and also Greeks, then Paul's gospel is not anti-Jewish.
+IA: If God's eschatological righteousness and wrath are revealed in the gospel, out of God's faithfulness toward his faith-full people,

---

122. See Wedderburn, *Reasons for Romans*, 141–42; Tobin, *Paul's Rhetoric in Its Contexts*, 384, 416.

123. See also Watson, *Paul, Judaism and the Gentiles*, 189–90. Watson argues that reading v. 16b in conjunction with the reference to the Roman situation in v. 15 makes sense of the unexpected assertion in v. 16b that the gospel is "for the Jew first, and also for the Greek." He regards this historically contextualized interpretation of v. 16b as more plausible than a "theological interpretation."

then Paul's gospel is not anti-Jewish but built on Jewish eschatological teaching and expectation.

IA4: If Paul's gospel is not anti-Jewish, then Paul does not need to be ashamed of it in Rome, where there are many Jewish-orientated Christ-believers.

C (confirming v. 16a): Paul is not ashamed of the gospel.

In this way, as a result of the cumulative strengthening created by the series of γάρ clauses in verses 16b–18, the confirming evidence in verse 16b is reinforced, and the relevance of verse 16a is in turn further increased. Finally, this has the knock-on effect of emphatically buttressing the claim in verse 15 regarding preaching the gospel to those in Rome, to which the entire strengthening chain leads back. Consequently, the claim in verse 15 is underlined as a highly salient and relevant point in Paul's communication, from which many potential implications are to be derived for the Roman addressees. The case for proposed series A—countering suspicions of anti-Jewish tendencies—as a construal of verses 15–16 is thus strengthened, since this series is fully compatible with the procedural strengthening account of γάρ in verses 17–18 laid out in series G. Conversely, since a procedural strengthening reading of γάρ in verse 18 lends little support to an anti-imperial construal of verses 17–18 (see series E), the validity of proposed series B, the anti-imperial reading of verses 15–16, is undermined. While the latter is a plausible construal of verses 15–16, it is inconsistent with the wider cotext.

6.2.8. Romans 1:18: Argumentative Implications

Our proposed reading of verse 18, based on the procedural guidance provided by γάρ, provides a way of understanding this verse so that there is no conflict between the communicative signal given by γάρ and our construal of the coherence and thrust of the argument. The statement in verse 18 is relevant in relation to verse 17 as a strengthening complex of assumptions that increases the cognitive effects to be derived from verse 17a. Specifically, it makes accessible assumptions that enable addressees to understand better in what way God's righteousness as revealed in the gospel is an expression of God's faithfulness toward his faith-full people. It is revealed as he deals with unrighteousness and injustice, fulfilling his commitment to save them.

This procedural reading of γάρ in verse 18 thus provides an answer to our third question. It compels us to interpret verse 18 in a close strengthening relationship with verse 17 and, in turn, with verses 16 and 15. It lends support to interpretations that seek to account for the relationship between verses 16–18 and Paul's claim in verse 15. The reading provides a coherent and integrated understanding of the entirety of verses 15–18, in keeping with the guidance given by the chain of γάρ clauses. It identifies verse 15 as highly salient in Paul's communication. The fact that this highly salient claim makes explicit reference to the believers in Rome also leads to the inference that the situation in Rome is uppermost in Paul's mind as he writes the letter. This begins to suggest an answer to our fourth question, namely, that the situation in Rome is directly related to Paul's purpose in writing.

The weighty theological material of verses 16b–18 is brought behind Paul's claim that he is not ashamed of the gospel, and thus also behind his assertion that he desires to preach it to those in the capital, in order to bolster these claims and give them persuasive punch. This suggests that Paul anticipates that his statement in verse 15 may raise implicit questions for some of his addressees and may not be accepted as valid without further evidence to strengthen it. This bolstering material therefore takes the form of pertinent aspects of Paul's gospel, specially tailored in order to persuade his Roman addressees that he does indeed have good reason to want to share it with them, because it is good, relevant news for them.

In verses 16–18, then, Paul presents tailored aspects of his version of the gospel, of its power to save, its universality, its eschatological character, and its Jewish-rootedness.[124] He does this in order to make clear that he is not ashamed of this gospel as something to be announced in Rome to the multicultural mix of Roman believers, many of whom have been influenced by the Jewish faith and who live in a minority situation within the dominant Greco-Roman culture. This suggests that what follows in the letter body is best understood as an expression of Paul's gospel specifically geared to this audience in Rome. We must wait for the discussion of 15:7–13 below to see how data from the rest of the letter lends further support to this construal of the epistle's purpose.

---

124. See Barclay, *Paul and the Gift*, 460.

6.2.9. Romans 1:19–32

There is not space here for a detailed examination of 1:19–32 in the light of my analysis of 1:15–18, nor of its place in the epistle's argumentation. Nevertheless, some observations on its relationship with 1:15–18, and its role in the progression of the argument, are in order. We have already ruled out Campbell's reading of 1:18–32. The procedural analysis of γάρ in 1:16–18 also sheds light on other interpretations of these verses. It suggests strongly that 1:18–3:20 cannot be read as an elaboration of the theme of the revelation of the wrath of God, with 1:18 as its heading.[125] Neither can verse 18 be viewed as an opening bracketing statement that finds its corresponding closing in 1:32, with verses 18–32 an explanation of what is implicit in the thematic statement of verses 16–17.[126] At the same time, Elliott's anti-imperial reading of verses 18–32, while respecting the close connection of verse 18 with verses 15–17, seems unlikely, with no explicit textual evidence to support it.[127]

When considering the question of the division of the text into sections, we need to heed Dahl's warnings regarding the inappropriateness of imposing rigid artificial divisions on the text.[128] Nevertheless, the occurrence of διότι in 1:19a brings to an end the tight fourfold strengthening chain of γάρ clauses in 1:16–18.[129] As a result, I suggest that what follows from verse 19 onward belongs less closely with what precedes it in verses 15–18 and should not be viewed as part of the cumulative buttressing found in verses 16–18 for the claim in verse 15.[130] In verse 19a, διότι introduces a reason why God's wrath is being revealed against the wickedness and unrighteousness of those who suppress the truth: it is because what can be known about God is plain to them. This statement in verse 19a then

---

125. *Pace* Dahl, "Missionary Theology in the Epistle to the Romans," 79.
126. *Pace* Wright, "Romans," 430.
127. Elliott, *Arrogance of Nations*, 6. Elliott argues that 1:19–32 is an "accurate catalog of misdeeds" of the Julio-Claudian dynasty.
128. Dahl, "Missionary Theology in the Epistle to the Romans," 79. See also Wedderburn, *Reasons for Romans*, 124.
129. I have not undertaken a detailed analysis of διότι, but suggest that it does not play the same procedural role as γάρ and does not guide toward the construction of an inferential strengthening series. Instead, it introduces a reason or cause and may communicate some semantic content in a way that γάρ does not.
130. See Linebaugh's analysis of vv. 16–18, on the one hand, and of vv. 19–32, on the other (Linebaugh, "Announcing the Human," 216).

6. γάρ as Communicative Signpost: Guidance in Tracing Paul's Argument   241

in turn becomes a springboard for the development of thought in verses 19–32, which traces the "history of sin" in the face of humanity's "creation-related knowledge of God."[131]

Based on our analysis of 1:15–18, the statement in verse 19a can thus be viewed as the basis of a fresh line of thought found in verses 19–32 (a basis that is itself strengthened by γάρ clauses in v. 19b and v. 20). Using material influenced by Jewish teaching, verses 19–32 trace the story of how humanity has refused to recognize its creator and has instead turned to idolatry. Such a reading of verses 19–32 shares elements in common with Jonathan Linebaugh's analysis of 1:16–32.[132] Paying careful attention to γάρ in verses 16b–18, Linebaugh interprets these verses as an "apocalyptic kerygma" that proclaims the "double apocalypse of divine righteousness and wrath" revealed in the gospel event.[133] In the context of this kerygmatic proclamation, verses 19–32 then represent a "targeted polemic" that catalogues the idolatry and immorality of all humanity, including Israel.[134] Although Linebaugh's identification of this proclamation in verses 16–18 differs from the more contextualized reading of these verses proposed above, and their relationship to verse 15, his recognition of a distinction between verses 16–18 and verses 19–32 is nevertheless compatible with this analysis.

I suggest that the parallels between this section and Wis 13–15 may be part of Paul's strategy for underlining that his gospel is not supersessionist but arises out of Jewish teaching and a Jewish worldview and is in continuity with it.[135] This is similar to his use in verses 17–18 of the Jewish eschatological concept of the two-sidedness of justice/righteous-

---

131. Linebaugh, "Announcing the Human," 216–17.
132. Linebaugh finds in 1:19–32 "the history of sin," within which Israel is allusively included (Linebaugh, "Announcing the Human," 216).
133. Linebaugh, "Announcing the Human," 224.
134. Linebaugh, "Announcing the Human," 216, 223.
135. For discussions of parallels and crucial differences between the two texts, through which Paul makes his point that Jews are included in the indictment of idolatry in Rom 1:18–32, see Linebaugh, "Announcing the Human"; Barclay, *Paul and the Gift*, 462–64; Watson, *Paul and the Hermeneutics of Faith*, 405–11. In contrast, see Zetterholm, "Non-Jewish Interlocutor," 58; Stowers, *Rereading of Romans*, 85–97. Linebaugh argues that there is continuity between Wisdom and Romans. Paul, however, situates his engagement with Wisdom within an "antithetical argument" in order to include Israel in the polemical critique and "establish the essential unity of humanity" (Linebaugh, "Announcing the Human," 217).

ness. But although in verses 19–32 Paul uses aspects of this Jewish critique of gentile idolatry, he adapts it to include elements that allude to Israelite disobedience, thus preparing the way for his fundamental claim that there is no difference between Jews and gentiles when it comes to the issue of rebellion against God (3:9, 22).[136] Moreover, I propose that this gradual introduction of a critique of Jewish sin and idolatry by means of allusions to stories from Israel's history and a modification of Wisdom's perspective may also arise from Paul's concern not to be perceived as anti-Jewish.

Thus in verses 16–18 pertinent aspects of Paul's gospel are presented, in Jewish conceptual terms (and citing Jewish scripture), as God's power to save all who are faith-full (*Jews first* and also Greeks), through the revelation of God's righteousness, which expresses his faithfulness in saving his faith-full people from injustice/unrighteousness.[137] In verses 19–32, however, the unrighteousness from which those who trust in God's righteousness are to be saved is exposed, not as that of their oppressors or enemies, but as none other than their own, whether gentile or Jewish. The enemy from which those who trust in God are to be powerfully delivered is not primarily Roman oppressors and imperial injustice, but their own ungodliness (1:18), which is further revealed later in Paul's argument as the power of sin (e.g., 3:9; 5:12–21; 7:13–25).[138] I suggest that Paul frames his gospel in this particular way at the beginning of Romans in order to allay suspicions of anti-Jewish tendencies and therefore of a gospel that may be shameful to proclaim in Rome (vv. 15–16a). His aim may be to redress the balance in the wake of the Galatian controversy, demonstrating that his gospel recognizes Jewish priority, while showing that this does not consist in a moral or ontological difference between Jews and gentiles in relation to sin.[139]

6.2.10. Summary: Questions Answered

In sum, the application of a procedural account to γάρ in 1:15–18 has thrown light on our four questions as follows:

---

136. See Barclay, *Paul and the Gift*, 463. Barclay draws attention to the echoes of "a biblical rebuke of Israelite idolatry" in Rom 1:23 (cf. LXX Ps 105:20).
137. The use of Jewish conceptual terms emphasizes the gospel's continuity with the Jewish faith (Walters, *Ethnic Issues in Paul's Letter to the Romans*, 74–75).
138. To which God has himself handed them over: 1:24, 26, 28.
139. For Jewish priority, see Barclay, *Paul and the Gift*, 459–61, 464.

1. The statements in verses 15–18 are bound together by the procedural guidance given by γάρ. Consequently, they should not be separated from one another in interpretation by the imposition of major section breaks in the text. The fourfold strengthening chain of γάρ clauses leads back to verse 15, supporting the claim in that verse and underlining its argumentative salience. In other words, many cognitive effects are to be derived from it for Paul's addressees. The fact that this reference to Rome is highly salient as Paul opens his argument suggests that the Roman destination of the epistle is central to his purpose in writing.

2. Verses 16–17 thus need to be interpreted as strengthening material within the context of Paul's desire to preach the gospel to those in Rome, rather than regarded as an isolated thesis statement that summarizes a gospel of justification by faith and thereby announces the epistle's theme. Nevertheless, since this material represents extracts of the Rome-relevant version of the gospel that Paul develops throughout the epistle, it is to be expected that we find here snatches of the themes to come. These verses are neither a digression, as Runge maintains, nor the heart of what Paul has to say, as Wright argues. Instead, verses 16b–18 represent a powerful theological rationale backing up the claim in verse 16a that Paul is not ashamed of the gospel. This in turn backs up the expression in verse 15 of his desire to preach the gospel to those in Rome. The manner in which Paul expresses this theological supporting evidence in Jewish-rooted yet multiethnic terms is shaped by what Paul perceives to be specifically relevant to his Roman addressees, and what he wishes to achieve among them. We should not allow its theological weight to distract us from the argumentative salience of the statement in verse 15, which it strengthens.

3. Verse 18 should be interpreted as part of the complex of assumptions in verses 16–18 marshaled to bolster Paul's claim in verse 15 and not as a heading for a new section describing God's wrath against humankind. The statement concerning God's wrath is to be understood as part of the revelation of God's righteousness that is nothing less than God's power to save his faith-full people who put their trust in him.

Whereas verse 18 looks backward to verses 15–17, in verse 19 a new phase of thought begins (though we should be wary of imposing sharp breaks on the text). While telling the story of humanity's sinfulness, verses 19–32 should not simply be viewed as the proof of humanity's guilt that paves the way for the presentation of the gospel solution in 3:21–26. Nor should they be regarded as a progressive acknowledgment of guilt through which individuals must pass before responding to the gospel. Instead, they can be understood as Paul's radical presentation, in the light of the revelation of God's righteousness in Christ, of just what it is that God's faith-full people, both Jews and gentiles, are delivered/saved from: not from unrighteous enemies, but their own ungodliness and unrighteousness, that is, the power of sin.

4. We can further suggest that a coherent account of the totality of the strengthening information in 1:16–18 may be provided by the proposal that Paul writes his letter, explaining his gospel, to counter a perception among Roman believers that this gospel may be anti-Jewish, a perception that not only threatens to bring it into disrepute, but also to exacerbate differences between torah-observant and non-torah observant believers in Rome, undermining unity.[140] Paul therefore emphasizes that his gospel is not shameful, and that it respects the priority of Jews in God's saving purposes, while insisting on the equality of Jews and gentiles both from the perspective of sin, and of God's mercy.[141] We shall see more clearly, however, when we come to consider the data in 15:7–13 and put it together with our findings from 1:15–18, that this concern to allay misgivings that his gospel is anti-Jewish is not in itself Paul's primary purpose. Instead, I propose that it is part of his more fundamental intention to build unity, between Jewish or torah-observant believers on the one hand, and gentile or non-torah-observant believers on the other, an intention that is already hinted at in the motif in verse 16b, "to the Jew first and also to the gentile."

In anticipation of our investigation of 15:7–13, then, at this point we can further tentatively hypothesize that Paul is responding to tensions caused by various kinds of ethnocentrism and partisanship among Roman believers.[142] These would be particularly related to torah observance and differing perspectives on the continuing role of Israel in God's purposes and thus exacerbated by the perception that his gospel is anti-Jewish. Paul thus uses Jewish themes and scripture in his theological rationale in verses

---

140. For disrepute, see Reasoner, *Strong and the Weak*, 235; Wedderburn, *Reasons for Romans*, 103–4; Tobin, *Paul's Rhetoric in Its Contexts*, 14, 73–77. For undermining unity, see Wedderburn, *Reasons for Romans*, 142. Cf. Tobin, *Paul's Rhetoric in Its Contexts*, 384, 416.

141. Barclay argues that the motif in 1:16b emphasizes both "the priority of the Jew in both salvation and judgment" and "the common position of Jew and Greek" (Barclay, *Paul and the Gift*, 464; see also 460).

142. Walters, *Ethnic Issues in Paul's Letter to the Romans*, 75; Russell, "Alternative Suggestion for the Purpose of Romans," 182–84.

16–18, and in his discussion of the story of humanity's sin in verses 19–32, to emphasize the Jewish foundation of the gospel.[143] At the same time, his insistence that all, Jews and gentiles, are accepted by God on the basis of faith-full trust in Christ hints at the fact that he aims to counter all forms of ethnocentrism and arrogance, Jewish and gentile (see the discussion of 15:7–13 in §6.3, below).

Following such a construal, Paul would be writing to counter various misperceptions and tensions among his Roman addressees, with the aim of building unity, as a witness to the power of the gospel. Such a hypothesis would account for all of the material in verses 16–18 in relation to verse 15 (and preceding). In order for this hypothesis to be plausible, however, it needs corroboration from evidence in the rest of the letter. With this in mind, we now turn to 15:7–13. We will see how our construal of the letter's purpose is further supported by a procedural analysis of γάρ in this passage and how this throws more light on the way the Roman situation shapes Paul's purpose and argument.

6.3. Romans 15:7–13: Bringing It All Together

This passage, occurring at the opposite end of the epistle's argument from 1:15–18, is potentially equally significant for determining the letter's direction and purpose. Romans 15:7 functions on one level as a conclusion to the whole argument of 14:1–15:6, and scholars' reading of that subsection determines to a certain extent their view of the role of 15:7–13.[144] For some who read the discussion of the weak and the strong as responding to a specific situation among the Roman believers, 15:7–13 serves as an argumentative key for the entire epistle.[145] There is a single occurrence of γάρ in 15:8. It is my contention that this plays a decisive role in identifying the thrust of Paul's argument, not only in these verses, but in the wider cotext. Its guidance helps shed light first on the identity of the weak and

---

143. In vv. 16–18 in particular, the theme of the revelation of God's righteousness and his wrath at unrighteousness. For the emphasis on the Jewish foundation of the gospel, see Barclay, *Paul and the Gift*, 460.

144. That 15:7–13 is the conclusion of 14:1–15:6 is highlighted, e.g., by the repetition in 15:7 of the imperative προσλαμβάνεσθε from 14:1.

145. E.g., Francis B. Watson, "The Two Roman Congregations: Romans 14:1–15:13," in Donfried, *Romans Debate*, 206–7 (see discussion below).

the strong, second on the identity of Paul's addressees more generally, and thus, third, on the situation in Rome that Paul writes to address.

Several important questions are raised by 15:7–13:

1. Whom is Paul addressing?
2. Is it the exhortation in verse 7, or the theological rationale of verses 8–9, that is most argumentatively salient in these verses, leading to most cognitive effects?
3. Does 15:7–13 represent the argumentative climax of the entire epistle?
4. How does our reading of 15:7–13 fit with our reading of 1:15–18?

I suggest that a procedural account of γάρ in verse 8, in helping us to answer these questions, has significant implications for the interpretation of the whole letter.

I will give a brief overview of scholarly opinion regarding the argumentative significance of these verses, and discuss their cotext, before examining pertinent exegetical issues. I will then propose a procedural analysis of γάρ in verse 8 and explore the exegetical and argumentative insights that this yields.

6.3.1. What Is the Argumentative Role of Romans 15:7–13?

Various scholars regard 15:7–13, and more specifically, either 15:7, or 15:8–9, as playing an important role in the argumentation of Romans. Barclay views 15:7–13 as a "framing passage" that matches 1:1–7 and emphasizes that the gospel is rooted in promises made to Israel, the realization of which includes the gentiles.[146] Jewett views the statement in verse 7b, "Christ welcomed you," as encapsulating the letter's main argument.[147] William Lane argues that the focus on the relationship between Jews and gentiles forms the letter's "dominant framework," Paul's specific aim being the reconciliation of Jews and gentiles in one church, within which the appeal for mutual acceptance in 15:7 features prominently.[148] Similarly, William Campbell understands 15:7 as "the climax of Paul's exhortation," which is "based on the work and example of Christ" (15:8–9) and resonates with the

---

146. Barclay, *Paul and the Gift*, 459–60.
147. Jewett, *Romans*, 889.
148. Lane, "Social Perspectives," 201.

conclusion of chapters 9–11.[149] Sarah Whittle, who reads Romans through the lens of the covenant-renewal narrative of Deuteronomy, and finds in it the theme of gentile inclusion in God's covenant with Israel, argues that the statement in 15:7–8 "sums up Paul's reading of Israel's history through the Deuteronomic narrative."[150] Watson's sociological approach leads him also to identify 15:7–13, and particularly 15:7, as a key to unlocking the situation of the Roman addressees and the epistle's purpose.[151]

Other scholars emphasize the importance of 15:8–9 rather than 15:7. Michael Bird finds in these verses the "pinnacle of the letter."[152] Dunn views 15:7 as an "opening call" for mutual consideration but argues that Paul's main concern is found in 15:8–9 in the underlining of "the twin themes of Christ as guaranteeing both the continuity of God's purpose to the circumcised and faithfulness of God to his covenant promises."[153] Wright, meanwhile, argues that verse 7 is a "paragraph-opening" containing elements to be developed, but that 15:8–12 represents the "theological climax of the whole letter," summing up its argument, within which verse 12 is climactic.[154] I will return to the question of the relative salience of verse 7 in relation to verses 8–9 below.

6.3.2. Cotext

Romans 14:1–15:13 is regarded by most as forming a single subsection within the major section of chapters 12–15.[155] The major section contains hortatory material that consists of specific ethical instructions and examples for life within the community of believers. These have as their foundation

---

149. Campbell, "Addressees of Paul's Letter to the Romans," 190. Russell regards 15:7–13 as "the polemical climax of Paul's epistle" (Russell, "Alternative Suggestion for the Purpose of Romans," 182).
150. Whittle, *Covenant Renewal*, 142.
151. Watson, "Two Roman Congregations," 206.
152. Bird, "Letter to the Romans," 198.
153. Dunn, *Romans 9–16*, 845.
154. Wright, "Romans," 746; Wright, *Paul and the Faithfulness of God*, 1494, 1455 n. 167.
155. E.g., Wright, "Romans"; Wilckens, *Der Brief an die Römer*, vol. 3; Cranfield, *Epistle to the Romans*, vol. 2. Reasoner shows that Dunn's analysis of 15:7–13 as a separate concluding section does not take account of the links between 14:1 and 15:7; 14:1 and 15:13; 14:17 and 15:13 (Reasoner, *Strong and the Weak*, 24–25, citing Dunn, *Romans 9–16*, 844–45).

and motivation the mercy of God, presented in the previous theological argument of chapters 3–11, in particular, the immediately preceding argument of chapters 9–11.[156] Within chapters 12–15, there is a switch in 14:1 to exhortations that address tensions between those characterized as "the weak" and "the strong."

In 15:1–2 Paul begins to draw together the exhortations of chapter 14 with a general exhortation to the strong to bear with the weaknesses of those who are not, looking to build the weak up, rather than pleasing themselves.[157] These exhortations are powerfully backed up in 15:3–4 by two γάρ clauses that contain a double dose of weighty theological material in verse 3 in the form of a christological example plus an authoritative citation from the LXX of Ps 69:9.[158] The aim of this buttressing theological framework is to persuade addressees to put the instructions in verses 1–2 into practice. The argumentative effect is to underline the salience of these exhortations, pointing toward them as main argumentative points, from which many relevant implications are to be derived. Verses 5–6 take the form of a prayer for unity among the Roman addressees, leading to united worship that glorifies God. This prayer, which also functions as an implicit exhortation to unity, sums up the thrust of the whole of the hortatory section from 14:1.

6.3.3. Exegetical Issues in Romans 15:7–9

15:7a: Διὸ προσλαμβάνεσθε ἀλλήλους,
15:7b: καθὼς καὶ ὁ Χριστὸς προσελάβετο ὑμᾶς εἰς δόξαν τοῦ θεοῦ.
15:8a: λέγω γὰρ Χριστὸν διάκονον γεγενῆσθαι περιτομῆς ὑπὲρ ἀληθείας θεοῦ,
15:8b: εἰς τὸ βεβαιῶσαι τὰς ἐπαγγελίας τῶν πατέρων,
15:9a: τὰ δὲ ἔθνη ὑπὲρ ἐλέους δοξάσαι τὸν θεόν,
15:9b: καθὼς γέγραπται,
Διὰ τοῦτο ἐξομολογήσομαί σοι ἐν ἔθνεσιν
καὶ τῷ ὀνόματί σου ψαλῶ.
15:10: καὶ πάλιν λέγει,

---

156. Barclay, *Paul and the Gift*, 508–11; Barclay, "Unnerving Grace: Approaching Romans 9–11 from The Wisdom of Solomon," in Wilk and Wagner, *Between Gospel and Election*, 107–9.

157. See Wilckens, *Der Brief an die Römer*, 3:100.

158. See Jewett, *Romans*, 880.

Εὐφράνθητε, ἔθνη, μετὰ τοῦ λαοῦ αὐτοῦ.
15:11: καὶ πάλιν,
Αἰνεῖτε, πάντα τὰ ἔθνη, τὸν κύριον
καὶ ἐπαινεσάτωσαν αὐτὸν πάντες οἱ λαοί.
15:12: καὶ πάλιν Ἠσαΐας λέγει,
Ἔσται ἡ ῥίζα τοῦ Ἰεσσαὶ
καὶ ὁ ἀνιστάμενος ἄρχειν ἐθνῶν,
ἐπ' αὐτῷ ἔθνη ἐλπιοῦσιν.

Romans 15:7 is introduced by διό, signaling that the exhortation that follows is a conclusion drawn from the preceding argument.[159] The concluding effect is reinforced by the repetition in verse 7a of the verb from the opening exhortation of 14:1. But whereas in 14:1 the exhortation was indirectly addressed to the strong in reference to their attitude toward the weak, here the use of the reciprocal pronoun ἀλλήλους makes the imperative more general in its scope.[160] The Roman addressees are urged to accept or welcome one another. This imperative is followed in verse 7b by a clause, introduced by καθώς, that presents as a model Christ's welcome or acceptance of believers. Whether καθώς is read as causal, or as introducing a comparison, the clause serves as an initial christological motivation for the imperative, lending it weight.[161] There is disagreement, however, over the referent of the pronoun ὑμᾶς in verse 7b. The textual variant ὑμᾶς is better supported by the external evidence than the variant ἡμᾶς and is "in harmony with the other instances of the second-person plural in the context" (vv. 5–7).[162] Most scholars therefore take ὑμᾶς as the original reading.[163] Depending on the position taken regarding the identity of the Roman addressees, some read the pronoun as referring exclusively to gentile believers and others to a mixed Jewish-gentile audience. The variant ἡμᾶς may have arisen precisely in an attempt to deal

---

159. Wilckens, *Der Brief an die Römer*, 3:105; Wright, "Romans," 746.

160. See Wilckens, *Der Brief an die Römer*, 3:105. The scope of Paul's address is here not precisely defined and we can infer from the preceding cotext that it extends to include everyone referred to directly or indirectly in 14:1–15:7.

161. For the causal reading of καθώς, see Käsemann, *An die Römer*, 369. For the comparative use, see Cranfield, *Epistle to the Romans*, 739; Jewett, *Romans*, 888–89.

162. Metzger, *Textual Commentary on the Greek New Testament*, 473.

163. See, however, Heinrich Schlier, *Der Römerbrief*, HThKNT 6 (Freiburg: Herder, 1977), 424.

with this ambiguity and to make better sense of the subsequent supporting theological statement in verses 8-9, which refers to the role of both Jews and gentiles in God's purposes.

The strengthening relationship indicated by γάρ in verse 8 is not as straightforward as in some instances. The extent of the strengthening premises needs to be determined, as well as the preceding element that is strengthened (see below).[164] The real difficulty associated with this occurrence of γάρ, however, lies with the exegetical complexities of the theological statement in verses 8-9a that it introduces. The infinitive clause of verse 9a is ambiguous.[165] Scholars are divided as to whether δοξάσαι should be read as dependent on the prepositional construction εἰς τό in verse 8b or as directly dependent on λέγω in verse 8a.[166] In the former case, δοξάσαι is parallel with βεβαιῶσαι in verse 8b. Christ's service to the circumcised is thus understood as having a dual purpose: confirming the promises to the fathers *and* leading the gentiles to praise God for his mercy.[167] In the latter case, δοξάσαι is parallel with γεγενῆσθαι, and Christ's service to the circumcised is understood as a separate event, not integrally linked with God's mercy shown to the gentiles. As Dunn notes, however, this second interpretation seems to contradict what Paul has argued earlier in the letter (see, e.g., 4:16, 9:8, 11:28-31).[168]

---

164. Cranfield claims that γάρ marks the relationship between vv. 8-12 and the imperative in v. 7 (Cranfield, *Epistle to the Romans*, 2:740). In contrast, Wilckens reads v. 8 alone as an explanation of the "christologische Begründung" of v. 7b (Wilckens, *Der Brief an die Römer*, 3:105).

165. Cranfield, *Epistle to the Romans*, 2:742. For an overview of interpretations, see Whittle, *Covenant Renewal*, 141.

166. For the former, see Barclay, *Paul and the Gift*, 460; Jewett, *Romans*, 892; Wright, "Romans," 747; Käsemann, *An die Römer*, 369. For the latter, see Cranfield, *Epistle to the Romans*, 742; Wilckens, *Der Brief an die Römer*, 3:106. Dunn, however, advocates a translation that preserves ambiguity (Dunn, *Romans 9-16*, 848).

167. τὰς ἐπαγγελίας τῶν πατέρων can be understood as referring first to the promises to Abraham (see 4:13-16), but also to the other patriarchs (see 9:7-13). Dunn suggests that the promises in view are those that included the blessing of the nations: Gen 12:2-3; 18:18; 22:18; 26:4; 28:14; Sir 44:21 (Dunn, *Romans 9-16*, 528). Whittle reads the expression also in relation to promises of covenant renewal in Deuteronomy (Whittle, *Covenant Renewal*, 142-46).

168. Dunn, *Romans 9-16*, 848.

6.3.4. A Procedural Analysis of γάρ in 15:8

Following a procedural account of γάρ, we can say that the statements in verses 8–9a are processed as a single complex of strengthening premises, since they are all grammatically dependent on λέγω (whether directly or indirectly). We can also identify the statement in verse 7b as the candidate for strengthening by the γάρ clause. Since verse 7b itself serves as a theological rationale for the exhortation in verse 7a, however, I suggest that the knock-on effect of any strengthening of verse 7b is, in turn, to increase the relevance of verse 7a.

A procedural reading of γάρ always directs us to a close consideration of the previous cotext and the accessing of previously communicated assumptions in the construction of a strengthening series. Thus, on a procedural reading, the *dual purpose* interpretation of verse 9a is to be preferred, because it is the most coherent with the preceding argument. This interpretation also serves as powerful theological strengthening for the exhortation to mutual acceptance in verse 7a, whereas the *single purpose* interpretation does not. This is because the former points to the interdependence between Jews and gentiles in God's purposes, in particular to the dependence of the gentiles on Christ's ministry to the Jews. In contrast, the *single purpose* interpretation provides no theological backup for the exhortation in verse 7a, and only weak backup for the theological motivation in verse 7b.[169] If we follow the *single purpose* reading, the statement in verse 8 regarding Christ's ministry to the Jews becomes a free-floating theological statement that does not contribute to argumentative coherence, in contradiction to the guidance given by γάρ regarding its argumentative role. In relevance-theoretic terms, it is questionable whether the *single purpose* interpretation achieves adequate relevance as a piece of strengthening evidence for the preceding material in verse 7. If we read γάρ as an indicator of procedural strengthening and assume that verses 8–9a function as strengthening premises for verse 7, only the *dual purpose* interpretation leads to adequate cognitive effects. Assuming a procedural strengthening function for γάρ thus supports the *dual purpose* interpretation.

---

169. Assuming that ὑμᾶς refers to at least some gentile addressees, if not exclusively so.

6.3.5. Light Thrown on the Identity of Paul's Addressees

Let us consider how a procedural analysis of γάρ in verse 8 sheds light on the wider argumentative questions raised in relation to 15:7–13. Once we assume that the information following γάρ in verses 8–9a is to be processed as strengthening premises, some proposed interpretations will be more coherent and logical than others. I propose that a procedural reading of γάρ illuminates the identity and ethnic make-up of Paul's addressees, by throwing light on the referent of ὑμᾶς in verse 7b. We need to test out the different possibilities in relation to this question, to see which is most compatible with a strengthening account. Since the *dual purpose* interpretation of 15:8–9a is strongly compatible with a procedural reading of γάρ, I will assume this interpretation as I work through a procedural analysis in relation to the question of the audience's ethnic make-up.

Interpretation H: ὑμᾶς referring to exclusively gentile addressees

On this reading, I propose that γάρ in verse 8 may trigger something like the following inferential series:

> **P (v. 7b):** Christ welcomed you [gentile believers in Rome] to the glory of God.
> **Q introduced by γάρ (vv. 8–9a):** Christ became a servant of the circumcised for the sake of God's truth, in order to confirm the promises to the patriarchs and in order that the gentiles[170] may glorify God for his mercy.
> **IA1:** The promises to the patriarchs include the promises to bless the gentiles through the patriarchs (especially Abraham) and their descendants. (Inferable from 4:16–17 in particular.)[171]
> **IA2:** If Christ became a servant of the circumcised for the sake of God's truth in order to confirm the promises to bless the gentiles and in order that the gentiles may glorify God for his mercy, then Christ welcomed the gentiles.

---

170. Since ἔθνη here stands in contrast with περιτομή, used as a metonym for Israel, I translate it as "gentiles."

171. See the use of βεβαιόω in conjunction with ἐπαγγελία in 4:16.

IA3: If the gentiles glorify God for his mercy because Christ welcomed the gentiles, then Christ welcomed the gentile believers to the glory of God.
C (strengthening v. 7b): Christ welcomed gentile believers in Rome to the glory of God.

Following a reading of ὑμᾶς as referring exclusively to gentiles, then, it is possible to construct an inferential series that results in the strengthening of the statement in verse 7b. The strengthening procedure is relevant as an explanation that increases the comprehensibility of this statement so that addressees adhere to it more strongly. But on this reading, the strengthening premise in verse 8a regarding Christ becoming a servant *of the circumcised* for the sake of God's truth seems of little argumentative relevance in the immediately preceding cotext. It does not provide evidence for the way Christ accepted/welcomed the gentiles. The strengthening series between verses 8b–9a and verse 7b is logically complete without it, achieving adequate cognitive effects and increasing the relevance of verse 7b.

Interpretation I: ὑμᾶς referring to both gentile and Jewish addressees

On this reading, I propose that γάρ in verse 8 may trigger the following series:

P (v. 7b): Christ welcomed you [Jewish and gentile believers in Rome] to the glory of God.
Q introduced by γάρ (vv. 8–9a): Christ became a servant of the circumcised for the sake of God's truth, in order to confirm the promises to the patriarchs, and in order that the gentiles may glorify God for his mercy.
IA1: If Christ became a servant of the circumcised for the sake of God's truth, this demonstrates that Christ welcomed/accepted the Jews. (Inferable from encyclopedic knowledge of concepts of circumcision and of servant/service.)[172]
IA2: The promises to the patriarchs include the promises to bless the gentiles through the patriarchs (especially Abraham) and their descendants. (Inferable from 4:16–17, etc.)

---

172. For circumcision, see 4.1.1 n. 12, above.

IA3: Christ welcomed the Jews in order to confirm the promises to bless the gentiles through the patriarchs. (Inferable from IA2 and from vv. 8–9.)

IA4: If Christ welcomed the Jews in order to confirm the promises to bless the gentiles through the patriarchs, and in order that the gentiles may glorify God for his mercy, then Christ's welcome of the Jews brings God's mercy and blessing to the gentiles, with the result that the gentiles glorify God for his mercy.

IA5: God's mercy and blessing to the gentiles demonstrates that God welcomed the gentiles. (Inferable from encyclopedic knowledge of concepts of mercy and welcome.)

IA6: If Christ's welcome of the Jews confirming the promises to the patriarchs brings God's welcome to the gentiles, with the result that they glorify God for his mercy, then God's welcome to the gentiles by means of Christ's welcome to the Jews brings glory to God.

C (strengthening v. 7b): Christ welcomed Jewish and gentile believers in Rome to the glory of God.

We see that a strengthening series based on interpretation I also leads to the strengthening of the statement in verse 7b so that it becomes more comprehensible and more relevant to addressees. Moreover, this second series is more strongly compatible with a procedural analysis of γάρ than the first, because it involves as strengthening premises not only the assumptions communicated in verses 8b–9a, but also those in verse 8a regarding Christ becoming a servant of the circumcised. It is thus better able to provide a coherent account of the information communicated in verses 8–9a in relation to the preceding cotext.[173] So a procedural strengthening account of γάρ confirms most strongly interpretation I, which posits a mixed Jewish-gentile audience, and is less compatible with a reading that insists on exclusively gentile addressees.

Since verse 7b is grammatically tightly connected with the exhortation in verse 7a and provides a theological motivation for it, the knock-on effect of the strengthening triggered by γάρ in verse 8 is to provide further backup for this exhortation, underlining its argumentative salience. Again,

---

173. Lane argues that the appeal to mutual acceptance, supported by the reference to the significance of the incarnation for both Jews and gentiles, would be pointless, if both groups were not represented in the Roman church (Lane, "Social Perspectives," 206–7). See also Wedderburn, *Reasons for Romans*, 32.

the strengthening provided by the γάρ clause in verses 8–9a is strongly compatible with a reading of verse 7a as an exhortation to Jewish and gentile believers to accept/welcome one another but less compatible with an interpretation that understands "one another" to refer to different groups of gentile believers. In this way, a procedural analysis of γάρ in 15:8 throws light on the question of Paul's addressees, supporting the view that they are a mixture of gentiles and Jews, even if most are gentile.

6.3.6. Light Thrown on the Argumentative Role of 15:7–13

Thus the inferential procedure triggered by γάρ in verse 8 contributes, via the strengthening of verse 7b, to the reinforcement and underlining of the exhortation to mutual acceptance in verse 7a, increasing its argumentative salience. Moreover, there is more to the strengthening than simply the inferential procedure. The information in verses 8–9a may additionally carry weight as a metarepresentation of commonly known and authoritative material within the Christian community. Some suggest that in the reference to Christ as servant in verse 8a, Paul may have in mind the tradition behind Mark 10:43–45.[174] The solemn introductory formula λέγω likewise draws attention to the authoritative nature of the material introduced. In this way, the authoritative character of the strengthening material brings a double dose of persuasive punch behind the exhortation in verse 7, convincing addressees more strongly of its validity and importance.

The strengthening material of verses 8–9a is followed in verses 9b–12 by a series of four citations from the LXX, all expressing the theme of the nations, or gentiles, praising God.[175] This provides further authoritative buttressing for the theological statement in verses 8–9a.[176] The quotation in verse 9b from Ps 18:49 is spoken from the perspective of a devout Jew singing God's praise among the gentiles.[177] The second and third citations, in verses 10 and 11, from Deut 32:43 and Ps 117:1, respectively, exhort gentiles to join God's people in praising him. The final citation, in verse

---

174. E.g., Jewett, *Romans*, 891; Dunn, *Romans 9–16*, 846.

175. Whittle views these citations as emphasizing the inclusion of the gentiles alongside Israel in the worshiping community (Whittle, *Covenant Renewal*, 135–39).

176. See Käsemann, *An die Römer*, 371.

177. Dunn, *Romans 9–16*, 853. The Jewish referent of *I* in this citation is understood variously; see Whittle, *Covenant Renewal*, 136.

12, is from Isa 11:10 and recapitulates the theme of Israel's Messiah bringing blessing (hope) to the gentiles.[178] Wright argues that this citation has "explosive political implications" and that Paul produces it as the "final move" in his whole argument.[179]

The cumulative effect of this weighty catena of scriptural support is to bring powerful theological backing first for the declaration introduced in verses 8–9a. The focus on the gentiles' worship of God alongside Israel in a messianic context provides support both for the statement that the gentiles glorify God for his mercy (v. 9a) and for the implication that the gentiles' experience of God's mercy is dependent on Christ's ministry to Israel (vv. 8–9a). The strengthening of verses 8–9a thus also has the knock-on effect of further increasing the relevance of verse 7b that Christ's acceptance of believers leads to God's glory. This in its turn increases the relevance of the exhortation in verse 7a, further increasing its argumentative salience.

The overall effect of the supporting catena plus strengthening procedure is therefore to increase the relevance of the exhortation to mutual acceptance. As a result, many cognitive effects are derived from verse 7a and addressees are forcefully persuaded to accept its desirability and motivated to put it into practice. Consequently, it can be understood as the main point of 15:7–13, representing the thrust of the argument, from which the greatest number of relevant implications arise for addressees.

This analysis throws into question Wright's view that the significance of verses 7–13 lies not so much in the exhortation in verse 7, as in the "theological climax" of verses 8–12.[180] A procedural account of γάρ in verse 8 points in the opposite direction. The material in verses 8–12 is indeed theologically weighty and a summary of various of the letter's themes but is nevertheless marshaled in the service of the concluding exhortation in verse 7, bringing persuasive ballast behind it. Verses 8–12 thus fulfill a *supporting* function in argumentative terms. The main cognitive effects or personal implications of the subsection are to be derived from the imperative "Welcome one another," addressed to Jews and gentiles. The grounding theological rationale of verses 8–12 does not itself generate new implications for addressees but represents assumptions that

---

178. For Whittle, this citation brings together "major themes" of the letter: "Christ as Davidic Messiah, the resurrected one, the one who rules the Gentiles, and in whom they have hope" (Whittle, *Covenant Renewal*, 139).

179. Wright, "Romans," 748.

180. Wright, *Paul and the Faithfulness of God*, 1494.

are already accepted, some of which have been communicated previously (see, e.g., 11:11–17 and 30–31). It is for this reason that the rationale may be perceived as a summary of the letter's theology.

This analysis supports the view of those who accord 15:7 special importance as the climax of Paul's exhortation. It suggests that those who read verses 8–9 as the focus of the subsection are allowing themselves to be distracted from Paul's main point by the theological significance of this supporting material. Similarly, Wright's reading of verse 12 as the "final move" in Paul's argument contradicts the guidance given by γάρ that indicates that verse 12 is relevant not in its own right, but as further support for verses 7–9. If we ignore this guidance, we risk missing the thrust of Paul's argument: gentile-orientated and Jewish-orientated believers are to accept one another in unity, bringing glory to God, because of what Christ has done for them, which binds them together inextricably in God's purposes.

The final verse in the subsection, 15:13, on the other hand, is introduced by δέ, indicating, I suggest, that the information that follows it is not to be processed as part of the strengthening rationale for verses 8–12. Instead, verse 13 is relevant in its own right, leading to fresh implications for addressees. The verse contains a prayer that parallels the one in 15:5–6, rounding off its subsection in a similar fashion, and drawing together many of the key concepts of the epistle.[181]

6.3.7. Light Thrown on the Purpose of the Epistle

The recognition of the argumentative salience of 15:7 at this very strategic closing point supports the view that the exhortation to mutual acceptance and unity among the Roman addressees, which arises out of the exhortations of 14:1–15:6, is central to an understanding of the epistle's argument and purpose. The salience of the exhortation is so marked, given its location in the argument, and the supporting information brought behind it so weighty, that it can be regarded as a summary not only of chapters 14:1–15:13, or chapters 12–15, but of the thrust of the entire letter. I suggest that the exhortation can be viewed as the epistle's most relevant point, from which multiple cognitive effects and behavior-transforming implications are to be derived.[182] Here at this pivotal

---

181. See Jewett, *Romans*, 887; Wright, "Romans," 744.

182. Barclay notes resonances of 1:16 in 15:8–9 (Barclay, *Paul and the Gift*, 460). According to a procedural reading, both 1:16 and 15:8–9, which emphasize that Paul

closing juncture, Paul spells out and sums up the practical personal and communal implications for Roman believers of the aspects of the gospel discussed in the epistle.

We have seen that a procedural account of γάρ confirms the view that Paul's Roman addressees probably include Jewish as well as gentile believers. The exhortation in verse 7 is best understood in terms of mutual acceptance and unity between torah-observant/Jewish-orientated believers on the one hand, and non-torah-observant believers/gentile-orientated believers on the other. The issue of relations between these two groups, which is bound up with an understanding of the continuing role of Israel in God's purposes, takes center stage at this crucial and highly salient point. From this we can infer that addressing the issue of unity among representatives of these differing perspectives is a key aspect of Paul's purpose in writing, as various scholars suggest.[183] We can conclude that his aim is to build bridges and mutual understanding between Jewish-orientated and gentile-orientated tendencies in Rome, confronting ethnocentrism and factionalism among believers.[184]

The hypothesis that Paul writes to address tensions and issues of unity in Rome accounts for the fact that Paul writes at such length. It seems unlikely that the apostle would write such a lengthy exposition of his gospel to the Roman believers as a self-introduction.[185] More plausible is the suggestion that he writes because he is motivated by reports of concrete problems or incipient tensions in Rome and wishes to provide teaching that strengthens the faith and builds up the community(ies) of believers there (see 1:11). These tensions are hinted at in the course of his argument in chapters 1–11 and then addressed more directly in chapters 12–15, and especially chapters 14–15, as we have seen.

---

places "Jew and gentile on a par on a distinctly Jewish foundation," serve as supporting theological rationales for what I suggest is the main point of Paul's argument, namely, to address problems and tensions in the Roman situation.

183. E.g., Esler, *Conflict and Identity in Romans*; Walters, *Ethnic Issues in Paul's Letter to the Romans*; Campbell, *Paul's Gospel in an Intercultural Context*; Russell, "Alternative Suggestion for the Purpose of Romans"; Wedderburn, *Reasons for Romans*; Wiefel, "Jewish Community"; Minear, *Obedience of Faith*. Bird provides an extensive list of variations on this hypothesis (Bird, "Letter to the Romans," 187).

184. We have seen that the factions are probably more complex than a straightforward Jewish-gentile division.

185. See Campbell, "Addressees of Paul's Letter to the Romans," 175.

I suggest that Paul's concern to demonstrate that his gospel is not anti-Jewish but rather affirms the priority and continuing role of Israel in God's salvific purposes in Christ is to be understood in relation to this unifying aim. Responding to misgivings that his gospel is dismissive of Israel and encourages a supersessionist perspective, he presents the gospel in a way that differs from his other epistles in emphasizing the continuity between the gospel and God's dealings with Israel.[186] He makes extensive use of Jewish scripture and other traditional material (e.g., in 1:19–32) and focuses on Israel's history and unique place in God's purposes.[187] In this way, he seeks to allay the fears and criticisms of Jewish-orientated and torah-observant believers, perhaps in the wake of the Galatian controversy, and to confront the incipient arrogance and potential supersessionism of non-torah-observant believers. At the same time, he continues to insist on the core of his faith-based gospel (as expressed in Galatians), namely, that there is no difference between Jew and gentile from the fundamental point of view of the justification of the ungodly, which is based on faith, that is, faith-full trust, in Christ. Paul is determined to show to Jewish-orientated and non-torah-observant groups alike that his gospel is not shameful or unworthy to be heard in Rome but reveals God's power to save all and God's faithfulness to his people, bringing righteousness/justice in the world. Paul's aim of building unity between believers who are divided over their relationship to the Jewish heritage also explains his repeated warnings against any kind of boasting and arrogance in human credentials, whether perceived moral superiority (2:1; ch. 14), torah observance (3:27–4:25) and Jewish "advantage," or a non-Jewish ethnocentrism with supersessionist tendencies (11:13–24).[188] Paul's Roman version of the gospel thus seems designed to counter various expressions of factionalism and ethnocentrism in the diverse multicultural Roman situation.[189] These tensions between differ-

---

186. See Johan C. Beker's comparison between Romans and Galatians. Johan C. Beker, *Paul the Apostle: The Triumph of God in Life and Thought* (Philadelphia: Fortress, 1980), 94–108.

187. Barclay, *Paul and the Gift*, 459–60.

188. See Russell, "Alternative Suggestion for the Purpose of Romans," 184; Walters, *Ethnic Issues in Paul's Letter to the Romans*, 79.

189. Russell, "Alternative Suggestion for the Purpose of Romans," 182–83; Walters, *Ethnic Issues in Paul's Letter to the Romans*, 75; Esler, *Conflict and Identity in Romans*, 358–59.

ent groups, if left unaddressed, threaten to throw into question the power and validity of the gospel.

The hypothesis that Paul addresses issues of, and threats to, unity among Roman believers fits well with our proposed construal of 1:15–18. We noted that the Rome-focused reading of the epistle's purpose suggested by a procedural account of γάρ in these verses needed to be corroborated by further evidence. Our analysis of 15:7–13 provides this. In both passages, the emphasis both on the inclusion of Jews and gentiles together in God's salvific purposes in the gospel, and on the priority of the Jewish people, suggests that Paul is addressing a specific situation of tensions in Rome arising from different stances toward the role of Jewish beliefs, traditions, and heritage for Christ-believers.

While our reading of 15:7–13 lends support to interpretations that identify a concern for unity as a key to the epistle's purpose, it does little to confirm an anti-imperial construal of the epistle. Although this reading makes sense of elements of 1:15–18, it is ultimately unsatisfying as an explanation of the data of the wider epistle. The fact that the key closing passage of 15:7–13 bears no obvious traces of an anti-imperial message undermines the plausibility of such a reading.[190]

6.3.8. Light Thrown on the Argument of the Epistle

If we view Romans as a presentation of Paul's gospel designed to counter factionalism and ethnocentrism and building unity among believers in Rome, we are able to make coherent sense of much of the data in the epistle. This reading accounts for the recurrent emphasis throughout on both the priority and the responsibility of Israel in God's purposes.[191] It explains the exploration of the universality of sin and ungodliness in Rom 1–3 and the interweaving of the theme of arrogance and boasting into this. Paul aims to undercut all pretension, Jewish and gentile, torah-observant and non-torah-observant, leaving all his addressees with an awareness that the injustice from which God brings deliverance in the gospel is not the

---

190. Wright's claim to find an argumentatively significant challenge to Caesar in 15:12 is questionable, as we have seen. See Barclay's critique (Barclay, *Paul and the Gift*, 456), and Wright's response to Barclay's criticism (Wright, *Paul and the Faithfulness of God*, 1307–9, responding to Barclay, "Why the Roman Empire Was Insignificant to Paul," *Pauline Churches*, 363–89).

191. See Barclay, *Paul and the Gift*, 464.

unrighteousness of others, but their own ungodliness. Furthermore, this construal of the epistle's purpose provides an explanation for the focus on God's righteousness and faithfulness, and on faith-full trust in Christ, as the sole criterion that counts when it comes to God's acceptance of the ungodly (chapters 3–5). It accounts for the exploration of the ambivalent role of torah, and for the implication that torah is fulfilled (rather than kept) in Christ, and thus in believers, through the Spirit's enabling (chapters 7–8).[192] It provides an explanation for the extended discussion of the role of Israel in God's continuing purposes, and of the interdependence of Jews and gentiles in those purposes, in order to bring mercy to all (chapters 9–11).[193] It makes sense of the exhortation to unity in diversity in 12:3–6, to love in 13:8–10, and of the exhortations to mutual acceptance in chapters 14–15. It accounts for the recurrent theme of arrogance and boasting in human criteria versus boasting and glorying in God. In short, as Campbell puts it, "Jews and Gentiles are inextricably intertwined in the purposes of God so that one may not boast over the other and so that one without the other cannot find the salvation of God."[194]

The conclusion that a concern for Jewish-orientated and gentile-orientated mutual acceptance shapes the letter's argument fits well with the view, argued for above, that 1:16–17 does not function as the letter's thesis statement. If Paul's aim in the letter is to address tensions in Rome, rather than to present an exposition of the gospel as summarized in 1:16–17, this accounts for the fact that parts of the letter do not fit obviously into the grid of 1:16–17. Once we assume a Rome-focused purpose, we are released from the interpretative grid that the so-called thesis imposes. This helps to answer Campbell's valid concerns about the circular and individualistic character of interpretations that take 1:16–17 as a starting point. An understanding of Paul's purpose as addressing disunity among torah-observant and non-torah-observant believers points to chapters 9–11 as the climax of the letter's theological argument, which serves as a compelling foundation for the hortatory section. The latter builds to its most relevant point in 15:7, from which multiple practical personal and communal implications are derived.

---

192. For torah as fulfilled rather than kept, see Whittle, *Covenant Renewal*, 125–29.
193. See Stephen Motyer, *Come, Lord Jesus! A Biblical Theology of the Second Coming of Christ* (London: Apollos, 2016), 189–92; Campbell, "Addressees of Paul's Letter to the Romans," 193.
194. Campbell, "Addressees of Paul's Letter to the Romans," 184.

6.3.9. Summary

In summary, a procedural account of γάρ in 15:7–13 has illuminated several important interpretative questions:

1. An understanding of the strengthening guidance γάρ gives helps us to resolve a major exegetical disagreement, providing support for the *dual purpose* interpretation of 15:8–9a.
2. The guidance γάρ gives supports a reading of ὑμᾶς in 15:7b as referring to both gentile and Jewish believers. This in turn lends weight to the view that Paul is addressing a mixed Jewish/Jewish-orientated and gentile/gentile-orientated audience in Rome.
3. Our analysis points to the exhortation in 15:7 as the most argumentatively salient and relevant point of the subsection 15:7–13 and of the section 14:1–15:13. The material in 15:8–12, on the other hand, serves as a powerful theological rationale that persuasively backs up the exhortation, reinforcing the cognitive effects of this exhortation by convincing addressees that it is crucial that they put it into practice.
4. The fact that this exhortation is made highly salient at this argumentatively crucial closing point leads us to infer that the issue of mutual acceptance and unity among Roman believers with different orientations is a key to understanding the epistle's purpose.
5. Taking the issue of unity between Jewish-orientated and gentile-orientated believers in Rome as the principal reason for the letter allows us to make sense of many facets of its argument and of the tensions within it. In particular, it makes sense of the Jewish-grounded version of the gospel that Paul gives. This can be explained as a response to the perception on the part of some that his gospel has anti-Jewish tendencies, a perception that threatens unity among believers in Rome. It also makes sense of his concern to quash boasting and arrogance.
6. The hypothesis of a situation among Roman believers where unity is at stake reinforces insights into the letter's purpose and argument suggested by our analysis of 1:15–18. The communicative guidance given by γάρ in both passages represents significant cumulative evidence pointing to the specific Roman situation as a key to understanding the particular shape and tailoring of the letter's theological argument.

7. An anti-imperial interpretation of the letter's purpose and argument, while Rome-focused, is not confirmed by the procedural analysis of 15:7–13.

6.4. Tracing the Path of Argument in Romans 1–4

Finally, drawing on the illumination provided by our analysis, I suggest the following partial sketch of the main points and flow of Rom 1–4 to illustrate how a procedural account assists us in tracing the path of Paul's argument. This is not comprehensive; it focuses only on those main argumentative points that are highlighted by buttressing γάρ clauses or chains. It does, however, show how an awareness of the strengthening role of γάρ clauses enables us to step aside from a traditional reading of this contested section and take a look at its argumentative thrust and contours with fresh eyes. It draws our attention to the particular argumentative salience of certain main points that give rise to many new cognitive effects for addressees. It also underlines the coherence of the argument, recognizing some significant moments of continuity that are neglected by the standard reading.

In this sketch, statements that are rendered highly salient by a subsequent strengthening chain of γάρ clauses are highlighted in bold. Other salient information (often introduced by connectives διό, οὖν, or δέ), communicating implications that are relevant in their own right though not supported by γάρ clauses, is also included at points such 3:1–8 to complete the skeleton of the argument. Buttressing γάρ clauses or chains are inset and preceded by the symbol ← to show their backward strengthening role. Subsection headings are presented in uppercase and represent a pause in the flow of thought.

1:13–18: PAUL IS EAGER TO PREACH THE GOSPEL IN ROME: HIS JEWISH-ROOTED GOSPEL IS RELEVANT TO JEWISH AND GENTILE BELIEVERS ALIKE

verse 15: **I eagerly desire to preach the gospel to you who are in Rome**

  ← verses 16–18: fourfold buttressing γάρ chain: God's righteousness saves all who are faith-full, Jew first and also gentile, from unrighteousness.

1:19a–32: ALL ARE UNGODLY, GENTILES AND JEWS ALIKE: THE STORY OF HUMANITY'S REBELLIOUS IDOLATRY

verse 19a: **what is known about God is plain to humanity**

    ← verses 19b–20: twofold γάρ chain: God has made it plain since the creation of the world

verse 20c: **So people are without excuse…**

2:1–16: NO ROOM FOR ARROGANT JUDGING BY CHRIST-BELIEVERS: JEWS AND GENTILES ALIKE WILL BE JUDGED BY GOD

verse 1a: **YOU are without excuse, whoever you are who judges [Jewish or gentile Christ-believer]**

    ← verses 1b–c: twofold γάρ chain: in judging others you condemn yourself

verses 6–10: **God will pay all people back according to their works … Jew first and also gentile**

    ← verse 11: γάρ there is no partiality with God.

        ← verses 12–15: threefold γάρ chain buttressing verse 11, which in turn buttresses 2:6–10.

2:17–28: NO ROOM FOR BOASTING IN THE JEWISH LAW: HEART CIRCUMCISION BY THE SPIRIT IS WHAT COUNTS, FOR JEWS AND GENTILES ALIKE.

verses 17–23: **You who call yourself Jew and boast in the law, dishonor God by breaking the law**

    ← verses 24–25: twofold γάρ chain

verses 26–27: **If the uncircumcised keep the law, their uncircumcision will be counted as circumcision and they will judge you, circumcised law-breaker**

    ← verses 28–29: γάρ … it is the person who is a Jew in a hidden way, circumcised in the heart by the Spirit, who receives praise not from human beings but from God.

3:1–8: GOD IS FAITHFUL TO HIS PROMISES TO THE JEWISH PEOPLE

verses 1–8: The Jews nevertheless have many advantages as God's people.

God is faithful [to his promises to them], even if some of them were unfaith-full. This does not mean that God condones unrighteousness, however. That is blasphemy!

3:9–20 BUT JEWS AND GENTILES ALIKE ARE ALL UNDER THE POWER OF SIN: THE ENEMY IS OUR OWN UNGODLINESS

verse 9a: **So are we Jews better off [when it comes to sin]? Not at all!**

> ← verse 9b: γάρ we have already made the charge that Jews and gentiles are all under the power of sin.

verses 10–18: scriptural proof of Jews as well gentiles under the power of sin.

verse 19–20a: **The whole world is under God's judgment. No one is made righteous by keeping the Jewish law**

> ← verse 20b: γάρ the Jewish law brings knowledge of sin.

3:21–26: GOD'S RIGHTEOUSNESS IS REVEALED APART FROM THE JEWISH LAW TO ALL WHO ARE FAITH-FULL, JEWS AND GENTILES ALIKE.

verses 21–22a: **God's righteousness is revealed apart from the Jewish law, through faithfulness**[195] **of Jesus Christ, to all who are faith-full**

> ← verses 22b–26: γάρ there is no difference [between torah-observant and non-torah observant]: all have sinned ... and are freely made righteous by God's grace through the redemption that is in Christ Jesus...

3:27–4:25: NO ONE HAS A BOAST, NOT EVEN ABRAHAM, WHO IS FATHER OF ALL THE UNGODLY WHO ARE FAITH-FULL, JEWS AND GENTILES.

verse 27: **Boasting is therefore excluded**

> ← verses 28–29: γάρ a person is made righteous by faith without works of the Jewish law. God is God of Jews AND gentiles.

verse 31: But we uphold the Jewish law.

---

195. See Morgan, *Roman Faith and Christian Faith*, 289.

4:1: **So what did our forefather Abraham find in this matter [of boasting in works of the law]?**

⟵ verse 2a: γάρ if Abraham was made righteous by works, he has a boast...

verse 2b: **But [he does] not [have a boast] before God**

⟵ verse 3: γάρ "Abraham was faith-full toward God and it was counted to him as righteousness."

verses 11–12: **Abraham was counted righteous by being faith-full toward God when he was uncircumcised, in order to be father of all the uncircumcised who are faith-full ... and father of the circumcised who follow his example of uncircumcised faith-fullness ...**

⟵ verses 13–15: threefold γάρ chain buttressing verses 11–12.[196]

There are no occurrences of γάρ in the remainder of chapter 4. The statement in verse 16, however, introduced by εἰς τοῦτο, is a reprise of the implication expressed in verses 11–12. This repetition further underlines the salience of the thought of verses 11–12.

From this sketch, we see that: (1) Rom 1:15; 2:6, 21–22a; 3:9; and 4:11–12 are made especially salient in the path of the argument by buttressing γάρ clauses. (2) The flow of argument in chapters 1–4 can be summarized thus: Paul's gospel is of vital importance to Roman believers (1:15): there is no difference between Jew and gentile as far as sin, judgment, and justification are concerned (2:6–10, 21–22a; 3:9) and no grounds for boasting. God's faith-full people are not delivered from unrighteous enemies, but from their own ungodliness, that is, the power of sin. As ungodly but faith-full children of Abraham (4:11–12), Jews and gentiles belong together in God's Jewish-rooted purposes. (3) In terms of continuity/discontinuity, 1:15–18 belong tightly together, as do 4:10–15. Furthermore, while pauses for breath may be taken at each of the suggested subsection headings, any formal imposition of breaks and headings is artificial and potentially misleading. What is striking is the overall argumentative continuity from 1:8 to the end of chapter 4. Although there is a switch in Paul's thought at 3:21, from exposing human ungodliness to explaining God's righteousness and

---

196. In contrast to the widespread tendency to divide the text between 4:12 and 4:13, our analysis suggests close continuity here.

Christ's faithfulness, this takes place as part of the larger continuing theme of no difference between Jew and gentile, and no grounds for boasting.

6.5. A Roman-Focused Reading

We can draw a number of conclusions from our application of a relevance-theoretic, procedural account of γάρ to Rom 1:15–18 and 15:7–13. We have seen that the connective serves as a crucial communicative clue at these pivotal points in the epistle's argument. This is especially important for us as secondary interpreters who are not party to all the contextual assumptions accessible to the letter's first addressees.

Not only does the guidance γάρ gives assist us in making exegetical decisions at the level of individual points of exegesis, but it also throws significant light on the epistle's wider argument. It helps us track, and pay attention to, the most salient argumentative points that carry the greatest number of potential cognitive effects or implications and are thus most relevant to addressees. It prevents us from becoming distracted by theologically weighty material that does not represent the main thrust of the argument, but rather provides a theological buttressing framework for the main points. By helping us to turn our focus away from supporting material toward the parts of the argument that give rise to the greatest fresh cognitive effects for addressees, a procedural account compels us to become more aware of the epistle as a piece of communication that is addressee-directed.

This understanding of γάρ and of the guidance it offers thus leads us away from a view of Romans as a timeless theological treatise that sets out Paul's theology. It throws into question, for instance, the traditional thesis reading of Rom 1:16–17 and the interpretative grid it imposes. Instead, it supports an interpretation of Romans in which the specific situation in Rome is the key for understanding the letter's purpose and argument. It compels us to read the epistle and its argument as context-specific and context-shaped, a tailored version of Paul's gospel written to build unity among his addressees. It suggests that we should read the whole of the argument of Romans in the light of this situation. This lends support to the view that the argumentative climax of the letter is to be found in 15:7–13. Furthermore, the guidance γάρ gives in 15:8 allows us to see the argumentative woods for the trees, focusing on the exhortation in 15:7 as crucially important, and provides support for the view that Paul's addressees must include Jewish as well as gentile addressees. In sum, a reading of γάρ as a textual and exegetical signpost throws light on major unresolved issues in the interpretation of Romans.

Furthermore, this procedural account challenges us in general to pay careful attention to the whole cotext and its previously communicated assumptions in the interpretation of disputed and argumentatively pivotal passages. It warns us against imposing artificial breaks on the text (e.g., at 1:16 and 1:18) that obscure the coherence of the argument, resulting in misleading or atomizing interpretations.

We have seen the danger of ignoring the important guidance provided by γάρ. The signpost is disregarded at our peril: the result may be an interpretation that takes us in completely the wrong direction, such as Campbell's construal of 1:18–32. Reading γάρ as a procedural indicator enables us to identify and rule out such interpretations. On the other hand, its guidance helps to confirm the validity of certain other interpretations, such as Wedderburn's, that argue for a context-specific explanation of the epistle's argument.

7
Relevance for Romans and Beyond

This interdisciplinary study has harnessed the theoretical framework of relevance theory in order to shed fresh light on the stubborn but neglected problem of the interpretation of γάρ in the letter to the Romans. We have found relevance theory to be a powerful tool for dispelling confusion related to the interpretation of γάρ and for illuminating the connective's communicative role, shedding light on argumentatively pivotal points in the epistle. By applying the innovative notion of procedural meaning to the connective, with its awareness of the role of inferencing and implicit information in interpretation, we have found a way beyond the inadequacies of both the traditional causal explanation and the loose approach to γάρ. Relevance theory opens up a consistent, contextually sensitive and cognitively grounded reading of γάρ. The result is that γάρ is accorded a significant role as a communicative signpost, guiding interpretation. This has many implications for the interpretation of Romans, not only at an exegetical level, but also in relation to wider unresolved questions relating to the letter's argument and purpose. More broadly still, it has a bearing on more general questions of Pauline interpretation, and biblical studies in general, and suggests various possibilities for future interdisciplinary interaction and research.

7.1. A Crucial Communicative Clue

7.1.1. A Consistent, Unified Account

The theoretical framework of the study was introduced in chapter 2. The research that was undertaken tested a procedural strengthening hypothesis for all occurrences of γάρ in Romans, adapting and extending this hypothesis in order to account for all the data. The findings of this research were presented, in the form of representative examples, in chapters 3 and 4. These chapters demonstrated, from a range of occurrences, both straightforward and complex, the validity of the procedural account and its ability to provide a unifying explanation for seemingly diverse uses of γάρ. By examining all instances, in both expository and hortatory material, the research ascertained that all can be consistently explained in terms of procedural instructions that guide addressees toward the inferential process of backward strengthening.

The connective can thus be said to have a core procedural function and should be regarded as a consistent communicative signpost. Rather than carrying conceptual meaning, γάρ is a procedural signal, constraining interpretation in a particular direction, thereby reducing ambiguity. It indicates that the information it introduces is to be processed as relevant in relation to previously communicated assumptions, rather than introducing fresh implications relevant in their own right. The connective raises expectations that the material it introduces will be relevant as strengthening premises for preceding claims. The inferential procedure it triggers consists of the subpersonal construction of a strengthening series of inferences involving the premises introduced by γάρ plus highly accessible contextual assumptions and yields a conclusion that reinforces previously communicated information. This results in the cognitive effect of strengthening; that is, it increases addressees' adherence to this previously communicated information. In this way, the guidance γάρ gives contributes to the persuasiveness of the argument.

7.1.2. A Flexible, Context-Sensitive Account

The findings presented in chapters 3 and 4 show that a procedural strengthening account of γάρ is not only unified and consistent, but also flexible and context-sensitive. The connective's core strengthening guidance works itself out differently in diverse cotexts in Romans. Given the cotext, addressees must infer in what way the strengthening procedure is relevant and in relation to which preceding information. The result of the procedure triggered by γάρ may be relevant as confirming evidence, a grounding rationale, a further explanation, an authoritative proof, a further specification, a clarifying adjustment to a previous claim, a parenthetical remark, and so on. In different types of argumentation, the strengthening procedure is likely to be relevant in different ways. In closely argued passages where the argument is developed logically by means of claims and supporting premises, it is likely to achieve relevance by means of the construction of a logically complete strengthening series. In passages where the main argumentative points are backed up by scriptural citations, it may achieve relevance as a proof that convinces by virtue of the authoritative source. In some highly rhetorical contexts, γάρ may contribute to a persuasive strengthening display even without triggering a full inferential procedure, if the display itself is enough to satisfy addressees' expectations of relevance. On occasion the connective's core strengthening guidance may be exploited with the secondary aim of achieving a particular rhetorical effect. For example, the association γάρ has with supporting material may function as a cover for the communication of salient but sensitive information (see 15:24).

Furthermore, the strengthening procedure achieves relevance in varying ways for different addressees, depending on their perspectives, background knowledge, and attitudes of skepticism or trust. Thus the strengthening triggered may be relevant to some as confirming evidence increasing the plausibility of a preceding claim, but to others as a further explanation increasing its comprehensibility. Full inferential series, especially more complex ones, will only be constructed where addressees are prepared to invest the processing effort required because the resulting cognitive effects will meet a felt need for more evidence. If, on the other hand, no implicit questions are raised for addressees by preceding claims, they may be content simply to accept the impression of strengthening that γάρ creates. This explains the fact that diverse addressees may derive differing inferential series, or indeed, none, on the basis of γάρ, and invest varying degrees of effort in interpretation.

Because of its flexibility, the procedural account is able to accommodate a range of explanations proposed by scholars for specific occurrences of γάρ in Romans, without dismissing it as a loose connective that simply takes its meaning from the cotext. Instead, γάρ functions as a broad interpretative constraint within which different addressees and interpreters work, as, using contextual information, they infer an interpretation relevant to them. The procedural account also makes sense of various observations regarding the uses of γάρ that are made, but not explained, by more traditional accounts. It provides an explanation for the fact that the preceding claim strengthened by the γάρ clause is on occasion not immediately adjacent to it but further back in the cotext. Similarly, it accounts for the fact that the strengthened information may have been communicated implicitly rather than explicitly in the preceding cotext.

7.1.3. An Account That Highlights Coherence

A procedural account of γάρ is, then, both consistent and contextually sensitive, two indispensable qualities for an exegetically useful reading of the connective. Furthermore, it also emphasizes the contribution that γάρ makes to a coherent understanding of Romans as a whole. A relevance-theoretic view regards the entire cotext of the epistle as accessible and potentially relevant contextual information that must be borne in mind in interpretation. The procedural guidance given by γάρ cements the coherence of the argument of particular subsections and, indeed, the wider epistle. This is because the search for a reinforcing inferential series between information introduced by γάρ and preceding communicated assumptions consolidates the close relationship between γάρ clauses and the previous cotext. In addition, the search for accessible contextual assumptions to deploy in the strengthening series frequently leads to the reactivation of assumptions communicated previously, whether in the immediately adjacent cotext or earlier in the letter. These assumptions are made more memorable by the reactivation. As a result, the whole argument becomes more comprehensible and coherent, as links between current claims and previously presented information are emphasized.

Furthermore, tight chains of γάρ clauses such as those in 1:15–18; 5:6–8; 7:14–15, 18–19; and 10:2–5 are particularly significant for the coherence of the argument. The effect of such chains is a cumulative backward strengthening, each γάρ clause functioning as a strengthening premise for the preceding, increasing the strengthening effects derived from it. The argumentative impact is to highlight the assumptions communicated at the head of the chain, to which the whole cumulative sequence leads back. Backed up as it is by the supporting weight of the strengthening sequence, the argumentative salience of this claim is underlined. It stands out as a main point from which many cognitive effects in the form of fresh implications are to be derived. Such salient claims are significant for the wider thrust and direction of the argument. A procedural account encourages interpreters to read chains of γάρ clauses as tightly knit and coherent complexes of thought that have an important role in underscoring key claims in the argument.

Although a procedural account shows that information introduced by γάρ achieves relevance as strengthening premises in relation to preceding assumptions, this information may also subsequently serve as a springboard for the further development of the argument (see 2:25). In such a case the content of the γάρ clause is processed first in relation to preceding information and is then itself picked up and built or elaborated on in the subsequent argument. We might characterize such material as looking in two directions: first, backward as reinforcing material, and second, forward as a foundation for further development. The double role that such information plays is to be distinguished, however, from the function of γάρ. The latter purely provides guidance toward backward strengthening. It does not direct the drawing of inferences in relation to the subsequent argument. What is clear is that an inferential procedural account of γάρ encourages close attention to assumptions communicated in the previous cotext and thus to the epistle as a whole as a single piece of coherent communication.

7.1.4. An Argumentatively Illuminating Account

The procedural guidance given by γάρ has a secondary effect that is of considerable argumentative significance. The connective flags up the fact that the strengthening premises it introduces function as background information that serves to increase the relevance and salience of preceding claims. This strengthening material plays second fiddle, in argumentative terms, to the claims that it strengthens. This is despite the fact that the strengthening premises often take the form of authoritative or generally accepted truths, whether familiar axioms from the ancient world, metarepresentations of Paul's own thought, scriptural citations, or other theological statements. Such material brings the additional weight of accepted authority behind the claims that are strengthened, lending them persuasive punch. Thus material that is theologically weighty is marshaled not as main points or steps forward in the argument, but instead in the service of more salient preceding claims, which represent the thrust of the argument. By facilitating the identification of relatively less salient background information, a procedural account of γάρ allows us also to track the main argumentative points that are thereby strengthened. It directs us to look away from strengthening material, which is frequently familiar, and toward the claims that are reinforced as the main argumentative implications, in order to gain optimal cognitive effects.

7.2. Interpretative Implications and Interdisciplinary Fruit

A procedural account of γάρ has multiple implications for the interpretation of Romans, both at the microlevel of the exegesis of individual verses, as we explored in chapter 5, and on the macroplane of the epistle's wider argument, as chapter 6 has demonstrated. Although γάρ is a small connective, it has a big interpretative impact, reducing ambiguity and assisting us in choosing between possible interpretations. The constraints it imposes upon the drawing of inferences are invaluable for modern interpreters, operating as we do in a secondary communication situation. This signpost thus demands our attention and respect. An approach to γάρ that dismisses it as a bland connector, used loosely, is to be rejected. If we ignore the guidance γάρ gives, treating it as an interpretative chameleon to be fitted in once an interpretation has already been decided upon, we deprive ourselves of an indispensable clue to a relevant interpretation. Like a driver who overlooks a road sign at a junction, we may find ourselves traveling in the wrong direction, and arriving at an unwanted destination.

7.2.1. Exegesis of Romans

This study leads to the conclusion that we need to give careful consideration to the procedural guidance provided by γάρ from the outset of the exegetical task, rather than reading the connective retrospectively in the light of a prior interpretation. As an indicator that instructs us to look backward in order to find the relevance of the information it introduces, it is a basic clue to the structuring and coherence of the argument. It compels us to pay attention to the preceding cotext as integral to the interpretation of information introduced by γάρ. It thus helps us trace where there is argumentative continuity rather than discontinuity, assisting us with identifying argumentative chunks of thought that should be held together and preventing us from interpreting γάρ clauses in isolation from what precedes. The connective cautions us against the imposition of breaks and section headings that obscure the inferential strengthening relationship between γάρ clauses and preceding claims.

The procedural instructions given immediately rule out interpretations that deny a strengthening connection between information introduced by γάρ and previously communicated assumptions. Similarly, the procedural account throws into question interpretations that assert that material introduced by γάρ represents a fresh implication or step forward in the argument, or a salient argumentative point, rather than supporting information. It likewise undermines readings that view the information in a γάρ clause as in contrast with, or antithetical to, the immediately preceding cotext. The guidance given is particularly helpful in the case of highly contested passages where the apparent ambiguity of the connective contributes to a plethora of readings. For example, it allows us to rule out Campbell's reading of Rom 1:18 as the beginning of the voice of the Teacher, supposedly in fundamental contradiction to Paul's gospel as programmatically stated in the previous verses. It also challenges traditional readings of 1:18 that view the verse as the introduction of a major new section in the argument. In the case of 4:1–2, we have seen that a procedural explanation of γάρ rules out Hays's alternative reading of 4:1, because of its lack of coherence with the direction of the argument in the immediately preceding cotext.

Given the limited scope of this study, it has not been possible to discuss all contested occurrences of γάρ in Romans. A procedural explanation of γάρ provides support, however, for certain interpretations of other highly disputed and argumentatively pivotal passages (e.g., 3:9 and 11:25–26) that argue that these verses must be interpreted in close relationship with their preceding cotext. A demonstration of the light a procedural account throws on the argumentative thrust of these passages and on the debates surrounding them could form the subject of a future study.

7.2.2. Unresolved Issues of the Wider Argument

In chapter 6 I argued that a procedural account of γάρ sheds significant light on the highly contested issues of the epistle's purpose and of the center of its argument. Putting together the findings of a procedural analysis of γάρ in two argumentatively pivotal passages, 1:15–18 and 15:7–13, we proposed that Paul wrote to address specific issues confronting his addressees in Rome and that his Roman version of the gospel is tailored to be relevant to that situation. More specifically, Paul aims to build unity among believers in a multicultural, multiethnic environment, where there are ethnocentric and factional tensions. These are fueled by perceptions about the implicitly anti-Jewish, supersessionist character of Paul's gospel in a situation where many believers have Jewish roots or have been influenced by the Jewish faith. The epistle's argument is thus shaped to address the question of the interdependent relationship of Jews and gentiles in God's purposes and of parity between Jews and gentiles as far as God's acceptance is concerned. It demonstrates that Jews and gentiles alike are ungodly, all under the power of sin, and justified by faith-full trust in Christ, even while Jews have priority both in God's saving purposes, and in his judgment.[1] Within this, chapter 11 is especially important as a theological climax that paints a breathtaking picture of the interdependent interweaving of Jews and gentiles in God's merciful purposes. Romans 15:7, meanwhile, with its summarizing and climactic exhortation to mutual acceptance, represents the argumentative thrust of the entire epistle, the most pertinent point, from which a multiplicity of fresh implications are to be derived for Paul's Roman addressees in their specific situation.

A procedural account of γάρ in 1:15–18 also throws light upon the so-called thesis statement of 1:16–17. It compels us to view these verses not as a summary of Paul's gospel of justification by faith, nor of the theme of the epistle, but rather as powerful theological support for Paul's claims that he desires to preach the gospel to those in Rome and is not ashamed to do this; 1:16–17 must be read within the context of these Rome-focused claims as specially tailored strengthening material that shows the relevance of Paul's gospel to those he writes to in Rome. Following a procedural account of γάρ, the verses cannot be read as a summarizing statement that announces and controls the letter's argument. These conclusions support Campbell's very valid concern that these verses should not be misused as a prior interpretative grid that is imposed upon the epistle's interpretation. Consequently, however, these verses should not be artificially set in isolation from the surrounding cotext, both preceding and subsequent. A procedural reading of γάρ shows that 1:18 in fact belongs with 1:16–17 as the final statement in the complex of strengthening premises. In this respect, the findings of this study present a major challenge to Campbell's controversial construal of the argument of Romans, as well as throwing into question some more standard interpretations.

While the procedural account affirms a Rome-specific reading of the letter's purpose, it does not support all Rome-specific interpretations. For example, the textual clues provided in the strengthening premises in 1:16–18, and more particularly in 15:8–9, do not provide strong support for an anti-imperial interpretation of the epistle such as Elliott's. Instead, the focus both on Jewish priority and on Jewish and gentile parity and inclusion (e.g., in the expression Ἰουδαίῳ τε πρῶτον καὶ Ἕλληνι in 1:16b and in the theological statement of 15:8–9) leads to the inference that Paul seeks

---

[1]. Barclay, *Paul and the Gift*, 464.

to address tensions in relationships between Jewish and gentile, or torah-observant and non-torah-observant, believers in Rome.

7.2.3. Broader Interpretative Implications

As well as throwing light on these specific contested issues, the findings of this study have other broader implications for our reading of Romans. We have seen that γάρ assists us in tracking the most relevant parts of the argument. A strengthening account of γάρ thus allows us to distinguish the argumentative woods from the trees, facilitating a focus on the argumentative thrust of the epistle. It prevents us from being sidetracked by the lure of theologically weighty information that, argumentatively speaking, functions as a buttressing theological framework for the most important argumentative implications that carry the argument forward. A procedural reading of γάρ thus discourages an interpretative preoccupation with strengthening theological explanations that risks confusing Paul's argumentative thrust with background information, albeit often authoritative, and doctrinally significant. Such a preoccupation contributes to a misleading "theological compendium" treatment of Romans. This sometimes gives rise to a distorted version of Paul's theology that is cut adrift from its contextual moorings and results in interpretations that are irrelevant in new interpretative contexts.

The thesis statement reading of 1:16–17 is one case in point. As Campbell rightly warns, the preoccupation with this material as a theological statement leads to an interpretative grid that is then imposed not only upon Romans, but also upon Pauline theology more generally.[2] Divorced from its argumentative and Rome-specific context and interpreted through the lens of a dominant, though oft-unacknowledged, individualistic Western construal of justification by faith, the statement is in danger of functioning as a distortion of the Pauline gospel.[3] The result may be an influential but truncated version of Paul's gospel that is opaque and irrelevant to believers in non-Western cultures, with negative repercussions for the comprehension and contextualization of the gospel.[4] It limits the relevance of the epistle, and of Pauline theology, in fresh contexts, neglecting significant

---

2. Campbell, *Deliverance of God*, 350.
3. Campbell, *Deliverance of God*, 7–8. See also Krister Stendahl, "The Apostle Paul and the Introspective Conscience of the West," *HTR* 56 (1963): 199–215.
4. See Russell, "Alternative Suggestion for the Purpose of Romans," 179–80.

aspects of Paul's argument that may be highly pertinent (e.g., the emphasis on family membership and solidarity in Rom 4, the exhortation to welcome the other in Rom 14–15, and the challenge to ethnocentrism and pretension throughout the letter). Furthermore, reading such material as timeless theological statements without due attention to their cotext and addressees encourages interpreters to read into the text what they are predisposed to find there, shaping it in the image of their own cultural presuppositions.[5] This impoverishes our reading of Romans, depriving the letter of its quality of otherness. Paying attention to γάρ and other communicative clues assists us in guarding against such distorting and limiting interpretative tendencies.

Related to this is another interpretative implication. A relevance-theoretic informed reading draws attention to the fact that the text, viewed as a communicative stimulus addressed to an audience, is not an autonomous object, complete in itself without a context. Instead, shaped by a communicator, it is a set of fragmentary and underdetermined clues pointing toward a relevant interpretation that must be inferred by addressees in a specific context. The procedural account takes us beyond the limitations of approaches that focus on the structure of the text itself, and on hierarchical units of discourse. It is not possible simply to limit ourselves to the linguistic code of the text in interpretation. Guided by its fragmentary clues, we must look beyond the text, making use of contextual information, in order to infer a relevant reading of Romans.

In this regard, a procedural reading makes us aware that both the first addressees, and we ourselves as secondary interpreters, inevitably engage in the drawing of inferences in the comprehension process. For secondary interpreters, contextual information will need to be drawn not only from assumptions communicated in the cotext, but also from plausible background assumptions about the probable historical situation in which the letter arose and to which it was addressed. While there can be no certainty about such background information, it is nevertheless possible to make informed judgments from historical data about basic assumptions that were probably accessible to the first addressees and to use these in order to arrive at the most coherent construal of all the textual data in the epistle.

---

5. See Campbell's apposite remarks regarding unacknowledged interpretive presuppositions and supposedly contextless, "theological" interpretations: "What ... must be recognized is that all interpreters have an envisaged 'context,' even if it is described as not being a context!" (Campbell, "Addressees of Paul's Letter to the Romans," 177).

Many of the implications drawn from this study of γάρ in Romans are highly pertinent to the study of other Pauline epistles. Comparative research remains to be undertaken on the use of γάρ in Paul's other letters and on the correlation between its use and the argumentative and persuasive character of different epistles. The line of argument of letters such as Galatians could fruitfully be reexamined in the light of a procedural understanding of γάρ. The study potentially also has multiple benefits for New Testament studies and biblical studies more generally. It challenges biblical scholars to give due consideration in interpretation to the role of both communicator intentions and addressees' inferential processes, to textual clues, cotext, and contextual information alike. It has the potential to bring together the sometimes polarized interpretative positions of those who insist on the author's intention, on the one hand, and those who argue for a reader-response perspective, on the other. It highlights the importance of taking all communicative clues into careful consideration as the starting point for exegesis. It fosters a respect for the coherence of texts as communicative wholes, guarding against atomizing interpretations. It encourages interpreters to remove their theological spectacles and take a fresh look at the argumentative thrust of biblical texts, reexamining their presuppositions regarding the most relevant and salient parts of the argument.[6] It recognizes a role for pertinent historical data in inferring a relevant interpretation and suggests a way of integrating such data into a plausible reconstruction of addressees' inferential processes.

The study has shown the fruitfulness of interdisciplinary collaboration. The application of innovative insights from cognitive pragmatics to a stubborn problem of biblical exegesis has proved to be a fertile undertaking. Harnessing a relevance-theoretic approach allows us to find a way forward out of the impasse of traditional explanations of γάρ to a more satisfying and exegetically useful explanation of the connective's communicative role. There are potentially many other fruit to be harvested from such interdisciplinary interaction. Innovative approaches and cutting-edge research from the fast-developing fields of linguistics and pragmatics have much to offer biblical studies, with the potential to throw fresh light on other old problems. Dialogue with these related disciplines and awareness of ongoing developments within them is, I suggest, not simply desirable, but necessary for the continuing vigor, validity, and relevance

---

6. Or, in the case of narrative material, the narrative eventline.

of biblical studies. Openness to new linguistic developments increases the intellectual rigor of biblical interpretation, as its established assumptions and methods are scrutinized, challenged, and strengthened in the light of new discoveries about human language, communication, and cognition.

The account of γάρ given in this study likewise makes a contribution to research in cognitive pragmatics. Specifically, it adds to the growing body of research applying relevance theory cross-linguistically. The results of the systematic analysis of occurrences of γάρ in Romans serve as a further exemplar of the way in which the notion of procedural meaning provides a compelling account of connectives in diverse languages. In addition, the study presents another example of the various ways in which different languages encode procedural meaning.

The findings of this study also have implications for the study of Koine Greek. The procedural reading of γάρ in Romans demonstrated here needs to be explored in relation to other Koine data. Its validity should be examined using other non-Pauline New Testament texts, including non-argumentative text types such as narrative material. If the account holds for other texts and text types, it has the potential to shed light on various exegetical ambiguities in other biblical texts, as it does in Romans. In addition, this account of γάρ should be explored in comparable contemporary extrabiblical material, such as the *Discourses* of Epictetus and the *Orations* of Dio Chrysostom.[7] From a lexicographic point of view, this study suggests that standard lexicon entries for γάρ such as those in BDAG need to be revised. A procedural understanding of γάρ requires us to reject the attempt to reduce γάρ to a single gloss or even several glosses. Instead, the connective needs to be explained in terms of core instructions that lead to diverse outworkings, depending on the particular cotext, and inferred from this.

Furthermore, the notion of procedural meaning throws open the door to a cognitively grounded, unified account of the function of other Koine Greek connectives. For example, a procedural account needs to be developed for δέ, οὖν, ἄρα, ἀλλά, and καί. The procedural role and distinct function of each will help to throw light on the function of all the others. Ideally, such research would have been undertaken in tandem with the analysis of γάρ, but that was beyond the scope of this limited study. Simi-

---

7. A *Thesaurus Linguae Graecae* search reveals 691 occurrences of γάρ in Epictetus's *Discourses* and 1860 occurrences in Dio Chrysostom's *Orations*.

larly, there is a need to explore the function of διοτί from a procedural point of view and establish its role in distinction to the procedural role of γάρ. More generally, a relevance-theoretic account of procedural meaning opens up the way for a more satisfactory explanation of other aspects of Koine Greek that are not adequately accounted for by traditional grammatical analysis. These include tense, mood, and aspect.[8]

In relation to Bible translation, the domain that triggered the initial impetus for this research, this study confirms that the translation of γάρ, and other New Testament connectives, into fresh languages, requires careful preparatory research. While γάρ in Greek communicates a broad inferential constraint, encompassing a wide range of types of strengthening, many other languages do not possess a single connective that covers this same range. Instead, a language may communicate strengthening guidance by means of several terms, depending on the more specific ways in which the strengthening procedure is relevant in different contexts.[9] Linguists and translators in a particular language need to begin by identifying the range of linguistic features used to give procedural guidance toward strengthening. Next, when undertaking exegesis of the biblical text, they must seek to understand the type of strengthening guidance γάρ primarily gives in a particular cotext and select the most appropriate linguistic feature that translates this. This may sometimes mean limiting the broad guidance given by γάρ to more specific strengthening guidance in a particular passage, reducing the interpretative choices available to addressees in the host language.[10]

In conclusion, at the broadest level, a relevance-theoretic approach encourages interpretation undertaken on a thoroughly communicative foundation, which respects the biblical text as shaped by a communicative intention and designed to produce effects on addressees. It affirms the validity of a variety of relevant interpretations, acknowledging the role of diverse perspectives and background knowledge in contribut-

---

8. See Sim, *Marking Thought and Talk in New Testament Greek*, 260; Sim, *Relevant Way to Read*, 118–19.

9. Modern English, e.g., introduces strengthening in a whole variety of different ways: *you see* to introduce a further explanation, *after all* to introduce confirming evidence that is already known, a colon to introduce a specification, etc. In spoken English, strengthening guidance is often given via intonation rather than by means of a lexeme.

10. As with all translation, the translation of connectives involves compromise.

ing to differing effects of the text, while recognizing the guiding role of communicator intentions in shaping it. It requires us to acknowledge the distinction between first addressees and secondary interpreters, recognizing that the text will be relevant in different ways to each. The awareness that all interpretation involves inferences involving contextual assumptions encourages an attitude of humility in the biblical interpretative task. We are compelled to recognize our limitations as secondary interpreters who cannot be certain of the contextual assumptions available to the first addressees and thus to hold onto our conclusions lightly. In the light of this, the direction offered by procedural indicators such as γάρ as a clue to communicator intentions is all the more valuable. Such communicator guidance functions as an anchor amid the uncertain currents of contextual information and audience perspectives. Despite the risks and uncertainties, the interpretative task ultimately remains worthwhile, because the text, shaped by a communicator, has continuing relevance; it is a stimulus to fresh cognitive effects provoked by someone and something that is Other, beyond ourselves.

Appendix A: Glossary

This glossary contains a combination of technical terms used within relevance theory, as well as more general terms, explaining the specific way that these are employed within this study. In some cases, the strict relevance theory definition has been adapted slightly.

argumentation: communication in which a communicator's overt aim is to persuade addressees of the validity or truth of certain claims. A communicator may make use of different kinds of strategies to achieve this aim, for example, rational/logical strategies, rhetorical devices, or the deployment of authoritative sources.

assertion: an explicitly communicated assumption by which the communicator represents a particular state of affairs as true.

assumption: a thought that is held by, or accessible to, an individual and is treated by that individual as a representation of the actual world.[1] An assumption may be explicitly stated, implicitly communicated or already held by the addressee as part of her background knowledge.

claim (interchangeable with assertion): an explicitly communicated assumption by which the communicator affirms that a particular state of affairs is true.

cognitive effects: "adjustments to the way an individual represents the world."[2]

comprehension mechanism: a posited cognitive mechanism that deals with the interpretation of language. The comprehension mechanism has as its input mental representations derived from a linguistic stimulus and

---

1. See Sperber and Wilson, *Relevance*, 2.
2. Clark, *Relevance Theory*, 363.

from contextual assumptions, and it computes inferences so as to arrive at the comprehension of a linguistic stimulus. It follows the relevance-guided comprehension heuristic.[3] In this study, the expression *comprehension processes* is used as a substitute for this more technical term.

contextual assumption: an implicit or background assumption accessible to the addressee and used in the interpretation of an utterance.[4]

cotext: the text (linguistic stimulus and communicated assumptions) that surrounds or accompanies a particular part of a text or communication under discussion, both preceding and following. The cotext is referred to by some scholars as the "literary context." The term may refer to a sentence, paragraph, section, or to the entire piece of communication, depending on what is pertinent in a particular case.

encyclopedic knowledge: the unique body of background knowledge, that is, mentally represented assumptions, stored in the mind of, and accessible to, an individual. This comes from the unique experiences of this individual and consists of contextual assumptions in the form of beliefs, memories, cultural information and values, and so on.

epistemic vigilance: a cognitive capacity on the part of addressees aimed at detecting false information. Relevance theory and cognitive scientists posit a suite of cognitive mechanisms that evaluate the reliability of a piece of communication, both in terms of the rational coherence of its content and the trustworthiness of its source.

explicit assumption: an assumption that is explicitly communicated in the text.

expository argumentation: argumentation in which the communicator aims to persuade addressees, by means of claims and supporting evidence, of the truth or validity of certain states of affairs.

γάρ clause: an explicitly communicated assumption, or set of assumptions, introduced by γάρ. The connective indicates that these assumptions are to be processed as strengthening premises. A γάρ clause may be a subsentential clause, a full grammatical sentence, or two or more conjoined

---

3. See Clark, *Relevance Theory*, 346–48.
4. See Sperber and Wilson, *Relevance*, 15–16; Clark, *Relevance Theory*, 224–27.

clauses that are inferred to belong together as a complex of strengthening premises.

hortatory argumentation: argumentation in which the communicator aims to persuade addressees, by means of exhortations and supporting rationale, to put into practice certain desirable actions.

implication: an assumption that is inferred from a series of premises. This series starts with an explicitly communicated premise and includes at least one implicit premise (contextual assumption) that is already held by the addressee or accessible to her. An implication represents a change in thought, and a fresh cognitive effect, for the hearer. An implication may be inferred by an addressee as the result of explicit or implicit communication and may or may not be intended by the communicator. An explicitly stated implication often represents a new thought or step forward in the line of argument.

logical argumentation: argumentation that achieves its aim of persuading addressees of the validity of certain claims primarily by the presentation of claims that are backed up by supporting premises, or evidence, are rationally coherent, and lead to certain logical conclusions.

mainline of the argument: the series of main points, or implications (leading to fresh cognitive effects), in an argument, each of which represents a new step forward in the development of the thought.

metarepresentation: a representation that represents another representation. In relevance theory terms, all verbal utterances are representations of thoughts. If a verbal utterance (or a thought attributed to a person or context) is later re-represented in another context, either as a citation or a paraphrase, this is a metarepresentation.

metatextual: used of a comment within the text/communication, which refers to communicated assumptions, to the manner of communication or to the communicator or addressees; in short, a comment that functions at a higher level of representation by referring to the communication itself, which in turn represents a state of affairs.

mutually manifest assumptions: those assumptions, contextual or communicated, that are accessible and capable of being held as true, by both communicator and addressees.

ostensive-inferential communication: transmission of information that involves, on the part of the communicator, an overt intention to communicate by means of a stimulus, and, on the part of the audience, inferences that are drawn in order to arrive at the comprehension of this stimulus.

premise: I use this term as relevance theory uses it, to refer to an assumption that is used in a process of inferences that leads to a conclusion. Thus a premise serves as support for a conclusion. This does not imply, however, as in strict logic, that the truth of a premise guarantees the truth of the conclusion. Instead, relevance theory talks in terms of nondemonstrable inferences, in which evidence may suggest a conclusion but does not guarantee its truth.[5] Premises may be entertained by addressees as a result of being explicitly or implicitly communicated or may be accessed from background knowledge.

procedure G: a posited strengthening inferential procedure, triggered by the connective γάρ (hence G), that takes place at the subpersonal level in the minds of addressees, as part of the comprehension process. The procedure processes a newly communicated assumption, or complex of assumptions, introduced by γάρ, as a premise that supports a previously communicated assumption. It searches for contextual assumptions made highly accessible by the new assumption to combine with it in a strengthening inferential series. This leads to a conclusion that independently confirms the previously communicated assumption, causing addressees to adhere to it more strongly.

propositional form: the disambiguated and filled-out form of an utterance that is semantically complete in the sense that it expresses a state of affairs and is capable of being true or false. It can thus serve as input into inferential processes and be stored in encyclopedic knowledge.

relevance-guided comprehension heuristic: the rule of thumb automatically followed at a subpersonal level by addressees' comprehension processes when drawing inferences in order to arrive at a relevant interpretation. This heuristic consists of two parts: (1) follow a path of least effort in computing cognitive effects; test interpretative hypotheses in order of accessibility; and (2) stop as soon as expectations of relevance are satisfied.[6]

---

5. Clark, *Relevance Theory*, 137–39; Sperber and Wilson, *Relevance*, 67–71.
6. Clark, *Relevance Theory*, 366.

rhetorical argumentation: argumentation that achieves its aim of persuading addressees to adhere more strongly to certain claims primarily by means of rhetorical features and devices (repetition, metaphor, parallelism, antithesis, chiasm, rhetorical questions, etc.), rather than by rational argument.

rhetorical effect: a persuasive effect created in a piece of argumentation by means of rhetorical devices and features that appeal primarily to the emotions and senses, rather than by rational argument consisting of claims and supporting premises.

rhetorical features/devices: formal features and literary/stylistic devices such as emphatic repetition, metaphor, rhetorical questions, antithetical parallelism, irony, and so forth that have a persuasive effect by creating an impression that affects emotions, rather than by the rational substantiation of claims.

strengthening effect: a cognitive effect, or change in thought, that consists of an existing assumption being held more strongly as valid, that is, adhered to more strongly, by an addressee.

strengthening procedure: an inferential procedure that involves the combination of explicitly communicated premises and implicit background assumptions in a deductive series, leading to a conclusion that causes addressees to adhere more strongly to a previously communicated assumption.

utterance: a linguistic stimulus consisting of a phonetic representation, given by a communicator in a particular situation. This linguistic stimulus serves as a clue to an assumption or thought that the communicator intends to communicate. This clue needs to be disambiguated and filled out in the context in order to represent the communicated assumption.[7]

---

7. See Sperber and Wilson, *Relevance*, 8–10.

Appendix B: Occurrences of γάρ in Romans

1:9	somewhat complex
1:11	straightforward
1:16a	somewhat complex
1:16b	somewhat complex
1:17	somewhat complex
1:18	problematic
1:19	straightforward
1:20	straightforward
1:26	straightforward
2:1b	straightforward
2:1c	straightforward
2:11	straightforward
2:12	straightforward
2:13	straightforward
2:14	somewhat complex
2:24	straightforward
2:25	problematic
2:28	somewhat complex
3:2	straightforward
3:3	problematic
3:9	straightforward
3:20	straightforward
3:22	somewhat complex
3:23	straightforward
3:28	straightforward
4:2	somewhat complex
4:3	straightforward
4:9	somewhat complex
4:13	problematic
4:14	somewhat complex

4:15	somewhat complex
5:6	problematic
5:7a	problematic
5:7b	problematic
5:10	straightforward
5:13	problematic
5:15	straightforward
5:16	straightforward
5:17	somewhat complex
5:19	somewhat complex
6:5	straightforward
6:7	problematic
6:10	somewhat complex
6:14a	straightforward
6:14b	straightforward
6:19	problematic
6:20	problematic
6:21	straightforward
6:23	somewhat complex
7:1	problematic
7:2	straightforward
7:5	somewhat complex
7:7	straightforward
7:8	somewhat complex
7:11	somewhat complex
7:14	somewhat complex
7:15a	somewhat complex
7:15b	straightforward
7:18a	somewhat complex
7:18b	straightforward
7:19	straightforward
7:22	problematic
8:2	straightforward
8:3	somewhat complex
8:5	somewhat complex
8:6	problematic
8:7b	straightforward
8:7c	straightforward
8:13	somewhat complex

8:14	straightforward
8:15	straightforward
8:18	problematic
8:19	somewhat complex
8:20	somewhat complex
8:22	somewhat complex
8:24a	straightforward
8:24b	straightforward
8:26	somewhat complex
8:38	somewhat complex
9:3	somewhat complex
9:6	straightforward
9:9	somewhat complex
9:11	problematic
9:15	somewhat complex
9:17	problematic
9:19	straightforward
9:28	straightforward
10:2	somewhat complex
10:3	straightforward
10:4	problematic
10:5	problematic
10:10	straightforward
10:11	straightforward
10:12a	straightforward
10:12b	straightforward
10:13	straightforward
10:16	straightforward
11:1	straightforward
11:15	problematic
11:21	straightforward
11:23	straightforward
11:24	straightforward
11:25	problematic
11:29	straightforward
11:30	somewhat complex
11:32	somewhat complex
11:34	straightforward
12:3	somewhat complex

12:4	somewhat complex
12:19	straightforward
12:20	straightforward
13:1	straightforward
13:3	somewhat complex
13:4a	straightforward
13:4c	straightforward
13:4d	straightforward
13:6a	somewhat complex
13:6b	straightforward
13:8	straightforward
13:9	straightforward
13:11	straightforward
14:3	somewhat complex
14:4	straightforward
[14:5]	somewhat complex
14:6	straightforward
14:7	somewhat complex
14:8	somewhat complex
14:9	straightforward
14:10	straightforward
14:11	straightforward
14:15	problematic
14:17	problematic
14:18	problematic
15:3	straightforward
15:4	somewhat complex
15:8a	problematic
15:18	somewhat complex
15:24	problematic
15:26	straightforward
15:27a	somewhat complex
15:27b	straightforward
16:2	straightforward
16:18	straightforward
16:19	somewhat complex

Bibliography

Primary Sources

Aland, Barbara, Kurt Aland, Johannes Karavidopoulos, Carlo M. Martini, and Bruce M. Metzger, eds. *The Greek New Testament*. 5th ed. Stuttgart: Deutsche Bibelgesellschaft; New York: United Bible Societies, 2014.

———, eds. *Novum Testamentum Graece*. 28th ed. Stuttgart: Deutsche Bibelgesellschaft, 2012.

Ambrosiaster. *Commentarius in epistulas paulinas*. Edited by H. J. Vogels. CSEL 81.1. Vienna: Hoelder-Pichler-Temsky, 1966.

Aristotle. *The Art of Rhetoric*. Translated by John H. Freese. LCL. London: Heinemann, 1926.

The Book of Jubilees. Translated by James C. Vanderkam. CSCO 511. Louvain: Peeters, 1989.

The Dead Sea Scrolls: Hebrew, Aramaic and Greek Texts with English Translations. Edited by James H. Charlesworth. Vols. 2 and 3. Tübingen: Mohr Siebeck; Louisville: Westminster John Knox, 1995–2006.

Dio Chrysostom. *Discourses LXI–LXXX*. Translated by Henry Lamar Crosby. LCL. Cambridge: Harvard University Press, 1951.

Epictetus. *The Discourses as Reported by Arrian: Fragments Books 3–4; the Encheiridion*. Translated by W. A. Oldfather. LCL. Cambridge: Harvard University Press, 1928.

———. *The Discourses as Reported by Arrian, the Manual and Fragments: Books 1–2*. Translated by W. A. Oldfather. LCL. Cambridge: Harvard University Press, 1925.

Euripides. *Cyclops; Alcestis; Medea*. Translated by David Kovacs. LCL. Cambridge: Harvard University Press, 1994.

Josephus. Translated by Henry St. J. Thackeray et al. 10 vols. LCL. Cambridge: Harvard University Press, 1926–1965.

Ovid. *Metamorphoses*. Translated by Frank J. Miller. 2 vols. LCL. Cambridge: Harvard University Press, 1916.
Plutarch. *Moralia*. Translated by F. C. Babbitt, W. Helmbold, et al. 15 vols. LCL. Cambridge: Harvard University Press, 1927–1969.
Rahlfs, Alfred, ed. *Septuaginta: Id est Vetus Testamentum Graece iuxta LXX interpretes*. Stuttgart: Deutsche Bibelgesellschaft, 1935.

Secondary Literature

Achtemeier, Paul J. "*Omne Verbum Sonat*: The New Testament and the Oral Environment of Late Western Antiquity." *JBL* 109 (1990): 3–27.
———. *Romans*. IBC. Atlanta: John Knox, 1985.
Adams, Edward. *Constructing the World: A Study in Paul's Cosmological Language*. Edinburgh: T&T Clark, 2000.
———. *The Earliest Christian Meeting Places: Almost Exclusively Houses?* LNTS 450. London: T&T Clark, 2013.
Anderson, R. Dean, Jr. *Ancient Rhetorical Theory and Paul*. CBET 18. Kampen: Kok Pharos, 1996.
Avemarie, Friedrich. "Israels rätselhafter Ungehorsam: Römer 10 als Anatomie eines von Gott provozierten Unglaubens." Pages 299–320 in *Between Gospel and Election: Explorations in the Interpretation of Romans 9–11*. Edited by Florian Wilk and J. Ross Wagner. WUNT 257. Tübingen: Mohr Siebeck, 2010.
Badenas, Robert. *Christ the End of the Law: Romans 10.4 in Pauline Perspective*. JSNTSup 10. Sheffield: JSOT Press, 1985.
Bakker, Stéphanie J. "On the Curious Combination of the Particles Γάρ and Οὖν." Pages 41–61 in *Discourse Cohesion in Ancient Greek*. Edited by Stéphanie J. Bakker and Gerry C. Wakker. ASCP 16. Leiden: Brill, 2009.
Barclay, John M. G. "Do We Undermine the Law? A Study of Romans 14:1–15:6." Pages 37–60 in *Pauline Churches and Diaspora Jews*. WUNT 275. Tübingen: Mohr Siebeck, 2011.
———. "Is It Good News That God Is Impartial? A Response to Robert Jewett, *Romans: A Commentary*." *JSNT* 31 (2008): 89–111.
———. *Jews in the Mediterranean Diaspora: From Alexander to Trajan (323 BCE–117 CE)*. Edinburgh: T&T Clark, 1996.
———. "Mirror-Reading a Polemical Letter: Galatians as a Test Case." *JSNT* 10 (1987): 73–93.

———. "Paul and Philo on Circumcision: Romans 2.25–9 in Social and Cultural Context." *NTS* 44 (1998): 536–56.

———. *Paul and the Gift*. Grand Rapids: Eerdmans, 2015.

———. "Unnerving Grace: Approaching Romans 9–11 from The Wisdom of Solomon." Pages 91–109 in *Between Gospel and Election: Explorations in the Interpretation of Romans 9–11*. Edited by Florian Wilk and J. Ross Wagner. WUNT 257. Tübingen: Mohr Siebeck, 2010.

———. "Why the Roman Empire Was Insignificant to Paul." Pages 363–89 in *Pauline Churches and Diaspora Jews*. WUNT 275. Tübingen: Mohr Siebeck, 2011.

Barrett, Charles K. *A Commentary on the Epistle to the Romans*. BNTC. London: Black, 1971.

Barth, Karl. *A Shorter Commentary on Romans*. London: SCM, 1959.

Bassler, Jouette M. "Divine Impartiality in Paul's Letter to the Romans." *NovT* 26 (1984): 43–58.

Bauer, Walter. *Griechisch-deutsches Wörterbuch zu den Schriften des Neuen Testaments und der übrigen urchristlichen Literatur*. Edited by Kurt Aland. 6th ed. Berlin: de Gruyter, 1988.

Baur, Ferdinand C. *The Apostle of Jesus Christ, His Life and Work, His Epistles and His Doctrine*. 2nd ed. London: Williams & Norgate, 1876.

Beker, Johan C. *Paul the Apostle: The Triumph of God in Life and Thought*. Philadelphia: Fortress, 1980.

Bird, C. H. "Some Γάρ Clauses in St. Mark's Gospel." *JTS* 4 (1953): 171–87.

Bird, Michael F. "The Letter to the Romans." Pages 177–204 in *All Things to All Cultures: Paul Among Jews, Greeks and Romans*. Edited by Mark Harding and Alanna Nobbs. Grand Rapid: Eerdmans, 2013.

Black, Stephanie. *Sentence Conjunctions in the Gospel of Matthew: καί, δέ, γάρ, οὖν and Asyndeton in Narrative Discourse*. JSNTSup 216. Sheffield: Sheffield Academic, 2002.

Blakemore, Diane. *Relevance and Linguistic Meaning: The Semantics and Pragmatics of Discourse Markers*. CSL 99. Cambridge: Cambridge University Press, 2002.

———. *Semantic Constraints on Relevance*. Oxford: Blackwell, 1987.

Blass, Regina. "Constraints on Relevance in Koine Greek in the Pauline Letters." Paper presented at a SIL International seminar in Nairobi, Kenya, May 1993.

———. *Relevance Relations in Discourse: A Study with Special Reference to Sissala*. CSL 55. Cambridge: Cambridge University Press, 1990.

Bornkamm, Günther. "The Letter to the Romans as Paul's Last Will and Testament." Pages 16–28 in *The Romans Debate*. Edited by Karl P. Donfried. Rev. and exp. ed. Edinburgh: T&T Clark, 1991.

———. "Revelation." Pages 47–70 in *Early Christian Experience*. New York: Harper & Row, 1969.

Burke, Seán. *The Death and Return of the Author: Criticism and Subjectivity in Barthes, Foucault and Derrida*. 3rd ed. Edinburgh: Edinburgh University Press, 2010.

Burridge, Richard. *Imitating Jesus: An Inclusive Approach to New Testament Ethics*. Grand Rapids: Eerdmans, 2007.

Campbell, Douglas A. *The Deliverance of God: An Apocalyptic Rereading of Justification in Paul*. Grand Rapids: Eerdmans, 2009.

———. "Douglas Campbell's Response to Robin Griffith-Jones." Pages 175–81 in *Beyond Old and New Perspectives on Paul: Reflections on the Work of Douglas Campbell*. Edited by Chris Tilling. Eugene, OR: Cascade, 2014.

———. "Rereading Romans 1–3." Pages 133–60 in *Beyond Old and New Perspectives on Paul: Reflections on the Work of Douglas Campbell*. Edited by Chris Tilling. Eugene, OR: Cascade, 2014.

Campbell, William S. "The Addressees of Paul's Letter to the Romans: Assemblies of God in House Churches and Synagogues?" Pages 171–95 in *Between Gospel and Election: Explorations in the Interpretation of Romans 9–11*. Edited by Florian Wilk and J. Ross Wagner. WUNT 257. Tübingen: Mohr Siebeck, 2010.

———. *Paul's Gospel in an Intercultural Context: Jew and Gentile in the Letter to the Romans*. SIGC 69. Frankfurt am Mainz: Lang, 1992.

Carston, Robyn. *Thoughts and Utterances: The Pragmatics of Explicit Communication*. Oxford: Blackwell, 2002.

Clark, Billy. *Relevance Theory*. CSL. Cambridge: Cambridge University Press, 2013.

Cranfield, C. E. B. *The Epistle to the Romans*. 2 vols. ICC. Edinburgh: T&T Clark, 1975.

Dahl, Nils A. "The Missionary Theology in the Epistle to the Romans." Pages 70–94 in *Studies in Paul: Theology for the Early Christian Mission*. Translated by Paul Donahue. Minneapolis: Augsburg, 1977.

———. "The One God of Jews and Gentiles." Pages 178–91 in *Studies in Paul: Theology for the Early Christian Mission*. Translated by Paul Donahue. Minneapolis: Augsburg, 1977.

Das, A. Andrew. "The Gentile-Encoded Audience of Romans: The Church Outside the Synagogue." Pages 29–46 in *Reading Paul's Letter to the Romans*. Edited by Jerry L. Sumney. RBS 73. Atlanta: Society of Biblical Literature, 2012.

———. *Solving the Romans Debate*. Minneapolis: Fortress, 2007.

Denniston, John D. *The Greek Particles*. Oxford: Clarendon, 1934.

Dijk, Teun A. van. *Discourse and Context: A Sociocognitive Approach*. Cambridge: Cambridge University Press, 2008.

Dodd, C. H. *The Epistle of Paul to the Romans*. MNTC. London: Hodder & Stoughton, 1932.

Donfried, Karl P., ed. *The Romans Debate*. Rev. and exp. ed. Edinburgh: T&T Clark, 1991.

Dooley, Robert, and Stephen Levinsohn. *Analyzing Discourse: A Manual of Basic Concepts*. Dallas: SIL International, 2000.

Dunn, James D. G. *The New Perspective on Paul: Collected Essays*. WUNT 185. Tübingen: Mohr Siebeck, 2005.

———. *Romans 1–8*. WBC 38A. Waco, TX: Word, 1988.

———. *Romans 9–16*. WBC 38B. Waco, TX: Word, 1988.

Edwards, Richard A. "Narrative Implications of *Gar* in Matthew." *CBQ* 52 (1990): 636–55.

Elliott, Neil. *The Arrogance of Nations: Reading Romans in the Shadow of Empire*. Minneapolis: Fortress, 2008.

———. *Liberating Paul: The Justice of God and the Politics of the Apostle*. Sheffield: Sheffield Academic, 1994.

———. *The Rhetoric of Romans: Argumentative Constraint and Strategy and Paul's Dialogue with Judaism*. JSNTSup 45. Sheffield: Sheffield Academic, 1990.

Esler, Philip. *Conflict and Identity in Romans: The Social Setting of Paul's Letter*. Minneapolis: Fortress, 2003.

Fantin, Joseph D. *The Lord of the Entire World: Lord Jesus, a Challenge to Lord Caesar?* New Testament Monographs 31. Sheffield: Sheffield Phoenix, 2011.

Fish, Stanley. "On King v. Burwell : What Is a Natural Reading?" *Huffington Post*, 29 June 2015. https://tinyurl.com/SBL4528a.

Fitzmyer, Joseph A. *Romans: A New Translation with Introduction and Commentary*. AB 33. New York: Doubleday, 1993.

Forbes, Chris. "Paul among the Greeks." Pages 124–42 in *All Things to All Cultures: Paul Among Jews, Greeks and Romans*. Edited by Mark Harding and Alanna Nobbs. Grand Rapids: Eerdmans, 2013.

Gamble, Harry Y., Jr. *The Textual History of the Letter to the Romans: A Study in Textual and Literary Criticism*. SD 42. Grand Rapids: Eerdmans, 1977.

Gathercole, Simon. *Defending Substitution: An Essay on Atonement in Paul*. Grand Rapids: Baker Academic, 2015.

———. *Where Is Boasting? Early Jewish Soteriology and Paul's Response in Romans 1–5*. Grand Rapids: Eerdmans, 2002.

Georgi, Dieter. "God Turned Upside Down." Pages 148–57 in *Paul and Empire: Religion and Power in Roman Imperial Society*. Edited by Richard A. Horsley. Harrisburg, PA: Trinity Press International, 2000.

Gibbs, Raymond W. *Intentions in the Experience of Meaning*. Cambridge: Cambridge University Press, 1999.

Gignac, Alain. "Le Christ, τέλος de la loi (Rm 10,4), une lecture en termes de continuité et de discontinuité dans le cadre du paradigme paulinien de l'élection." *ScEs* 46 (1994): 55–81.

Griffith-Jones, Robin. "Beyond Reasonable Hope of Recognition? Prosōpopeia in Romans 1:18–3:8." Pages 161–74 in *Beyond Old and New Perspectives on Paul: Reflections on the Work of Douglas Campbell*. Edited by Chris Tilling. Eugene, OR: Cascade, 2014.

Gutt, Ernst-August. *Translation and Relevance: Cognition and Context*. Manchester: St. Jerome, 2000.

Harbeck, J. A. "Mark's Use of 'Gar' in Narration." *Notes on Translation* 38 (1970): 10–15.

Hays, Richard B. *Echoes of Scripture in the Letters of Paul*. New Haven: Yale University Press, 1989.

———. "Have We Found Abraham to Be Our Forefather according to the Flesh? A Reconsideration of Rom. 4:1." *NovT* 27 (1985): 76–98.

Heckert, Jakob A. *Discourse Function of Conjoiners in the Pastoral Epistles*. Dallas: SIL International, 1996.

Hellholm, D. "Enthymemic Argumentation in Paul: The Case of Romans 6." Pages 119–79 in *Paul in His Hellenistic Context*. Edited by Troels Engberg-Pedersen. Edinburgh: T&T Clark, 1994.

Hengel, Martin. "Der vorchristliche Paulus." Pages 177–291 in *Paulus und das antike Judentum*. Edited by Martin Hengel and Ulrich Heckel. WUNT 58. Tübingen: Mohr Siebeck, 1991.

Horn, Laurence R., and Gregory E. Ward, eds. *Handbook of Pragmatics*. BHL. Oxford: Blackwell, 2004.

Hurtado, Larry W. "Oral Fixation and New Testament Studies? 'Oral-

ity,' 'Performance' and Reading Texts in Early Christianity." *NTS* 60 (2014): 321–40.
Iten, Corinne. *Linguistic Meaning, Truth Conditions and Relevance: The Case of Concessives*. New York: Palgrave MacMillan, 2005.
Jervell, Jacob. "The Letter to Jerusalem." Pages 61–74 in *The Romans Debate*. Edited by Karl P. Donfried. Minneapolis: Augsburg, 1977.
———. "The Letter to Jerusalem." Pages 53–64 in *The Romans Debate*. Edited by Karl P. Donfried. Rev. and exp. ed. Edinburgh: T&T Clark, 1991.
Jewett, Robert. *Romans: A Commentary*. Hermeneia. Minneapolis: Fortress, 2007.
Johnson-Laird, Philip N. *Mental Models: Towards a Cognitive Science of Language, Inference, and Consciousness*. Cambridge: Cambridge University Press, 1983.
Jülicher, Adolf. "Der Brief an die Römer." Pages 223–335 in vol. 2 of *Die Schriften des Neuen Testaments*. Edited by Wilhelm Bousset and Wilhelm Heitmüller. 3rd ed. 4 vols. Göttingen: Vandenhoeck & Ruprecht, 1917.
Karris, Robert. "Romans 14:1–15:13 and the Occasion of Romans." Pages 65–84 in *The Romans Debate*. Edited by Karl P. Donfried. Rev. and exp. ed. Edinburgh: T&T Clark, 1991.
Käsemann, Ernst. *An die Römer*. HNT 8a. Tübingen: Mohr, 1973.
Keck, Leander. "The Post-Pauline Interpretation of Jesus' Death in Rom 5,6–7." Pages 237–48 in *Theologia Crucis—Signum Crucis: Festschrift für Erich Dinkler zum 70. Geburtstag*. Edited by C. Andersen and Günther Klein. Tübingen: Mohr Siebeck, 1979.
Klauck, Hans-Josef, and Daniel P. Bailey. *Ancient Letters and the New Testament: A Guide to Context and Exegesis*. Waco, TX: Baylor University Press, 2006.
Klein, Günther. "Paul's Purpose in Writing the Epistle to the Romans." Pages 29–43 in *The Romans Debate*. Edited by Karl P. Donfried. Rev. and exp. ed. Edinburgh: T&T Clark, 1991.
Kuehner, Raphael, and Bernhard Gerth. *Ausführliche Grammatik der griechischen Sprache*. Vol. 2. 3rd ed. Hannover: Hahn, 1966.
Kümmel, Werner G. *Introduction to the New Testament*. Translated by H. C. Kee. Rev. ed. Nashville: Abingdon, 1975.
———. *Römer 7 und das Bild des Menschen im Neuen Testament*. TB 53. Munich: Kaiser, 1974.

Kuss, Otto. *Der Römerbrief übersetzt und erklärt*. 3 vols. Regensburg: Pustet, 1957.
Lagrange, Marie-Joseph. *Saint Paul, Épître aux Romains*. EBib. Paris: Lecoffre, 1916.
Lampe, Peter. *From Paul to Valentinus: Christians at Rome in the First Two Centuries*. Translated by Michael Steinhauser. Minneapolis: Fortress, 2003.
Lane, William L. "Social Perspectives on Roman Christianity during the Formative Years from Nero to Nerva: Romans, Hebrews, 1 Clement." Pages 196–244 in *Judaism and Christianity in First-Century Rome*. Edited by Karl P. Donfried and Peter Richardson. Grand Rapids: Eerdmans, 1998.
Larsen, Iver. "Notes on the Function of γάρ, οὖν, μέν, δέ, καί, and τέ in the Greek New Testament." *Notes* 5 (1991): 35–47.
———. "The Use of γάρ and the Meaning of Fire in Mark 9:49." *Notes on Translation* 8 (1994): 33–39.
Levinsohn, Stephen H. *Discourse Features of New Testament Greek: A Coursebook on the Information Structure of New Testament Greek*. 2nd ed. Dallas: SIL International, 2000.
———. *Textual Connections in Acts*. SBLMS 31. Atlanta: Scholars Press, 1987.
Levinson, Stephen C. *Pragmatics*. CSL. Cambridge: Cambridge University Press, 1983.
Linebaugh, Jonathan A. "Announcing the Human: Rethinking the Relationship between Wisdom of Solomon 13–15 and Romans 1.18–2.11." *NTS* 57 (2011): 214–37.
Longacre, Robert E. *The Grammar of Discourse*. 2nd ed. New York: Plenum, 1996.
Longenecker, Richard N. "The Focus of Romans: The Central Role of 5:1–8:39 in the Argument of the Letter." Pages 49–69 in *Romans and the People of God: Essays in Honor of Gordon D. Fee on the Occasion of His Sixty-Fifth Birthday*. Edited by Sven Soderlund and N. T. Wright. Grand Rapids: Eerdmans, 1999.
———. *Introducing Romans: Critical Issues in Paul's Most Famous Letter*. Grand Rapids: Eerdmans, 2011.
Luther, Martin. *Lectures on Romans*. Translated by Wilhelm Pauck. LCC 15. London: SCM, 1961.
MacKenzie, Ian. *Paradigms of Reading: Relevance Theory and Deconstruction*. New York: Palgrave Macmillan, 2002.

Matsui, Tomoko. "Semantics and Pragmatics of a Japanese Discourse Marker *Dakara* (so/in Other Words): A Unitary Account." *Journal of Pragmatics* 24 (2002): 867–91.

McKechnie, Paul. "Paul among the Jews." Pages 103–23 in *All Things To All Cultures: Paul Among Jews, Greeks and Romans*. Edited by Mark Harding and Alanna Nobbs. Grand Rapids: Eerdmans, 2013.

Metzger, Bruce M. *A Textual Commentary on the Greek New Testament: A Companion Volume to the United Bible Societies' Greek New Testament (4th rev. ed.)*. 2nd ed. Stuttgart: Deutsche Bibelgesellschaft; New York: United Bible Societies, 1994.

Meyer, Paul W. "Romans 10:4 and the 'End' of the Law." Pages 78–94 in *The Word in This World: Essays in New Testament Exegesis and Theology*. Edited by John T. Carroll. Louisville: Westminster John Knox, 2004.

Michel, Otto. *Der Brief an die Römer*. KEK 4. Göttingen: Vandenhoeck & Ruprecht, 1978.

Minear, Paul. *The Obedience of Faith: The Purposes of Paul in the Epistle to the Romans*. SBT 2/19. London: SCM, 1971.

Moeschler, Jacques. "Connecteurs pragmatiques, inférences directionnelles et représentations mentales." *Cahiers Chronos* 12 (2005): 35–50.

Moo, Douglas J. *The Epistle to the Romans*. NICNT 5. Grand Rapids: Eerdmans, 1996.

Morgan, Teresa. *Roman Faith and Christian Faith: Pistis and Fides in the Early Roman Empire and Early Church*. New York: Oxford University Press, 2015.

Motyer, Stephen. *Come, Lord Jesus! A Biblical Theology of the Second Coming of Christ*. London: Apollos, 2016.

Moyise, Steve. "Quotations." Pages 15–28 in *As It Is Written: Studying Paul's Use of Scripture*. Edited by Stanley E. Porter and Christopher D. Stanley. SymS 50. Atlanta: Society of Biblical Literature, 2008.

Nanos, Mark D. *The Mystery of Romans: The Jewish Context of Paul's Letter*. Minneapolis: Fortress, 1996.

———. "To the Churches Within the Synagogues of Rome." Pages 11–28 in *Reading Paul's Letter to the Romans*. Edited by Jerry L. Sumney. RBS 73. Atlanta: Society of Biblical Literature, 2012.

Neusner, Jacob. *What Is Midrash?* GBS. Philadelphia: Fortress, 1987.

Newman, Barclay M., Jr. *A Concise Greek-English Dictionary of the New Testament*. Stuttgart: Deutsche Bibelgesellschaft; New York: United Bible Societies, 1993.

Osiek, Carolyn. "The Oral World of Early Christianity in Rome: The Case of Hermas." Pages 151–72 in *Judaism and Christianity in First Century Rome*. Edited by Karl P. Donfried and Peter Richardson. Grand Rapids: Eerdmans, 1998.

Pattemore, Stephen. *The People of God in the Apocalypse: Discourse, Structure, and Exegesis*. SNTSMS 128. Cambridge: Cambridge University Press, 2004.

Paulsen, Henning. *Überlieferung und Auslegung in Römer 8*. WMANT 43. Neukirchen-Vluyn: Neukirchener Verlag, 1974.

Perelman, Chaïm, and Lucie Olbrechts-Tyteca. *The New Rhetoric: A Treatise on Argumentation*. Notre Dame: University of Notre Dame Press, 1969.

Porter, Stanley E. "How Can Biblical Discourse Be Analyzed? A Response to Several Attempts." Pages 107–16 in *Discourse Analysis and Other Topics in Biblical Greek*. Edited by Stanley E. Porter and D. A. Carson. JSNTSup 113. Sheffield: JSOT Press, 1995.

———. *Idioms of the Greek New Testament*. BLG 2. Sheffield: Sheffield Academic, 1992.

———. "An Introduction to Other Topics in Biblical Greek Language and Linguistics." Pages 84–88 in *Biblical Greek Language and Linguistics: Open Questions in Current Research*. Edited by Stanley E. Porter and D. A. Carson. JSNTSup 80. Sheffield: JSOT Press, 1993.

———. *The Letter to the Romans: A Linguistic and Literary Commentary*. New Testament Monographs 37. Sheffield: Sheffield Phoenix, 2015.

Porter, Stanley E., and Andrew W. Pitts. "Greek Language and Linguistics in Recent Research." *CurBR* 6 (2008): 214–55.

Porter, Stanley E., and Christopher D. Stanley, eds. *As It Is Written: Studying Paul's Use of Scripture*. SymS 50. Atlanta: Society of Biblical Literature, 2008.

Reasoner, Mark. *The Strong and the Weak: Romans 14.1–15.13 in Context*. SNTSMS 103. Cambridge: Cambridge University Press, 1999.

Rhyne, Clyde Thomas. *Faith Establishes the Law: A Study on the Continuity between Judaism and Christianity, Romans 3.31*. SBLDS 55. Missoula, MT: Scholars Press, 1981.

Rijksbaron, Albert, ed. *New Approaches to Greek Particles*. ASCP 7. Amsterdam: Gieben, 1997.

Robertson, A. T. *A Grammar of the Greek New Testament in the Light of Historical Research*. 3rd ed. London: Hodder & Stoughton, 1919.

———. *A Short Grammar of the Greek New Testament: For Students Familiar with the Elements of Greek.* 4th ed. New York: Hodder & Stoughton, 1908.

Rodriguez, Daniel. "On Γαρ'd: Dialogue in LXX Isaiah and Romans." *Modular Aggregation of Principles for Bible Translation*, 2014. https://map.bloomfire.com/posts/2237610-on-d.

Rodríguez, Rafael, and Matthew Thiessen, eds. *The So-Called Jew in Paul's Letter to the Romans.* Minneapolis: Fortress, 2016.

Rudolph, Michael A. "Reclaiming ΓΑΡ: The Semantic Constraints and Structural Significance of ΓΑΡ as an Intersentential Conjunction in Romans Through Hebrews." PhD diss., Southeastern Baptist Theological Seminary, 2014.

Runge, Steven. *A Discourse Grammar of New Testament Greek.* Peabody, MA: Hendrickson, 2010.

———. *Romans: A Visual and Textual Guide.* HDC. Bellingham, WA: Lexham, 2014.

Russell, Walter B. "An Alternative Suggestion for the Purpose of Romans." *BSac* 145 (1988): 174–84.

Sanday, William, and Arthur C. Headlam. *A Critical and Exegetical Commentary on the Epistle to the Romans.* ICC. Edinburgh: T&T Clark, 1902.

Sanders, E. P. *Paul and Palestinian Judaism: A Comparison of Patterns of Religion.* London: SCM, 1977.

Sasamoto, Ryoko. "Japanese Discourse Connectives *Dakara* and *Sorede*: A Re-assessment of Procedural Meaning." *Journal of Pragmatics* 40 (2008): 127–54.

Sbisà, Marina, Jan-Ola Östman, and Jef Verschueren, eds. *Philosophical Perspectives for Pragmatics.* Amsterdam: Benjamins, 2011.

Schiffrin, Deborah. *Approaches to Discourse.* Oxford: Blackwell, 1994.

———. *Discourse Markers.* Cambridge: Cambridge University Press, 1987.

Schlier, Heinrich. *Der Römerbrief.* HThKNT 6. Freiburg: Herder, 1977.

Schmithals, Walter. *Der Römerbrief: Ein Kommentar.* Gütersloh: Mohn, 1988.

Seifrid, Mark A. "Unrighteous by Faith: Apostolic Proclamation in Romans 1:18–3:20." Pages 105–45 in *The Paradoxes of Paul.* Vol. 2 of *Justification and Variegated Nomism.* Edited by D. A. Carson, Peter T. O'Brien, and Mark A. Seifrid. WUNT 2/181. Tübingen: Mohr Siebeck, 2004.

Sicking, C. M. J., and J. M. van Ophuijsen. *Two Studies in Attic Particle Usage.* MS 129. Leiden: Brill, 1993.

Sim, Margaret. *Marking Thought and Talk in New Testament Greek: New Light from Linguistics on the Particles ἵνα and ὅτι*. Eugene, OR: Pickwick, 2010.

———. *A Relevant Way to Read: A New Approach to Exegesis and Communication*. Cambridge: Clarke, 2016.

Slings, Simon R. "Adversative Relators Between PUSH and POP." Pages 101–29 in *New Approaches to Greek Particles*. Edited by Albert Rijksbaron. ASCP 7. Amsterdam: Gieben, 1997.

Sperber, Dan, and Deirdre Wilson. "Précis of Relevance: Communication and Cognition." *Behavioral and Brain Sciences* 10 (1987): 697–754.

———. *Relevance: Communication and Cognition*. 2nd ed. Oxford: Blackwell, 1995.

Sperber, Dan, Fabrice Clément, Christophe Heintz, Olivier Mascaro, Hugo Mercier, Gloria Origgi, and Deirdre Wilson. "Epistemic Vigilance." *Mind & Language* 25 (2010): 359–93.

Stendahl, Krister. "The Apostle Paul and the Introspective Conscience of the West." *HTR* 56 (1963): 199–215.

———. *Paul among Jews and Gentiles*. Philadelphia: Fortress, 1976.

Stowers, Stanley K. *The Diatribe and Paul's Letter to the Romans*. SBLDS 57. Chico, CA: Scholars Press, 1980.

———. "*Peri Men Gar* and the Integrity of 2 Cor. 8 and 9." *NovT* 32 (1990): 340–48.

———. *A Rereading of Romans: Justice, Jews, and Gentiles*. New Haven: Yale University Press, 1994.

Stuhlmacher, Peter. *Paul's Letter to the Romans: A Commentary*. Louisville: Westminster John Knox, 1994.

———. "The Purpose of Romans." Pages 231–42 in *The Romans Debate*. Edited by Karl P. Donfried. Rev. and exp. ed. Edinburgh: T&T Clark, 1991.

Swartz, S. "Hiding the Light: Another Look at Luke 8:16–18." *Notes on Translation* 8 (1994): 53–59.

Thistleton, Antony C. *Discovering Romans: Content, Interpretation, Reception*. London: SPCK, 2016.

Thorsteinsson, Runar M. *Paul's Interlocutor in Romans 2: Function and Identity in the Context of Ancient Epistolography*. ConBNT 40. Stockholm: Almqvist & Wiksell, 2003.

Thorsteinsson, Runar M., Matthew Thiessen, and Rafael Rodríguez. "Paul's Interlocutor in Romans: The Problem of Identification." Pages 1–37 in *The So-Called Jew in Paul's Letter to the Romans*. Edited by Rafael Rodríguez and Matthew Thiessen. Minneapolis: Fortress, 2016.

Thrall, Margaret E. *Greek Particles in the New Testament: Linguistic and Exegetical Studies*. NTTS 3. Leiden: Brill, 1962.

Tobin, Thomas H. *Paul's Rhetoric in Its Contexts: The Argument of Romans*. Peabody, MA: Hendrickson, 2004.

Turner, Nigel. *Syntax*. Vol. 3 of *A Grammar of New Testament Greek*. Edinburgh: T&T Clark, 1963.

Unger, Christophe. "Epistemic Vigilance and the Function of Procedural Indicators in Communication and Comprehension." Pages 45–73 in *Relevance Theory: More Than Understanding*. Edited by Ewa Wałaszewska, Agnieszka Piskorska. Newcastle upon Tyne: Cambridge Scholars Publishing, 2012.

———. "On the Cognitive Role of Genre: A Relevance-Theoretic Perspective." PhD diss., University of London, 2001.

Vorster, Johannes N. "Strategies of Persuasion in Romans 1:16–17." Pages 152–70 in *Rhetoric and the New Testament: Essays from the 1992 Heidelberg Conference*. Edited by Stanley E. Porter and Thomas H. Olbricht. JSNTSup 90. Sheffield: JSOT Press, 1993.

Wallace, Daniel B. *Greek Grammar Beyond the Basics: An Exegetical Syntax of the New Testament*. Grand Rapids: Zondervan, 1996.

Walters, James C. *Ethnic Issues in Paul's Letter to the Romans: Changing Self-Definition in Earliest Roman Christianity*. Valley Forge, PA: Trinity Press International, 1993.

Watson, Francis B. "By Faith (of Christ): An Exegetical Dilemma and Its Scriptural Solution." Pages 147–63 in *The Faith of Jesus Christ: Exegetical, Biblical and Theological Studies*. Edited by Michael F. Bird and Preston M. Sprinkle. Milton Keynes: Paternoster, 2009.

———. *Paul and the Hermeneutics of Faith*. London: T&T Clark, 2004.

———. *Paul, Judaism and the Gentiles: Beyond the New Perspective*. 2nd ed. Grand Rapids: Eerdmans, 2007.

———. "The Two Roman Congregations: Romans 14:1–15:13." Pages 203–15 in *The Romans Debate*. Edited by Karl P. Donfried. Rev. and exp. ed. Edinburgh: T&T Clark, 1991.

Wedderburn, Alexander J. M. "The Purpose and Occasion of Romans Again." Pages 195–202 in *The Romans Debate*. Edited by Karl P. Donfried. Rev and exp. ed. Edinburgh: T&T Clark, 1991.

———. *The Reasons for Romans*. Edinburgh: T&T Clark, 1988.

Whittle, Sarah. *Covenant Renewal and the Consecration of the Gentiles in Romans*. SNTSMS 161. Cambridge: Cambridge University Press, 2015.

Wiefel, Wolfgang. "The Jewish Community in Ancient Rome and the Origins of Roman Christianity." Pages 85–101 in *The Romans Debate*. Edited by Karl P. Donfried. Rev. and exp. ed. Edinburgh: T&T Clark, 1991.

Wilckens, Ulrich. *Der Brief an die Römer*. 3 vols. EKKNT 6. Neukirchen-Vluyn: Neukirchener Verlag, 1978–1982.

———. *Der Brief an die Römer: Studienausgabe*. Ostfeldern: Theologie Patmos Verlag, 2014.

———. "Die Rechtfertigung Abrahams nach Römer 4." Pages 33–49 in *Rechtfertigung als Freiheit: Paulusstudien*. Neukirchen-Vluyn: Neukirchener Verlag, 1974.

———. "Über Abfassungszweck und Aufbau des Römerbriefes." Pages 110–70 in *Rechtfertigung als Freiheit*. Neukirchen-Vluyn: Neukirchener Verlag, 1974.

Wilk, Florian. "Rahmen und Aufbau von Römer 9–11." Pages 227–53 in *Between Gospel and Election: Explorations in the Interpretation of Romans 9–11*. Edited by Florian Wilk and J. Ross Wagner. WUNT 257. Tübingen: Mohr Siebeck, 2010.

Wilson, Deirdre. "The Conceptual-Procedural Distinction: Past, Present and Future." Pages 3–31 in *Procedural Meaning: Problems and Perspectives*. Edited by Victoria Escandell-Vidal, Manuel Leonetti, and Aoife Ahern. Bingley: Emerald, 2011.

———. "Relevance and the Interpretation of Literary Works." *UCL Working Papers in Linguistics* 23 (2011): 69–80.

Wilson, Deirdre, and Dan Sperber. "Relevance Theory." Pages 607–32 in *The Handbook of Pragmatics*. Edited by Laurence R. Horn and Gregory E. Ward. Oxford: Blackwell, 2004.

Winer, Georg B. *A Treatise on the Grammar of New Testament Greek: Regarded as the Basis of New Testament Exegesis*. Edinburgh: T&T Clark, 1870.

Wire, Antoinette C. "'Since God Is One': Rhetoric as Theology and History in Paul's Romans." Pages 210–27 in *The New Literary Criticism and the New Testament*. Edited by Elizabeth S. Malbon and Edgar V. McKnight. JSNTSup 109. Sheffield: JSOT Press, 1994.

Witherington, Ben, III. *Paul's Letter to the Romans: A Socio-rhetorical Commentary*. Grand Rapids: Eerdmans, 2004.

Wolter, Michael. *Röm 1–8*. Vol. 1 of *Der Brief an die Römer*. EKKNT 6.1. Neukirchen-Vluyn: Neukirchener Verlag, 2014.

———. *Paulus: Ein Grundriss seiner Theologie*. Neukirchen-Vluyn: Neukirchener Verlag, 2011.

———. *Rechtfertigung und Zukünftiges Heil: Untersuchungen zu Röm 5, 1–11*. BZNW 43. Berlin: de Gruyter, 1979.

Wright, N. T. *The Climax of the Covenant: Christ and Law in Pauline Theology*. Edinburgh: T&T Clark, 1991.

———. *The New Testament and the People of God*. Christian Origins and the Question of God 1. London: SPCK, 1992.

———. *Paul and the Faithfulness of God. Parts I–IV*. 2 vols. Christian Origins and the Question of God 4. London: SPCK, 2013.

———. "Paul and the Patriarch: The Role of Abraham in Romans 4." *JSNT* 35 (2013): 207–41.

———. *Paul for Everyone: Romans, Part 1; Chapters 1–8*. London: SPCK, 2004.

———. "Paul's Gospel and Caesar's Empire." Pages 160–83 in *Paul and Politics: Ekklesia, Israel, Imperium, Interpretation; Essays in Honor of Krister Stendahl*. Edited by Richard A. Horsley. Harrisburg, PA: Trinity Press International, 2000.

———. "Romans." Pages 393–770 in *Acts; Introduction to Epistolary Literature; Romans; 1 Corinthians*. NIB 10. Nashville: Abingdon, 2002.

———. "Romans 9–11 and the 'New Perspective.'" Pages 37–54 in *Between Gospel and Election: Explorations in the Interpretation of Romans 9–11*. Edited by Florian Wilk and J. Ross Wagner. WUNT 257. Tübingen: Mohr Siebeck, 2010.

Wuellner, Wihelm. "Paul's Rhetoric of Argumentation in Romans." Pages 128–46 in *The Romans Debate*. Edited by Karl P. Donfried. Rev. and exp. ed. Edinburgh: T&T Clark, 1991.

Zahn, Theodor. *Der Brief des Paulus an die Römer*. KNT 6. Leipzig: Deichart, 1910.

Zakowski, Samuel. "She Was Twelve Years Old: On Γάρ and Mark 5:42." *Glotta* 92 (2016): 305–17.

Zerwick, Maximilian. *A Grammatical Analysis of the Greek New Testament*. Translated by Mary Grosvenor. 4th ed. SubBi 39. Rome: Pontifical Biblical Institute, 1993.

Zetterholm, Magnus. "The Non-Jewish Interlocutor in Romans 2:17 and the Salvation of the Nations: Contextualizing Romans 1:18–32." Pages

39–58 in *The So-Called Jew in Paul's Letter to the Romans*. Edited by Rafael Rodríguez and Matthew Thiessen. Minneapolis: Fortress, 2016.

Ziesler, John A. *Paul's Letter to the Romans*. London: SCM, 1989.

Zufferey, Sandrine. *Lexical Pragmatics and Theory of Mind: The Acquisition of Connectives*. Amsterdam: Benjamins, 2010.

Ancient Sources Index

Hebrew Bible/Old Testament			Psalms	
			18:49	255
Genesis			26:10	109
2–3		86	62:12	76
12:2–3		250	69:9	248
15		175	105:20 LXX	242
17:9–14		181	106:32–33	52
18:18		250	117:1	255
22:18		250		
26:4		250	Proverbs	
28:14		250	11:31	137
			24:12	76
Leviticus				
18:5		196–98	Isaiah	
19:18		83	8:14	188
			11:10	256
Numbers			13:6–14:8	233
14:28		117	28:16	188
21:18		52	45:23	117–18
			49:18	117
Deuteronomy		247, 250	52:5	126
8:17		196	59:15–18	233
9:4		196		
10:17		76	Jeremiah	
30		197–98	22:24	117
30:11–14		197		
30:12		196	Ezekiel	
30:12–14		198	5:11	117
30:14		74		
30:15		200	Habakkuk	
30:19		200	2:4	215, 235
32:43		255		
			Zephaniah	
2 Chronicles			1:14–2:3	233
19:7		76	3	233

Malachi

1:2	148
Mal 4:1–5	233

Deuterocanonical Books

Wisdom of Solomon

13–15	241

Sirach

44:19–20	185
44:19–21	185
44:21	250

1 Maccabees

2:52	181

Pseudepigrapha

Jubilees

15:25–28	185, 127

Ancient Jewish Writers

Josephus, *Bellum judaicum*

7.45	218

Josephus, *Contra Apionem*

2.282	218

New Testament

Matthew

1:18–23	52
2:1–6	52
2:16–18	52
3:1–3	52

Mark

10:43–45	255

Luke

4:16–21	53

Acts

9:11	46
15:3	163
21:39	46
22:3	46

Romans

1	223
1–3	260
1–4	13, 132, 204, 227, 231, 263, 266
1–8	143
1–11	63, 65, 80, 212, 258
1:1–5	233
1:1–7	207, 246
1:1–15	62, 207
1:1–16	207
1:1–17	207, 213
1:3	177
1:3–4	235
1:5	208
1:6	49
1:6–7	208
1:7	50
1:8	266
1:8–10	229
1:8–12	207
1:8–15	162, 208–10, 215
1:9	233, 289
1:10–14	215
1:11	208, 221, 258, 289
1:13	162, 208, 209
1:13–15	208, 213
1:13–18	263
1:14	208, 210
1:14–2:16	210
1:14–17	211
1:15	50, 263, 266
1:15–17	24
1:15–18	14, 24, 203, 206, **207–45**, 260, 262, 266–67, 272, 275–76
1:16	14, 257, 268, 289
1:16–17	10, 13–14, 22, 61, 191, 205–6, 261, 267, 276–77
1:16–18	10, 22, 263
1:16–20	61

Ancient Sources Index

1:16–32	241	2:17–24	126–27, 130, 177
1:16–15:13	205	2:17–28	264
1:17	10, 67, 289	2:17–29	125, 127
1:18	3, 9–14, 22, 24, 205, 242, 268, 275–76, 289	2:21–22	126, 266
		2:23	125–26, 128–30, 133
1:18–2:16	228	2:24	125, 126, 128, 129, 289
1:18–3:20	205–6, 225, 227–28, 231, 240	2:24–25	264
		2:25	10–12, 124, **125–31**, 166, 170, 272, 289
1:18–4:25	205, 225, 229		
1:18–32	24, 224–25, 230, 240–41, 268	2:25–27	131
		2:25–29	126–27, 130
1:19	264, 289	2:26	130
1:19–20	264	2:26–27	264
1:19–32	**240–42**, 243, 259, 264	2:26–29	131
1:20	264, 289	2:28	289
1:23	242	2:28–29	264
1:24	242	3	51, 174
1:24–31	66	3–5	261
1:26	88, 242, 289	3–11	248
1:28	242	3:1–8	263–64
2–4	85	3:2	289
2:1	76, 125–26, 259, 264, 289	3:3	289
2:1–5	125, 127	3:8	55
2:1–16	14, 116, 264	3:9	3, 242, 265–66, 275, 289
2:5	233	3:9–20	265
2:6	76–78, 266	3:10–18	265
2:6–10	77–78, 264, 266	3:19–20	265
2:6–16	127	3:20	265, 289
2:7	77, 137	3:21	266
2:7–10	76–77	3:21–22	12, 197, 265
2:8	77	3:21–26	142, 175, 193, 204–5, 243, 265
2:9	77–78		
2:10	77–78, 137	3:21–31	174, 183–84, 205–6
2:11	**76–79**, 171, 264, 289	3:21–4:25	175, 231
2:12	9, 11, 289	3:21–5:21	132
2:12–13	129, 131	3:22	12, 37, 69, 181, 242, 289
2:12–14	131	3:22–23	36
2:12–15	264	3:22–26	75, 265
2:12–16	126	3:23	36, 289
2:13	289	3:27	133, 175, 178–79, 182, 265
2:13–15	127	3:27–28	180, 184–86
2:14	289	3:27–30	176
2:17	125, 129, 133	3:27–31	23, 175–76, 184, 187, 212
2:17–22	129	3:27–4:1	180
2:17–23	264	3:27–4:25	186, 259, 265

Romans (cont.)

Reference	Pages
3:28	181–82, 289
3:28–29	182, 265
3:29	182, 185
3:29–30	176, 182
3:30	181, 183–84
3:31	174, 265
4	52, 174–76, 182, 266, 278
4:1	23, 201, 266, 275
4:1–2	173, **174–87**, 201, 275
4:1–12	176
4:2	3, 23, 266, 289
4:2–10	182
4:3	266, 289
4:3–25	180
4:5	142
4:9	289
4:10–15	266
4:10–17	182
4:11–12	266
4:12	266
4:13	12, 266, 289
4:13–15	266
4:13–16	250
4:14	289
4:15	290
4:16	250, 252, 266
4:16–17	252–53
4:18	142
4:20	142
4:25	142
5	154, 204
5–8	70, 132–33, 204
5:1–5	132
5:1–11	132–33, 141
5:1–7:6	71
5:1–8:39	85
5:2	141
5:2–3	133
5:2–5	134
5:3–4	133
5:3–5	134
5:4	141
5:5	131–37, 140–42
5:5–7	141
5:5–10	134, 141
5:6	166, 290
5:6–7	3, 12, 124, **131–42**, 166
5:6–8	133–34, 141, 170, 272
5:6–11	133–34
5:7	166, 290
5:7–8	140
5:8	133–34, 139–40, 142, 290
5:9	141
5:10	141, 290
5:12	72
5:12–21	85, 154, 242
5:13	290
5:15	290
5:15–21	72
5:16	290
5:17	290
5:19	290
5:20	85
6	63, 65, 85, 149, 154–55
6–8	51
6:1	55, 155, 177
6:1–3	155
6:1–14	154
6:1–8:39	132
6:5	290
6:7	290
6:10	290
6:12–14	154–55
6:13	157–58, 160, 167
6:13–14	157
6:13–23	154
6:14	149, 160, 290
6:15	55, 155
6:15–23	154–55
6:16–18	157
6:16–19	160
6:17	153, 156
6:17–18	156–58, 160
6:18	153, 155–56, 159
6:19	166–67, 290
6:19–20	124, 166
6:20	166, 290
6:20–21	159
6:20–22	159–60

Ancient Sources Index

6:20–23	159	7:19	104, 290
6:21	153, 155, 160, 290	7:19–20	100, 102
6:22	110, 153, 155, 159–60	7:20	103, 105
6:23	97, 290	7:21	87
7	61, 66, 85, 149, 206	7:21–25	72, 86
7–8	261	7:22	12, 87, 290
7:1	50, 52, 85, 124, **148–53**, 166–67, 290	7:23	87
		7:25	71
7:1–6	85, 149	8	61, 63, 66, 85–86, 132
7:2	290	8:1	71–72, 73
7:4	85	8:1–4	194
7:5	85–86, 88, 92, 290	8:1–11	70–71, 85
7:7	55, 86, **87–89**, 90, 91, 94, 104–5, 177, 290	8:2	**70–74**, 290
		8:2–7	61
7:7–8	90–91	8:3	71, 290
7:7–11	92, 94	8:3–4	10
7:7–12	86–87, 90, 94–95	8:5	290
7:7–13	86	8:6	290
7:7–14	72	8:7	290
7:7–20	62, 84–86, 103–6, 119	8:13	290
7:7–25	23, 70–72, 85–86	8:14	291
7:8	**90–91**, 92, 105, 290	8:15	291
7:8–10	92	8:17–30	15
7:8–11	95	8:18	9, 11–12, 291
7:9–10	92	8:19	291
7:10	91–94, 105, 193	8:20	291
7:11	**91–94**, 96, 104, 290	8:22	11, 291
7:12	87, 94, 100, 105	8:24	291
7:12–14	193	8:26	291
7:13	55, 86, 94–100, 105–6	8:31	177
7:13–16	100	8:31–39	133
7:13–20	86, 94, 106	8:38	291
7:13–25	86, 242	9–11	74, 143–44, 188, 204, 212, 247–48, 261
7:14	11, 87, **94–98**, 99, 100, 106, 290		
7:14–15	170, 272	9:1–2	55
7:14–20	106	9:1–3	193
7:14–22	61	9:1–5	143
7:15	**98–100**, 102–4, 113, 136, 290	9:3	177, 291
7:15–16	98	9:5	177
7:15–20	98	9:6	143, 148, 291
7:15–23	98	9:6–13	144
7:16	100, 103, 105	9:6–29	143
7:17	86, 100–101, 103, 105	9:7–9	144, 148
7:18	290	9:7–13	250
7:18–19	**100–103**, 170, 272	9:8	250

Romans (cont.)

Reference	Pages
9:8–9	144
9:9	291
9:10	143–47
9:10–12	143–44
9:11	10, 124, 166, 291
9:11–12	**143–48**
9:11–13	145
9:13	143, 148
9:14	177
9:15	291
9:17	10, 291
9:19	291
9:28	291
9:30	177
9:30–31	189
9:30–33	74, 188, 201
9:30–10:1	193
9:30–10:4	196
9:30–10:13	51, 187
9:31	188
9:31–32	192
9:32	189
9:33	188
10	61, 188
10:1	188–89
10:1–4	196
10:1–5	23
10:1–13	15, 74, 187, 201
10:2	187–89, 291
10:2–4	189, 195
10:2–5	187, 200–201, 272
10:3	188–89, 191–95, 201, 291
10:4	23, 74, 291
10:4–5	3, 11, 173, **187–202**
10:5	23–24, 291
10:5–6	187, 196–97, 199, 201
10:5–8	196, 198–99, 200–201
10:5–9	10, 196
10:5–10	196
10:5–13	74, 187, 196
10:6	23–24, 188, 196–98
10:6–7	198
10:6–8	196, 198, 201
10:9	74–76
10:10	**74–76**, 291
10:10–13	61
10:11	188, 291
10:12	291
10:13	74, 291
10:16	291
11	61, 276
11:1	45, 291
11:11–17	257
11:11–32	23
11:13	48, 50
11:13–24	259
11:15	291
11:17–24	204
11:21	291
11:23	291
11:24	291
11:25	3, 9, 23, 291
11:25–26	275
11:28	291
11:28–31	250
11:30	291
11:30–31	257
11:32	291
12	66, 80
12–13	64, 80, 107
12–15	63, 206, 247–48, 257–58
12:1	80
12:1–2	107, 204
12:1–15:13	63, 65, 80, 106
12:3	291
12:3–6	261
12:4	291
12:9–21	80
12:14–21	52
12:19	292
12:20	292
13	51
13:1	**80–82**, 292
13:1–7	61, 66, 80, 82
13:3	292
13:4	292
13:6	292
13:6–7	82
13:8	**82–84**, 292

13:8–9	171	15:7–13	15, 24, 203, 205, 207, 237, 244, **245–63**, 267, 275
13:8–10	82, 212, 261		
13:9	82, 292	15:8	23–24, 267, 292
13:11	292	15:8–9	10, 205, 276
14	51, 61, 66, 248, 259	15:8–12	24, 212
14–15	51, 58, 63, 107, 204, 213, 258, 261, 278	15:14–15	162
		15:14–21	161–62
14:1	108–9, 119, 247–49	15:14–33	161–62
14:1–6	115	15:14–16:27	62
14:1–11	84	15:16	48
14:1–12	62, 106, 118, 119	15:16–21	162
14:1–15:6	245, 257	15:17–19	162
14:1–15:7	249	15:18	292
14:1–15:13	51, 107–8, 247, 257, 262	15:20	208
		15:22	162, 229
14:2	108	15:22–33	161
14:3	**108–10**, 118–19, 292	15:23	161–62
14:3–4	116	15:23–24	161–65
14:3–11	61	15:24	124, **161–67**, 271, 292
14:4	110–11, 116, 119, 292	15:24–27	163
14:5	**110–11**, 112–14, 122, 292	15:26	292
14:5–6	120	15:27	11, 292
14:6	**111–12**, 113–15, 119–20, 292	15:28	163
14:7	118, 120, 136, 292	15:28–29	162
14:7–8	118	15:30	164
14:7–9	**112–15**, 116, 120–21	16	51, 162
14:7–11	171	16:2	292
14:8	88, 119–20, 292	16:13	52
14:9	120, 292	16:17–20	55
14:9–11	119	16:18	292
14:10	118, 120, 292	16:19	292
14:10–11	**116–18**		
14:11	292	1 Corinthians	
14:12	118, 120	1:26–27	135
14:15	292	16:6	163
14:17	247, 292		
14:18	292	2 Corinthians	
15	51	1:16	163
15:1–2	248	5:15	113
15:3	248, 292	10:9–10	53
15:3–4	248	11:22	45
15:4	292		
15:5–6	248	Galatians	
15:5–7	249	1:13–14	45
15:7	267	1:15–16	46

Galatians (cont.)
2:7–8	46
6:12–13	185

Philippians
3:1–11	185
3:5	45

1 Thessalonians
5:27	53

Hebrews
2:11	88

Greco-Roman Literature

Dio Chrysostom, *Orations*	280
Epictetus, *Discourses*	280
1.12.9	52
1.29.3	52
2.12	52
2.26.1–2	100
Euripides, *Medea*	100
Ovid, *Metamorphoses*	
7.19–20	100
Seneca, *Epistulae morales*	
108.22	218

Modern Authors Index

Achtemeier, Paul J.   53, 210–11
Adams, Edward   48, 51–52, 64, 80
Anderson, R. Dean, Jr.   211, 225
Avemarie, Friedrich   188–90, 197
Badenas, Robert   24, 74, 187–88, 190, 193, 197–99
Bailey, Daniel P.   208
Bakker, Stéphanie J.   16
Barclay, John M. G.   42, 44, 46–47, 49, 51, 55–58, 63–64, 76, 88, 107–8, 111, 127, 129, 131–32, 136, 143, 176, 178–79, 184, 186, 188–90, 193, 197, 201, 212, 217, 225, 227, 232, 236, 239, 241–42, 244–46, 248, 250, 257, 259–60, 276
Barrett, Charles K.   85, 101, 125–26, 134, 138, 144, 155–56, 162, 205, 227
Barth, Karl   213–14
Bassler, Jouette M.   76
Bauer, Walter   12, 89
Baur, Ferdinand C.   47, 55, 204
Beker, Johan C.   259
Bird, C. H.   3,
Bird, Michael F.   58, 205, 214, 247, 258
Black, Stephanie   3–6, 18, 20–21, 40, 85
Blakemore, Diane   18–19, 28, 33, 35–36, 40, 44, 67, 81, 84, 89, 115, 168
Blass, Regina   4, 19, 32, 35–38, 40, 44, 59, 68–70, 115, 168
Bornkamm, Günther   63, 223, 227
Burke, Seán   41
Burridge, Richard   80
Campbell, Douglas A.   13–14, 22, 24, 53, 55, 57–58, 125, 132, 175, 177, 188, 190, 204–6, 210, 214–15, 221, 224–27, 240, 246–47, 275–77

Campbell, William S.   43, 48, 50, 58, 107, 190, 197, 218, 246–47, 258, 261, 268, 278
Carston, Robyn   28, 68
Clark, Billy   28–29, 283–84, 286
Clément, Fabrice   63
Cranfield, C. E. B.   8, 10, 58, 71, 73–77, 81, 85–87, 95, 98, 101, 108–9, 112, 125–27, 130, 132–34, 137–38, 144–45, 149, 155, 159, 162, 175–76, 178–79, 188–91, 196, 204–5, 207, 210–11, 213–15, 223, 226–27, 247, 249–50
Dahl, Nils A.   56, 182, 211, 229–32, 240
Das, A. Andrew   47, 49, 51, 107, 150
Denniston, John D.   1, 6, 10, 16, 150–51
Dijk, Teun A. van   18
Dodd, C. H.   225
Donfried, Karl P.   47–48, 52, 56, 58, 63, 207–8, 212, 245
Dooley, Robert   64
Dunn, James D. G.   9–13, 22, 48, 56, 58, 65, 71–72, 74–76, 80–81, 83, 85–90, 94–95, 102, 108–10, 113, 116, 118, 125–30, 132–34, 137, 144–45, 148–49, 154–55, 159, 161–63, 175–76, 178, 182, 185, 187–91, 193, 195–96, 204–5, 208, 210, 212, 214, 223, 225, 247, 250, 255
Edwards, Richard A.   3
Elliott, Neil   1, 13–15, 22, 47, 57–58, 76, 80, 85, 125, 177, 198, 204, 206–8, 211, 213, 217, 219, 221, 224, 229–30, 232–33, 240, 276
Esler, Philip   42, 47–48, 50–51, 58, 258–59

Fantin, Joseph D. 20, 40, 42, 45
Fish, Stanley 41
Fitzmyer, Joseph A. 110, 204–5, 208, 225
Forbes, Chris 46
Gamble, Harry Y. 51
Gathercole, Simon 132–34, 137–38, 179
Georgi, Dieter 219, 232
Gerth, Bernhard 1, 5
Gibbs, Raymond W. 41
Gignac, Alain 187
Griffith-Jones, Robin 225–26
Gutt, Ernst-August 36
Harbeck, J. A. 15
Headlam, Arthur C. 227
Heckert, Jakob A. 4, 17
Heintz, Christophe 63
Hellholm, D. 63, 124, 154
Hengel, Martin 45–46
Horn, Laurence R. 27, 29
Hurtado, Larry W. 52–53
Iten, Corinne 18
Jervell, Jacob 56
Jewett, Robert 7, 48, 51, 52, 57, 71, 74–77, 80–81, 86, 98, 100–102, 108, 110–11, 113, 125, 127–28, 131–35, 137–38, 144, 148–50, 154–56, 159, 161–63, 177–79, 181–82, 185–87, 190–91, 196, 198, 204–5, 208, 213, 215, 223, 227, 232, 246, 248–50, 255, 257
Johnson-Laird, Philip N. 20
Jülicher, Adolf 120, 149, 156
Karris, Robert 58, 63
Käsemann, Ernst 11–12, 23, 65, 71, 74, 77, 85–87, 94, 97–98, 100, 102, 106, 108–9, 112–13, 120–21, 126, 132–34, 144–45, 147, 149, 150, 154–56, 159, 162–63, 174, 178, 187–91, 196–99, 204–5, 211–12, 214, 223, 249–50, 255
Keck, Leander 131–32, 139
Klauck, Hans-Josef 208
Klein, Günther 131, 208
Kuehner, Raphael 1, 5
Kümmel, Werner G. 55, 85–88, 90, 92, 95, 98, 174
Kuss, Otto 159
Lagrange, Marie-Joseph 88, 144, 156, 163, 174, 190, 225
Lampe, Peter 48, 51–52
Lane, William L. 48, 218, 246, 254
Larsen, Iver 4, 15
Levinsohn, Stephen H. 15–17, 20, 40, 64
Levinson, Stephen C. 18
Linebaugh, Jonathan A. 76, 224, 227, 240–241
Longacre, Robert E. 64, 65
Longenecker, Richard N. 47, 56, 58, 204
Luther, Martin 204, 214
MacKenzie, Ian 41
Mascaro, Olivier 63
Matsui, Tomoko 18
McKechnie, Paul 45
Mercier, Hugo 63
Metzger, Bruce M. 111, 135, 249
Meyer, Paul W. 74, 187–97
Michel, Otto 128
Minear, Paul 48, 51, 204, 211–13, 258
Moeschler, Jacques 18
Moo, Douglas J. 87, 110
Morgan, Teresa 214–15, 235, 265
Motyer, Stephen 261
Moyise, Steve 63, 79
Nanos, Mark D. 49, 107
Neusner, Jacob 52
Newman, Barclay M., Jr. 88
Olbrechts-Tyteca, Lucie 62, 79
Ophuijsen, J. M. van 6
Origgi, Gloria 63
Osiek, Carolyn 52
Östman, Jan-Ola 27–28
Pattemore, Stephen 18, 27, 29–30, 38–45, 50, 53
Paulsen, Henning 71
Perelman, Chaïm 32, 62, 79
Pitts, Andrew W. 20, 40
Porter, Stanley E. 5–7, 16, 17, 20, 40, 45, 49, 63, 110, 174, 204, 225
Reasoner, Mark 52, 64, 107–8, 111, 135, 212, 244, 247
Rhyne, Clyde Thomas 174, 187, 190
Rijksbaron, Albert 6, 16

Modern Authors Index

Robertson, A. T.   1, 5
Rodriguez, Daniel   47, 226
Rodríguez, Rafael   55, 76, 107, 125, 204
Rudolph, Michael A.   4, 78, 91
Runge, Steven   3, 17, 20, 40, 228–29, 243
Russell, Walter B.   58, 244, 247, 258–59, 277
Sanday, William   227
Sanders, E. P.   9, 45
Sasamoto, Ryoko   18
Sbisà, Marina   27–28
Schiffrin, Deborah   18, 40
Schlier, Heinrich   249
Schmithals, Walter   80, 217
Seifrid, Mark A.   204–6
Sicking, C. M. J.   6
Sim, Margaret   20–21
Slings, Simon R.   16
Sperber, Dan   28–33, 41, 63, 79, 283–84, 286–87
Stanley, Christopher D.   45, 63
Stendahl, Krister   204, 213, 277
Stowers, Stanley K.   3, 42, 47–49, 52, 76, 86, 100, 125–27, 130, 132, 175, 177, 182, 241
Stuhlmacher, Peter   212
Swartz, S.   15
Thiessen, Matthew   47, 55, 57, 76, 107, 125, 204
Thistleton, Antony C.   205
Thorsteinsson, Runar M.   47, 55, 57, 76, 107, 204
Thrall, Margaret E.   3
Tobin, Thomas H.   51, 205, 207, 212, 217, 218, 237, 244
Turner, Nigel   4
Unger, Christophe   39, 68
Verschueren, Jef   27, 28
Vorster, Johannes N.   48
Wallace, Daniel B.   2, 5–6
Walters, James C.   50–51, 58, 242, 244, 258–59
Ward, Gregory E.   27
Watson, Francis B.   23, 45, 47, 51, 55–58, 64, 85, 86, 107, 125, 127, 133, 144, 176–77, 181, 185, 187, 190, 196–97, 199, 204, 214–15, 217, 236–37, 241, 245, 247
Wedderburn, Alexander J. M.   47, 50, 58, 211–12, 214, 217–18, 221, 223–24, 229–30, 233–34, 236–37, 240, 244, 254, 258, 268
Whittle, Sarah   83, 162, 187, 196–97, 200, 205, 247, 250, 255–56, 261
Wiefel, Wolfgang   48, 57–58, 218, 258
Wilckens, Ulrich   8–9, 12, 22, 56, 64, 71, 72, 80–81, 86, 95, 101, 107, 126, 132–35, 144–45, 149, 174, 177, 179, 187, 190–91, 193–94, 208–9, 211, 214, 217, 223–24, 247–50
Wilk, Florian   9, 43, 74, 188, 248
Wilson, Deirdre   1, 18, 28–33, 35, 41, 43, 45, 79, 283–84, 286–87
Winer, Georg B.   1, 5, 16
Wire, Antoinette C.   51
Witherington, Ben, III   162, 211
Wolter, Michael   7, 11–13, 46–47, 55–58, 71, 73, 85–87, 95, 98, 100, 102, 127, 129, 132–34, 136–39, 141, 149, 152, 155, 159, 174, 178–79, 181, 207–8, 214, 217, 225
Wright, N. T.   1, 7, 9–10, 23–24, 44, 48, 57, 64, 71, 85–90, 94, 98, 101, 106–7, 112, 115, 120–21, 127, 131–34, 144, 147, 155–56, 159, 174–79, 182–84, 186–87, 189–91, 193, 196, 198, 200, 204–5, 213–15, 221, 223–24, 227–28, 232, 235, 240, 243, 247, 249–50, 256–57, 260
Wuellner, Wihelm   207
Zahn, Theodor   175
Zakowski, Samuel   3, 20
Zerwick, Maximilian   75, 132, 191, 225
Zetterholm, Magnus   47, 217–18, 241
Ziesler, John A.   58, 126
Zufferey, Sandrine   18

www.ingramcontent.com/pod-product-compliance
Lightning Source LLC
Chambersburg PA
CBHW032031300426
44117CB00009B/1018